Citizen Hughes

Students a ... Research

Citizen Hughes

Michael Drosnin

Hutchinson

LONDON   MELBOURNE   SYDNEY   AUCKLAND   JOHANNESBURG

For my family,
for my friends,
for all who kept
the faith.

Hutchinson & Co. (Publishers) Ltd
An imprint of the Hutchinson Publishing Group
17–21 Conway Street, London WIP 6JD
Hutchinson Publishing Group (Australia) Pty Ltd
16–22 Church Street, Hawthorn, Melbourne, Victoria 3122
Hutchinson Group (NZ) Ltd
32–34 View Road, PO Box 40-086, Glenfield, Auckland 10
Hutchinson Group (SA) Pty Ltd
PO Box 337, Bergvlei 2012, South Africa
First published in USA by Holt, Rinehart and Winston 1985
First published in Great Britain 1985
© Michael Drosnin 1985
Printed and bound in Great Britain by Anchor Brendon Ltd,
Tiptree, Essex.

British Library Cataloguing in Publications Data

Hughes, Howard, *1905–1976*
    Citizen Hughes: in his own words
    Howard Hughes tried to buy America
    1. Hughes, Howard
    2. Millionaire—United States—
       Biography
    I. Title
    II. Drosnin, Michael
    338′ .04′ 0924   HC 102.5H8

    ISBN   0 09 161130 X

Designed by Susan Hood

"There was nothing either above or below him. . . . He had kicked himself loose of the Earth. . . . His intelligence was perfectly clear—concentrated, it is true, upon himself with horrible intensity, yet clear. . . . But his soul was mad. . . .

"Everything belonged to him—but that was a trifle. The thing was to know what he belonged to, how many powers of darkness claimed him for their own."

—Joseph Conrad
Heart of Darkness

Contents

Author's Note

This book is based primarily on nearly ten thousand previously hidden internal documents of the Hughes empire, including more than three thousand pages of the billionaire's own handwritten memoranda, all of which were stolen from his Romaine Street headquarters on June 5, 1974.

All of these papers were seen by me in their original form. I personally photographed all the memos that Hughes himself wrote and photocopied the memos sent to him by his aides, executives, and attorneys. A number of originals in both categories were retained for purposes of verification.

I have tried, so far as possible, to tell the story revealed in these documents in Hughes's own words—to present his true story in his own voice—by weaving his memos into a narrative that places them in dramatic and historical context. Some of the memos have been internally rearranged or edited to eliminate material extraneous to specific points being made in the text. In no case has the editing altered the substance of the memos.

All details of the narrative are based on the documents themselves, on hundreds of interviews with persons who had direct knowledge of the events, on sworn depositions and testimony filed in numerous court cases, and on thousands of government records obtained through the Freedom of Information Act. Among the persons who cooperated were several in Hughes's organization, including two of the billionaire's personal aides who had never before granted an interview.

In reconstructing scenes and events, I have tried to check every detail with at least two sources. My goal was to create a sense of being there—with Hughes in his penthouse or with the president in the White House—without forsaking historical accuracy. In every instance, I attempted to interview all persons involved and to check their accounts against all available records.

Detailed notes on each chapter, some notes on the illustrations, and a special note on authenticity, appear at the end of the book.

Citizen Hughes

The Great Hughes Heist

No one called it a third-rate burglary. There was no need to—no one got caught. Besides, a nation still transfixed by Watergate hardly noticed the June 5, 1974, break-in at 7000 Romaine Street in Hollywood.

The target, a hulking block-long two-story building, looked like an abandoned warehouse. It had no name. But for a quarter-century 7000 Romaine was the nerve center of a vast secret empire. It belonged to Howard Hughes.

The burglars were not only after his money but also his secrets. At the height of his wealth, power, and invisibility, the phantom billionaire commanded his empire by correspondence, scrawling his orders in thousands of handwritten memos, hearing back from his henchmen in memos dictated to his aides, dealing with outsiders only through the Romaine switchboard, which kept verbatim transcripts of all incoming calls.

And the Romaine vaults safeguarded all those memos, all those transcripts, all of Hughes's personal and corporate files, all the secrets of a mystery man who was known to have dealings with the CIA, the Mafia, and the White House and whose hidden empire seemed to reach everywhere.

The fortresslike steel-and-concrete building was said to be impregnable. Published accounts detailed a fail-safe security system that included laser-beam surveillance, X-ray detection devices, and electronic alarms to alert a private army before anyone could even get near the burglarproof safes. Entry was by appointment only, and few outsiders were ever allowed through the four-combination, push-button-lock doors.

But in the early morning hours of June 5, 1974, persons unknown managed to get in uninvited. No alarms blared, because there was no working alarm system. No private army opened fire, because there was no private army. Romaine was a Hollywood façade, protected only by a single unarmed security guard.

The guard, Mike Davis, had just completed his rounds outside the building. It was 12:45 A.M.

"As I opened a side door," he would later tell the police, "someone came from behind and jammed a hard object into my back. I never actually saw a gun. I just assumed they were armed. I knew I wasn't."

"Let's go, we're going in," Davis said the burglars ordered, pushing him ahead of them. They told the guard to lie facedown on the floor. Blindfolded and gagged, his wrists taped cross-handed, Davis said he saw nothing but thought he heard four men, the two who came up behind him and two more who arrived soon after, dragging in a two-tank acetylene torch on a clattering steel dolly.

He heard them send a lookout upstairs, where the only other person in the building was manning the switchboard in a soundproof room and didn't hear a thing.

"If the doors are open, you can hear a pin drop," explained the oblivious operator, Harry Watson. "If they're closed, you could drop a bomb and I wouldn't hear it. That night my doors were closed and I wouldn't have heard a tank come through."

The burglars took their time, moving through the maze of offices in the sprawling building as if they had a treasure map. According to Davis, they first led him straight to Kay Glenn's office. Glenn was managing director of Romaine and chief deputy to Bill Gay, one of three top executives who ran the Hughes empire through its holding company, Summa Corporation. There the burglars peeled open a safe in the top drawer of a filing cabinet, removing thousands in cash and unidentified documents.

At the same time, Davis said he heard the pop and crackle of a blowtorch. Directly across the hall, the safecrackers burned a gaping hole through the steel doors of a walk-in vault. "Looky here, this is it!" the guard heard one exclaim.

Before they were finished, the burglars had torched another large safe, pried open three smaller ones, and ransacked several offices, including that of Nadine Henley, Hughes's longtime personal secretary and a member of Summa's ruling triumverate.

Finally, Davis said, the intruders marched him upstairs and entered a second-floor conference room where the billionaire's personal files had been assembled at the orders of his general counsel, Chester Davis, the third member of Summa's top command.

"This is a piece of cake," said one of the burglars, prying open a file cabinet, and the guard said he could hear them tell each other, "Take this, not those. Yeah, those are the good ones," as they dropped folder after confidential folder into cardboard boxes on the floor.

Almost four hours after they had arrived, the burglars trussed Davis around the knees and ankles with surgical tape, left him lying on a couch in a basement furniture warehouse, and vanished.

He did not leap up after them. "If I could have freed my arms and legs and pulled the blindfold off and jumped one of them for the sake of Hughes, I wouldn't have done it," the guard later explained. "I knew the security at Romaine was lousy, and I tried to tell all the top people, but no one seemed to care. And I was only getting crumbs, while they were getting a whole loaf of his bread."

So, as ordered, Davis lay still on the couch. About half an hour after the burglars had escaped, he loosened his bonds and hobbled back up to Kay Glenn's office. There he phoned upstairs to the still oblivious switchboard operator, who called the police.

Detectives combed the cavernous Hughes headquarters without finding a solid clue. There were no identifiable fingerprints, the abandoned acetylene tanks could not be traced, and no one in the nearly deserted industrial district had seen the burglars. One of the cops who surveyed the scene was later quoted as saying, "They knocked off Romaine like it was a corner delicatessen."

The police revealed only that $60,000 had been taken although some press reports placed the figure as high as $300,000. The Hughes organization, of course, said nothing. In fact, taking immediate control of the case, Summa dispatched a representative to police headquarters to censor all announcements.

So there was no public mention of the other missing items, but in a bulletin sent to law-enforcement agencies, the Los Angeles police also listed as stolen a bizarre grab bag including two large Wedgwood vases, a pink-and-blue ceramic samovar, an antique wooden Mongolian eating bowl, and Nadine Henley's butterfly collection.

No one was told about the solid-gold medallion found in a basement trash bin, where it had been inexplicably discarded by the burglars.

And not a word was said about the big secret of the break-in: the secret papers of Howard Hughes had disappeared.

There was virtually no powerful force in this country, indeed in the world, that did not have an interest in the missing files, that did not have reason to steal them, that did not have reason to fear their loss. There was circumstantial evidence to suggest that the CIA, the Mafia, even the White House was behind the break-in. There was still stronger evidence that Hughes had "stolen" his own files to safeguard them from subpoena.

Certainly both the timing of the break-in and the ease with which it was accomplished raised immediate questions about the Great Hughes Heist. The burglars were not the only ones after his private papers.

Just three days before the break-in, the Securities and Exchange Commission had subpoenaed all the documents at Romaine relating to Hughes's 1969 takeover of Air West. Nothing more directly threatened the billionaire. Hughes himself and two of his top aides had been indicted for conspiring to manipulate the airline's stock, defrauding shareholders of $60 million. President Nixon, his confidant Bebe Rebozo, and his brother Donald had all been implicated in the deal, and Hughes faced a possible twelve years in jail.

"Hughes and his agents may have been motivated to make it appear that there was a theft in order to avoid complying with our subpoenas," suggested a secret SEC report.

Just six days before the break-in, a federal judge had ordered Hughes to surrender five hundred memos demanded by his former chief of staff, Robert Maheu. Ousted in a 1970 palace coup, Maheu was at war with the new high command and had filed a seventeen-million-dollar slander suit against Hughes for calling him "a no-good, dishonest son of a bitch who stole me blind." The bitter legal battle had already produced charges of Hughes-CIA skulduggery, secret payoffs to Richard Nixon and Hubert Humphrey, and a proposed million-dollar bribe to Lyndon Johnson. Maheu claimed the subpoenaed memos would confirm all his allegations.

He also suspected that Hughes had arranged the burglary to get rid of the damning documents, but Summa officials claimed that Maheu himself had masterminded the break-in and hinted to police that he may have done it in cahoots with the Mafia. For years Hughes's intelligence network had been trying to link Maheu to the Mob, to find proof that he had conspired to loot the billionaire's Las Vegas casinos. While the FBI also considered Maheu a suspect, it raised the possibility that the Mafia had acted on its own.

"We may indeed have an effort on the part of organized crime to gain information regarding Mr. Hughes through this break-in," concluded a confidential FBI report. "This could be to calibrate the stockholder or otherwise obtain useful documents for pressure purposes: e.g., to maintain organized-crime status in Nevada."

Meanwhile, both the Senate Watergate Committee and the Watergate special prosecutor were probing a concealed $100,000 "contribution" from Hughes to Nixon by way of Rebozo. There was substantial evidence that the cash not only bought the president's approval of the Air West takeover but also won Attorney General John Mitchell's go-ahead on Las Vegas hotel purchases that violated antitrust laws.

In fact, Senate investigators believed that the Hughes connection had triggered Watergate. It all began, they theorized, with Nixon's fears that Democratic party chairman Larry O'Brien had learned of the Rebozo payoff—and perhaps a great deal more—while employed as the billionaire's Washington lobbyist. The Senate committee demanded that Hughes appear in person and surrender his files, and the special prosecutor issued several subpoenas just weeks before the break-in.

Now the FBI saw a possible Watergate link to the Romaine heist. A Los Angeles police report log noted: "Received call from Karis, FBI—states home office in Washington interested; they feel Watergate is involved."

And the CIA, in its own list of "possible culprits," after Maheu, the Mafia, and "foreign government—not necessarily USSR," also suggested that the Hughes break-in had been "politically motivated to aid or deter Watergate investigation."

But the Agency itself was also suspect. Shortly before the burglary, Senate investigators got the first official hint that Maheu, while working for Hughes, had orchestrated a CIA-sponsored plot to assassinate Fidel Castro with the help of two leading Mafiosi. It was the CIA's dirtiest secret, and Maheu had revealed it to Hughes in a phone call that may well have been transcribed and stored at Romaine.

And all of these probes were coming to a head when Romaine was looted and the secret papers vanished.

"If you go on the theory that someone wanted to find out what Hughes knew, or wanted to make sure no one else found out, everyone but the Loch Ness monster was suspect," commented a detective assigned to the case.

Adding to the mystery, the Romaine heist was the sixth unsolved burglary of a Hughes office in just four months. In February 1974 there was a break-in at the billionaire's Las Vegas headquarters. No documents were reported taken, although police found filing cabinets rifled, desks ransacked, and papers strewn on the floor. In March, burglars struck another Hughes office in Las Vegas. At about the same time, the New York law offices of Hughes's chief counsel, Chester Davis, were hit. Again no papers were reported missing. In Washington there was a break-in at Mullen & Company, a public relations firm owned by Hughes lobbyist Robert F. Bennett, who also fronted for the CIA and employed Watergate burglar E. Howard Hunt. File drawers were left open, but once again no papers were reported stolen. And finally, in April, Hughes's office in Encino, a Los Angeles suburb, was entered through the roof. This time the thieves made off with a voice scrambler, a sophisticated device that was used to secure telephone conversations with Bennett's Washington office and CIA headquarters in Langley.

It was against this background that Los Angeles police began to investigate the new heist at 7000 Romaine. In a confidential report written several weeks after the break-in, LAPD detectives noted some curious aspects of the bizarre case:

- "The building is taped and wired for an electrical alarm system, but it had not been operative for one year. Without knowledge of this fact, it appears the alarm is operative."
- "The physical layout of this building and the type of material kept in each office is not general knowledge, even within the organization."
- "Although only one large Mosler walk-in vault was torched, there are 18 additional vaults on the same floor which were not attacked."
- "Three of the offices were entered with keys. One of the most important was that of Kay Glenn. Investigating officers tried to shim this door and others and found it was not possible."

Even more troubling were the results of polygraph examinations administered to the Hughes employees. Mike Davis, the lone security guard on duty the night of the break-in, failed to appear three times and finally refused to take a lie-detector test. "I just don't believe in it," he explained. "A man should be trusted on his word." Davis was fired. The only witness to the burglary was now himself a suspect.

His boss, Vince Kelley, Summa's West Coast security chief, did take a polygraph—but failed. He "displayed guilty knowledge to all four examiners who reviewed the tape," according to the police report. A later FBI report on Kelley's test was more explicit: "He was asked about prior knowledge, where the stolen property was located, and if he was present during the robbery. He 'failed miserably' when answering all these questions."

To clear himself, Kelley arranged a second polygraph test through a private eye, who found him "clean." What Kelley didn't mention was that the same private eye and two of their mutual friends had been involved in one of the five earlier Hughes break-ins, the Encino job, and had actually ended up with the stolen scrambler.

Yet although he had failed to report the earlier theft, failed to install a burglar alarm at Romaine, failed his lie-detector test, and then chose a pal connected with one Hughes burglary to clear him of complicity in another, Kelley was not dismissed. He remained West Coast security chief.

Adding to this strange puzzle, Kelley's boss, Ralph Winte, the man in charge of security for the entire Hughes empire, had himself been involved in plotting the theft of another cache of secret Hughes papers. E. Howard Hunt had just recently revealed in sworn Senate testimony that he had plotted with Winte to seize a stash of Hughes's memos by busting open the safe of Las Vegas newspaper publisher Hank Greenspun, in a joint venture between the Hughes and Nixon forces, approved by Attorney General Mitchell.

An FBI report on Romaine, noting Winte's role in that aborted break-in, mentioned that when called before a Watergate grand jury Winte "became so nervous and nauseated that he did not testify." Yet Winte, like Kelley, not only kept his job but also worked closely with the Los Angeles police in its Romaine probe.

Still, the police could not help but note that the entire Hughes security apparatus—from the Romaine guard to the top command—was now suspect. The LAPD report on the break-in concluded that "someone within the corporation set up or supplied information for this burglary." The conclusion seemed both obvious and inevitable: the Great Hughes Heist had been an "inside job."

But who was the inside man, who were the burglars, who was behind them, and who had the stolen secret papers?

The police remained baffled. The FBI was soon drawn into the case, and a top-secret task force was set up at the CIA. The directors of both agencies huddled with each other in Washington, sent emissaries to the chief of police in Los Angeles, finally even briefed the president of the United States and pledged a million dollars to the quest—all in a desperate effort to track down the burglars and recover, if need be buy back, Howard Hughes's dangerous secrets.

But the break-in was never solved, and none of the stolen papers were ever found. The papers were still missing, and the mystery still remained, when I began my own investigation years later.

What follows is the true story of the Great Hughes Heist and of how I found the secret papers of the world's most secretive man.

"Got a guy that tells me he can put us right into Howard Hughes's stash," said the Jiggler to the Pro.

That's how it all began. Early in May, over lunch in a Los Angeles drugstore. Sitting in the booth across the table, the Pro just smiled.

Funny little guy, the Jiggler. Always had some "big deal" going. He'd come by, talking out of the side of his mouth, acting tough, telling the Pro about his latest scores. But the Pro knew he was small change, the lowest order of thief, just a key-jiggler who hung around parking lots at public swimming pools and private country clubs, breaking into empty cars, snatching wallets and watches from the glove compartments.

And here he was talking about taking Howard Hughes. Sitting in some damn drugstore, talking about the all-time fucking ultimate Big Score.

"Okey-dokey," said the Pro. "We'll hit Hughes first, then knock over J. Paul Getty. Maybe take the Rockefellers too."

The Jiggler didn't laugh. He knew that this Hughes job was for real. He could just feel it.

"Look," he told the Pro. "Look, I've stumbled into one hell of a thing. This red-headed guy says he can put us right into Hughes's stash. He wants to meet. He wants to talk right now."

The Pro was intrigued. Not buying, but definitely intrigued. "No names," he told the Jiggler, looking hard across the table, letting him feel the stare.

"No names," the Jiggler assured him. "Red, he don't know your name. I ain't told him nothing."

So they took the freeway to Red's place, and the Pro was impressed. It was on the better side of Hollywood, an expensive apartment with lots of good jewelry lying around and closets full of hot suits, Red being a fence. But Red himself was a real sleaze, and the Pro saw scam, not score.

Red asked him about opening vaults, big walk-in jobs, asked if he could handle it. The Pro said he could bust anything. They talked for an hour, but no one mentioned Hughes.

A couple of weeks later, the Jiggler was back. Told the Pro that Red was ready to *show* him something.

"What do ya know about 7000 Romaine?" asked Red. The Pro said he'd never heard of it. "That's Howard Hughes's stash," said Red. "I got an inside man who can put us in the place."

"I thought you were going to *show* me something," said the Pro.

"I am," said Red. "I'm gonna show you the inside of Hughes's stash."

The three of them—Red, the Jiggler, and the Pro—drove over to Romaine late that evening, pulled into the parking lot out back. An impatient guy was waiting nervously outside the building, motioning them to come over, not openly waving his arm but making a surreptitious little gesture with his hand held close to his side.

Mr. Inside opened the door without ceremony. Red and the Jiggler slid in. The Pro couldn't believe what was going down. He'd had more trouble breaking into a vending machine. Something smelled wrong. He remained outside.

Red came back to the door, said, "Come on, come in."

"I don't have my tools," said the Pro.

Red said, "No, just come in and look around."

Mr. Inside joined them. "Just make yourself at home," he told the Pro, inviting him in. "Don't worry. There's no one else here."

The Pro couldn't resist. He went in and right away came face-to-face with a solid wall of Mosler walk-in vaults. A block-long hallway lined with nineteen massive old steel-doored floor-to-ceiling safes. The Pro figured he must be dreaming. Or maybe he'd died and gone to heaven.

"What do you think this joint will go for?" he asked Mr. Inside.

"At least a million," said the inside man. "Millions. No telling how much. Some of those vaults are filled to the ceiling with silver dollars. There's cash everywhere."

The Pro looked around at Red and the Jiggler. He felt like one of the Beagle Boys inside Scrooge McDuck's money bin.

It was only later, after he left, that the Pro began to wonder who was really behind this job and what they were really after. And one other thing. Was he being called in as a professional or set up as a fall guy?

But a week later the Pro was back at Romaine, casing the joint, taking it apart.

Again, he was there just to look, get the layout, size up the safes, open everything that was unlocked—the offices, the desks, the filing cabinets—light-finger everything, see what Hughes had hidden away in his fabled fortress.

The place was a maze, dark and eerie. A concrete hallway ran the full length of the building, leading off into numerous side corridors with sudden turns and hidden passageways, all studded with vaults and lined with doors, all of them unmarked, with no hint of what lay on the other side.

The Pro began to check out the vaults. One was unlocked, but it had not been entered for so many years that it was still hard to pull open the heavy steel door. It creaked and grated with a noise that echoed throughout the vast empty building, and when he was finally able to peer inside, the Pro was more than disappointed. The big vault was filled with cans of film, hundreds of them, the prints and negatives of Hughes's old movies. Nothing else. Not a single silver dollar.

But in an office next door, in the first drawer of the first filing cabinet he opened, the Pro spotted the tip of a red money wrapper. He slid it out, saw that it was marked "$10,000," and pushed it back in. Bingo! Right then and there, the Pro was committed.

This might be the come-on for a setup, but he had to go ahead. And in a desk drawer in the same office he found keys to the rest of the building.

Starting down the hallway he tried one door after another, excited now, like a kid on a treasure hunt. First he entered a conference room, empty except for two glass-walled cubby-hole offices, both of them filled with model airplanes. Nothing else. Just model airplanes.

Across the hall he fumbled with the mess of keys and finally opened the door to another room. Inside were three cases of liquor, old bottles of whiskey and wine that had belonged to Hughes's father, dead half a century, and at least a hundred gift-wrapped packages, none of them ever opened, the ribbons still tied, most with cards still attached, birthday and Christmas presents sent over the years to the indifferent billionaire.

Leaning against one wall were eight or ten pictures of Jane Russell, oil paintings on wood, four feet tall, one depicting the buxom actress nearly nude, all of them scenes from her first movie, a 1941 Hughes production, *The Outlaw*.

It went on like that as the Pro reeled from one bizarre room to the next, only to discover discarded furniture, rolls of carpet, parts of old movie sets, odd cartons filled with cheap watches or cigarettes or bars of soap, scores of aviation trophies, plaques, and medals, motion-picture equipment, and finally in one room down at the far end of the hall some valuable antiques—Tiffany lamps, marble statues, bronze figurines, ceramic quails—side by side with cartons of junk: more soap, rolls of paper towels, and dozens of scrapbooks filled with old newspaper clippings about Hughes's public exploits dating back to the 1930s.

Nothing made any sense. The Pro had burglarized every kind of company in creation, but he had never before encountered anything remotely like this. Romaine was not a corporate headquarters but a warehouse of Hughes memorabilia. The Pro was dismayed. There was obviously cash here, even some valuables, and he did not know what was hidden in the other eighteen locked vaults, but what was out in the open made it look less like a money bin than his grandmother's attic. It was like Hughes had stored away his life in this cavernous old place.

The Pro started back down the hall, and between the antiques room and a row of computer banks unlocked another door. It led into a small dark room cluttered with cartons, several bulky humidifiers, a cot, and a rollaway bed. As the Pro shone his flashlight over to the far wall he saw an open closet, looked inside, and nearly fell over in a dead faint.

For one horrible moment he felt the presence of Howard Hughes. Actually thought he saw him standing there in the closet. In fact, it was just his old clothes, eight or nine double-breasted suits hanging there, along with one white sports coat and an old leather flight jacket, the clothes not merely hanging but sagging from the hangers, rotting on them, obviously untouched for decades.

On a shelf above lay an assortment of brown glass medicine bottles and several hats, snap-brim Stetsons and a couple of white yachting caps. On the floor below was a pair of old tennis shoes and a half-dozen pairs of aged wingtip brown oxfords with the toes curled all the way up. The Pro couldn't tear his eyes away from that closet. It was the curled-up shoes that really got to him.

He spent at least twenty minutes standing in that haunted room, staring at that decaying wardrobe, feeling about as frightened as he had ever felt in his life but unable to leave, repeatedly looking over his shoulder, expecting Hughes to materialize at any moment, to walk out of the shadows of that closet, or worse yet, to reach out and pull him in there.

Suddenly he felt less like a burglar than a grave robber, opening up a pharaoh's tomb, fearing the mummy's curse.

Now completely drawn into the Hughes mystique and the madness of this place, the Pro made his way up a flight of metal stairs leading to the second floor, half afraid to find out what was there but compelled to look. At a landing halfway up, there was a safe built into the wall. It seemed like an odd place to have one, and although the building was filled with larger, more imposing vaults, he noted it as a prime target. For now, however, he continued upstairs.

He entered another block-long hallway running the full length of the second floor, also lined with unmarked doors. Most of the offices were empty, but the Pro spotted loose cash, perhaps a thousand in twenties, fifties, and hundreds, inside a desk of an office he knew belonged to the Romaine paymaster; saw a couple of other rooms that looked promising; and then opened a set of heavy walnut double doors with big brass knobs.

Inside was a reception room with four wall safes, beyond that a large plush office, and beyond that a thirty-foot-long beige-carpeted conference room rich with dark wood paneling and lined with leather-bound law books.

In the center of that room stood a twelve-foot-long mahogany table, and on that table in very neat rows were ten piles of white paper with typewritten memos and ten piles of yellow legal-pad pages with handwritten messages. All the yellow papers were signed "Howard."

His heart pounding, the Pro leafed through them. He saw numbers in the millions, talk of dealings with mobsters and politicians, names like Nixon, Humphrey, Kennedy, Johnson. He felt not only Hughes's presence now, but also his power.

And he knew that whatever else was hidden away at Romaine, whatever lay behind the steel doors of those locked vaults, these secret papers were the real prize.

June 5, 1974. The night of the break-in.

The Pro knew something was wrong the instant he arrived. There was a stranger leaning against the wall, just inside the door. A man he'd never seen before.

"Who the fuck is that?" he demanded. Mr. Inside, standing next to the stranger, said, "That's my partner."

The Pro looked around to his own partners, the Jiggler and another man he had brought in for the big job, a professional safecracker he had worked with before. This wasn't the plan. He had been expecting to find Red waiting there with Mr. Inside. Now, instead, this mystery man.

Was he a cop? A Hughes operative? Some secret agent? Was he going to bust the Pro right now or blow him away the minute he walked out the door? Whoever this guy was, whoever was really behind this job, the Pro was now certain there was a lot more to it than he had been told.

But it was too late to back out now, and he wanted to go ahead. He'd never have another chance to take off Howard Hughes.

He sent the mystery man upstairs with the Jiggler, supposedly to stand guard outside the one occupied room, to make sure that the switchboard operator didn't walk in on the break-in, but really to have the Jiggler keep watch over this stranger. The two of them, both wearing handkerchief masks, stood there nervously shoulder to shoulder all night.

Meanwhile, the Pro and his partner went to work.

They went straight to the office where the Pro had spotted the $10,000 bank wrapper the night he cased the joint, laid a four-drawer filing cabinet on its back, peeled open a fire safe in the top drawer with a wedge and a hammer and a crowbar—and immediately hit paydirt. Six bundles of hundred-dollar bills, $10,000 in each, eight bundles of fifties each worth $1,000, and perhaps $500 more in small bills.

The Pro dumped it all into his tool satchel, a dark blue gym bag with white plastic handles, and also threw in two gold Juvenia watches each worth a grand. Not a bad haul. More than seventy big ones from the first safe they popped.

They left behind several hundred thousand dollars in series-E bonds—worthless paper, all nonnegotiable—and headed across the hall to a row of six walk-in vaults.

Mr. Inside pointed to one of the old Mosler safes, said it was stuffed with silver dollars, hundreds of bags, thousands in each, all of them old coins worth five bucks apiece. Dragging the two-tank acetylene torch over to the vault, the Pro lowered his goggles and went to work, burning through the ten-foot-high double steel doors until he had cut a hole big enough, and then clambered right in.

The vault was stacked wall to wall, practically floor to ceiling, all the way back ten feet deep. But not with silver dollars. Climbing over boxes and trunks and assorted debris, the Pro rummaged through the dark safe, shining his flashlight in every direction in an increasingly frantic search for the treasure, only to find another bizarre collection of Hughes's personal effects: hundreds of hearing aids stashed in several wooden fruit crates; boxes upon boxes of old correspondence, letters and Christmas cards sent to him in decades past; numerous footlockers filled with old screenplays; another trunk of scrapbooks and several crammed with pilot logs; scores of silver-cup flying trophies and a gold cup from a golf tournament; more hearing aids; and a large ceremonial plate from William Randolph Hearst.

The Pro could have remained in that vault all night without getting a full inventory. Only three items really caught his attention. A seven-millimeter solid silver pistol with a card that read, "Captured from Hermann Goering." A pair of German SS binoculars in a black leather case. And a huge cut-glass bowl bearing the inscription *To Howard Hughes from Hubert Horatio Humphrey*, with the vice-president's seal etched below. He left that behind, taking only the pistol and the binoculars.

It seemed pointless to attack the seventeen remaining vaults.

The Pro instead moved down the hallway, forcing a couple of doors along the way just to make it look more like a routine prowl, left his partner to check out the antiques collection, and as if drawn by some supernatural force returned to the little room where he had discovered Hughes's old clothes, wasting valuable time staring again at that haunted closet.

Finally, he started up to the second floor, where the secret Hughes papers lay waiting, where the mystery man had been sent hours earlier, suddenly quite worried again about this half-forgotten stranger and what plans of his own he might have for the break-in, or for the Pro.

But halfway upstairs on the landing he once more encountered that oddly placed wall safe and had to bust in. He quickly punched out the combination lock, opened the steel door, and discovered a whole hidden room, ten feet wide, fifteen feet long, but only four and a half feet high. He crawled in.

The room was filled with green-and-brown boxes, Campbell's soup cartons, perhaps two hundred of them stacked wall to wall, all of them stuffed with old canceled checks. Personal checks signed by

Hughes and made out to various restaurants and nightclubs—the Brown Derby, the Stork Club, and El Morocco—corporate checks from RKO and TWA, thousands upon thousands of checks from the 1920s through the 1950s, all neatly piled in the soup cartons.

They were clearly of no value, but the Pro was entranced. He spent fifteen minutes hunched over in that crawlspace, poring through the checks like some addled bookkeeper until his back ached so badly he had to leave.

Up on the second floor, the mystery man and the Jiggler still stood guard shoulder to shoulder. "We'll clear a hundred grand easy," the Pro told them as he went back to work.

For forty-five minutes he and his partner struggled with the Romaine paymaster's safe, unsuccessfully trying to punch, peel, or pry it open. Finally, they had to lug the acetylene tanks upstairs and burn their way in, turning the small office into a smoke-filled blast furnace, but pocketing another $10,000 in cash as well as Hughes's personal credit cards, his old pilot's license, and an expired passport. In a secretary's office that adjoined the room, they pried open a file cabinet and found a few hundred dollars more.

The Pro and his partner were sopping wet now from the heat of the torch work, from the sheer physical labor, and from the tension; and they were right down to the wire for time. It was almost four A.M. now—the deadline they had set for their getaway—and they knew that the cleaning crew arrived before dawn. His partner wanted to bust some more safes, but the Pro wanted only to get the secret papers and get out.

They headed for the big conference room, where Mr. Inside now joined them. Gesturing toward the documents spread out on the mahogany table, he said, "Let's take these." It was the first time anyone had said anything about the papers. It seemed almost an afterthought.

"I'll hold on to them," the inside man continued, still entirely offhand, "and if anything goes wrong, use them for blackmail, keep them for insurance to buy our way out."

"Okey-doke," said the Pro, as he gathered up the billionaire's personal papers from the table and swept them into a big cardboard box he had found in the Jane Russell room downstairs.

"There are more in those cabinets," said Mr. Inside, pointing to four locked five-drawer file cabinets standing side by side against the rear wall, next to a row of windows that looked out on the Romaine parking lot.

The Pro busted the locks easily with a screwdriver and opened drawer after drawer stuffed with thousands more white typewritten documents and yellow handwritten memos, grabbing armful after armful of confidential folders and dropping them all into cardboard Transfile cases until the cabinets were bare. The Pro, his partner, and Mr. Inside carted them all downstairs to a first-floor warehouse space that backed onto a rear loading dock, and on the last trip down took along the Jiggler and the mystery man.

It was well past four in the morning now, well past their deadline, as they all gathered around a Ping-Pong table in the large open warehouse area. The Pro emptied his blue gym bag onto the table, dumped out the cash, and made the big count. It all came to just under $80,000.

"Not exactly a million, but a damn good night's work," said the Pro, and divided the loot into five equal stacks. Everybody took one, the Pro taking his last. About $500 remained in loose bills. He pushed it toward the others, and while they hesitated, the mystery man quickly reached out and pocketed it all.

Unzipping his fly, the Pro took a leak. His partner and the Jiggler also urinated on the floor. And having looted and defiled the sacred Hughes sanctuary, they loaded the billionaire's secret papers into a stolen Ford van and vanished into the night.

Holed up alone at his hideout, the Pro had no idea what forces he and his cohorts had unleashed. He had no idea that they had hit Romaine just days after the SEC and Maheu subpoenas, that Watergate investigators were also after the files, that the president, the CIA, and the Mafia were all now suspect, and he also had no idea who was really behind the break-in.

But he did know who had the stolen secrets. He did.

It had been a tense ride away from Romaine. With his partner at the wheel, the Pro sat up front holding a gun on his lap, keeping a constant eye on the mystery man, who was sitting in the back next to the Jiggler, his hand in a brown paper bag gripping a pistol that lay on top of his share of the loot. Behind them all, in the rear of the van, lay Transfiles and cartons filled with the stolen documents.

The stranger was supposed to get the papers, take them on behalf of Mr. Inside, who had gone his own way after the heist. That was all understood. But who was this mystery man, and what else did he have in mind?

The Great Hughes Heist

All night the Pro had been waiting for the stranger to make his move. Now, at close quarters in the getaway van, it felt like *High Noon.* They were all on edge from the heist, the adrenaline really pumping now as they made their escape, watching for the cops, waiting to hear the wail of the sirens, see the flashing red lights; but mainly they were watching each other, wondering who would start shooting first.

And all the while the Pro's mind was racing. Why had he been brought in on this job? There was nothing of value in the vaults, and they hardly needed a professional to bust into some filing cabinets. Did they want a vault torched just to divert the police? Divert them from what? Why was there no alarm, why were keys for the entire building just lying in a desk drawer, why had everything been made so damn easy?

And, above all, why had the secret papers been so conveniently assembled and left right out in the open? Had Hughes plotted to "steal" his own files, only to have them actually stolen? Because whatever was up, the Pro had already decided to turn the tables on whoever was behind the heist.

It was a notion that had begun to take hold from the moment he first saw the papers, that had grown along with his suspicions about his cohorts, that had become a fixation as he became increasingly obsessed with Hughes, and that had finally seized him in the last moments of the break-in when Mr. Inside suddenly announced that *he* would keep the papers. At that instant, the Pro knew that the secrets, not the money, had been the true object of the break-in all along and decided to hold on to the papers himself.

Now, in the van, there was no one but the mystery man to stop him. The Pro looked back again at his adversary. The stranger shifted nervously, his hand still inside the bag, still gripping the pistol. The Pro knew he could take this guy, whoever he was. And whoever was behind him, whoever had masterminded this job, wasn't in the van.

They were headed north into the valley, going to Encino, but the Pro was not about to drive into a trap, go to some unknown place where anyone—cops *or* robbers—might be waiting. Instead, they stopped at a street corner and the Pro suggested that the stranger get out.

"What about the papers?" asked the mystery man. He was clearly scared shitless. The Pro, still holding his gun on his lap, said that he would personally deliver them to Mr. Inside. They stared at each other for a moment. The stranger took a quick look at the other two men, the Jiggler and the Pro's partner. Outnumbered three-to-one, he didn't argue.

It wasn't until the Pro was alone in the van, alone with the papers, driving home as the sun came up, that it really hit him. He actually had all of Howard Hughes's secrets. He locked himself inside his garage and stayed up all that day and all through the next night listening for radio reports of the burglary and reading through thousands of private Hughes papers, getting totally drawn into the power of that strange secret world.

The following morning he left to meet with Mr. Inside, as they had arranged, at a Los Angeles coffee shop. On the way, he picked up a copy of the *Times*. The heist was front-page news: "GANG FLEES WITH $60,000 AFTER 4-HOUR RAID ON HUGHES OFFICE." There was no mention of stolen papers.

But as he sat in his car reading the newspaper, the Pro discovered that this was not the first Hughes break-in, that there had been a string of recent burglaries at Hughes's offices around the country, that just days before he was brought in on this caper the office in Encino had been hit and a voice scrambler stolen. Encino. The same place he had dumped the mystery man.

Were the break-ins connected? Who was behind it all? What were they really after? And who, the Pro wondered, was going to come after him?

He was relieved to find Mr. Inside waiting alone at the coffee shop. "Are the papers safe?" the inside man immediately asked. "I want them back." He was tense, but the Pro had put him at ease simply by showing up, and now he readily agreed to turn over the hot documents.

"Of course," said the Pro. "No problem." He made detailed arrangements for the transfer—time, date, place—and immediately cut off all further contact.

He bought three steamer trunks at three different shopping centers, filled them with the Hughes papers, padlocked each, and put them all into storage at three different warehouses under three different assumed names. All except for one manila folder of handwritten memos, which he stashed away in a hidden panel in the basement of his hideout.

He had no set plan. Just a thought. Hughes would pay well to get back his papers. The Pro decided to ransom them for one million dollars.

But it wasn't really money he was after anymore. He wanted the million, all right, but what he really wanted was the chance to go one-on-one with Howard Hughes. In his fantasy, the Pro now saw himself, a man from the streets, sitting at the same table with the richest man in America, sitting there as an equal, knowing that he had the hidden billionaire's most prized possession, all his secrets, all in his own handwriting, knowing that in this one game not Hughes but the Pro would be holding all the cards.

It became his obsession. He wanted above all to play pair poker with Howard Hughes.

Ten days after the break-in, a man calling himself Chester Brooks phoned Romaine. He asked to speak to Kay Glenn, Nadine Henley, or Chester Davis. Attorney Davis was contacted but said he didn't know a Mr. Brooks.

Two days later, Chester Brooks called back. This time he added, "It is about the burglary and it is urgent." And he offered convincing proof. He invited the Hughes executives to take a look at the white envelope on the green trash can under the tree in the park across from their other office in Encino.

Nadine Henley looked out her window and spotted the envelope. Fearing a booby trap, she called the police bomb squad, which retrieved the package. It was definitely explosive.

Inside was a memo in Hughes's handwriting on a sheet of yellow legal-pad paper. Addressed to Robert Maheu, the June 6, 1969, memo read:

> Bob—
>
> I would be ecstatic at the prospect of purchasing Parvin in the same manner as Air West. Do you think this really could be accomplished? I just assumed that the cries of monopoly would rule it out.
>
> If this really could be accomplished, I think it would be a ten strike and might change all of my plans.
>
> Please reply. Most urgent,
>
> Howard

The document not only established Chester Brooks's credentials—thus providing the first lead to the missing papers—but also raised some troubling questions. Hughes and two of his top aides were at that very moment under criminal investigation in the Air West case. And here the billionaire was suggesting that Parvin-Dohrmann, which owned several Las Vegas casinos, be acquired "in the same manner as Air West."

Moreover, Parvin was then a known Mob front controlled by Sidney Korshak, a Beverly Hills attorney identified by the Justice Department as one of the country's most powerful organized-crime leaders. Hughes had dealt with him before, and Korshak's name was to surface again in the Romaine break-in saga.

But, for the moment, it was the mysterious Chester Brooks who held center stage. He had instructed the Hughes executives to signal their interest by placing a classified ad in the *Los Angeles Times* with the message "APEX-OK" and a telephone number written backward. It was done. Three days later he called again and spoke to Nadine Henley in a conversation recorded by the police.

First Brooks had a message for Hughes: "It may please him to know that this is not part of any conspiracy through the Maheu people, and we wish this man no personal harm of any, any kind."

Next he tried to put some heat on Henley: "There was quite a bit more money that was said to be taken than actually was. You might bring that to his attention. It seems that maybe he's got some people in his own company who dabbled somewhat."

And then Brooks got down to business: "The total price we're interested in procuring is one million dollars. We want it in two separate drops. The first one of which will be $500,000 for half of the documents. The second one will follow in a three-day period."

He concluded the ransom demand with a warning: "If there is at any time any breach of trust, the negotiations will stop at once.

"We'll call you tomorrow and you can either give us a yes or a no," added Brooks.

Henley stalled for time. "This is not money I could just pull out of my hat," she said, noting that Hughes himself would have to be contacted. "It takes me a little time to get in touch with the man, sometimes, you know."

"Well, that's your responsibility," replied Brooks. "We won't call but one more time."

As arranged, Brooks called back the next day for Henley's answer. The police were waiting. A helicopter and a fleet of squad cars were poised on alert, all set to close in as soon as the call could be traced. They got the first three digits in just a few seconds, started to focus the dragnet on North Hollywood . . . and never got any closer than that.

Nadine Henley was not there to receive the call. "All righty," said Chester Brooks, and hung up. He never called again.

The Pro was left sitting with his million-dollar haul. He decided to wait Hughes out. Wait until he was ready to sit down at the table and ante up for the big game. Wait until Hughes came after him. He waited for days, he waited for weeks, he waited for months, all the while hearing his TV blare news of Hughes, Maheu, Nixon, Rebozo, Watergate, wondering which if any of them had ordered the break-in, watching all these forces swirl about the hidden billionaire while he sat there with all of the man's secrets.

And while the Pro waited, unknown to him, the biggest secret of all began to leak out.

When the final ransom call came, Nadine Henley and the entire Hughes high command were aboard a mystery ship in Long Beach harbor, at the world's most exclusive bon-voyage party.

And while they waited in vain for Chester Brooks to call back, the mystery ship—the *Hughes Glomar Explorer*—set sail on a top-secret mission to a point in the Pacific 750 miles northwest of Hawaii.

The *Glomar* was known to the world as a futuristic deep-sea mining vessel that Hughes had built to scoop up the oceans' vast untapped mineral wealth. Kay Glenn knew better. The mining venture was simply a cover. And the three-hundred-and-fifty-million-dollar ship actually belonged not to Hughes but to the CIA.

Only a handful of people knew that, and on July 1 Glenn discovered something none of them knew.

A document outlining the *Glomar*'s true mission was missing. It was apparently now in the hands of the unknown burglars who had looted Romaine a month earlier. The security breach could not have come at a more sensitive time. The *Glomar* had just arrived at its destination and was about to reach a giant claw three miles underwater to recover a sunken Russian submarine from the bottom of the Pacific Ocean.

Glenn's boss, Bill Gay, called CIA Director William Colby to give him the news. Colby called FBI Director Clarence Kelley. Kelley called William Sullivan, head of the Bureau's Los Angeles office.

And Sullivan went directly to LAPD headquarters to confer with Los Angeles Police Chief Ed Davis.

When Sullivan emerged from his secret meeting with Chief Davis, he went downstairs to brief the detectives handling the Romaine investigation. He told them that "national security" was involved. He did not mention the *Glomar* or the Russian sub. But he did instruct the cops not to look at the stolen Hughes papers if they recovered them.

"We were supposed to close our eyes, seal the documents in a pouch, and deliver them unread to the FBI," said one detective who was at the meeting. "That's actually what they told us. I don't know how we were expected to find the stuff with our eyes closed."

Romaine was no longer a local police case. While lower-level officers were left to stumble about blindly, CIA general counsel John Warner met secretly with Chief Davis and Los Angeles District Attorney Joseph Busch.

"It's clear that Busch and Davis believed they were really doing something big for national security," recalled a prosecutor who became privy to the details. "But for the guys actually handling the investigation it was a disaster. Nobody knew what was up. The Hughes people were so goddamn mysterious, we couldn't get a thing out of them, then the FBI steps in and starts playing cat-and-mouse—saying it's your case, but don't ask what's going on—and lurking behind everything there's the CIA."

Indeed, some local law-enforcement officials wondered if the CIA had invented the "national security" claim to sabotage their investigation, to keep them from finding Hughes's secrets.

Meanwhile, back in Washington, a hastily formed CIA task force noted that "the burglars may well have been hired by the Corporation itself" and wondered if the *Glomar* document was really missing at all.

Perhaps the entire *Glomar* scare was merely a ploy to cover up Hughes's theft of his own files and at the same time bring the CIA into his battle against Maheu. "Hughes may attempt to place the blame for the burglary on Maheu," reported the task force, "simultaneously attempting to ascertain how strongly the Agency feels about the loss of the sensitive document, and hope that the Agency may offer to intercede in the Maheu trial."

But the CIA had to assume that the *Glomar* memo was in fact stolen, had to recognize that even the Russians might have it, and William Colby had to tell that to the president.

It must have been an odd meeting. In less than a month Richard Nixon would be forced out of office; his dealings with Hughes were under heavy scrutiny; and Colby knew that the president had reason beyond the *Glomar* to worry about the Romaine heist: the missing secret papers might contain a whole brace of "smoking guns."

Indeed, the CIA suspected that the White House itself might be behind the break-in. In its first list of "possible culprits," the Agency suggested that the burglary was "politically motivated to aid or deter Watergate investigation," and among "possible customers" the CIA included "anti-impeachment forces if documents are embarrassing."

But Colby claimed to recall no mention of Watergate in his meeting with Nixon, and very little talk of Romaine. "Obviously it was a major difficulty, obviously I was responsible to the president and kept him advised as to what was going on. I'm sure we discussed the potential exposure of the *Glomar* project. But I can't remember any particular discussion of the break-in. I'm just saying it would be quite normal for me to keep him advised of something like that."

And if Nixon had more than the *Glomar* on his mind, Colby too had other worries. Not only was the Castro assassination plot threatening to blow, but the Hughes organization also had a virtual monopoly on highly classified spy satellites and provided cover for CIA agents working abroad.

"Obviously we had other contracts with elements of the Hughes empire—research things and technology, and things like that—and to the extent that any of those . . ." Colby's voice trailed off. "But I don't know what was stolen," he continued. "I'm not sure anybody knows precisely what was taken. So I certainly can't say that any other project was compromised. I just don't know."

Only one thing was certain: the missing secret papers had to be recovered.

While the *Glomar* lowered its giant claw, and Colby huddled with Nixon, and the entire Hughes-CIA-FBI intelligence network went on red alert, two unlikely new characters joined the show. Leo Gordon, a sometime actor and screenwriter, and Donald Ray Woolbright, a sometime used-car salesman known to police as a petty thief.

Their alleged meeting late in July turned the Great Hughes Heist into an "Upstairs, Downstairs" melodrama, with Woolbright and Gordon playing the lowlife subplot in the running saga of powerful men in desperate pursuit of great secrets. Before it was over, Wool-bright would be indicted by a grand jury that heard Gordon as its star witness. The following account of their meeting is based on Gordon's testimony.

"I don't know whether I should tell you this," Woolbright began hesitantly, pacing the actor's living room. "But I've been beating it around in my head for days, and I've been walking the walls with it. I have something that's very big and I don't know quite how to handle it."

The car salesman was agitated. He couldn't sit still.

"Who is the most important man you can think of in the world today?" he suddenly asked.

"Kissinger," replied Gordon.

"How about Howard Hughes?" suggested Woolbright. "What would you say if I told you I had two boxes of Howard Hughes's personal documents?"

Gordon, who had seen newspaper accounts of the break-in, guessed that the documents must have come from Romaine. Woolbright, he claimed, simply nodded.

It was fitting that the Romaine mystery should take its next odd B-movie twist in Leo Gordon's living room. An aging Hollywood veteran, Gordon had played the second-level heavy in a long string of third-rate movies with titles like *The Restless Breed*, *Gun Fury*, and *Kitten with a Whip*; appropriately, he had also appeared in *The Man Who Knew Too Much*. His was one of those nameless leathery faces that had flickered through every TV action series from "Gun-smoke" to "The Untouchables." As an actor, he almost always played the bad guy. His specialty was death scenes; spliced together they would run at least three hours.

Woolbright also had a tough-guy image. But his was not manu-factured in Hollywood. A product of the north St. Louis slums, the car salesman had run up a hometown police record almost as long as Gordon's list of screen credits. He had twenty-six arrests, on charges ranging from burglary and fencing to assault and carrying a concealed weapon. But for all his arrests, Woolbright had never done any time, and his only conviction was for a petty misdemeanor. Back in St. Louis, police called him a "nickel-and-dimer," a street hustler with no real stature in the criminal community. And they could not believe that Woolbright was even remotely involved in the Hughes heist.

"If he did it," said one officer, "it would be the equivalent of a sandlot ballplayer going to the major leagues and hitting a home run in the World Series his first time at bat."

Then how did the used-car salesman come to have the billionaire's secret papers? He said he got them from "Bennie."

According to Gordon, Woolbright told him this strange tale. Woolbright said he was just sitting home one night when he got a call from a St. Louis man named Bennie. And that Bennie—whom he had met at a friend's funeral two years earlier and never seen again—said he represented four other men from St. Louis who had pulled the Romaine job "on commission." Now Bennie wanted Woolbright to ransom the purloined papers back to Hughes.

It was, by Gordon's account of Woolbright's odd tale, quite a haul. "There was stuff about political payoffs—Nixon, I think—and references to Hubert Humphrey as 'our boy Hubert,' " claimed the actor. "Files on Air West and TWA. A complete rundown on *everything* happening in Las Vegas. And a hell of a lot about the CIA." All of it handwritten by Hughes himself.

But the ransom attempt had fallen through. The would-be bagman was out of a job. Then Woolbright allegedly began thinking about Clifford Irving and figured that if Irving wangled $750,000 for a bogus autobiography, the real goods should be worth at least as much.

"That's why he came to see me," explained Gordon. "He thought that because I'm a professional writer, I'd be able to help him peddle the papers."

Still, Gordon was a very odd choice. Although he often played the villain as an actor, Gordon was in fact quite close to the forces of law and order. A familiar face around police headquarters, he had written more than twenty scripts for "Adam 12," a TV series glorifying two fictional squad-car cops. The license plates on Gordon's own car read ADM-12, he had an honorary police badge, and his best friend was an investigator for the district attorney's office.

Why would a bagman for the hottest burglars since Watergate risk spilling the beans to an ersatz cop? Why would the burglars entrust their valuable booty to Woolbright, a man their supposed contact had met only once? It made no sense.

Yet Gordon's account would soon become central to the entire Romaine case, and new characters drawn into the drama did confirm the Woolbright connection.

The actor first took his new partner to see a Hollywood business manager, Joanna Hayes, but she told them nobody would buy hot

Hughes papers from a used-car salesman. So they went instead to see a lawyer Gordon had heard was "well connected."

Woolbright showed the lawyer, Maynard Davis, a memo supposedly written by Hughes, and Davis placed a call to his "Uncle Sidney"—Sidney Korshak, reputed to be one of the most powerful organized crime leaders in the country.

As it happened, Los Angeles police believed that Korshak may have played a role in the Romaine heist. According to an LAPD report, Hughes security chief Ralph Winte said he had "received information that there were possibly two attorneys involved, Sidney Korshak and Morris Shenker . . . if a sale [of the papers] was made, it would be through these attorneys."

But Davis claimed his Uncle Sidney was out of town when he called, and swore he never discussed the Hughes papers with him.

Gordon said he and a dispirited Woolbright left the lawyer's office and went to a nearby coffee shop. "Well, we tried our best shot and I guess we're too lightweight to handle it," the car salesman reportedly said. "It's too big for us. I'll just have to give this stuff back to the people and forget it."

If Woolbright was discouraged, a large team of FBI men, CIA agents, and LAPD detectives was equally disheartened. Two months had passed since the burglary without a breakthrough, and the *Glomar* was completing its top-secret mission under threat of sudden exposure.

Finally, "Adam 12" Gordon tipped off the police. When his weird tale of the Woolbright connection flashed through law-enforcement circles, the reaction was immediate and seemingly decisive. The FBI told the LAPD to have Gordon reestablish contact with Woolbright and sent word to Chief Davis that there was a million dollars in CIA funds available to buy back Hughes's dangerous secrets.

"Payoff: This option unquestionably rankles," noted a CIA report, "but must be considered a mere pittance when weighed against the time, effort, and monies expended to date on *Glomar*."

With the million in hand, the FBI and CIA prepared an elaborate scheme: "Informant being operated by LAPD would meet with chief suspect Woolbright within the next couple of days for the sole purpose of indicating that the informant has a possible interested eastern buyer. LAPD informant will introduce seller to Los Angeles attorney, who would then give name of New York attorney who had client interested in stolen merchandise. Bureau agent from Los Angeles division would be identified as assistant to New York attorney, and would be available to fly to Los Angeles with $100,000 with which to negotiate a buy. Stipulation would be not to buy package unseen, but rather to examine individual pieces of merchandise. It is believed that this procedure would enable undercover agent to examine all merchandise. $100,000 to be placed in safety-deposit box in Los Angeles bank as 'show money' to be utilized by undercover agent in buy transaction."

That was the plan. Yet despite the trappings of high-level intrigue and high finance, what followed was low comedy.

On police orders, Gordon met with Woolbright at an all-night restaurant near his home. But the actor had not been given any lines. His instructions were simply to renew contact. No one had told him what to say. Left to improvise, Gordon concocted an odd story. He told Woolbright that movie star Robert Mitchum would put up the money for the stolen papers. The meeting ended indecisively.

Detectives hurriedly arranged for Gordon to confer with federal officials, but hours before the scheduled strategy meeting, Woolbright called and demanded an immediate rendezvous. The Mitchum story had not gone over. "All right, I'll level with you," said Gordon. "The police are onto it. The Feds are onto it. They know about me, and they know about you, and all they're interested in right now is recovering those documents because national security is involved."

Woolbright, according to Gordon, took the news quietly but issued a warning: "The people I'm dealing with are not the nicest people in the world. If this goes wrong, it might take a few years, but we'll pay the piper."

Gordon claims they then struck a deal: Woolbright would get one folder to verify that he had the documents; Gordon would supply $3,500 front money. "He told me he was leaving immediately, then added, 'But my God, don't tell the police—if I show up with a tail I'm a dead man.' "

Later that evening, Gordon met for the first time with a government representative. The official said his name was Don Castle, but never showed any identification and refused to say which federal agency he represented. He told Gordon to get word to him through the police when Woolbright called back.

The call came two weeks later. Woolbright said he was "still working on it." Gordon was taken for a second meeting with Castle at a North Hollywood hotel. "When this goes down I want a controlled situation," said the mysterious agent. Then he added with a laugh, "Maybe we'll get the right folder and solve this whole thing for three or four thousand dollars."

It was not to be. Gordon said he never saw or heard from Woolbright again. Nor did he ever have further contact with the mysterious Don Castle.

"They dropped me like a hot potato after that last meeting," complained Gordon. "It was really strange. It was like I had the Hope diamond, and *zap*, all of a sudden it was glass."

The great search for the stolen Hughes secrets had come to an abrupt end.

Why, after gearing up so intense a recovery effort, after bringing in the heads of the CIA, the FBI, and the LAPD, even alerting the president of the United States, why, after pledging a million dollars to the quest, did everyone simply give up after entrusting the entire mission to a second-string movie actor?

Apparently because Hughes's secrets were thought to be so dangerous that finally nobody wanted to find them.

In the weeks that followed the failure of Operation Gordon, the FBI and CIA met to plot a new investigation of the Romaine heist, starting from scratch—and instead quietly decided to drop the whole case.

An FBI report classified "secret" spelled it all out:

"Bureau agents met October 31, 1974, with representatives of sister federal agency regarding status of instant case and ramifications of contemplated investigation.

"Conference at Los Angeles included discussion of possibilities of embarrassment to sister federal agency in the event of direct and full field investigation of theft by FBI."

But it was not only the CIA that might be embarrassed.

"In view of the possibilities of direct investigation and inquiry with some of the nationally known personalities involved with Howard Hughes interests, which might lead to disclosure, it is recommended that no further investigation be conducted by the FBI unless the other interested federal agency is in agreement with the above-mentioned interviews."

It was not. Although the *Glomar* secret remained at risk, top officials of the CIA decided to abandon the investigation. The Agency had learned from a "fairly reliable source" what was stolen from

Romaine and passed the unsettling information along to the FBI:

"Property taken included cash, personal notes, and handwritten memoranda by Howard Hughes; correspondence between Hughes and prominent political figures, etc. The personal papers are said to be sufficient in volume to fill two footlockers and are filed in manila-type folders and catalogued in some fashion. The contents are said to be highly explosive from a political view and, thus, considered both important and valuable to Hughes and others."

Political dynamite. Already a president had been driven from office amid speculation that Watergate was triggered by his dealings with Hughes. God only knew what else might be revealed in those stolen documents, what other powers might be implicated in which dirty deals. Neither the FBI nor the CIA wanted any part of it.

Top officials met at Langley late in November to close out the case: "It was finally decided that the Agency would do nothing but monitor the case and request nothing from the FBI except what the FBI is doing: i.e., the FBI is monitoring the Los Angeles Police Department. At the current time the Los Angeles Police Department is not conducting a current investigation, so in effect they are doing nothing at this time."

And that's how the official investigation ended. With the CIA watching the FBI do nothing, and the FBI watching the Los Angeles police do nothing, all of them now afraid to find Howard Hughes's dangerous secrets, fearing to embarrass "prominent political figures" and "nationally known personalities," fearing to find secrets best left untold.

It was like the final scene from *Raiders of the Lost Ark*. No one wanted to find the Romaine raiders, much less open the lost Hughes ark.

It was almost two years later when I entered the case, looking only for the answers to a few questions about the *Glomar*.

Woolbright was about to come to trial, and I assumed that the Romaine break-in had been solved, the burglars arrested, the loot recovered. But I had not made more than a few phone calls before I realized that something was terribly wrong: obvious leads had never been followed; obvious questions had never been asked; the Hughes organization had never come clean with the cops or the FBI; the CIA had tampered with the grand jury. Even the prosecutor handling the case was not at all sure the lone defendant was guilty, had no idea who actually staged the break-in, much less who was ultimately behind it, and indeed was not at all certain that there had even really been a break-in.*

And, of course, the stolen secret papers had never been found. I was determined to get them. It was clear that everyone else had abandoned the quest.

I cannot tell here how I cracked the Romaine case, how the trail finally led to the Pro, how I tracked down the man with the stolen Hughes secrets, because I promised to protect him as a confidential source.

It was less Sherlock Holmes than a lot of legwork, and a bit of luck, following up leads the police had failed to, going down several blind alleys, playing one hunch and then another, just pulling at all the loose threads until the whole strange mystery finally unraveled. And when I had put it all together, when the evidence seemed absolute, I went looking for the man who had the secrets that the FBI and the CIA had been afraid to find.

"I can prove that you did it," I told the Pro.

We were sitting alone in the back of a bar. It was the first time we had met. I could see a gun stuck into the waistband of his pants. It wasn't well concealed.

"I'm going to write a book," I continued. "It's either going to be about you and the break-in or it's going to be about Howard Hughes. It's your choice. But if it's going to be a book about Hughes, I'll need your help. I'll need the papers."

The Pro said nothing. Not a word. He just threw me a hard look and waited for me to go on. I confronted him with the evidence. He listened without comment.

I hadn't scared him. I got the feeling no one ever had. Except Howard Hughes. I tried to keep the conversation going, to ease the tension, and as we talked I began to realize that this thief was totally obsessed with Hughes, that the obsession had nearly destroyed him, and that the secret papers he wouldn't admit to having had become a curse.

That was my way in. He actually *wanted* to unload those dread

---

*Eventually, after two trials and two deadlocked juries, all charges against Woolbright were dismissed. No one else has ever been charged with any aspect of the burglary.

documents. But how could I get him to give them to me? One thing I knew about people with secrets: deep down they all really wanted to tell. What good was it to have pulled off this great caper if no one knew he had done it?

I had to get him to trust me. We spent the next two days together. We talked for fourteen hours straight the first day, in the bar, in a hotel lobby, walking the streets, sitting in a park. We slept five hours and met again the next day for breakfast. Again, we talked nonstop all day and into the night.

He wanted to talk about Hughes. For two years he had been wanting to talk about Hughes, wanting to tell what he alone knew. But first he wanted to know more about me, why I'd come after him.

I told him who I was. A former reporter for the *Washington Post* and the *Wall Street Journal*, now a free lance on assignment from *New Times* magazine. I told him how I had gotten into the Romaine story, searching for the answer to another unsolved mystery, a top-secret military project that supposedly involved the *Glomar* and a fantastic plot to deploy missiles at the bottom of the ocean.

None of that got to him. What got to him first was the discovery that I had been in jail. That I had done more time than he had.

"What were you in for?" asked the Pro.

"Protecting a source," I said. "Refusing to give up a guy to a grand jury."

He liked that. We began to talk about his crime. He still wasn't admitting anything, but I talked about the break-in as if he had done it, I talked about the papers as if he had them, and gradually he began to talk about it that way too. I told him I didn't think he had done anything wrong, that in fact I admired what he had done, thought that he had pulled off one of the great capers of all time, and that he had gotten hold of something truly important, secrets the American people had a right to know.

"What does that make me?" asked the Pro. "An investigative thief?"

"Precisely," I told him. "And the real criminal is Hughes. He tried to steal our entire country."

"I don't know," said the Pro, taking exception. "I like the guy. You know, I really liked him."

He sounded a bit wistful. Howard Hughes was dead. He had died just a few months earlier. Without ever exactly saying he had committed the break-in, without ever exactly admitting he had the secret papers, the Pro began to tell me his fantasy—his long-nurtured plan to play pair poker with Hughes.

"In my own mind I saw myself actually sitting there in the penthouse playing cards with Hughes," he said. "I was suddenly his equal for that moment. Maybe I'd be blown away the minute I walked out the door, but there I was, a guy from total nowhere, playing a winning game with Howard Hughes."

For two years he had sat on those hot stolen secrets, waiting to see who would come after him, waiting for Hughes to ante up for the big game. But no one had come. And now Hughes was dead. So was the fantasy.

I had to give him a new fantasy. And suddenly I realized that the Pro himself had already come up with it. Instead of playing pair poker, he could play investigative thief.

I mentioned Daniel Ellsberg. The Pro wasn't at all sure he approved of what Ellsberg had done. Like most criminals, he was a hard-line patriot. Still, he began to warm to the role, to feel important, perhaps even noble.

"If you had the papers, where would you stash them?" he asked me. Before I could answer, he tore a piece of paper from my notepad, crumpled it up into a little ball, and, holding it in front of me, asked, "Where would you hide *this*? It's not so easy to hide something so that no one could ever find it. Not even something as small as this. Where would you hide three steamer trunks?"

"Where did *you* hide them?" I asked in reply.

"Sealed in a wall," said the Pro, openly admitting for the first time that he had the stolen papers. "Built right into the wall of a house, and the people that're living there don't even know it. Been in that wall for almost two years."

"Are you sure they're still there?" I asked, not because I doubted it but because I wanted him to. As long as those papers were safely immured, they would remain beyond my reach.

"Pretty interesting that the FBI and the CIA and Hughes all stopped looking, that nobody ever came after you," I observed. "Have you ever wondered why?"

"Sure," said the Pro. "What're you getting at?"

"I was just wondering if they found what they were really after. I mean, you haven't actually *seen* the papers for a couple of years. Maybe they're not in that wall anymore."

The Pro shrugged it off, but he was clearly disturbed. I had to make him wonder if the papers were gone, if he had already lost his treasure without even knowing it. I had to play on his paranoia until he could no longer live with the doubt, until he just *had* to go into that wall and get those papers back out.

Several times over the next few hours he asked me if I really thought they might be gone. "Who knows?" I replied. "It would sure explain an awful lot."

It was late into the evening of the second day when the Pro suddenly said, "Okay, I'm gonna get them out. I'll show them to you."

Just like that. It was hard to believe. It had been much too easy. I began to wonder if he really had the Hughes papers, if this was all a scam, if I had been playing him or if he had been playing me, if I had followed another false trail. Or, even if he really did have them, if he was simply trying to keep me from unmasking him by making a promise he never intended to keep.

I didn't yet understand how desperately he wanted to get rid of the curse. I never really would. Not until I had the papers myself.

I returned from that trip to write my story about the break-in, uncertain now if I had actually solved it. Several times over the next few months I talked to the Pro, pay phone to pay phone, and each time he said he would show me the papers. But not quite yet.

Finally, I went ahead with the magazine article, presenting the case as unsolved, raising questions about who was behind it, never mentioning the Pro, not quite sure how he really fit into it all, also not wanting to put an X on the treasure map.

But there was a hidden message in that story, one that made clear I knew far more, and to make sure that the Pro didn't miss it, I delivered a copy of the magazine to him personally.

He read the story all the way through, turned back to an illustration up front, a picture of a safecracker opening a Pandora's box, a vault spewing out all manner of strange and terrible secrets, and, pointing to the burglar, he said, "Hey, that's me."

That's what got him. Not my story. Not my hidden message. That picture. It had memorialized the break-in, had finally given him some recognition, had made his adventure seem meaningful again. He kept looking at that picture all day.

The next day we went hunting together.

He was testing me, seeing whether I would go out into the woods alone with him, a shotgun in his hand, whether I would risk that after threatening to nail him, and as we walked through the trees toward a river he asked me if I had told anyone what I knew. I said I had not.

"Don't you think it's pretty dangerous to tell me that?" he asked.

"Not really," I replied. "Who else are you going to find to take those damn papers off your hands?"

I had never gone hunting before, had never shot anything but a tin can, but I was lucky now and shot down a duck, and while the recoil nearly broke both my jaw and my shoulder, I knew I had passed some important rite, had successfully entered his territory.

As we were walking, we talked politics, and the Pro told me he had received a letter from Richard Nixon thanking him for his support of the president's Vietnam policy. It was dated June 5, 1974.

We got to talking about Watergate. "Square Johns," said the Pro. He said it with real contempt. "You don't get a bunch of retired spies and FBI agents to do a break-in," he added. "If you want to do a break-in, you get yourself some burglars."

And all the while I kept wondering if this Nixon supporter, this Hughes admirer, this oddly vulnerable professional thief with right-wing ideas and left-wing instincts was really going to give me his stolen secret papers.

While we were sitting by the river, he told me he would. And this time I knew that he meant it.

I told him that I also had to know the full story of the break-in, that I would protect him, keep his name out of it, go to jail myself if necessary rather than give him up, but that I had to know who was really behind the heist.

"I don't know," said the Pro.

He told me how it all came down, about the Jiggler and Red and Mr. Inside, and about the mystery man who suddenly appeared the night of the break-in. He told me details only one of the burglars could know, but there was one detail he could not tell me: who was ultimately behind it.

"I never knew," he said. "I wasn't supposed to end up with the papers. I always figured that whoever was behind it would come after me. No one ever did.

"Except you."

My instructions were to go directly from the airport to a massage parlor. That's what the Pro told me a few weeks later, when he called to say he was ready to show me the papers.

"Just ask for Honey," he said. "She'll take good care of you."

The parlor was on the outskirts of town, along a seedy commercial strip, and inside it was decorated with oil paintings of nude women, all painted with real passion by a convict whose fantasies had clearly run wild while he was locked up in prison. The artist was a friend of the Pro's, and the Pro owned a piece of the parlor.

I asked for Honey. She smiled invitingly and took me through a beaded curtain to a back room. "Aren't you going to take off your clothes?" she asked. I hesitated, wondering first if she had mistaken me for a regular customer, then wondering if this was the punch line of a practical joke, if the Pro had lured me into coming for his papers only to leave me naked in his whorehouse. On the other hand, this could be merely a prudent security measure. What better way to make sure I wasn't wired or armed?

I stripped down to my shorts. "Don't be shy," said Honey, and I took them off too. She checked me out, went through my clothes, and when I was dressed again she led me out a back door. We got into a car parked behind the parlor and drove to a garden apartment a few miles away. It was empty, and without explanation Honey drove off, leaving me there alone.

At first I just sat anxiously on the edge of an armchair, waiting to see who would appear, what would happen next. I waited ten minutes, fifteen, half an hour. Nothing happened. A clock in the kitchen showed a different hour than my watch, so I picked up the phone to call for the right time. The line was dead.

Tired and tense, I stretched out on a couch, but as soon as I lay down I felt something hard sticking into my back. Reaching between the cushions, searching for the source of my discomfort, I pulled out a gun. A black nine-millimeter Browning semiautomatic. It was loaded.

Hurriedly, I stuffed the pistol back between the cushions, sat upright at the other end of the couch, then realized that my fingerprints were all over that gun. Alarmed by the thought, I wiped the gun clean with my shirttail and again shoved it back where I had found it, all my senses now on full alert.

At that instant, I heard the door open. In walked the Pro. He had been parked out front all along, waiting to see if I had been tailed. He said he was going to take me to see the papers.

We drove quite a distance, and while I wasn't familiar with the area, it seemed that he doubled back several times, always with an eye on the rearview mirror. Finally, we made a few quick turns, drove through a shopping center, and pulled into a motel. The room was empty. No secret papers. We stayed there an hour or so, watching TV, then left.

"You didn't really think I was going to give them to you, did you?" asked the Pro as we got back into his car. I just looked at him, full of anger. He laughed.

"Well, I am," he said. "I don't know why, but I am. Either you're the most sincere guy I ever met or the best con man in the world. Anyway, I'm gonna give them to you. I wouldn't if Hughes was still alive. If you had come while he was alive, I wouldn't of even talked to you. I wouldn't of talked to Colby or Hoover. I wouldn't of talked to Nixon. Only Hughes."

We drove for a while in silence and finally pulled into another cheap motel out in the middle of nowhere. As soon as we walked in the door, I saw three padlocked steamer trunks.

The Pro opened them without ceremony. It was the end of his adventure, and the beginning of mine, his escape from the hold that Hughes had kept over him for more than two years, and my heedless rush into that same harrowing embrace.

Two of the trunks were crammed with white typewritten documents, and the third was filled with thousands of yellow legal-pad pages, handwritten memos signed "Howard." It was Hughes's "in" box and "out" box for an entire era, virtually everything his henchmen had sent him, virtually everything Hughes himself had ever dared to put down in his own hand, a complete documentary record of his dealings stolen from his fortress and then sealed in a wall, unseen and untouched by any outsider except the Pro, until now.

All that night, all through the next day, and all through the next night I sat up in that motel room reading those documents, at first afraid to stop, not knowing whether I'd ever get to see them again, then unable to stop, completely drawn into the stark power of the story revealed in these strange secret papers.

It was "political dynamite," all right. But hardly what the FBI or the CIA could have feared or even imagined. The memos were at once a cold-blooded tale of an entire nation's corruption and an intimate journal of one man's descent into madness. The great secret that Howard Hughes had kept hidden was not this or that scandal, not this payoff or that shady deal, but something far more sweeping and far more frightening—the true nature of power in America.

1 Mr. Big

Remote control.

There was no need to venture out, not even to stand up. The little silver-gray box had invisible power, and its four oblong buttons controlled everything. At the slightest touch it sent out a special high-frequency signal, silent to the human ear, but capable of activating an immense circuitry that reached almost everywhere.

Howard Hughes gripped the rectangular instrument.

Alone in the darkened bedroom of his Las Vegas penthouse hideaway, lying naked on a double bed, propped up by two pillows, and insulated by a layer of paper towels from the disheveled sheets that had not been changed for several months, Hughes pushed one button. Again. And again.

The television channels flipped by in rapid succession.

Hughes checked out the full gamut of stations on the color TV that flickered at his feet. Then, satisfied, he set aside his Zenith Space Commander.

It was just after two A.M. on Thursday, June 6, 1968. ABC was dark. NBC had also signed off for the night. Only channel 8, the local CBS affiliate that Hughes himself owned, was still on the air to broadcast the grim news.

Robert F. Kennedy was dead.

Hughes had been awake for two nights, gripped by the video spectacle. He had watched Kennedy claim victory in the California presidential primary, smiling, joking, earnest, vibrantly alive. He had heard the shots just minutes later, muffled at first by the noise of the still cheering crowd, then distinct and unmistakable. He had seen Bobby lie bleeding on the cold cement floor.

It was a shared national experience. The shock and horror—the agonized moans of disbelief, the panic, the hysteria, the tears—spread in waves through the throng of stunned campaign workers and was instantly transmitted to millions across the country. Everywhere people watched television and waited, listening to hospital bulletins, reliving the immediate tragedy in endless replays that also revived painful memories of Dallas.

Through it all, for almost twenty-six hours, Hughes had kept his TV vigil, and now he watched a red-eyed Frank Mankiewicz walk slump-shouldered into the floodlit hospital lobby to confirm everybody's worst fears. Biting his lip to hold back the tears, the press secretary bowed his head for a moment, then read a brief statement: "Senator Robert Francis Kennedy died at 1:44 A.M. today. He was forty-two years old."

Mankiewicz spoke softly, but the fateful announcement blared from Hughes's television, its volume turned to the highest level to accommodate the partially deaf billionaire. News of the tragedy continued to reverberate in his room.

But Hughes was no longer listening. He reached over to a bedside night table, grabbed a long yellow legal pad, and, propping it up on his knees, scrawled a fevered memo to his chief of staff, Robert Maheu.

"I hate to be quick on the draw," wrote Hughes, "but I see here an opportunity that may not happen again in a lifetime. I dont aspire to be President, but I do want political strength. . . .

"I have wanted this for a long time, but somehow it has always evaded me. I mean the kind of an organization so that we would never have to worry about a jerky little thing like this anti-trust problem—not in 100 years.

"And I mean the kind of a set up that, if we wanted to, could put Gov. Laxalt in the White House in 1972 or 76.*

"Anyway, it seems to me that the very people we need have just fallen smack into our hands. Also, if we approach them *quickly* and skillfully, they should be as anxious to find a haven with us as we are to obtain them. . . .

"So, in consideration of my own nervous system, will you please

---

*Paul Laxalt, then the obscure but very cooperative governor of Nevada, now a U.S. Senator who was Ronald Reagan's campaign chairman and is perhaps the president's closest friend.

move like lightning on this deal—first, to report to me whom you think we want, of Kennedy's people, and second to contact such people with absolutely no delay the minute I confirm your recommendation. I repeat, the absolutely imperative nature of this mission requires the very ultimate in skill. If it is not so handled, and if this project should leak out, I am sure that I will be absolutely crucified by the press. . . .

"However, I have confidence that you can handle this deal, and I think the potential, in manpower and in a political machine all built and operating, I think these potentials are just inestimable, and worth the risk—provided you move *fast.* Please let me hear *at once.*"

Hughes lifted his ball-point pen, read the memo over carefully, and signed it "Howard." He slipped the two-page message into a large manila envelope, then snapped one long fingernail smartly against a brown paper bag hanging at his bedside as a depository for used Kleenex. It made a sharp noise, summoning from an adjoining room one of the five male attendants who served him in rotating shifts around the clock. The Mormon aide licked the flap, sealed the envelope, and carried it to an armed security guard stationed just outside, separated from the Hughes suite by a locked door that had been specially installed in the hotel hallway. The guard, in turn, took an elevator nine flights down, walked a few yards, and delivered Hughes's memo to Robert Maheu at his home next door to the hotel.

Maheu, an outwardly genial former FBI agent whose soft round features masked a toughness only hinted at by his cold black eyes, apparently failed to fully grasp the nature of his new mission. In a follow-up message later that morning, Hughes impatiently explained his orders while a presidential jet flew Kennedy's body back to New York to lie in state at St. Patrick's Cathedral, where 150,000 people waited in a line stretching more than a mile for a glimpse of the coffin.

"Bob," wrote Hughes, "I thought you would understand. I want us to hire Bob Kennedy's entire organization—with certain exceptions, of course, I am not sure we want Salinger and a few others. However, here is an entire integrated group, used to getting things done over all obstacles. They are used to having the Kennedy money behind them and we can equal that. This group was trained by John Kennedy and his backers, and then moved over to R.F.K. when John died.

"It is a natural for us. I am not looking for political favors from

Bob—

I hate to be quick on the draw, but I see here an opportunity that may not happen again in a lifetime. I dont aspire to be President, but I do want political strength. I want the kind of strength Pan American used to have in the days of Sam Pryor.

I have wanted this for a long time, but somehow it has always evaded me. I mean the kind of an organization so that we would never have to worry about a jerky little thing like this anti-trust problem — not in 100 years!

And I mean the kind of a set up that, if we wanted to, could put Gov. Laxalt in the White House in 1972 or 76.

Anyway, it seems to me that the very people we need have just fallen smack into our hands. Also, if we approach them quickly and skillfully, they should be as anxious to find a haven with us as we are to obtain them.

If we do not move quickly, they may make other tie-ups just to avoid losing face by being in the position of

standing around with no
job in sight. They may
easily make other arrangements
just in deference to their
pride, and once announcing
same, they will be much more
difficult to deal with.

So, in consideration
of my own nervous system,
will you please move like
lightning on this deal —
first, to report to me whom
you think we want, of
Kennedy's people, and second
to contact such people with
absolutely no delay the minute
I confirm your recommend-
ation. I repeat, the absolutely
imperative nature of this mission
requires the very ultimate in
skill. If it is not so handled,
and if this project should leak out,
I am sure that I will be
absolutely crucified by the press,
under the astute handling of
Mr. Salinger.

However, I have con-
fidence that you can handle
this deal, and I think the
potential, in manpower and in
a political machine all built and
operating, I think these potential
are just inestimable, and worth
the risk — provided you move
fast. Please let me hear at
once, Howard

them. I expect you to pick our candidate and soon. I repeat, I dont want an alliance with the Kennedy group, I want to put them on the payroll."

Maheu understood. And he delivered. Not the entire Kennedy team, but its leader, Bobby's campaign manager, Larry O'Brien. Before the month was out, Maheu had made contact. A few days later, O'Brien—a central figure in American politics, a White House insider who had already directed two successful presidential campaigns and was about to take command of the Democratic party— was in Las Vegas talking terms. Soon he was "on the payroll."

Moving with the cold audacity of a grave robber, Hughes had switched O'Brien from Camelot to his own dark kingdom almost as effortlessly as he switched television channels. And he had done it without ever leaving his room. By remote control.

To a nation of mourners focused on the public passion play, this hidden backstage drama would have seemed a blasphemy, its language alone an outrage. There was no hint of sorrow, no sign of any emotion, only a terrible urgency to close the "deal." For two days Hughes had watched a tragedy and seen only an "opportunity."

He had also seen what the mourners missed. Power in America was not an Arthurian romance of martyred princes and loyal knights honor-bound to an ideal, but a marketplace where influence and allegiances were bought and sold.

There was nothing unusual about the O'Brien transaction, except for its macabre backdrop. Richard Nixon, Hubert Humphrey, Lyndon Johnson—virtually every major political figure of the era, including even Bobby Kennedy himself—also had a Hughes connection, as did scores of lesser national leaders and local potentates. Hughes had appraised them all with the cool detachment of an investment analyst. "I have done this kind of business with him before," he had said of Johnson. "So, he wears no awe-inspiring robe of virtue with me." Humphrey was "a candidate who needs us and wants our help," and thus "somebody we control sufficiently." Bobby Kennedy, on the other hand, "would get too much support from others," but might win, "so lets cover our bets." Only Nixon ("my man") got the ultimate accolade: "he I know for sure knows the facts of life."

Camelot was a trifle. Howard Hughes had long ago set out to buy the government of the United States.

"Try to determine who is the real, honest-to-God, bagman at the White House," he once ordered his henchman Robert Maheu. "And please dont be frightened away by the enormity of the thought. Now,

6/6/68

Bob –

   I thought you would understand. I want us to hire Bob Kennedy's entire organization — with certain exceptions, of course. I am not sure we want Salinger and a few others. However, here is an entire integrated group, used to getting things done over all obstacles. They are used to having the Kennedy money behind them and we can equal that. This group was trained by John Kennedy and his backers, and then moved over to R.F.K. when John died.

   It is a natural for us. I am not looking for political favors from them. I expect you to pick our candidate and soon. I repeat, I dont want an alliance with the Kennedy group, I want to put them on the payroll. Please read my last message again.

   Many, many thanks and please! let me hear!

                JN.

I dont know whom you have to approach, but there is somebody, take my word for it."

Hughes spoke the language of power stripped of all pretense. What set him apart, finally, more than his money, more than his megalomania, more even than his mystery, was his blunt buy-the-bastards approach. It was not that Hughes cynically bought politicians—others also went to market—but that he innocently demanded a bill of sale. All who did business with him knew that they had made not merely a deal, but had entered into a virtual Faustian pact.

"I am determined to elect a President of our choosing this year, and one who will be deeply indebted, and who will recognize his indebtedness," the billionaire had declared earlier in 1968, preparing for an orderly transition of power. "Since I am willing to go beyond all limitations on this, I think we should be able to select a candidate and a party who knows the facts of political life."

He ordered repeated payoffs to presidents, presidential candidates, senators, congressmen, and governors, caring nothing about party labels or political ideologies, not at all caught up in personal charisma or campaign rhetoric, guided only by his own golden rule: "find the right place, and the right people, and buy what we want."

When his agents approached the government on a businesslike basis, the payoffs often succeeded. But Hughes was driven by his fears and phobias to seek what even his money could not buy and no matter how much power he acquired, he was never satisfied.

"I have given a full lifespan of service to this country, and taken very little for my personal pleasure or glorification," complained the unappreciated patriot. "If I dont rate better than this shoddy treatment, it is pretty sad."

Citizen Hughes. He bought politicians but never voted. He railed bitterly against taxes but paid none at all for seventeen consecutive years. His empire produced strategic weapons of the nuclear age, but he fought atomic testing in his own backyard.

Citizen Hughes. He tried to buy the government of the United States but instead helped bring it down.

Neither Hughes nor anyone else could have known it at the time, but the long slide toward Watergate started with the memo he wrote the night that Bobby Kennedy died.

That memo brought Larry O'Brien into the Hughes orbit, and their relationship came to obsess Richard Nixon, who feared that the hated Kennedy gang would discover his own hidden dealings with the billionaire. For years it has been rumored that the Hughes-

Nixon-O'Brien triangle triggered Watergate. New information disclosed in this book now makes it clear that Nixon inspired the break-in in a desperate effort to cover up his Hughes connection.

Hughes had so carefully hedged his bets, had channeled so much secret cash to so many rival powers, that such a collision was inevitable.

If others more sophisticated, less paranoid, managed to acquire more actual power, still it was Hughes who became the very symbol of hidden power, it was Hughes who brought down a president, and it was Hughes who forced the eternal question: Is there a Mr. Big?

He was only trying to protect himself.

There were dangers everywhere, and he was so vulnerable. The world was dealing with a façade. The real Howard Hughes lay hidden in a self-made prison, a naked old man in terrible pain and terminal terror, living like an inmate in the back ward of a mental institution, looking like a corpse laid out on a slab in the city morgue.

He was a figure of gothic horror, something ready for or just risen from the grave. Emaciated, practically skeletal with only 120 pounds stretched out over his six-foot-four-inch frame, and hardly a speck of color about him anywhere, not even in his lips, he seemed not merely dead but already in decay. Only the long gray hair that trailed halfway down his back, the thin, scraggly beard that reached midway onto his sunken chest, and the hideously long nails that extended several inches in grotesque yellowed corkscrews from his fingers and toes seemed still to be growing, still showing signs of life. That, and his eyes. Sometimes they looked dead, blank. But other times they gleamed from their deep-sunk sockets with surprising, almost frightening intensity, fixed in a hard, searching, penetrating stare. Often, however, they seemed to stare in, not out.

Hughes was in pain. Physical pain. Mental pain. Deep, unrelenting pain. Many of his teeth were rotting black stumps, some just dangling loose from his puffy, whitened, pus-filled gums. A tumor was beginning to emerge from the side of his head, a reddened lump protruding through sparse strands of gray hair. He had bedsores festering all down his back, some so severe that eventually one shoulder blade—the bare bone—would poke through his parchmentlike skin. And then there were the needle marks. The telltale tracks ran the full length of both his thin arms, scarred his thighs, and clustered horribly around his groin.

Howard Hughes was an addict. A billionaire junkie. He was shooting up massive amounts of codeine, routinely "skin-popping" more than twenty grains daily, sometimes three or four times that much, regularly taking doses thought lethal. He had been hooked for two decades, ever since a 1946 plane crash, when his doctor prescribed morphine to ease the pain of what everyone thought would be his final hours. As he instead recovered, the doctors substituted codeine, and through the years Hughes demanded ever-larger doses, finally setting up a byzantine illegal supply operation, getting prescriptions filled under assumed names at various Los Angeles drugstores.

Often now he would awaken in the terrors of withdrawal and begin his day by reaching down to the black metal box by his bedside where he kept his stash and his unsterilized hypodermic needle. Immediately mixing a fix, he would dissolve several white tablets in his pure bottled Poland Spring water, then jab the spike into his wasted body. Sometimes he prolonged the ritual by "double-pumping," injecting half the white fluid, then drawing it back up into the syringe with his blood, letting the needle dangle for a moment before he shot the full load back into his system. Then he would relax, and in the first warm flush of relief and satisfaction now and then softly sing a little jingle to himself, a little scat bebop routine he remembered from the old days. "Hey-bop-a-ree bop. Hey-bop-a-ree-bop." And finally maybe even a quiet chuckle.

There were other drugs, and the codeine was not the worst of them. Hughes was also gobbling massive quantities of tranquilizers, up to two hundred milligrams of Valium and Librium at a single shot, ten times the normal dose. Blue bombers. And when he wasn't shooting codeine, he was swallowing fistfuls of Empirin #4, a prescription compound containing codeine, aspirin, caffeine, and a synthetic pain-killer called phenacetin. It was not the codeine but the phenacetin that was doing the real damage, ravaging his already shrunken kidneys. Eventually it would kill him.

Already he had the smell of death around him. He rarely washed. He never brushed his teeth. Most of the time, instead of walking to the bathroom, he stayed in bed and urinated into a wide-necked mason jar, insisting that the filled jars be kept and stored in his bedroom closet. Moving his bowels was a far more complex operation. He was chronically, terminally constipated and routinely spent a large part of his day, often five or ten hours at a time, sitting on the toilet without results, despite huge doses of powerful laxatives. In the end, he usually gave it up and had to once again submit to the humiliation of an enema administered by one of his nursemaids.

So there he was, sprawled naked on his unmade bed. Mr. Big. Like the portrait of Dorian Gray, his was the true but hidden face of power in America. All the inner corruption made visible. And like that portrait, Howard Hughes too had to be locked away, concealed from public view.

No one knew what he looked like. No one knew how he lived. No one—not the man in the street, not the businessmen or politicians who dealt with him, not the presidents who treated him as an equal, not even his own top executives—had the slightest inkling of what Howard Hughes had become.

No one had seen him for almost a decade.

And like Dorian Gray himself, Hughes presented a public image that remained forever young, fixed in an earlier, more innocent time. The picture most people still had of Hughes was from his last public appearance. Vigorous and vital—if no longer Jimmy-Stewart boyish, still handsome, his dark hair slicked back and parted down the middle, a commanding presence, a tall supremely confident tycoon, looking a bit like a leading man from a 1940s movie, but far more rugged, more forceful, more dangerous, radiating power. In short, Hughes as he had appeared in his last newsreels.

Indeed, his whole life seemed as if it had been played out in a dazzling series of newsreels.

Orphaned a millionaire at age eighteen. Heir to an ever-expanding fortune based on a tiny drill bit his father had invented. Holder of an absolute monopoly on the device needed to extract from the ground virtually every drop of oil in the world. Sole owner of an enterprise that would pour out hundreds of millions of dollars!

Hughes in Hollywood. The teen-age tycoon come to Tinseltown, using his sudden wealth to pursue his passions: movies, airplanes, and women. 1930: Grauman's Chinese Theater. Not yet twenty-five, he leaps into national prominence with the most expensive movie in history, *Hell's Angels*. Then a whole string of big hits: *The Front Page*, *Scarface*, *The Outlaw*. Hughes at his own openings, a seemingly endless succession of screen goddesses on his arm, including two he himself made into sex symbols. Jean Harlow, the Platinum Blonde. Jane Russell, the Buxom Bombshell. A fabulously rich, somewhat notorious playboy-producer high-stepping through the Great Depression!

Hughes the Flying Ace. The daring young pilot in his leather flight jacket, a fedora tilted rakishly across his forehead. Standing beside racing planes he himself designed and built. Breaking all the records. 1935: a new land speed record. 1936: the cross-country record. 1937: a second transcontinental dash that breaks his own record. Capping it all, in 1938, a stunning around-the-world flight. Now an international hero, he comes home to ticker-tape parades down Broadway in New York and in Chicago, Los Angeles, and his old hometown, Houston. The toast of a country enraptured by men making history in the skies. A Lindbergh with uncounted millions!

Then, suddenly, tragedy—and scandal. 1946: near death in a dramatic plane crash. Hughes, test-piloting an air force reconnaissance plane of his own design, loses control and smashes the sleek XF-11 into Beverly Hills. 1947: barely recovered, he's unceremoniously hauled before a United States Senate investigating committee, accused of war-profiteering and political payoffs!

Hughes on trial. Caught in the glare of the klieg lights. Charged with winning war contracts by plying Pentagon brass and the president's son with bribes, booze, and broads. At the center of the controversy, a gigantic plywood seaplane—the "Spruce Goose." Hughes's Folly. An eighteen-million-dollar pile of lumber that's never left the ground. Undaunted, Hughes faces down the senators. Stalks out of the hearing room with a daring promise: "If the flying boat fails to fly, I will leave the country and never come back!"

Long Beach harbor. November 2, 1947. Hughes at the controls of the "Spruce Goose," dwarfed by the outsized airplane, five stories tall, far bigger than anything ever flown. He says he will only taxi it on the water this time out, but the cameras are rolling anyway. And, suddenly, the amazing thing is aloft! Hughes gets it seventy feet up in the air, flies it a mile across the bay!

That was his last newsreel. Indeed, Hughes was rarely seen in public again. His fame was at its peak. There was even a brief "Hughes-for-President" boom. But at the moment of his greatest triumph, he withdrew.

It was the beginning of a long retreat, and of a sudden series of defeats. The now hidden Hughes seemed to be losing control of his empire, a piece at a time. All his hobbies had become big corporations: the movies, RKO; the shop where he built his racing planes, Hughes Aircraft; his love of flying, TWA. His toys had outgrown him. First he had to surrender direct control of the aircraft company after an ultimatum from the Pentagon. Then he was forced to sell RKO. Finally, in 1957, crisis.

He was about to lose TWA, the enterprise closest to his heart. It was Hughes versus the Bankers. He wanted a new fleet of jets and needed their money. They wanted control. He wouldn't share it. At the peak of the crisis, the one man he trusted, the one man he needed, his right-hand man, Noah Dietrich, the gruff CPA who had run his business empire since 1925, his surrogate father, suddenly abandoned him. Almost simultaneously, Hughes found himself forced into a new partnership. He got married.

It was all too much. Instead of setting up house with his new wife, the young actress Jean Peters, Hughes retreated into a bungalow at the Beverly Hills Hotel, stripped off his clothes, and began his descent into total seclusion—and madness.

Nothing mattered more now than the isolation. In fact, when it came to a choice between holding on to his beloved TWA and losing his absolute privacy by appearing in court, he gave up control of the airline.* No longer in control of it, he didn't want it at all. In May 1966, he sold TWA.

For $546 million.

It was the biggest check ever to go to one man at one time, more money than the greatest of the old robber barons had amassed in their lifetimes. Now the big question was: What would he do with the incredible windfall?

Fortune magazine tried to puzzle out the phantom's new "mission": "A mystery now surrounds Hughes's plans for the half-billion dollars he received. It is possible only to speculate about what he will do with it. He seems to have something big and surprising on his mind, and whatever it is, it doubtless was a major factor in his decision to sell. Has he some new kind of interest, cultivated in his own isolated world?"

Actually, the only "mission" Hughes had in mind was to find a new place to hide. He had to flee California, his home for four decades, to escape state taxes. So, in July 1966 he left his bedroom for the first time in five years and set out across America, a fugitive with half a billion dollars.

On the train trip to Boston, alone in his private railroad car Hughes

---

*Hughes's refusal to appear in court ultimately had a $137 million price tag. The bankers had filed suit in June 1961 after a battle for dominance that began when they imposed a voting trust over his TWA stock in December 1960. As part of the lawsuit, they demanded that Hughes appear for a deposition. His refusal led a federal judge to find him in default in May 1963, and more than five years later damages were set at $137 million, which with interest escalated to $145 million.

scribbled some notes for a message to Jean Peters, trying to explain to his wife why he had left her behind at their home in Bel Air, trying to make her understand his "mission."

"Originally I had no faintest thought of proceeding," he wrote. "At the last minute you started wearing a long face. I said, 'Why?' You said because I would fail to complete the mission. I would goof out like last time."

There had been an argument. Marital strife caused by the strain of Hughes's maddening indecision, his constant alerts and endless delays, and perhaps the fact that they had shared a bed for less than a year of their ten-year marriage, that Jean had seen him only by appointment for the past five years.

"At the last minute I could not face the possibility of reverting to a telephone relationship," Hughes continued. "So, I delayed. You let me know at once that the closeness and trust we had achieved was destroyed.

"So, I reinstated my plans—with your promise to trust and believe in me.

"Where did I do the wrong thing?" he asked, approaching the delicate question of leaving without her.

"The crux of the whole deal is that, if you come, we have no option or choice. From that point on, we are irrevocably committed to the place where we land. If I go alone—or if you go alone, either of us can look around—describe what we see—what is available—and where. Then, the die is not cast until the other arrives."

It made perfect sense. He had to go alone. They had been over that several times.

"I had to go. I told everybody we were leaving. I dont want to fail. But I will not leave you upset"—he started to write "My Sweet Adorable One," then crossed it out. Too effusive.

"Honey!" he continued, "I want to do what you want me to do. I am boxed into a corner. I have the distinct feeling you dont want me to go ahead with any of this. But if I stop now I feel this may not be what you want either. I will be quitting once more.

"I hope this is the start of the road back," Hughes concluded, seeming out of his confusion to have drawn new strength, a new determination to put things right.

Then, inexplicably, he scrawled four more words—"cut your head off"—and underlined it with an angry slash.

It now stood out plainly: "*cut your head off.*"

The rage was unmistakable. But whose head was Hughes after?

His wife's? Or his own? He may not have been entirely sure himself. But the notes he made on the train ride to Boston give the best picture of Hughes's state of mind as he began his quest.

It was, of course, unthinkable to send the handwritten message to Jean Peters. And not merely because of its shocking postscript. Hughes never sent his wife a letter in his own hand. Much too risky.

Instead, he summoned one of his attendants in the next railroad car, and from his notes dictated a message for the Mormon to memorize and recite to his wife. The courier left the train at the first stop, San Bernardino, and drove back to Bel Air to deliver the farewell. It was a more controlled, simpler message that the Mormon gave Jean. Something to the effect that Hughes loved her dearly and looked forward to the day they would be back together.

One thing Hughes definitely did not want mentioned was his destination. That was a secret. Even from his wife.

Anyhow, Boston was just a stopover. It was not the end of the line. Hughes had traveled three thousand miles just to decide where he really wanted to go.

At four A.M. on Sunday, November 27, 1966, Thanksgiving weekend, a locomotive hauling just two private railroad cars pulled into an obscure desert junction on the outskirts of Las Vegas.

Howard Hughes had come back across America to make his Last Stand. He had found his new mission. He would make Nevada his kingdom, and use his half-billion-dollar windfall to create a world he could control completely. He had stopped running, but he had not stopped hiding.

Hughes emerged from his ten-year retreat defiantly determined to exercise his full power while remaining a total recluse.

Now, in the predawn blackness of the Nevada desert, he began to take charge. It was only a few short steps from his railroad car to the waiting van. He could have walked. Instead, like an Oriental pasha—or a spoiled child—he demanded to be carried the few steps on a stretcher.

The curtained van whisked Hughes to his new hideout, the Desert Inn Hotel, a gaudy gambling emporium smack in the middle of the Las Vegas Strip, perhaps the most garish, most public place in the universe. It was certainly no Hole-in-the-Wall, no Walden Pond, but it was somehow just right.

The Wizard of Oz had come to the Emerald City.

At the Desert Inn, the entire top floor was reserved and waiting. His aides snuck Hughes upstairs during the early morning lull, carried him down the hall, and parked the stretcher in a bedroom of a suite picked at random. There was another bedroom in the same suite and six more empty suites on the vacant penthouse floor, but Hughes had no interest in checking them out. He stayed put in the room first picked blindly—and never emerged for the next four years.

Indeed, he rarely left his bed. And yet, in these four years Hughes had his greatest impact on the nation, making his unseen presence felt in corporate boardrooms, in political back rooms, even in the Oval Office of the White House.

He was now more than a billionaire, with $750 million cash on hand and other assets worth at least as much. *Fortune* magazine would soon name him the richest man in America. And he had power even beyond his vast wealth. He was the sole owner of the Hughes Tool Company, with its monopoly on the device needed to drill all oil wells. He was sole trustee of the Hughes Aircraft Company, a top-ten defense contractor with strong CIA ties, manufacturer of all spy satellites that circled the globe and of the first spacecraft that landed on the moon. And beyond his real power was the power of his myth.

His long disappearance had only increased it. Hidden from view, unseen for a decade, now known best of all for being unknown, Hughes had become the perfect vehicle for everyone's fantasies.

If the popular image was still the fictional Hughes created by Harold Robbins in his 1961 best-selling novel *The Carpetbaggers*— the lone adventurer, the romantic hero, the appealingly eccentric tycoon—by now a darker, more sinister image was also beginning to take hold.

An aura of scandal had settled around him, his payoffs to politicians were rumored if not known, and he arrived in Las Vegas— "Sin City," the center of Mob power—just as the James Bond movies reached a peak of popularity. In the lurid atmosphere of the late 1960s, some now imagined that Hughes was an evil genius with a master plan for world domination—Dr. No, Blofeld, and Goldfinger all rolled into one.

The vision was of an archvillain in his hidden domain, surrounded by war-room electronics and gleaming computer banks, his eyes fixed on a huge blinking map of the world, sitting at the controls of a sophisticated array of advanced technology, commanding vast private armies.

Instead, there was Hughes, naked in his bedroom, unwashed and disheveled, his hair halfway down his back, sprawled out on a paper-towel-insulated bed, staring at his overworked television, with no device more sophisticated than his Zenith Space Commander. Next door, his command center, a hotel living room, was manned by five Mormon nursemaids: former potato-chip salesmen, construction workers, and factory hands, lackeys with no special skills, not even shorthand, equipped only with one console telephone, an electric typewriter, and a four-drawer filing cabinet.

The real Mr. Big was surrounded only by filth and disorder. Mountains of old newspapers, brittle with age, spread in an ever-widening semicircle on the floor around his bed, creeped under the furniture, and spilled into the corners of his cramped fifteen-by-seventeen-foot room, mixed together haphazardly with other debris—rolls of blueprints, maps, *TV Guides*, aviation magazines, and various unidentifiable objects.

A narrow path had been cleared from his bed to the bathroom, then lined with paper towels, but the tide of trash overran even that, topped off by numberless wads of used Kleenex the billionaire wielded to wipe off everything within reach, then casually cast upon the accumulated rubbish. It was all united in a common thick layer of dust that settled in permanently over the years. The room was never cleaned. Hughes did not want his Mormon aides stirring things up or disturbing his junkpiles, which continued to grow unchecked.

Amid this incredible clutter, set apart in pristine splendor, stood stack after stack of neatly piled documents. They covered every available surface. Thousands of yellow legal-pad pages and white typewritten memos piled with absolute precision on the dresser, two night tables, and an overstuffed armchair, all within easy reach of Hughes on his bed. He compulsively stacked and restacked these papers, often for hours at a time, taking a sheaf and whacking them down to align one side, then another, endlessly repeating the process until not a page was a millimeter out of place. That was vital.

These special papers were the instruments of *his* power.

For the four years Howard Hughes made his Last Stand in Las Vegas, he commanded his empire by correspondence. It was the only time in his life that the world's most secretive man regularly risked writing down his orders, plans, thoughts, fears, and desires.

Hughes himself emphasized that the handwritten memos were unique.

"My men will tell you I dont write five letters a year," he wrote his new right-hand man, Robert Maheu, toward the beginning of their pen-pal relationship.

"I have been notorious through the years for conducting all of my business orally, usually by telephone. I am sure you have heard of this characteristic.

"When I started sending you long hand notes, my people protested long and loud," Hughes continued, recalling how bitterly the Mormons had fought this sudden departure, not wanting to lose their role as his exclusive channel to the world outside.

"They wanted to retype my messages at least, and correct mistakes in composition, and spelling, etc.

"I said no, that there was not time, and that I would ask you to return the messages so they would not get out of my hands in that condition.

"Listen, Bob, in the Senate investigation of me, the material they dredged out of my own files was the only scrap of evidence that permitted them to get their foot in the door," Hughes concluded, still enraged by that violation twenty years earlier, a triumph that had left him permanently scarred.

"I assure you I learned my lesson from that incident, and I watch what accumulates in the files very carefully."

Yes, he had to retain absolute control of his secret papers—"the very most confidential, almost sacred information as to my very innermost activities."

His only real correspondent, Maheu, would have to return them. And Hughes would not even send copies to his other top executives, men he had not seen for a decade and no longer spoke to even by phone. Instead he had his Mormons read them the memos, so that these hallowed documents never left the penthouse.

He carefully trained these trusted attendants to be robot transmitters of his great secrets.

"I have thought of you," he explained in an oft-repeated catechism, "as non-eavesdroppers, as impersonal, completely loyal, enforced listeners to secret, privileged transmissions—in the same posture as the telegraph operator used to be in, when he was forced to transmit all kinds of highly personal and confidential material.

"I remember when the difference between a small-town non-professional operator and a metropolitan, highly trained operator was easily recognizable, because the small-town operator would react to the message as if it were addressed to him, while the good operator would never bat an eye or react in any way, no matter how startling the text of the message might be.

"Your posture in the transmission of messages," he added, "is as sacred and impersonal as an electronic machine."

Secure that his secrets were safe with his robots, that his dispatches could not possibly fall into hostile hands, Hughes daily scrawled out his orders on reams of yellow legal-pad paper, scheming through sleepless nights to control a world he feared to face, unleashing a blizzard of memoranda, sometimes more than a hundred pages in a day.

And here they were, all neatly stacked around his bed, in precise piles that had multiplied and grown to perilous heights. Hughes reached out one spindly arm, grabbed a sheaf at random, and began riffling through his papers. The dark secrets of his life were casually mixed in with the dark secrets of America.

Alone in his dimly lit room, leaning back on a couple of pillows, Hughes reread a few memos, leafed through the pile and skimmed a few more, all the while unconsciously crossing his toes, one over the other, starting from the little toe and working his way in, an old habit that now caused his long toenails to click, a constant counterpoint to the sound of the papers he shuffled.

Hughes was oblivious to the discordant sounds, completely caught up in reading his memos. Here was one about bribing a president. There another about buying a new airline. Next a reminder to get more codeine—had it been done? A few pages later, a complaint about taxes. Here his comments on a TV show. Followed by something about buying the network. Hughes continued to rummage through his papers, reliving past terrors and triumphs, chewing over schemes he had hatched the day or the week or the year before.

Suddenly he stopped and stared intently. This was important, and it hadn't been handled, at least not to his satisfaction. Hughes, who was obsessed with his image, realized it had been sullied badly—"your sponsor is far from the popular idol he once was," he noted sadly to his Mormon aides.

But he had a plan, and here it was, a whole new way to present himself to the world:

"I want the Hughes activity to be presented to the public, in a massive new publicity and advertising campaign, as the only example of competitive enterprise still functioning and holding out against the onrushing hordes of corporate giants.

"In other words, the one 'corner grocery store,' proprietor-managed type of old fashioned business activity still holding out against the overpowering pressure of the new corporations with their executives, managers, stockholder intracacies of control, politics, proxy battles, institution ownership, etc. etc.—all of the interlocking cross currents and intrigue that go to make up the modern U.S. industrial giant—the corporation, the Establishment."

That was how he saw himself, as David, not Goliath, as the lone survivor of the American Dream. He had to get that message out to the world.

Meanwhile, continuing to root through his documents, Hughes fished out another plan that had not quite gotten off the ground. Just another "mom-and-pop" operation the proprietor of the last "corner grocery store" had in mind. A grandiose vision of a global Las Vegas, with Hughes at the center, bookie to the entire world:

"I once told you I was interested in acquiring one of the book-making establishments in town," he wrote his chief aide.

"Well, I dont see any point in buying just one of these books. It is my hope that the damndest book operation anyone ever conceived of can be developed.

"Are you aware that any of dozens of businessmen in the country can pick up the telephone and call their broker, either at his office or at home, or even out at a restaurant, and say: 'Charley, buy me 50,000 U.S. Steel at the market.'

"So, what I have in mind is a system of credit research by which every man of substance, in the entirety of the U.S., will be catalogued and listed with all the truly significant information necessary to appraise his ability to pay and his integrity.

"I want to see a development under which a wealthy man can phone from London to a certain phone number in Las Vegas and identify himself and place a bet on just about anything—a horse race at Hollywood Park, a track meet in Florida, a football game in New York, an election, at the state or national level, the passage of some bill up in Congress—just about anything.

"Also, I want to see a development which will permit a man to phone from London and, after placing a bet on some event, such as mentioned above, to say: 'Put $10,000 on the line at the Sands.'

"In fact, when the man on the phone requests the bet, the clerk could hit one of those recording timers, which would be heard over the phone. So, the exact instant of the bet would be recorded, and the clerk could say over the phone to the customer: 'Your bet is made, at 12:36:04.' Then, a few seconds later, the clerk could say: 'Your play occurred at 12:36:12—you won with a natural, eleven. Do you want to bet again?'

"There are many refinements of this deal that could be worked out as you go along.

"Do you know why I think this kind of play would catch on? Because men, simply by nature, like to show off. I can just see some minor league V.I.P. out to dinner with some very attractive young protagonist of the opposite sex, and he picks up the phone, brought to his table at Twenty-One, and he makes a five or ten thousand dollar bet over the phone.

"Then he turns to his girl and says: 'Well, I just won ten thousand in Vegas—let's spend it!'

"Look how that would impress the female! She would reason that he must be a pretty wealthy and a pretty trustworthy man to be able to persuade the Las Vegas gambling fraternity to extend credit and take his bet orally, by phone, all the way across the country.

"Now, I urge you not to disclose *anything—not to anyone*—not even the slightest hint—of this 'play by phone' concept."

Rereading his memo, squinting at his own scrawl, Hughes wondered why this grand scheme had never gone anywhere. It seemed to make such perfect sense laid out so plainly in such meticulous detail. He made a mental note to get it back on track and meanwhile continued to rummage through his papers, grabbing another thick sheaf from the night table.

He was getting tired, but he could not sleep. He usually stayed up until dawn. His body flagged, but his mind reeled on, a runaway engine that could not stop and therefore *had* to find something, *anything* to work on, work over, work to death. He seemed to believe that he worked best at the outer limits of his endurance, pushing himself often for days without sleep, as if his mind, by feeding on his emaciated body, consuming it, gained some special power.

"I work around the clock, holidays mean very little to me, since I work just about all the time," he explained.

"I have absolutely nothing but my work. When things dont go well, it can be very empty indeed.

"I do not indulge in sports, night clubs, or other recreational activities, and since, in fact, I do not do much of anything else at all, except my work, just what do you suggest I do, crawl off in a corner some place and die?"

That was, of course, pretty much what he had done. And quite often, Hughes was not really working at all. He was simply caught in a catatonic daze, playing with his long hair, pulling it up over the top of his head, then letting it fall, or stacking and restacking his memos. When he was working, it was often furious but wasted motion. He would spin his wheels, digging himself deeper into a rut over some entirely trivial or totally imaginary matter. But he was always torturing himself, and at that he worked very hard.

Sometimes he'd reach into his stacks of memos and torture himself with memories. Here was one. A close encounter with grave danger only narrowly escaped. God, it was horrifying even to recall it! Still, he picked up the memo and went back in time.

It was the day Lyndon Johnson "abdicated," and while Hughes had mentioned in passing something about picking a new president—"selecting one of the candidates and nursing him into the White House," those were his words—he was instead fixated on a real crisis much closer to home.

All his enemies were conspiring against him.

"Please dont declare war upon me so early in the day," Hughes had written in a plea to Robert Maheu. "I am well aware that this is not anything that is important to you, but merely something you were pressured into doing by certain groups here. I am speaking of the Easter Egg Hunt."

The Easter Egg Hunt. There were plans—no, a plot!—to hold it at his hideout, the Desert Inn.

"I have been told, however, that although there are a number of people in Las Vegas who favor this event, there is a more powerful group who are dedicated to discrediting me and that this second group will stop at nothing."

Not only was this "second group" so diabolical as to plot the hunt, but it was also about to launch a "gossip campaign" against him.

"The substance of this story (and it has already been fed to certain Hollywood columnists, who very fortunately are friends of mine from my motion picture days) the substance is that: I am ashamed for my sinful past (adventures with females, etc.) and I am having a backlash here, manafest in my extreme isolation from social contact, presumably for the purpose of putting temptation out of reach, and an intensive and very expensive campaign to reform the morals of Las Vegas. I am supposedly waiting to start a real all-out war against the normal customs of Las Vegas—such as: topless show girls, etc. etc., dirty jokes, dirty advertisements, etc."

But that was not the real danger. No, the real danger was the egg hunt.

"Now, I am further informed, and this is what really has me worried, that this militant group plans to stage a really viscious all-out juvenile riot at our Easter party.

"I am not eager to have a repetition, in the D.I., of what happened at Juvenile Hall when the ever-lovin little darlings tore the place apart. I am sure your reply to that will be that, with our better-trained security force, such a thing just could not happen. However, my information is to the effect that our opponents hope we do set this riot down, because they feel they can get more publicity if we do."

Of course. The billionaire's guards could not club down the kiddies, not even if they really ran amok and rushed his penthouse retreat.

"[Q]uietly explore alternate possibilities such as: Moving it to the Sunrise Hospital and making it a charity event. We could start the ball rolling by donating 25 or even $50,000. I just want to see it moved to a place where, if something goes wrong, it will be a black mark against Las Vegas—not a black mark against us."

His was no ordinary paranoia. It had sweep and grandeur, but he could also focus its full intensity on the smallest incident and bring all his terror to bear. And while his paranoia encompassed virtually everything, it really zeroed in on all forms of "contamination." Unwashed and living in filth, he was forever cleaning the space around him.

Nothing obsessed him more than the purity of fluids, and he had discovered something shocking about the Las Vegas water system, which he set out in another anguished memo:

"This water system will comprise the only water system in the world where the outlet of the sewage disposal plant plus tons of raw, untreated sewage flows right into a small, stagnant pool of water, and then flows right back out again, through a screen to remove the turds, and then into our homes to be consumed by us as drinking water, washing water, and water to cook with."

Well, not exactly by "us." Hughes himself drank only bottled water and insisted that it be used in cooking his meals. He had done so for twenty years. Indeed, he drank only one brand, Poland Spring water, only from quart bottles, and only if bottled in its original plant in Maine. As for washing, that was no big problem, since he rarely washed at all. Still, the local water pollution upset him deeply.

"It is not so much the technical purity or impurity, it is the revolting, vomitous unattractiveness of the whole thing. It is sort of like serving an expensive New York Cut steak in one of our showrooms and having the waiter bring the steak in to a customer in a beautiful plate, but, instead of the usual parsley and half a slice of lemon and the usual trimmings to make the steak attractive—instead of this, there is a small pile of soft shit right next to the steak. Now, maybe technically the shit does not touch the steak, but how much do you think the patron is going to enjoy eating that steak?

"I think he would lose his appetite very fast."

Hughes himself never had much of an appetite. He generally ate only once a day, at some odd predawn hour, and took forever to get down his meal, often requiring that a bowl of soup be reheated several times. Sometimes he did not eat at all for days, other times he subsisted for weeks on desserts alone. But he was very picky about the preparation of his food, especially about any possible "contamination."

Earlier he had dictated a three-page single-spaced memorandum titled "Special Preparation of Canned Fruit":

"The equipment used in connection with this operation will consist of the following items: 1 unopened newspaper; 1 sterile can opener; 1 large sterile plate; 1 sterile fork; 1 sterile spoon; 2 sterile brushes; 2 bars of soap; sterile paper towels."

Hughes carefully outlined nine precise steps to be followed religiously: "Preparation of Table," "Procuring of Fruit," "Washing of Can," "Drying of Can," "Processing the Hands," "Opening the Can," "Removing Fruit," "Fallout Rules While Around Can," and "Conclusion of Operation."

Each step was intricately detailed. For "STEP #3 Washing of Can" he instructed: "The man in charge turns the valve in the bathtub on, using his bare hands to do so. He also adjusts the water temperature so that it is not too hot or too cold. He then takes one of the brushes, and, using one of the bars of soap, creates a good lather, and then scrubs the can from a point 2 inches below the top of the can. He should first soak and remove the label, and then brush the cylindrical part of the can over and over until all particles of dust, pieces of the label, and, in general, all source of contamination have been removed. Holding the can in the center at all times, he then processes the bottom of the can in the same manner, being very sure that the bristles of the brush have thoroughly cleaned all the small indentations on the perimeter. He then rinses the soap. Taking the second brush, and still holding the can in the center, he again creates a good lather and scrubs the top of the can, the perimeter along the top, and the cylindrical sides to a point 2 inches below the top. He should continue this scrubbing until he literally removes the tin protection from the can itself."

Before opening the now immaculate fruit can, the billionaire's servitor, following Step #5, had to "process": "This action will consist of washing and rinsing the hands four distinct and separate times, being extremely careful to observe the four phases in each washing. That is to say, the man first must brush every minute particle and surface of his hands and fingers. He then puts each finger tip into the palm of the opposite hand and cleans each finger by rotating and pressing the fingers against the palm. He then interlocks the fingers and slides them together. The last phase is grasping the palms together and wringing them."

The can and the man both now thoroughly scrubbed, it was time to remove the fruit, which required that "Fallout Rules" be observed: "While transferring the fruit from the can to the sterile plate, be very sure that no part of the body, including the hands, be directly over the can or the plate at any time. If possible, keep the head, upper part of the body, arms, etc. at least one foot away."

There was a postscript: "This operation must be carried out in every infinitessimal detail, and HRH would deeply appreciate it if the man follow each phase very slowly and thoughtfully, giving his full attention to the importance of the work at hand."

The fruit was now ready to be dished up to Hughes, who did not bathe or shower for months at a stretch, and dined on a bed whose sheets were changed just a few times a year, in a room that was never cleaned.

Yet this memo was merely one in a long series, all part of an elaborate set of rituals the billionaire had dictated over the years, and which by now filled a thick and constantly updated looseleaf binder kept in the penthouse. Its purpose—to prevent the "backflow of germs."

The invisible threat required special vigilance. It had been a central preoccupation for more than a decade, and even before Hughes drifted into seclusion he would neither shake hands nor touch doorknobs. Now he demanded that everything his Mormons delivered to him be handled with Kleenex or Scott paper towels, "insulation" to protect him from "contamination."

The five Mormon nursemaids were his only human contact. Yet even they were not allowed to enter his room unbidden or to speak to him until he spoke first. There was no socializing, no idle chitchat. Hughes kept his door closed most of the time and rarely talked to them at all, instead communicating by memo even with these men in the next room. In part, it was because he was nearly deaf and refused to wear a hearing aid. To be heard, the Mormons would have to stand close and shout. Hughes didn't want them that close, and both his body odor and breath were so rank that they didn't want to get near him.

Still, he needed to control their every movement. None had been allowed a day off since joining his retinue, and while they finally bargained for a twelve-day-on, four-day-off schedule in Las Vegas, Hughes often ignored the man on duty, preferring to call back an escaped Mormon to perform some absurd task, such as measuring the slippage of his pillow. At times they were all on "stand-by."

"The moment each man arrives at home from his duties at the hotel, call and give him the following message," Hughes had dictated when he first established the standby rules. " 'HRH said he would be extremely and deeply grateful if you would be kind enough to remain at home without leaving for even one fraction of a second for any reason whatsoever, no matter how great the emergency might be.' "

The Mormons were his little polygamous family, all the family Hughes had left now, and he needed to keep them around. He was cut off from everyone else. Even his wife.

He would never see Jean Peters again. They spoke almost every day on the telephone and each time had the same conversation. Hughes kept trying to persuade Jean to move to Las Vegas, to live in one of the two mansions he had bought for her—one a $600,000 palatial estate in town, the other a five-hundred-acre ranch nearby—telling her that life would be perfect in Nevada, that she would love the clean air. And Jean kept agreeing to come, if Hughes would just leave his penthouse and move into their new home first.

It was a standoff. Hughes could not leave his hideout, could not share his life. He wanted his wife close by, under his control, but he could no longer actually live with her. Instead, he secretly bought a "surveillance house" across the street from her home in Beverly Hills and kept his wife under watch while each night he tried to persuade her to come to Las Vegas.

In his own way, he seemed to love her, and the nightly phone calls were important. Sometimes he fretted that she would not be in or refuse to talk when he called at some predawn hour.

"Please call Mrs. and ask her if it will be convenient for me to call tonight and ask her what is the latest that would be convenient," he scribbled to his Mormons one Christmas Eve.

"Remind her this is my birthday."

And when he had his wife on the phone again, he would once more beg her to join him and assure her that he would soon emerge from his seclusion. "He said that he felt himself to be like someone on a track being pursued by the engines," Jean later recalled. "It was almost his mania to get everything settled and then start to build his dream world."

But, in fact, there was no room in his "dream world" for Jean, no room for anyone else at all. Certainly no room for a rival. What Hughes dreamed of was a world in which only he existed, and often he wrote out entire scripts for his henchmen to follow in dealing with threats to his solipsist vision, such as the sudden arrival in Las Vegas of another multimillionaire.

"Now, I think No. 1 on the list for this year is Mr. K-1," wrote Hughes in 1967, hatching a plot to dispose of his new rival, Kirk Kerkorian, who had just announced plans to build the biggest hotel-casino in town.

"I want your idea of how he would react if you were to see him and say something like this:

" 'Kirk, I have just had a long talk with Howard.

" 'I dont have to tell you that when he sold his interest in TWA, he picked up the largest check that any single individual ever carried out of Wall St. Since that time he has moved very slowly. He has made investments in Las Vegas, but nothing else.

" 'Now, Kirk, what this is all leading up to is that I just see you two friends of mine embarking on a course that can only lead to a disastrous collision.

" 'Howard wants to buy your land and persuade you not to build this hotel. I think his friendship (and he has very few friends) is yours for the asking, and I think it would be worth so much more to you that there would be no comparison.

" 'The way he figures it, if he had had even the most remote idea that you were planning to do this, he would have located somewhere else. I know for a fact that he made an all-out study to see if it would be possible to relocate now, but you see he just could not dispose of his property here without wrecking the economy of the entire state.' "

It was Kerkorian who would have to get out. Howard Hughes had to be alone in his kingdom, his power unchallenged and absolute.

But locked in his room with all his grand schemes, with all his great fears, with his absolute need for absolute power, Hughes needed a go-between, one trusted man who could take the visions he scrawled in his memos and make them a reality in the dangerous world outside.

And the billionaire had found that man—his new remote-control instrument—Robert Aime Maheu.

They would make the Big Movie together, Hughes producing, directing, and writing the screenplay, Maheu out on the stage playing Hughes to the world.

"I spent the whole night writing the script. Every word—every move—every tear—every sigh. All the stage directions are carefully worked out. I could get $10,000 for a script as good as this at 20th Century Fox. So, I want to see what comes of it, but I am afraid I know what the last scene is right now, and I am afraid it is not you and me walking into the setting sun with the package under our arms."

Still, it was quite a spectacle the two of them were about to put on.

2 Bob and Howard

It was not love at first sight. The courtship had lasted twelve years, and they never really saw each other. In fact, in the beginning Robert Maheu did not even know that he was working for Howard Hughes.

Private-eye Maheu was sitting in his recently opened Washington office on a spring day in 1954, when his phone rang. It was a matrimonial case. Not his usual line. The sign on the door said ROBERT A. MAHEU ASSOCIATES. But there weren't really any associates quite yet, and although the office was just a couple of blocks from the White House, it wasn't all that grand. Desk, swivel chair, hat rack, and not much else. In fact, Maheu was sharing the space (and the telephone) with an accountant. Still, he was beginning to attract some very interesting cases. Like the guy now on the phone.

It was a local lawyer. Big firm. Had a job for Maheu on behalf of a client he wouldn't name. Wanted all the dirt on one Stuart W. Cramer III, a real blueblood, son of a wealthy industrialist who played golf with Ike. The kid had just married a young Hollywood starlet. Name of Jean Peters. What the unnamed client wanted was a complete rundown, but mainly he wanted to know if this Cramer was mixed up with any of the intelligence agencies.

As Maheu had told the lawyer right off, he didn't normally take matrimonial work. He was no ordinary private eye. But this case was actually right up his alley. Maheu was a *very* private eye—private enough to be getting a $500 monthly retainer from the CIA. Under-the-table money to handle jobs too dirty for the Agency to handle itself. Pimping for Jordan's King Hussein. Producing a porn flick starring a look-alike of Indonesia's President Sukarno. Odd jobs like that.

So he took the Cramer case. It was not exactly that he needed the work, but it looked like a piece of cake for a man with his connections, and a few extra bucks wouldn't hurt. In truth, Maheu was in a bit of a bind. Nearly $100,000 worth. That Dairy Dream strike-it-rich-quick scheme had really turned into a nightmare. Which was why he had gotten into this spy-for-hire racket in the first place.

Or, at least that's the way Maheu would later tell it. After a dazzling career with the FBI, mainly counterintelligence work in World War II, he suddenly quit the Bureau in 1947 to take advantage of a big business opportunity. Dairy Dream. Exclusive U.S. rights to a new process for canning pure cream. A great success that suddenly turned sour with the terrible discovery that the cream had a very limited shelf life. The cost of retrieving it from supermarkets across the country was ruinous. Busted, Maheu went back to work for the government as chief of security at the Small Business Administration, but his take-home hardly covered the interest on his debt. So he became Robert A. Maheu Associates.

But it is not at all clear if Maheu was a down-at-the-heels, feet-on-the-desk gumshoe trying to look big-time, or a big-time front for the CIA trying to look like a sleazy bankrupt shamus. The year he quit the FBI, 1947, was the same year the CIA got started, and Dairy Dream may have been only an unfortunate side venture. In any event, by the time he took the Cramer case Maheu was not only on the Company's payroll, he was already deep into high-stakes international intrigue.

The Case of the Greedy Greek was a classic tragedy. At least for Aristotle Onassis. In his hubris, the tycoon had made a secret deal with the dying king of Saudi Arabia that gave him a virtual monopoly on shipping oil from the Persian Gulf. It was Maheu's mission to scuttle that contract. Ostensibly he was working for Onassis's blood rival Stavros Niarchos. But the CIA was definitely in on it and so was then Vice-President Richard Nixon, and while not even the players seemed to be sure who was using whom on whose behalf, Big Oil was probably pulling the strings to make the world safe for Aramco. Still, it was Maheu's show. He bugged Onassis's offices in New York, Paris, and London, got proof that the contract had been bought with a bribe, exposed the scandal in a Rome newspaper secretly owned by the CIA, and finally journeyed to Jidda, where he personally presented his evidence to the Saudi royal family and killed the whole deal. Not bad for a private peeper on his first big job.

And he still found time to handle the Cramer case. Turns out the kid did have some kind of ties with the CIA. Liaison for Lockheed, apparently. What else Maheu dug up is unknown, but within months Cramer III and Jean Peters had separated, Jean was back in Hollywood seeing Howard Hughes, and in 1957 the former Mrs. Cramer became the new Mrs. Hughes.

By that time Maheu had figured out that the billionaire was his unnamed client and, in fact, was getting regular assignments. Fixing a city council race. Helping a would-be blackmailer recognize his mistake. That kind of thing. Finally, the same year Hughes got married, Maheu even got to speak to him.

Hughes was in Nassau, escaping his new wife while he pondered a Caribbean real-estate coup, and he called long-distance, summoning his gumshoe down to the Bahamas. Wanted Maheu to slip $25,000 to the Bay Street Boys. On that mission, cooling his heels in a hotel lobby, Maheu also caught a quick glimpse of his mystery client—from the back, as Hughes was about to enter an elevator, berating his hapless Mormon aides for their failure to have the door open and waiting.

Maheu recognized the voice. He would come to know it all too well. But that trip to Nassau was Hughes's last public appearance, and it was as close as Maheu would ever get to seeing him. He would, however, begin to spend a lot of time out in Los Angeles tending to Hughes's problems, especially with women.

Like the Case of the Captive Slave Girls. In the summer of 1959, Hughes, now in complete seclusion, holed up in the Beverly Hills Hotel, seeing no one, not even his wife, suddenly decided to add seven Miss Universe contestants to his harem. For years he had been stashing mistresses in safe houses all around Los Angeles, under surveillance and under guard, and although he had never seen some of them he still had several on standby. Now he wanted more. Fast.

He awakened Maheu in the middle of the night, sent him out to Long Beach with orders to offer the beauty queens movie contracts. All seven were lured into hotel suites and kept there awaiting promised screen tests. Hughes, however, seemed to lose interest, and after weeks without contact the girls started drifting away. When the billionaire discovered his loss, he flew into a rage and assigned a dozen of his operatives to keep the last, Miss Norway, from leaving.

Maheu apparently had no role in that part of the caper, but he did claim credit for hushing it up years later when it came to the attention of a Senate committee. "The files, Howard," Maheu later told Hughes, "contained very devastating evidence pertaining to Miss Norway, a participant for Miss Universe, who claimed that she had virtually been held a captive, and a tape which a former private investigator working for you had sold to the Committee, wherein a certain girl was talking to her boyfriend and claiming that she was being held captive, that she was under constant surveillance, etc. All of this evidence was completely destroyed in my presence, and we never had one bit of publicity."

Maheu was becoming a valued operative, an essential part of the strange new hierarchy of nursemaids, bodyguards, and business executives Hughes was gathering around him. The billionaire was no longer content to share his gumshoe. It came to a head when Maheu tried to return to Washington to be with his wife, who was about to give birth to their fourth child. Hughes was as intent on holding onto him as he had been on keeping Miss Norway.

In a furious series of phone calls Hughes insisted that Maheu stay. Told him he had once seen a woman walking in the park with a basket on her head stop just long enough to have a baby, then walk on with the baby in the basket. Finally, pulling out all the stops, Hughes demanded that Maheu shut down his detective agency, join him full time, and become his "alter ego."

Maheu, however, was not quite ready for complete monogamy. It was not his wife who was the real competition. It was the CIA.

The Agency had another odd job for Maheu. To set up a Mob hit of Fidel Castro. For months the CIA had been trying to eliminate the new Cuban leader with poison cigars, LSD, exploding seashells, and a powerful depilatory to make his beard fall out. Now, in the summer of 1960, they decided to bring in some real pros. So they called in Maheu, "a tough guy who can get things done." His mission—to make contact with the Mafia and arrange a $150,000 contract murder.

In the first week of November 1960, five men gathered in a suite at the Fountainbleu Hotel in Miami Beach. Maheu had no need to introduce his CIA case officer James O'Connell to his Mafia pal John Roselli. They had already met, at a party in Maheu's home. Roselli, the Syndicate's silver-haired "ambassador" to Las Vegas and Hollywood, introduced the two strangers. Chicago Mob boss Sam Giancana and the Mafia's former man in Havana Santos Trafficante. The daisy chain was almost complete, and Trafficante said he could line up a Cuban to make the hit.

But already there were problems. Just a few days before the big sit-down, Giancana got word that his girl, singer Phyllis McGuire, was two-timing him in Las Vegas with comedian Dan Rowan. To keep Giancana in Miami and on the job, Maheu had sent an operative to bug Rowan's room, the wireman had been busted by a hotel maid, and the Las Vegas sheriff had called in the FBI. Giancana thought that was so funny he almost choked on his cigar laughing.

And now, up in the Fountainbleu, there was real discord. The CIA man O'Connell told the mobsters he wanted Castro gunned down in a "gangland-style killing." Like in "The Untouchables." The Mafiosi, however, wanted this hit done with the dignity befitting a patriotic enterprise. Giancana rejected the standard rub-out as "too dangerous" and suggested poison pills. Roselli also favored something "nice and clean," no "out-and-out ambushing," perhaps a secret poison that would disappear without a trace. Like in "Mission Impossible."

It took the CIA's Technical Services Division months to perfect the botulinum toxin. Ultimately—just weeks before the April 1961 Bay of Pigs invasion—Maheu would pass the deadly capsules to a sweating Cuban standing in the doorway of the Boom Boom Room at the Fountainbleu.

But long before the pills were passed, indeed shortly after the big sit-down adjourned, Maheu received an urgent phone call. Holed up in his hotel room, trying to put together a rush job to kill Castro, trying to mediate between the Mob and the CIA, trying to keep the jealous Giancana in Miami, trying to get his wireman out of jail in Las Vegas, trying to keep himself from being indicted for the bugging, trying to ward off the Las Vegas sheriff and a very suspicious J. Edgar Hoover, trying to keep the lid on all the leaks, trying to hold the whole damn thing together, Maheu suddenly also had to deal with Howard Hughes.

Hughes was in a jealous rage. He wanted to know just what Maheu was doing down in Miami, and he wanted him back in Los Angeles immediately. Now Maheu really had a problem. The Castro plot was the most closely held secret in CIA history, known to no more than a dozen people directly involved, perhaps not including the president of the United States. Maheu asked the CIA if he could tell Hughes. The answer from Langley—sure, go right ahead. Apparently without a second thought.

Maheu hurried down to a phone booth—not on orders from the Agency, but from Hughes, who always insisted on stringent security measures—and told the billionaire that he was on a top-secret mission to "dispose of Castro in connection with a pending invasion of Cuba."

Hughes received the news sitting naked on a white leather chair in the "germ-free zone" of his Beverly Hills Hotel bungalow, a pink napkin on his lap for the sake of modesty, surrounded by mountains of dirty Kleenex. The thirteenth person made privy to the assassination plot. He took it all in over the phone held to his hearing-aid box, then told Maheu to fly right back to Los Angeles. Immediately. He promised to keep him there no more than forty-eight hours, then let him return to his mission in Miami.

But the Castro murder would have to be his final fling. After that, the billionaire expected absolute fidelity.

Maheu returned from the Cuban debacle just in time to take on his most critical mission for Hughes. He was now the man in charge of the most important thing in the billionaire's life—keeping him hidden. Hughes had become the object of an intense manhunt. His battle with the bankers over TWA had exploded into an all-out war. An army of process servers was trying to slap him with a subpoena, trying to force him out of hiding and haul him into court. It was Maheu's job to keep them at bay.

He brought all the black arts of his clandestine world into play, deploying doubles, creating false trails, renting hideaways in Mexico and Canada, making TWA think Hughes was here, there, and everywhere, while the billionaire just lay on his bed in Bel Air.

Maheu himself moved out to Los Angeles, leaving his other clients behind in Washington. Now Robert A. Maheu Associates had only one client: Howard Hughes. The one-time private eye was not only in charge of secrecy but also secret money. He emerged as the billionaire's top bagman, a position heralded by his attendance as Hughes's representative at the 1961 Kennedy inaugural, where he flew in with a planeload of Hollywood stars and purchased four boxes at $10,000 apiece.

It was a key role, but their relationship was still one-sided. Hughes continued to play the field, while Maheu remained monogamous. For all his new power, he was still just the house dick, a glorified gumshoe, certainly no rival to the top executives in the empire. The long courtship might never have achieved real intimacy had it not been for the billionaire's sudden move to Las Vegas in 1966.

Bob and Howard

Robert Maheu was waiting out in the Nevada desert at four A.M. when Howard Hughes arrived. He had handled security for the big move and averted a major crisis when the train fell behind schedule, threatening to bring the recluse to his secret rendezvous point in broad daylight. Maheu commandeered a private locomotive and got Hughes into town before dawn.

But he missed his last chance to see his phantom boss.

Out in the dark silent desert, Maheu again heard the cracked, reedy voice he had come to know so well, heard it barking commands, giving detailed instructions about the delicate transfer from the train to the van, knew that any second he would finally get to see the hidden man whose bidding he had done for a dozen years, his eyes straining against the darkness to catch sight of the figure he had fleetingly glimpsed just once ten years earlier, the mystery man no one had seen since, the phantom billionaire.

But, just as Hughes was about to emerge, just as the first vague outlines of his image began to materialize at the door of the train, Maheu suddenly spotted two points of light in the distance, the headlights of a car approaching the remote railroad junction. He was so intent on shielding Hughes from strangers, he had been drawn so far into Hughes's secret world, that he missed the one moment he could see Hughes himself.

Again, at the Desert Inn, the vigilant bodyguard turned away at a critical instant, and by the time he turned back Hughes had vanished forever into his penthouse.

All Las Vegas, all the world, thought that Maheu was dealing with Hughes personally, saw him go up the elevator to the secret ninth floor, assumed that he was seeing its sole occupant, but in fact they never had and never would meet face-to-face. Maheu never got closer to Hughes than the adjoining room and had no more idea of what he looked like or how he lived than the rest of the world outside. Hughes, for his part, had never seen Maheu at all.

Yet, within months, the two men would exchange solemn vows and enter into a bizarre marriage.

It was Moe Dalitz who finally brought them together. The hatchet-faced proprietor of the Desert Inn, a senior member of organized crime, was running a gambling emporium, not a retreat. He wanted to rent the penthouse to high rollers, and he wanted Hughes out by Christmas. When the recluse failed to budge, Dalitz threatened to march upstairs and drag him out into the street if he was not gone by New Year's Eve.

Once more Maheu came to the rescue. He persuaded one of his former clients, Teamster boss Jimmy Hoffa, to call Dalitz, a key recipient of union pension-fund loans, and prevail upon the mobster to grant Hughes a reprieve. That bold move only bought a few weeks, however. Dalitz was adamant. Hughes had to go.

Faced with eviction, the billionaire decided to become his own landlord: he would buy the hotel.

Again, Maheu's connections proved handy. He arranged the big deal through his erstwhile partner in the Castro plot, the Mafia's ambassador to Las Vegas, John Roselli. Dalitz and his three principal partners from the Cleveland Mob were ready, indeed eager to sell. All of them were in hot water with the Feds. Everything seemed set, but neither Maheu nor the mobsters was prepared for Hughes's favorite pastime, negotiating endlessly at odd hours, haggling like a hostile pawnbroker over every nickel and dime. The deal changed daily, the bargaining dragged on for months.

Maheu went up and down the Desert Inn elevator like a yo-yo, meeting with the Dalitz group downstairs, winning another concession, only to be presented with new demands from the penthouse. Five times the mobsters cut their price before Hughes finally gave his approval and Maheu shook hands on the deal.

Then Hughes suddenly spotted an item that displeased him: a fifteen-thousand-dollar quibble on a thirteen-and-a-quarter-million-dollar deal.

Maheu went back up to the penthouse, sat down in the adjoining room, and furiously scrawled a letter of resignation.

"Howard," he wrote, "you have finally succeeded in insulting my intelligence. You have also compromised so many of my friends and contacts that I find it impossible to continue working for you.

"I am leaving for Los Angeles in the morning.

"As I have told you repeatedly, you have nothing to fear from me except that I intend to charge you my going rate through March 14, 1967.

"I wish you a lot of luck, including the very *remote* possibility that you may be lucky enough to select a successor who will have equal loyalty.

"In sincere friendship, Bob."

Within minutes Hughes sent word from his lair. He would go ahead with the deal as agreed, without the fifteen-thousand-dollar discount. And he begged Maheu to stay in Las Vegas at least long enough to receive a phone call the next morning.

Precisely at eight A.M. the phone rang in Maheu's hotel room. For the next two hours Hughes proceeded to cajole him, to beg him never to threaten to leave again, to become his right-hand man forever, to accept a half-million-dollar base salary, to be his one and only, to be faithful to him alone. They exchanged vows. It was virtually a formal marriage ceremony—"till death do us part." Hughes said they would spend the rest of their lives together and made Maheu promise never to leave him.

Until now they had known each other only as disembodied voices on the telephone, but with their marriage began an incredibly intimate pen-pal relationship, a daily exchange of love letters and letters of lost love, interspersed with plans for multimillion-dollar deals and plots to buy the government of the United States. An epic domestic quarrel that soon had the newlyweds bickering like an old married couple and would ultimately disrupt the domestic affairs of the entire nation.

SCENES FROM A MARRIAGE: Act I

"I regret last night as much as I assume you do, perhaps I regret it more.

"Anyway, I have only one desire now and that is my sincere wish that you and I, in deference to what I hope remains of our friendship, take steps best calculated to avoid any chance of a repetition.

"To this end, Bob, and with the assurance of continued friendship, I want to ask that you place in my hands completely the resolution of such problems as may exist between us."

———

"First of all, I hope you understand that you do not have an exclusive to sleepless nights.

"For some strange God damned reason which I'll never comprehend, everyone seems to believe me except you. When I told you that I would be with you for the duration and that I would not leave you—that is *precisely* what I meant. I *did not* say and did not *intend* to say that I was leaving you.

"The only conclusion I can reach is that you do not believe me and in reality perhaps you are sub-consciously trying to find a successor for me.

"As I have told you repeatedly—I am committed to you but you are not to me."

———

"Well, Bob, I will be very happy to believe you about everything. I think a good starting point would be for you to affirm your original promise to stay with me permanently, and without the necessity of my getting down on my knees and begging you to do it."

———

"How in the world you can interpret my statement that I want to be with you in Las Vegas or wherever in hell you choose to go for the duration of our lives—as an act of hostility—I'll never know.

"You will never know how much it upsets me when I do something which disturbs you. I try so hard to please you and meet all of your demands.

"Howard, please let me know *immediately* if you are satisfied that this horrible incident is over."

———

"Thanks very much, but no thanks!

"I have just read your message which breathes hostility out of every line.

"I dont think that relationships entered to at the point of a shotgun are any good."

Interspersed with the "love letters" were fights on the phone, back-and-forth calls late into the night, and first thing the next morning more memos recapitulating the phone fights, followed by handwritten notes fighting about the recapitulations.

"I am returning your message for reference," wrote Hughes. "At the top of page 2, the underlined portion puzzles me. The only time I mentioned anything that might be interpreted this way was very recently when I said that I got the feeling from you that you no longer had the same enthusiasm for this position that I had sensed at the start of our relationship.

"Then I reminded you of the remark you made, which caught me by complete surprise, the remark that you had a deep instinctive feeling that we were headed on a collision course, and that perhaps we should be best advised to end it now in a friendly way. I never will forget this remark and the calmness with which you said it, because I was literally dumbfounded with surprise. Anyway, I re-

I regret last night as much as I assume you do, perhaps I regret it more.

Anyway, I have only one desire now and that is my sincere wish that you and I, in deference to what I hope remains of our friendship, take steps best calculated to avoid any chance of a repetition.

To this end, Bob, and with the assurance of continued friendship, I want to ask that you place in my hands completely the resolution of such problems as may exist between us.

First of all, I hope you understand that you do not have an exclusive to sleepless nights.

For some strange God damned reason which I'll never comprehend, everyone seems to believe me except you. When I told you that I would be with you for the duration and that I would not leave you — that is precisely what I meant.

did not say and did not
intend to say that I was
leaving you.

The only conclusion I can
reach is that you do not believe
me and in reality perhaps you are
sub-consciously trying to find a
successor for me.

As I have told you
repeatedly — I am committed to
you but you are not to me.

Well, Bob, I will be
very happy to believe you about
everything. I think a good
starting point would be for
you to affirm your original
promise to stay with me
permanently, and without the
necessity of my getting down on
my knees and begging you to do
it.

How in the world you can interpret my statemet that I want to be with you in Las Vegas or wherever in hell you choose to go for the duration of our lives — as an act of hostility — I'll never of know.

You will never know how much it upsets me when I do something which disturbs you. I try so hard to please you and meet all of your demands.

Howard — Please let me know immediately if you are satisfied that this horrible incident is over.

Thanks very much, but no thanks!

I have just read your message which breathes hostility out of every line.

I dont think that relationships entered to at the point of a shotgun are any good.

minded you of this and I said I wondered if you were having a return of these feelings. You said: 'not in the least!'

"So, Bob, I am sure you will agree that on no occasion have I suggested that we part on friendly or unfriendly terms. I would not dream of making a remark like that. As a matter of fact, I live in constant fear that some chance remark I may make will be misinterpreted by you, and that you will get angry as you did once before that I remember. The time you told me you were a volatile Frenchman and that you had to let off steam once in a while.

"So, you see I would not dream of suggesting that you leave, because I would be afraid you would call my bluff and take me up on it.

"I am afraid those are your lines in this drama," concluded Hughes, "so please dont accuse me of stealing them."

"Howard," Maheu wrote in reply, scrawling his response on the reverse side of the billionaire's plea, "please let's knock off this horrible exchange of negative notes because we have too many important things to accomplish in a short period of time.

"I have no desire to leave and I would most certainly never think of taking advantage of your obvious desire not to get rid of me.

"Seven years ago I promised you I would phase out from all other clients. This, I have done. For God's sake, Howard, when will you realize that you are my *only* 'boss'! I truly don't know where in the hell I'd go or what I would do if you decided to 'kiss me off.'

"So—*please*—stop talking in terms of worry—because I would leave *only* if it were an accomodation to *you*. It may be difficult for you to believe this. I am sorry we do not have an opportunity to discuss these things in person. I could convince you of my dependency upon you in a matter of minutes.

"Anyway—let's forget who's to blame for what and move forward."

It was never over that easily. Hughes needed the fights. He often seemed to court battle with Maheu, seeking to draw him closer, to get him more emotionally involved, to make their relationship more intimate, an intimacy that could be attained only through combat. It was hardly acceptable for Hughes to tell his only friend, "I love you, Bob." So, instead there were the fights, and the inevitable postmortems.

"I dont consider it an unavoidable occupational hazard that you and I have to be at each others' throats like yesterday," wrote Hughes in the cold light of a new day.

"When we have an episode like that, I feel ashamed and disgusted with myself for my contribution to it. So even if you are able to brush it aside the next day and take it as a part of the game (which I admire), I am not able to do likewise."

Remorse mingled with bitterness, a true sense of loss with a terrible yearning for the golden old days of peace and harmony, that lost idyll of first love that never really existed.

"Whenever I suggest that our relationship be altered or improved in some manner, you always say there is nothing wrong with it," Hughes continued.

"But I can't buy this, Bob, I remember too clearly how it was when we first came to Nevada.

"Every new project that came up seemed to move more quickly and successfully than anyone could have anticipated.

"Also, you did not object to working at night.

"But the thing that impressed me the most was the speed with which you functioned. Perhaps I am simply more impatient than most people.

"This is probably why I started doing business by phone when most people were using the mail.

"Anyway, when I first got to know you, I remember thinking to myself—

'This is the real "get dunner" I have been looking for!'

"Bob, you lead a very active life.

"You have a lot of people around you—your family, friends, and others.

"I have absolutely nothing but my work.

"When things dont go well, it can be very empty indeed.

"I would like to make a real effort to restore things to the way they used to be, and I promise to do my share.

"I cannot tell you how truly grateful I will be if you can find it in your heart to do likewise."

It was a marriage that was not only always on the brink of collapse from internal tensions but also under constant attack from outside by rival courtiers. Maheu's sudden rise to power, his new intimacy with Hughes, was a shock to other top executives in the empire. When Hughes eloped to Las Vegas he left several would-be brides at the altar, all of them now united in jealous hatred of Maheu.

It was a conspiracy of the once-betrothed. In Los Angeles, there was Bill Gay, who ran the Romaine Street command center and the Mormon palace guard. In Houston, there was Raymond Holliday, who controlled the purse strings as chief executive of the Hughes Tool Company. In Culver City, there was Pat Hyland, who ran the Hughes Aircraft Company. In New York, there was Chester Davis, who handled the TWA case and had parlayed it into an appointment as general counsel.

Maheu was vigilant in spotting potential threats to his new marriage. Yet for all his experience as a clandestine warrior, he never recognized the true dimensions of the conspiracy. He ignored his obvious rivals and fixated instead on Hughes's lead attorney in Houston, Raymond Cook, who seemed to be gaining back-channel control over all the key power centers.

"I've had a bellyful of Cookie-Boy," Maheu told Hughes.

"First of all—make no mistake about it—for many years Cook has been attempting to take over your entire empire—*even* at the exclusion of Howard Hughes.

"I met this 'bum' for the first time in 1954. In less than one hour, he was making derogatory statements about you that I could not believe.

"Dietrich can tell you about an approach Cook made in an attempt to put you out of circulation in 1957.

"As time progressed I became more and more aware of the necessity to protect you from these 'demons.' By *these*, I mean Cook and his crowd.

"I think it is only fair for me to remind you that at age 25 I received the highest award our country can give for setting up a counter-intelligence system. When I was 27, I was given the prime responsibility for convincing the Germans that the invasion was going to take place in Southern France rather than Normandy.*

"Anyway, Howard—you have quite often told me that I was resented in certain circles of your organization because of my FBI background. The Cook group certainly has justification for resenting me. When I decided that to protect you to the fullest extent, the time had come to 'penetrate' the group, it was perhaps the most simple assignment we've ever undertaken. They are 'weak', they drink too much, and they talk too much. But more important, they are not loyal to you and to each other.

---

*Maheu's claim of a central role in D-Day is at least an exaggeration. While he did do counterintelligence work for the FBI during World War II, and he was handling a Vichy double-agent, there is no available evidence to support his boast of diverting the Nazis from Normandy.

"Anyway, they are now engaged in an all out effort to discredit me and my people in your eyes. They somehow know that you were ill recently, and they are attempting to accomplish their '*goal*' before something happens to you.

"In the meantime, they are trying to assure themselves of receiving the *first* telephone call when this occurs so that Holliday and Cook can fly immediately to Las Vegas—seize all your papers and take over. The reason for moving in so many lawyers from Houston on a permanent basis is to be ready for the big day.

"Howard, I hate to be so brutal and lay it on so coldly but those are the facts.

"There is no doubt that Cook is behind all this and unfortunately Holliday is so weak that he cannot cope with the push from Cook.

"All of these stupid problems could be eradicated instantly by the choice of a strong man as your *top guy*—whether it be me or someone else."

What Maheu failed to recognize was that the last thing Hughes wanted was a "strong man" as his "top guy." Such a man could endanger the billionaire's own power. In fact, Hughes wanted no one in overall authority, and far from seeking peace and order in his empire, he provoked and encouraged the internal power struggle, playing one top executive against another to keep them all off-balance.

And he feared Maheu most of all, as he confided to his counsel Chester Davis: "Chester, stated simply, with the explosiveness and unpredictability of my relationship with Bob, and with his well known characteristic of 'given an inch, take a mile,' I dont want to place him in a position which I may find, in the light of later scrutiny, has penetrated too far. In other words, Chester, I would not ever want to be faced with the problem of cutting Maheu back or reducing his authorities. He is, as you know, a very strong-willed individual."

But if Hughes feared Maheu most it was only because he now depended on him so completely, largely because he neither liked nor trusted any of his other top executives.

He had not spoken to Cook for a decade, had once actually fired him, and often saw his legal advice as condescending and contemptuous personal assaults: "Raymond! If you would treat me as something other than a cross-breed between an escaped lunatic and a child, you would be surprised how much better we would get along!"

He had never met Pat Hyland, had not seen Raymond Holliday since the late 1950s, and was now so estranged from them—the only real businessmen in his empire—that he relied on lower-echelon informants to keep tabs on both the Hughes Tool Company and the Hughes Aircraft Company.

"My men, upon whom I rely for all of my factual data concerning the entire Culver City operation, do not include Pat Hyland," the billionaire told Maheu. "Hyland has become completely unpredictable lately. I have no confidence in him.

"My confidantes inside the H.A.C. and H.T.Co. organizations put their very lives in jeopardy with some of the disclosures they make to me, and if they thought this information went to anybody—no matter whom—they would not continue to inform."

Of all his ministers-in-exile, none was more completely banished or more taken by surprise than the chief Mormon, Bill Gay. The heir apparent after Hughes's split with Dietrich, Gay had created the palace guard and gained in power as Hughes withdrew into seclusion. Once the field commander of the germ-warfare campaign, he suddenly became the most prominent casualty of that war when his wife fell ill in the late 1950s and Gay was banned as a dangerous carrier. Now he was frozen out completely.

Hughes never told Gay why, but he poured out his bitterness to Maheu. It was Gay who was responsible for looking after Jean Peters, and it was therefore obviously Gay who was responsible for the failure of his marriage:

"Bill's total indifference and laxity to my pleas for help in the domestic area, voiced urgently to him, week by week throughout the past 7 to 8 years, have resulted in a complete, I am afraid irrevocable loss of my wife.

"I am sorry, but I blame Bill completely for this unnecessary debacle.

"And this is only the beginning. If I compiled here a complete list of the actions or omissions in which I feel he has failed to perform his duty to me and to the company, it would fill several pages.

"I feel he has let me down—utterly, totally, completely."

Alone in his penthouse, estranged from all his key men, cut off even from his wife, scarred by a long string of past divorces—from his first wife,* from his first right-hand man Dietrich, from all his original executives and operatives—Hughes was now desperate to make a success of his new but already terribly troubled marriage to Maheu.

---

*Ella Rice, who Hughes married in 1925, and divorced in 1929.

"Bob," he wrote, "this uncertainty, distrust, and these accusations are bringing my entire operation to a halt and tearing me apart inside.

"I am not trying any further to debate who is right and who is wrong.

"Kuldell left me, Dietrich left me, Ramo and Wooldrich, Frank Waters and Arditto all left me, so lets say the incompatibility is probably on my side.*

"Anyway, right or wrong, I know one thing, and that is that this situation must be resolved and now."

Time and again Hughes tried to get to the root of his problems with Maheu, endlessly examining and analyzing, always talking about their "relationship."

SCENES FROM A MARRIAGE: Act II

"Bob—I am afraid I have lost the magic touch with which we used to find accord and harmony in almost everything we did.

"Somehow I cannot seem to reach you the way I used to.

"When I say I cannot seem to establish the relationship we used to have, you say I am imagining things."

"We shall never solve the problem of the 'relationship we used to have' unless we *both* try.

"It sure as hell doesn't help when I have to spend half of my time explaining off situations which did not exist in the first place."

"I agree it takes two to quarrel. It also takes an effort on the part of both parties to maintain a compatible relationship. However, I think in all fairness that I worry more and give more attention to this problem than you do. I suppose this is normal since I am bottled up here and my whole life is one of correspondence."

"You know, Howard, I do not envy in the least the lonesomeness which you must experience in the penthouse. Perhaps our relation-

*Robert C. Kuldell, general manager of Hughes Tool Company when Hughes inherited it, fired in 1938; Simon Ramo and Dean Wooldridge, top scientists at Hughes Aircraft who quit in 1953 and founded TRW, Inc.; Frank Waters and James Arditto, Hughes's political lawyers who both quit and filed suit against Hughes in 1961.

ship would instantaneously become a better one if I could hope that you might not envy the constant clobbering to which I am exposed from the penthouse."

"I used to be able to communicate with you and not be frightened for fear that each word I spoke or wrote might be the one that would cause you to get angry with me and wind up with my stomach tied up in knots. Please, Bob, let us go back to the environment of friendship that used to exist between us. That is all I ask."

"As to our relationship, Howard, I am afraid that I will always have a reasonably short fuse.

"I realize that many times things I say are illustrative of a short-tempered Frenchman, to which I plead guilty, but you must never, please, feel that you cannot bounce back and flip me on my ass.

"Perhaps even more important is that I sincerely believe, and hope you concur, that two dear friends should never go to sleep without all problems between them during the day having been resolved."

"Lets make a fresh start and bury all past differences.

"I know you are not completely satisfied with my conduct, in so far as it relates to you, and I can submit a list of quite a few items of grievance I wish, at the proper time, to take up with you.

"However, in spite of these short-comings, I am ready, if you are, to make a real, true, maximum effort, an all-out attempt to reconcile our differences.

"I want to turn over a new leaf with you."

They kissed and made up a thousand times, turned over a new leaf and started fresh every other day, but still the fights continued. Hughes was beside himself.

"I only hope you utilize your strategic powers of psychiatric suggestion as effectively on our opponents as you do upon me," he pleaded with his underling.

"I dont know why I am always placed in the position of being neglectful, irresponsible, ungrateful, and generally unworthy in the day to day progress of my relationship with you, Bob.

"It is almost like some massive chess game in which you seem never to miss an opportunity to place me at a disadvantage whenever the chance presents itself."

For a while it did look as though Maheu had the billionaire checkmated, using his emotional hold over Hughes to gain ever greater power, the volatile Frenchman whose hot-tempered outbursts had Hughes cowed, the Jesuit manipulator whose Svengali-like powers had Hughes under his spell.

Hughes, in his desperation to win Maheu's heart, now offered his regent the keys to the kingdom and a palace to go with it.

"I am prepared to give you the highest order of responsibility and authority in the Hughes Tool Company," he declared. "By that I mean you will outrank all other executives of the company, and you will have only me to contend with.

"If I place you in this position of authority over the entire worldwide activities of the company, not just the Nevada Division, but the entire Hughes Tool Company, if you assume this position of authority, then, more than ever, I must have a clean-cut understanding with you as to what my position in this picture is going to be.

"You will simply have to realize and to accept one basic fact, Bob, and that is that, as long as I am alive and able to do so, I intend to retain the final authority for myself.

"Now I dont think this is so damned bad from your standpoint.

"Anyway, you are stuck with me."

At the time, that did not seem too high a price to pay. Especially given the $600,000 French Colonial mansion Hughes built for Maheu just off the third fairway of the Desert Inn golf course. Jealous rivals called it "Little Caesar's Palace." A modified plantation house with a touch of Las Vegas–style splendor, the mansion had two tennis courts, an indoor-outdoor swimming pool, a patio shielded from the evening chill by an invisible warm-air curtain, a private screening room, parquet flooring, and twin curved stairways that could have come out of Tara. But most important of all, it had a direct telephone line to Hughes in his penthouse hideout half a mile away.

Anyone who had seen the two men talking—Maheu in a custom-made suit flashing gold-and-diamond RAM cufflinks, seated at a big polished desk in the paneled office of his new mansion, Hughes sprawled out naked on his paper-towel-insulated bed in a cramped, filthy, darkened room surrounded by debris—would have assumed that Maheu was the billionaire, and wondered why he was engaged in marathon conversation with an obviously deranged derelict.

4/30/68

Bob —
    I agree it takes two to quarrel.
It also takes an effort on the part
of both parties to maintain a
compatible relationship. However, I
think in all fairness that I worry
more and give more attention to this
problem than you do. I suppose
this is normal since I am bottled
up here and my whole life is one of
correspondence.

10/8 — 5 P.M.   1969?

Bob —
    I don't know why I am
always placed in the position
of being neglectful, irresponsible, ungrateful, and
generally unworthy in the
day to day progress of my
relationship with you, Bob.

    It is almost like some
massive chess game in
which you seem never
to miss an opportunity
to place me at a dis-
advantage whenever the
chance presents itself.

While Hughes lay huddled in his somber seclusion, Maheu flashed through Las Vegas with flamboyant relish, flew about the country in a private Hughes jet, entertained royally on his oceangoing yacht, hobnobbed with movie stars and astronauts and Mafia dons, dropped in for state dinners at the White House, and played tennis with Nevada's governor.

Now, to top it off, he had been offered overall command of Hughes's entire empire. Everything was going according to plan.

Or so it seemed. But if Maheu looked and lived like the billionaire, Hughes in fact still was. And as he had warned Maheu when he dangled before him the keys to the kingdom, "You are stuck with me."

The battle for control was not over. It had hardly begun. No sooner had Hughes promised Maheu full command than he was gripped by a growing paranoid fear that Maheu would take over completely. He never exactly withdrew the offer, but neither did he ever actually give Maheu the job. Instead he suggested a "trial arrangement," an "informal gentlemens' understanding," a "word of honor agreement" they would for the moment just keep to themselves.

Maheu was perplexed. "Howard, as to the over-all informal authority, what good does it do unless the officers of your company are so notified?" he asked. "They certainly have no reason for taking my word on a matter of such significance."

Hughes was enraged by Maheu's doubts. "If you want our relationship to endure at all I besiege you not to adopt your present attitude," he shot back.

"I deny that I have failed to implement our confidential gentleman's agreement. I emphatically deny that I have broken our agreement in any way whatsoever. This is just one more in a long string of assumptions you have reached in your own suspicious mind. I contend that our agreement is 100% in full force and effect. If anybody violates our word of honor agreement, it will be you and not I."

The phantom top job became a major battleground.

"Howard," wrote Maheu, taking a tough stand, "the agreement that we discussed and in which both of us concurred, was that I would be in charge of all the divisions of the Hughes Tool Co. If you have changed your mind, it is as simple as telling me so.

"I have made it very clear that I have no intent of accepting any position in your company unless you are the only one to whom I am responsible, and unless it is in fact the top position. If we cannot reach that understanding, then I want to accept several directorships which have been offered to me for some time with very favorable stock options.

"I think we must also remember, Howard, that it was not I who ever asked for the top job under you, but it was always you who offered it."

Maheu's threatened infidelity, his open toying with side affairs, his constant "Dear John" letters, drove Hughes into a jealous frenzy.

"You say: 'It was not I who ever asked for the top job, but you who offered it,' " Hughes replied.

"I think this is a fairly accurate appraisal of our relationship. In other words, it is *always* I who am forced to ask you to do this or that, and it is always I who must ask you to overlook something which has offended you.

"I dont see what you gain by this chip-on-the-shoulder attitude.

"Bob, the only thing I can say in summary is that you seem constantly to place me in a position where I must beg you not to leave or beg you not to work for somebody else or beg you not to make outside investments.

"I just wonder how you would like it and how long you would endure the type of insults that you administer to me daily.

"Suppose I were to hover on the brink of asking you for your resignation, and suppose I were to repeat this attitude over and over, how would you feel?

"I suppose you will answer this by saying you are explosive by nature. But Bob, I am just as easily disturbed as you are."

Hughes was, in fact, more than disturbed. He brooded about Maheu's constant bullying and threatened betrayal late into the night, carefully reviewing their entire relationship more in sadness than in anger, composing a heartfelt memo before deciding to let passions cool overnight.

"I have been working for the last three hours writing you a long message," he informed Maheu. "I feel very intensely and very bitterly about what you intend to do.

"I think it is important enough to give it fresh consideration in the morning. So why dont you get a good night's sleep and I will send you this message in the morning."

At the crack of dawn, he hit his estranged helpmate with his pained letter of lost love:

"Bob, I feel worse than you have any idea about my instinctive realization that you do not intend to remain with me.

"Anyway, tragic as this is to me, I assure you I will have no bitterness about it if you will only try to do it in as considerate a manner as possible.

"On numerous occasions, I have endeavored to turn over a new leaf with you and tried to get to the bottom of the flaw in our relationship and correct it.

"Time and time again I have plead with you to help me find out what was bugging you and eliminate it so that we could have a really trusting relationship in both directions.

"You have always insisted that nothing was the matter and that I could rely on your remaining with me the rest of your life.

"Yet now you are doing something obviously intended as a severance of our relationship.

"I have sensed some frightening incident like this.

"You see, you have penetrated into my activities to an extent where practically every single phase of my life is dependent upon you. You have handled it this way and you have resented any contact I have with outsiders.

"This would be OK if you were likewise completely dependent on me. But this is not the case. By your skillful handling of things, the major part of my daily life seems to flow through Maheu Associates.

"You have carefully kept your firm alive. I told you on numerous occasions that the one thing I could not accept was a part time arrangement. I certainly have paid on a full time basis.

"It seems to me that, in your view, you are still Robert A. Maheu Associates, and I am just a client."

Just a client. What a sad, brutal realization. He had allowed himself to be swept away, to fall for, become totally dependent on a man who considered him just another client.

Hughes's deep insecurity about Maheu's fidelity touched every aspect of their relationship. The phantom top job offer became a running battle, one of many in their ongoing battle for control, not so much over the empire as over each other. It would turn even the most trivial disputes into titanic emotional struggles.

Even a golf tournament.

It was no ordinary tournament, the one in dispute here. It was the Tournament of Champions, a Las Vegas institution that had long been a trademark of the Desert Inn. But no more. Hughes had ordered it out almost immediately upon buying the hotel in 1967, afraid that he would be contaminated by the hordes of spectators and, worse yet, spotted by the television cameras supposedly covering the golf match.

Maheu had tried to dissuade him. "What in the hell are you worried about?" he had asked. "I think we can control the scanning of cameras and increase the security so that you can be safe 'in your castle'— which you damn right deserve. My only suggestion is that we make you a *hero* rather than the *'prisoner of war.'* "

Maheu had kept at him, but Hughes was adamant.

"I have been your whipping boy long enough," he exploded, as the golf fight again aroused dangerous passions. "I dont intend to take any more abuse on this subject. I will not have the tournament at the Desert Inn because, to do so, would place me in the position of having refused to have it at the D.I. up to this time."

So the golf tournament had been transferred to Moe Dalitz's California resort, Rancho La Costa. In the years since, however, Hughes had grown increasingly worried that he would be blamed for the loss of this prestigious event. And now, in April 1969, Maheu was at La Costa on a do-or-die mission to bring the tournament back—not back to the Desert Inn, but back to Las Vegas.

. The plan had been to close the deal and announce the coup on national television. But Maheu had failed in his mission to La Costa. Failed to recapture the golf match, and ruined the entire plot.

The plot against Jack Nicklaus and Arnold Palmer. Hughes had been scheming against them ever since the two top pros had refused to participate in the uprooted Tournament of Champions in early 1968. He saw it as a deliberate slap in the face and a grave peril.

"I think it would be the very worst public relations for these men to cancel out," Hughes had written when the crisis began. "A lot of people may feel that this is the very first setback we have suffered. At best, you may be sure the newspaper writers will be very hostile about it and they will blame us in print all over the country."

National disgrace. But it was more than that, more even than a good excuse to pick another fight with Maheu. Golf was a sensitive subject for Hughes. He had once dreamed of himself *being* a Nicklaus or Palmer, indeed had put it at the top of his list. While still in his early twenties, Hughes told Noah Dietrich: "My first objective is to become the world's number one golfer. Second, the top aviator, and third I want to be the most famous movie producer. Then, I want you to make me the richest man in the world." Only the golfing crown had eluded him. And now he was not willing to let Palmer and Nicklaus also slip away.

At first he plotted to snare them both. "It will be considered by everybody here that this is a terrible insult to me personally," wrote Hughes. "I had already come to the conclusion that some kind of a special deal will have to be made with N. and P. So I have decided to offer the two players a contract to appear in a feature motion picture."

After more brooding, Hughes changed his mind. He would make only one of them a star.

"Re: golf," he wrote, "I am willing to forget Nicklaus, but I am not willing to forget Palmer. I insist we take steps, more than ever, to insure Palmer's participation.

"Now, look, Bob, I am going to get Palmer some way, so why not save us both a lot of grief and help me with it," he cajoled Maheu, who kept pressing him to bring the tournament back to the Desert Inn. "I am not willing to move it back here. I am not going to be pressured into it by Nicklaus's refusal.

"I am willing to talk movies to Palmer. In some ways it would be easier to handle than with the two Prima Donnas in one film. Since we are only shooting for one player, I think a short subject (about ½ hour) should be enough. I very definitely do not think we should tell him it will be a short subject, but I also do not feel we should tell him it will be a full length motion picture."

The more he brooded, however, the less willing Hughes became to offer Palmer even a short subject. Why make either Nicklaus or Palmer a star, when instead he could make it hot for both of them?

"I have just worked out a plan for doing without Nicklaus permanently—as to Palmer, I dont know," wrote the billionaire, unveiling his latest scheme.

"I want to consider opening a massive book on the P.G.A. Golf Tour and certain other selected sporting events. I want our book to become the bible in determining odds. That is the key to the deal. I want our book to be the last word in determining the odds on any player, and thus the determining factor in the standing of that player in his sport."

The plot to entice Nicklaus and Palmer had evolved into a plot to destroy them. Not content to fix the odds, Hughes decided to really fix their wagons. He would find a new man and make *him* a star.

"Ever since Nicklaus' and Palmer's rejection of our invitation, I have taken a sacred vow to find another golfer and groom him to supplant and far exceed these two. I have been determined to shove these two bastards into the background. Well, I have watched every bit of golf news avidly, and with my intimate knowledge of the game, I have settled on Casper as our man."

Billy Casper was a real comer. Hughes would build him up, leave Nicklaus and Palmer far behind, and win by proxy the golfing crown that had eluded him in his youth.

"Now, I read some encouraging news," he continued with vindictive glee. "Nicklaus and Palmer are at the low-point of an all-time record slump that started exactly 8 months ago—about when they gave us the brush. So, my reaction to that is: it couldn't happen to a nicer guy!"

But there was no time to gloat. Hughes had bigger fish to fry. He planned to make himself the global impresario of golf, just take over the entire sport.

"It is my desire to establish Las Vegas as the Golf Capitol of the World," he declared. "I am prepared to put up purses that will far exceed anything yet—$500,000 and even $1,000,000 tournaments!"

But the first crucial step in the whole grand scheme was to bring the Tournament of Champions back to Las Vegas. And Maheu had failed in his mission to La Costa.

"I told you it was mandatory to announce, no later than the conclusion of play today, that the tournament would be returned to Las Vegas," complained Hughes, hammering away at his henchman long-distance.

"I said if this was not done the public here would turn against me in force.

"So, here we are Bob, the first bitterness that has existed between us in a long time, and I dont want it to happen again."

Maheu absorbed the diatribe over a telephone that seemed glued to his ear. Hughes had kept him on the line almost the entire day, as always unable to bear his absence or his freedom. Maheu had missed the golf match, he had missed the awards ceremony, he had missed the big postgame gala. All he had seen of La Costa was the inside of a phone booth. Now he exploded. He had been busting his ass trying to put the big deal together while Hughes just sat back watching the tournament on television, and if Hughes had others more qualified to handle it, he was more than welcome to give them this plum.

Well, it had taken long enough, but Hughes finally had Maheu exactly where he wanted him. Boiling in a phone booth. The grandiose golf schemes no longer mattered. It was once more time to discuss their relationship.

"Quote more qualified than I unquote," wrote Hughes. "This is a well-worn phrase in your vocabulary, Bob, you have used it often.

"I dont know anybody more qualified than you are, Bob, but I sure as hell know some people who are easier to get along with than you are. It is a fact, Bob, that I have never in my entire life tried as conscientiously, as hard, or as dilligently to get along with anybody as I have with you.

"When I first started writing my messages to you, it was for one reason only. I was afraid that, on the telephone at one time or another, I was going to lose my temper. So I started writing messages to you in order that I could read them over word by word and pick out any slight details I felt you might consider offensive.

"It is too bad that, after taking all of these pains, I should write you a message which does not contain any slightest suggestion of criticism, yet apparently I have somehow offended you.

"Anyway, to return to the Golf Tournament, you will see that I did not even remotely suggest I have anybody more qualified to handle it. I certainly have learned by now not to say anything as dangerous as that to you.

"I just feel there are about 500 other matters requiring your skillful handling, and I also feel, in spite of the denials that I know you will make, that you and I are separated by a wider chasm today than at any time recently.

"And if the word I used before, the word 'bitterness' does not describe your feelings, it sure as hell describes mine.

"Incidently, what right have you to say I am sitting here comfortably watching TV while you suffer at some dancing function in La Costa?

"In other words, how—just how do you know I am comfortable? Maybe I am sitting here wracked with pain, how the hell do you know any different?

"I am sure that most unbiased people would certainly prefer to be dancing at La Costa, at the presentation ceremonies of the golf tournament, rather than confined to a bed watching TV—and most particularly, if the subject on TV is a critical unpleasant one."

It just killed Hughes to see Maheu traipsing about, whether to La Costa or to Cape Canaveral.

If with the golf tournament Hughes took something trivial and

made it seem momentous, with the Apollo space shots—the quest
to land a man on the moon—Hughes took something truly momentous and made it seem trivial. Merely an excuse for another fight
with Maheu. Once again, it was triggered by what Hughes saw as
Maheu's maddening wanderlust.

"I am not eager for you to attend the event at Canaveral," wrote
the billionaire, stifling his man's dangerous urge to roam.

"I view this purely and simply as a situation where you have asked
to do something which you personally want to do. And which will
take you away from my orbit for a certain period of time, and then
return you later with all of the attendant risks of illness, accident,
airplane highjacking, airplane accident in the over crowded skies,
etc., etc., ad infinitum.

"One thing is not a matter of risk or uncertainty, one thing is sure,
it will sap a certain measure of your strength right at a time when
you are the key man and the very fulcrum upon which my entire
world depends.

"Bob, you are always asking me what happens to you if I die.
Have you ever thought of what would be the outcome to me if
something should happen to you?

"Bob, you are handling absolutely everything that is most important to me, and many of these matters, such as the $137,000,000
TWA judgement, are being handled by persons completely unknown
to me and according to a strategy totally unknown to me.

"This is unavoidable, and I am not asking that it be any different.
I only want you to know that, if anything should happen to you, I
would not even know where to begin trying [to] pick up the pieces.

"So, please just bear that in mind when the time comes for you
to leave for Florida."

The space shots should have been moments of triumph and celebration. Hughes had played a key role in the historic quest. His
empire had built the first spacecraft that landed on the moon, and
the Hughes Surveyor sent back to earth the first close-ups of the
moon's surface via the Hughes Early Bird communications satellite,
which would also broadcast the astronauts' moon walks to the world.
But it all brought no joy to the penthouse. Once more, as with the
golf tournament, Hughes could not bear being confined to his bed,
relegated to watching the big event on television, while Maheu was
down at the launch, hobnobbing with the astronauts. After all, Hughes
had once himself been hero of the skies. So space shots were always
touchy.

Even on the day men walked on the moon. Especially then. Maheu did not try to escape Hughes's orbit for the big one. Instead, he spent weeks personally producing a TV show celebrating Hughes as a space pioneer and planned to run it on the Las Vegas station Hughes owned right before the moon walk. But on the eve of the landing came word from Mission Control—abort! Suddenly, at the last possible moment, without explanation, Hughes canceled the show.

"You are the captain of the ship and I will follow your advice," wrote the grounded Maheu, "but I cannot help but tell you that you are making the mistake of your life, which otherwise would have been the greatest thing that has happened since your arrival here. Cancelling the program at this late date will result in repercussions from which you will never recover.

"I might also add, Howard, that it is evident to me that I should be prepared to become just another zombie in your stable, and not have another original thought."

Captain Hughes refused to be intimidated. "Bob, my reason for withdrawing from this is purely one of timing," he explained. "I believe, with good cause, that I will be accused of attempting to cash in on somebody else's bravery.

"Bob, lets put the shoe on the other foot—If I am to be the so-called Captain, what good is it if you ignore my deep conviction and raise so much hell that I have to do it your way or face the consequences of bad feeling from you and threatened reprisals or horrible 'repercussions' tomorrow?"

Maheu did not understand. He seemed to have the strange idea that Hughes had canceled the TV show for the pure pleasure of shooting him down. Just to provoke another fight. They argued bitterly all night and into the morning of the moon landing, and they were still at it when Neil Armstrong took "one small step for a man, one giant leap for mankind."

"Howard, please give this little boy from Maine an opportunity to prove to you whether he is right or wrong," pleaded Maheu, still trying to save his show while the rest of the world watched the space spectacular.

"If you are the gambling man that I think you may be, I am prepared to make a little wager with you. If I fall on my face on this caper, I will continue working for you for the rest of my life at no cost to you, and if you are wrong you will double my salary as long as I work for you."

Hughes had no interest in the wager.

"Your proposed bet is just absurd," he wrote. "You would not be able to get along with me working for free.

"We can't even get along when you get paid."

It was true. By now their marriage had turned into a nonstop brawl, with both partners weary of the battle but continuing to slug it out, as if by habit. It didn't take anything as sensitive as space shots or golf tournaments to get them going. Even routine business could become the flash point.

Maheu started the fireworks one Fourth of July with a simple request for decisions on several pending projects. There was nothing provocative about his memo, and he even apologized for intruding on the holiday weekend.

"If you feel that the above items should not have been mentioned on the 4th of July," he wrote, "you might attribute it to the fact that I am under sedation as a result of a stupid accident I had yesterday. My leg is in a complete cast."

Hughes was not sympathetic. He saw Maheu's routine request as a vicious attack and responded with a blast at his crippled lieutenant.

"I work around the clock," he began defensively. "There are only so many hours and the day is gone.

"Regarding your apology for disturbing me on the 4th of July weekend, this was not necessary. As you are aware, holidays mean very little to me, since I work just about all the time.

"There is only one thing that occurs to me, Bob. Whenever you call something like this to my attention, I get the impression that, instead of merely calling my attention to something you fear I may have forgotten, you are seeking to place me in a posture of guilt.

"It is almost as if we were playing some kind of game.

"I have no desire to pick a quarrel with you. I *did* get your message last nite. It *did* raise hell with my evening. I had *not* forgotten any of the items mentioned. I did *not* resent being reminded of them. I think it was just the ominous, warning tone of your reminder that disturbed me. The snide, sarcastic language.

"Bob, I dont think I merit this kind of insulting language from you, and, since you are always talking about maintaining the respect of your associates, how do you think this sounds to my staff?

"Someday, when you have time, just come out with it and tell me exactly and fully how stupid you really think your associate is.

"Anyway, I am sick of fighting with you when you are supposed to be on my side."

The sedated, injured Maheu was stunned.

"I have cast my entire business life in your hands which, of course, also means the future of my family," he replied. "How in the world can you deduce from perhaps a poorly worded message that I think you are stupid? Honest, Howard, if I didn't have respect for you as a human being and for your intelligence, I can assure you that I would not be here thoroughly dependent on one man.

"Please knock this off because I become very emotionally disturbed when I feel that I am the cause of upsetting you."

Hughes was not really all that upset. In fact, never in the entire tormented history of their stormy relationship was he happier than when Maheu injured himself. Finally, they were both bed-ridden. Now he had Maheu all to himself. And he was making the most of it.

"I am sorry about your knee, and I have no desire to add to your problems," he wrote solicitously. "On the other hand, I have urgent problems which simply cannot be put aside."

The list of problems was truly staggering.

"Please give me some word on Parvin, Franklin's statement, Laxalt, Cannon, and Bible's efforts on behalf of Lake Mead water, my request not to permit a high-rise on the Bonanza site, the threatened hotel on the Zoong property, the threatened hotel on Convention Center Drive, the three parcels of real estate, your efforts via the Justice Dept. to acquire Stardust, my communication via Rebozo to Pres. Nixon, my request to you for some revision of the allocation of Army helicopter business to Bell, that should not wait another five minutes, possible acquisition of the Riviera.

"Bob, the above list includes eleven items, which, relying solely upon my memory, eleven items that I have entrusted to your sole and exclusive handling, are overdue for a report.

"P.S.—I have not included the TWA judgement, which brings the list to twelve, for your easy remembrance."

Each day began with a similar get-well message.

"How is your knee this morning?" Hughes would inquire, and then launch into another diatribe.

"Bob, please do not take offense at this, but I would appreciate it very much if you would review a list of the projects in work and dictate a brief status report on each.

"You tell me nothing about anything. Nothing about any progress in the TWA affair for a year, nothing about the water system, nothing about the future plans of the AEC, and half a dozen other projects I have asked you to take over.

"Bob, I must be the least informed executive in the whole damned country concerning his own business. I have to learn more from the news media than anyone I know in a comparable position. This *must end* or I will, in my own defense, be forced to set up an investigative organization to inform me of what is happening in my own organization. This surely would be an all time high in embarrassment and I ask you not to make it necessary.

"I am sorry to complain this way, Bob, but honestly, I sometimes think you are so busy with your very full and complex life, that you perhaps forget I am living in a virtual vacuum.

"Perhaps, while you are staying off your knee, Bob, and unable to keep some of your appointments for meetings, etc., it may give you an opportunity to work on some of the projects and problems I have mentioned, many of which can be advanced by your efforts via the phone.

"I hope you are feeling better."

"I thank you, Howard, for inquiring about my knee," replied Maheu from his bed. "It continues to be very painful, particularly at night when I make abrupt turns while sleeping which causes me to awaken repeatedly.

"Howard, I truly have been trying to keep you informed. If you feel that these matters give you a reason to control me via some investigative organization within your complex, please be my guest. It might do you some good to find out about some of my accomplishments from another source."

"Are you and I going to embark on another voyage of hostility?" Hughes shot back.

"I have no desire to quote control you, but Bob, I do not intend to learn about my business affairs from the news media any longer. If I desired to spy on you, I would ask someone to do it, and I certainly would not tell you about it beforehand.

"How is your knee, Bob? Please be careful about getting up. Knowing your restless nature, I have been worrying very, very much about the liklihood of your injuring your knee permanently."

It went on like that for a month, until Hughes learned that, unfortunately, Maheu had recovered, and quickly moved to keep him from returning to his full and complex life.

"Bob, are you well enough—I mean your knee—to go to a meeting?" he asked innocently. "I assumed you might be well enough because somebody told me you were up the other night."

They were no longer joined as shut-ins, but they were still joined in unholy matrimony.

SCENES FROM A MARRIAGE: Act III

"Now, Howard, I am getting pretty damned disturbed about what seems to be developing into a compulsive need to give Bob hell. We never talk about the small miracles we pull.

"I am really trying to do a job for you in innumerable areas, but I have to get the feeling when I hit the sack tonight that I do not have your backing and that perhaps I should indulge in the sure-fire way of gaining your complete confidence—DO NOTHING OR SCREW UP THE DETAIL.

"Howard, I really feel very badly about having to speak so frankly, but as they say that's how the cookie crumbles, and they happen to be your cookies, so you can crumble them any way you choose."

––––––––

"I dont desire this unhappiness on your part. I am the one who suffers the most from it.

"It does not make me feel happy, and it certainly does not benefit my health to quarrel with you.

"I do not claim it is a one way street by any means. I will try to improve."

––––––––

"Howard, until now, and I repeat now, I have been genuinely interested in protecting our flanks wherever they may be. I have been concerned about a 12:01 AM closing on the Slipper, protecting your image in Ecuador, choosing a Presidential candidate, making sure that all of your investments to date in Las Vegas run profitably, keeping a door open in the Bahamas, stopping the Boulder City Council from passing a resolution condemning our position on nuclear tests, preventing the White House from revealing the contents of your letter to the President—the contents of which to date I know nothing—but which they claim could prove embarrassing.

"If all of these things are unimportant then perhaps you should tell me precisely what you expect me to do, because I've just about lost my courage in trying to exercise my own judgement. Honest to

Christ, Howard, you make it impossible for me to know what you want, how you want it, where you want it, and when you want it."

"Do I detect in your last message a slight hint of your uncertainty with respect to the future and what it may hold for the two of us?

"If so, I think it is about time you lay it all on the line with no reservations.

"I think our relationship needs re-examination and re-clarification, either as worthless or as deserving of your loyalty and allegiance."

"Howard, you certainly have my loyalty, devotion, and friendship. It is inconceivable that anything could ever happen which could cause this to change.

"I am referring to many years of continued, consistent dedication and loyalty which I defy you to find in any other human being. If all of this has been in vain, then I feel sorry indeed—not for myself but for you. I say I feel sorry for you because if you, in fact, don't recognize it when you really have it, then you must be a terribly unhappy person."

"I must say I am astounded. A month or two ago I asked you if there was not something under the surface that I was unaware of. I said you seemed preoccupied and I feared an explosion one of these nights that would wreck our relationship. You told me I was imagining things.

"I want earnestly, Bob, to achieve immediately a better relationship with you. I know we have been over all of this ground before, and I know that getting you to admit that there could be any improvement is next to impossible.

"But I want to try anyway."

"Howard, you keep referring to a better relationship. I have no problem in this area, but by indirection you keep sending little messages which indicate that you have certain apprehensions about establishing such a relationship.

"Every time I make a suggestion to help you accomplish what I genuinely believe is your sincere desire, I get dropped on my head.

"I constantly beg for guidance. It just happens that I get none, but do receive an over-abundance of criticism. My oujai board is beginning to runneth over, because I am beginning to realize that when I dip my cup into the liquid fuel I am drinking from a seive I end up having nothing to taste."

Maheu was losing his grip. Within a year, the erstwhile CIA tough guy had been driven to drink and was crying for mercy, his Machiavellian schemes seemingly forgotten as he was drawn further and further into an overwhelmingly intimate and terribly troubled relationship with Hughes.

Despite all the strains and bickering, they were still together, about to embark on a series of missions that would shake the country. But as they set off to buy America, both had to wonder—could this marriage be saved?

3 The Kingdom

Shortly after Thanksgiving 1967, Nevada Governor Paul Laxalt got a sudden chill—as if he had seen a ghost. The Ghost of Thanksgiving Past.

In the year since Howard Hughes had made his holiday-week pilgrimage to Las Vegas, Laxalt had been haunted by a hidden fear. Without once meeting him, the governor had granted Hughes nearly feudal rights, doing everything in his power to help the unseen billionaire become Nevada's biggest private employer, its largest landowner, and king of its one industry, gambling.

Laxalt waived all the rules, placed Hughes above the law, and let him seize full control of four major casinos. No individual had ever before owned even one, but all were licensed at the governor's command despite the billionaire's refusal to submit a photograph, fingerprints, or the detailed personal and financial records required by Nevada law. Nobody even dared to suggest that Hughes make a personal appearance.

In addition to the casinos, the recluse now owned four resort hotels, most of the land on the Las Vegas Strip, a vast amount of other real estate, two airports, one airline, and a local television station. It all came to almost $100 million, an investment Hughes had to protect. He bought local politicians wholesale, imposing his will on officials from the courthouse to the statehouse, and seemed to have enormous influence over the silver-haired Republican governor.

Laxalt had allowed an invisible man to control Nevada more completely than anyone has ever controlled a sovereign state. And now he was haunted.

Hughes, on the other hand, was quite pleased. "I think Laxalt can be brought to a point where he will just about entrust his entire political future to his relationship with us," wrote the phantom. "I think that is the way it should be and the way it can be."

In fact, Hughes had promised to make the obliging governor president of the United States.

"I am ready to ride with this man to the end of the line, which I am targeting as the White House," he declared. "I think we must convince him beyond a shadow of a doubt that I intend to back him with unlimited support right into the White House in 1972."

Paul Laxalt for president! At the time it seemed just another bizarre notion hatched in the unreal world of the penthouse. But even as Laxalt nurtured his hidden relationship with Hughes, he was also developing a special relationship with the newly elected governor of a neighboring state, Ronald Reagan. One that would make him the future president's closest friend, his chief political adviser, and his national campaign chairman.

But even when Laxalt became one of the most powerful men in the country, Howard Hughes would still be there to haunt him, as he haunted Laxalt now.

Visions of the White House could not still his fears. The governor could not forget that he was dealing with a phantom, that he had never seen Hughes, had not even spoken to him. That nobody had. Not since he supposedly arrived in Las Vegas, indeed not for an entire decade.

Dread thoughts, which the governor might have repressed forever if no one had discovered the strange midnight meeting of his Gaming Control Board. In late November 1967, several of the state's top regulatory officials gathered like a secret coven at the witching hour, roused sleeping colleagues with a conference call, and by 1:30 A.M. had formally approved the impatient billionaire's fourth casino license. When the incredible story leaked, a few legislators were sufficiently shocked to demand a full investigation.

Laxalt could no longer suppress his fears. They came tumbling out, one chilling thought after another. What if Hughes was not really up in the penthouse? What if Hughes had been replaced by an imposter? What if Hughes did not in fact exist?

The governor was frantic. On December 11, 1967, Laxalt secretly summoned his gambling czars to the state capitol in Carson City. All agreed that something must be done.

This was a job for the FBI.

"It was the unanimous consensus of this entire group," the chief agent in Las Vegas reported to J. Edgar Hoover, "that some effort should be made to enable the Nevada state authorities to know for certain that HOWARD HUGHES actually is alive and that they are actually licensing a 'live individual.'

"Even though everything appears to be 100% above board," continued the FBI memo, "no one, including the Governor of the State of Nevada, has ever personally seen, talked with, or discussed any licensing matters with HOWARD HUGHES. There is grave concern among the Nevada gaming authorities and Governor LAXALT that a great 'hoax' could be being perpetrated. . . ."

Still, it was inconceivable to actually confront the phantom financier. Early on, the gaming board had timidly asked his lawyer, Richard Gray, if just one member might see the billionaire. His reaction was troubling, in retrospect.

"Mr. GRAY lost his composure and indicated that if the authorities would require this then Mr. HUGHES would probably withdraw from the State of Nevada," the FBI report recounted. "No further effort was made to pursue a personal meeting with HOWARD HUGHES."

All the state ever got was a power of attorney supposedly signed by the recluse. Now the governor took this treasured scrap and nervously handed it over to the FBI for authentication. Was the signature genuine, had the phantom left any fingerprints?

"Nevada gaming authorities do not desire to do anything of an official nature with the results of this examination," the surreal report concluded, "other than to satisfy in their own minds that HOWARD HUGHES exists and that they are dealing with him."

If the question was more than embarrassing, the answer was truly a rude shock.

J. Edgar Hoover had not become a national institution by sending his G-men in pursuit of ghosts. The director took one look at Laxalt's pitiful plea and unceremoniously scrawled, "We should have absolutely *nothing* to do with this. H."

Case closed.

Hughes would continue to haunt Nevada as long as Laxalt remained in office, and the governor would continue to do his bidding, but Laxalt would never get to see him, nor would he ever get any real proof that he was dealing with a "live individual."

Howard Hughes, of course, was alive, right there on the ninth floor of the Desert Inn. Had Laxalt managed to meet him, however, he probably would have had the shock of his life.

Naked and disheveled, his hideously long fingernails tracing patterns on color-coded maps, the phantom of the penthouse sat in bed busily plotting to buy the rest of Nevada.

He had not come to Las Vegas with a master plan. He had come only because he didn't know where else to go and because he had been there before and liked it. He liked the all-night ambiance, he liked the showgirls, he liked the whole tone and feel of the place. In the early 1950s, before he went into seclusion, he used to fly in regularly for a night or a few days or a few weeks, catch the shows, perhaps pick up a showgirl, dispatching one of his lackeys to arrange the assignation, always ordering him to first get a signed release. He rarely gambled, just occasionally dropped a nickel in a slot machine, but he cruised the casinos and was a familiar figure at ringside in the showrooms, and he kept coming back.

Others now speculated as to why Hughes had come back again. All were certain he had some great "mission"—to reform the loose morals of Las Vegas, to clean out the Mob, to join up with the Mob. In fact, Hughes had no plans at all when he arrived, except to find a safe place to hide. And, in a real sense, that was still all he was after.

At first, it was safe enough to hide in his blacked-out bedroom, behind a closed door, behind his phalanx of Mormons, behind a locked partition in the hallway, behind an armed security guard on an otherwise vacant and sealed-off penthouse floor. Then he had to own the entire hotel. To protect himself. Having bought the Desert Inn, he had to buy all the surrounding hotels on the Strip. Again, for self-protection. Now he had to buy the rest of Las Vegas. For the same reason.

Desperate to control his own little world, Hughes bought increasingly greater control of the world outside, expanding his domain in concentric circles, only to discover that the more he owned, the more he needed to protect, so that each new acquisition generated the need for further acquisitions to protect those that came before.

Atop his desert command post, Hughes loomed over the Las Vegas Strip, snatching up its gaudy hotels and gambling casinos like some demonic demigod playing an outsized Monopoly game. Had he looked out his window, he could have seen it all: miles of improbable flash set down by mobsters in the middle of nowhere, with eighty-foot

signs blinking STARDUST and SANDS and CAESAR'S PALACE, a fabulous
façade for the bare bones of capitalism, pure money with no product,
as skeletal as Hughes himself, the garish front as much a mirage as
his own public image.

It was a cheap, loud, vulgar place, and Hughes never set eyes on
it during his entire stay. His windows had been blacked out the day
he arrived, and not once did he peel back the masking tape, pull up
the blinds, and look outside. Never in four years.

Hughes had his own vision, and he didn't want it sullied.

"I like to think of Las Vegas in terms of a well dressed man in a
dinner jacket, and a beautifully jewelled and furred female getting
out of an expensive car," he wrote, conjuring up a more acceptable
image. "I think that is what the public expects here—to rub shoulders
with V.I.P.'s and Stars, etc.—possibly dressed in sport clothes, but
if so, at least good sport clothes. I dont think we should permit this
place to degrade into a freak, or amusement-park category, like
Coney Island.

"Dont misunderstand me about the clothes," he quickly added.
"I am not suggesting that our entire staff go out and blow themselves
to a new wardrobe at the hotel's expense. (That is intended to be a
joke.) I am not thinking of what our employees wear, and I am
certainly not thinking of spending any unnecessary money. So lets
make do with the present uniforms.

"I was thinking more of the impression given in the advertisements,
etc.," he continued, trying to get back to his vision, but suddenly
sidetracked by another disturbing thought.

"One thing is certain—if you permit Jai-Lia to come in here you
will never get them out, and it is a dangerous crowd filled with
communists from Cuba.

"Anyway, the point I am trying to make is that you well know
(from my resistance to the Monorail, for example) that I see Las V.
as being just one notch in class distinction above the amusement
park category. For this same reason I am bitterly opposed to dog-
racing. I would not oppose horse racing in a few years if we are cut
into it.

"Bob, ever since I arrived here I have been fighting attempts to
down-grade the Strip into some kind of freak show—an amusement
park—a cross between Coney Island and the Hudson Palisades Park.
If one of these sideshows is allowed, there will be 3 or 4 or six and
then we will have a real avenue of merry-go-rounds and roller
coasters.

"I have certainly made no secret with you of my feelings that the Las Vegas strip does not have much class (in fact, I was laughed at once when I said it had a certain degree of class), but nevertheless it does have just that small difference in class distinction between an amusement park and a place which is garish, but like no other place in the entire world.

"I dont think I would like to live here or center all of my future plans around this pivot point if Freemont Street is going to be moved to the Strip."

Class. They may have laughed at him once, but Hughes was now determined to make Las Vegas a real high-class place, and there was no room in his vision for the honky-tonk atmosphere that had already overrun downtown, much less for monorails, dog racing, or (God forbid) jai alai.

In fact, Hughes had more than a vision. He had a plan. A mission. He would "make Las Vegas as trustworthy and respectable as the New York Stock Exchange—so that Nevada gambling will have the kind of a reputation that Lloyds of London has, so that Nevada on a note will be like Sterling on silver."

Real class. But his plans went still further.

"We can make a really super environmental 'city of the future' here—No smog, no contamination, efficient local government, where the tax-payers pay as little as possible, and get something for their money."

There it was. Hughes Heaven—no contamination, no taxes, and lots of class. There was, of course, one other requirement: he had to own it all.

He already owned the Desert Inn, the Sands, the Castaways, and the Frontier, all nicely clustered in the center of town. Now he was eyeing the Silver Slipper, a low-class "grind" casino just across the street, and its huge next-door neighbor, the Stardust, which alone would nearly double his holdings.

"I feel there is something very important and very significant about being in a position of 100%, admitted undisputed leadership," wrote Hughes.

"I know you tell me that such a position has already been achieved," he chided Maheu, who urged restraint, "but if you asked ten different people, you would probably get ten different opinions.

"Bob, stated briefly, I am certain that there is great value in any entity which is clearly, indisputably the *world's* greatest and largest gambling operation.

"So, I am talking about a clear cut leadership of such magnitude that the word of mouth report would become accepted throughout the world. So that when anybody thinks or speaks of gambling, the reaction would be automatic, just like the reaction to Sterling on silver.

"But, what is most important of all, is that it will put to rest this gnawing urge I have for a slightly stronger position," he concluded, reassuring his regent, "and when this urge is satisfied, I am positive our relationship (yours and mine) will improve immeasurably.

"I am certain, Bob, that the removal of this one thorn in my side will leave us with a really harmonious prospect for the future."

Hughes had to have the Silver Slipper and the Stardust, and he also wanted the Silver Nugget and the Bonanza and Bill Harrah's clubs in Reno and Lake Tahoe and perhaps the Riviera and . . . well, just about every hotel and casino in Nevada. But for now the Slipper and the Stardust were a must.

Up in Carson City, Paul Laxalt was getting worried again. If Hughes had a gnawing urge, the governor still had a gnawing fear. The legislative probe stirred up by Hughes's last casino license was coming to a head, and two new purchases right now might be dangerous. Laxalt asked Maheu to ask his hidden boss to slow down.

"Because of the developments of the last few days and a concerted effort to make multiple licensing a political football, the Governor respectfully requests that you refrain from any additional acquisition at this time," Maheu wrote Hughes. "He thinks that if we wait a few months until the atmosphere has changed that the situation would be entirely different. He is preparing a long confidential memorandum for your consumption. Anyway, Howard, he pointed out his great devotion to you and begs of you to hold still until at least you have had a chance to absorb his comments."

Hughes could not hold still. He was upset by Laxalt's wavering support, and he was angry.

"Do you think maybe it is just barely possible that the Gov. is cooling just a little bit toward me?" he wondered, feeling unappreciated. "Maybe now that I have contributed the 100 million to the sagging Vegas economy and stopped the run on the bank (so to speak) is it just possible he has decided I am more of a liability than an assett?"

The more Hughes brooded on Laxalt's ingratitude, the angrier he got. Hold still? Hell, he would take his money where it was appreciated.

"I can only call the shots as I see them, Bob," he fumed. "I think this multiple ownership howl is a lot of shit.

"I will lay you ten to one that if I tell the Gov. that I will be willing—unhappy but willing—to divert our investments elsewhere if that is really what he wants, but I wish to be very sure he realizes the situation. I have at least another hundred and fifty million to invest. Since moving here, I have turned down three very attractive investments simply because they were not in Nevada.

"Now, if the Gov. looks at this fairly I dont think he will want to see me put 40,000,000 in a hotel-casino in Venezuela where I have an unbelieveable offer. I think he may prefer not to have multiple licensing up to a point. But when it reaches the spot where he has to stand by and see us plant 40,000,000 down in Venezuela, I dont think he will go for it. Not when he need only pick up the phone to keep the 40 right here."

But why wait for Laxalt to pick up the phone? Hughes had a bold idea: he would call Laxalt! That should buck him up. Yes, he would do it. It had been a long time, but Howard Hughes was now ready to reach out and touch someone.

To soothe the nervous governor, the phantom placed a phone call to the statehouse. It was the first time he had talked to anyone outside his inner circle since coming to Nevada, and the conversation was banner headline news throughout the state: "GOVERNOR TALKS TO HUGHES." Something like the Second Coming.

"It was one of the most interesting conversations of my life," Laxalt proclaimed, seemingly dazzled by the billionaire's grasp of state affairs and his big plans for Nevada. The governor, however, failed to mention what Hughes himself considered most important.

It was not the Stardust, it was not the Slipper, it was not the threat of a legislative probe or the growing resistance to his casino-buying spree. It was not even his plans to make Laxalt president. It was something far more important than all that. It was the water. Hughes was in an absolute frenzy about the water.

"When I spoke to Gov. Laxalt," he complained a few days later, "I told him I was truly and urgently alarmed at the way the authorities were rushing ahead into the so-called 'Southern Nevada Water Project.' I told him I felt the entire plan simply was not palatable. That the water might be treated with sufficient chlorine so that it would meet the minimum test requirements and be technically drinkable—just as they boast that you can drink the effluent of the Los Angeles sewage disposal plant.

"But that is not the point. This is a resort, and we have to make the air and the water etc. not just non-poisonous but attractive, tasty, palatable. We are in competition with other resorts and if it becomes known that our new water system is nothing but a closed-circuit loop, leading in and out of a cesspool, our competitive resorts will find this out and they will start a word-of-mouth and publicity campaign that will murder us.

"Anyway, it is not the actual purity of the water that counts. In this case, where we are considering a resort, the question is how many tourists will be dissuaded from coming to Las Vegas by the word-of-mouth campaigns of Hawaii, Florida, and all the other U.S. resorts sneering at the spectacle of people swimming, bathing, and drinking water which is nothing more or less than diluted piss and shit."

Hughes had gone on at some length and with considerable passion about the purity of fluids, and Laxalt had been quick to agree with him.

"The Gov. said he was aware of this situation and was 'sick about it,' " the billionaire continued, recalling their conversation. "Those were his words. I said I felt no matter how far the present program had progressed, it had to be changed. I urged him to see what could be done to hold it up temporarily while he and I try to find some solution.

"I have not heard a word in reply, and it appears everything is going right ahead," complained Hughes, for the moment more puzzled than angered by Laxalt's inexplicable failure to scuttle the multimillion-dollar water project. "Why haven't I heard from him?"

Not only was the governor strangely silent about the water but he also remained reluctant to ram through two more casino licenses for Hughes. Obviously it was going to take more than a phone call to get Laxalt fully motivated. In order to expand his domain and make his new kingdom a fit place to dwell—to protect himself by becoming absolute sovereign and banishing all contamination—Hughes would have to make at least one additional purchase. He would have to buy Laxalt.

"Now, to make the Laxalt deal work, we have to find a means of motivation," he wrote.

"When I have a real tough assignment like this, I search about for two ingredients: 1. A man who can do the job if he truly wants to. And, 2. A means of furnishing a consideration to this man which will be of such a nature and such an amount as to be well nigh overpowering in its effect upon the man.

"Now, Bob, I think Laxalt can be brought to a point where he will just about entrust his entire political future to his relationship with us. I think that is the way it should be and the way it can be.

"I think we must convince him beyond a shadow of a doubt that I intend to back him with unlimited support right into the White-House in 1972. I think I must even set up some legal entity charged with doing this job, and said intity must be self perpetuating, so that, in [the] event of my death, or change of political objectives, the financial support for Laxalt will continue uninterrupted.

"Anyway, to return to my original thought, if we can truly convince the Governor that his future destiny lies with me, then I am positive that, with a little coaching from me at the time, he will have no difficulty in accomplishing our objective."

An eternal "Laxalt-for-President" slush fund. That should motivate the governor, indeed have an overpowering effect upon him. Hughes, however, was not content to let it go at that. As in all his acquisitions he needed one-hundred-percent control, and he was worried that others might get their hooks into the man he was grooming to be Leader of the Free World.

"I am fearful that somebody or some company may be getting to Gov. Laxalt on a sub-rosa basis," wrote Hughes.

"[W]e must show enough interest to keep the Gov. solely and exclusively devoted to our interests. The first time he ties up with somebody like K[erkorian] or Crosby of Mary Carter Paint or any other source of financing, I think we will be forced to pull out of here lock stock and barrell. I am ready to ride with this man to the end of the line, which I am targeting as the White House in 1972," he reiterated, "but there is no room in our program for a second angel."

No, Hughes could not share his governor. And it would be four years before he could promote Laxalt from the statehouse to the White House. In the interim he had to find some means of keeping Laxalt devoted. Perhaps promise him a second term as governor, maybe just offer to put him on the payroll. Or why not both? Hughes was ready to let Laxalt write his own ticket.

"Any time you will tell me to go ahead," he informed Maheu, "I am prepared to make a personal phone call to Laxalt and tell him it is my desire that he remain governor and that I promise unlimited support for this campaign, and, further, that should he fail to be

Now, to make the Laxalt deal work, we have to find a means of motivation.

When I have a "real tough" assignment like this, I search about for two ingredients: 1. A man who can do the job if he truly wants to. And, 2. A means of furnishing a consideration to this man which will be of such a nature and such an amount as to be well nigh overpowering in its effect upon the man.

Now, Bob, I think Laxalt can be brought to a point where he will just about entrust his entire political future to his relationship with us. I think that is the way it should be and the way it can be.

I think we must convince him beyond a shadow of a doubt that I intend to back him with un-limited support right into the White-House in 1972.

elected governor for another term, I want him to accept a position in private industry which I know will meet his requirements, no matter how extreme they may be.

"I am positive I can sell this to Laxalt.

"Please call the Governor and simply tell him that I wanted to be sure he understands that I do want him to become one of the very top executives of my company."

Maheu was soon sending Hughes regular progress reports on the secret job negotiations:

"I had a very fine meeting with the Governor. I truly believe that I can convince him to join your organization permanently as a top executive in charge of all your Nevada operations or anywhere else you may choose to assign him."

"Governor Laxalt has started to ask me precisely what his assignment will be in your organization," Maheu reported a few weeks later, as Hughes stalled on the details.

The talks dragged on for years, and the governor continued dickering for a job almost the entire time he remained in office. As late as June 1970, Maheu noted: "Laxalt is very anxious to discuss his future employment with us and I really believe we owe him the courtesy of sitting down with him at a very early date."

Rather than accept the job Hughes kept dangling just out of reach, however, Maheu speculated that the governor would instead rejoin his family law firm, which received at least $180,000 from the billionaire while Laxalt was in office.

"My guess is that he will hit us for a retainer with the understanding that we have priority on all of his time but allow him to build a law practice at the same time," Maheu reported after another meeting with the governor.

Ultimately Laxalt would send Hughes a handwritten letter suggesting his availability as a private attorney, but noting that the long-discussed job would be such a blatant conflict of interest that he dare not go directly on the billionaire's payroll.

"Dear Howard," wrote the governor as he prepared to leave the statehouse, ". . . I fear that a direct contract relationship with you might be misinterpreted. I would dislike, as would you, to have anyone think that the cooperation of our administration with you during the past four years was on a 'quid pro quo' basis. . . .

"I've decided to open a law office in Carson City. . . . If you should ever have need of any assistance from me, I'll be happy to provide it."

any time you will tell
me to go ahead, I am
prepared to make a per-
sonal phone call to Laxalt
and tell him it is my
desire that he remain governor
and that I promise un-
limited support for this
campaign, and, further, that,
should he fail to be elected
governor for another term,
I want him to accept a
position in private industry
which I know will meet
his requirements, no matter
how extreme they may be.

I am positive I can sell
this to Laxalt.

Governor Laxalt has started to ask me precisely
what his assignment will be in your organization.

Laxalt is very anxious to discuss his future
employment with us and I really believe we owe him the courtesy of sitting down with him at a very early date.

My guess is that he will hit us for a retainer
with the understanding that we have priority on all of his
time but allow him to build a law practice at the same time.

Almost immediately upon leaving office, Laxalt did in fact start collecting legal fees from Hughes that would total at least $72,000.

But all that was far in the future as Hughes plotted early in 1968 to expand his domain. With the governor no longer a problem, Hughes began to present himself as a benefactor to the other citizens of Nevada. He would build the world's largest hotel in Las Vegas, a spectacular one-hundred-and-fifty-million-dollar resort, "a complete city within itself." He would create the world's greatest airport in the Nevada desert, make it the new "gateway to the West," and build a high-speed railway to whisk passengers from the Jet Air Terminal to downtown Las Vegas. He would endow a new medical school for the University of Nevada, promising "$200,000 to $300,000 per year for 20 years." He would bring new industry to the state, indeed he would move the Hughes Tool Company and the Hughes Aircraft Company and the Howard Hughes Medical Institute to Nevada, make it the headquarters of his entire empire.

In fact, the only thing Hughes would actually ever build in Nevada was Maheu's new mansion, and indeed he would do his best to block *all* new hotels, *all* new industry, *all* "competition." But as each day brought some fresh report of Hughes's intended good works, nobody seemed ready to refuse him a couple of more mere gambling casinos.

With Laxalt firmly behind his plans to acquire the Stardust and Silver Slipper, with all opposition to his Monopoly game melting before his munificence, Hughes began to worry that a horde of freeloaders would also be licensed.

"I am informed that, since word has gotten out that our applications will be approved, everybody and his little dog is filing for a gaming license because they all reason that if the Commission passes ours they cannot very well refuse somebody else. So what I want is a report on those applications which are nearest to being considered favorably, in order that we may take whatever preventive measures may be indicated.

"Bob, competition is moving in on all sides on a rampant basis," he added. "Every time somebody starts the preparation for the opening of a new casino I suffer very substantially."

It was agony. Hughes could no longer enjoy the prospect of expanding his empire. He could only dread the "excessive competition, or the threat of future excessive competition, or competition of a type which I consider harmful." He demanded that Maheu "cast an evil spell" on all rivals to his power.

Maheu was not optimistic. "Unfortunately, Howard, our problem is one of changing the philosophy which permeates the entire area, and that is going to take some time. It is generally known that for the last six months, there has not been one room available in Las Vegas on any weekend, and, as a result, many people don't even attempt to come to the city."

Hughes was unmoved. It was that kind of thinking that led to disaster, and he could prove it.

"I just cannot go along with your philosophy and that of the community, which seems to be: lend a helping hand to everybody who wants to build a new hotel or casino, the more the merrier!

"Please remember, Bob, that it was this philosophy, that there is no bottom to the barrell—it was this philosophy that led to the 1929 stock market crash and seven of the worst years this country ever faced.

"It was this same philosophy that led to the construction of a miniature golf course on every corner in Los Angeles, and the horrible, tragic crash of this industry—taking with it all the little people involved."

First the Great Depression. Then miniature golf. Next the ruin of Las Vegas.

"You say you can't get a room. Well, Bob, that is just the way it ought to be. Do you think for one minute that '21' and El Morrocco in New York would be such a success if they were not jam-packed to the roof so that it is impossible to dance or even to breathe in there?

"People only want to go where it is impossible to get reservations—they only want to go where it is crowded and where everybody else is trying to go. Please believe me, I know from bitter experience.

"The first time it is not, as you say 'impossible to get a room' in Las Vegas, then you better start worrying, because serious trouble is ahead—and not very far ahead."

In fact, Hughes already saw serious trouble all around him. These threatened new hotels and casinos were not merely dangerous competition, they were something far worse—contamination! Soon he would be surrounded by impure water, swarms of mosquitoes, carnival freaks, and filthy animals.

"Bob, there are almost ten new hotels announced. The one that troubles me the very most is the new Holiday Inn right smack in front of the Sands. To make it much worse, they are planning to make it a Showboat sitting in a huge lake of water. A Showboat with a pond of stagnant infested water.

"If they are considering using water from Lake Mead, the effluent in the water would smell to high heaven. Jesus! when I think of that lake of sewage disposal on the front lawn of the Sands. Ugh! It may even smell up our Sands Golf Course. Whatever the source of the water, there would be the additional problem of mosquitos. They would not be able to have water running in and out, so it would become stagnant and an ideal place to breed mosquitos.

"If this crumby hotel cannot be stopped, I would just as soon sell at a loss the Sands."

But there was no escape. Even as the Showboat threatened to befoul the Sands, another monstrosity was going up right next door to the Stardust—the Circus-Circus. It was something straight out of Hughes's worst nightmare.

"The aspect of the Circus that has me disturbed is the popcorn, peanuts, and kids side of it," he wrote, describing with horror a Norman Rockwell vision of Americana. "And also the Carnival Freaks, and Animal side of it. In other words, the poor, dirty, shoddy side of Circus life. The dirt floor, sawdust and elephants. The part of a Circus that is associated with the poor boys in town, the hobo clowns, and, I repeat, the animals. The part of a circus that is synonymous with the common poor man—with the freckled face kids—the roustabouts driving the stakes with three men and three sledge hammers, etc., etc.

"It is the above aspects of a circus that I feel are all out of place on the Las Vegas Strip," he continued, returning to his own vision of a high-class resort. "After all, the Strip is supposed to by synonymous with a good looking female all dressed up in a very expensive diamond studded evening gown and driving up to a multi-million dollar hotel in a Rolls-Royce. Now, you tell me what, in that picture, is compatible with a circus in its normal raiment, exuding its normal atmosphere and its normal smell."

For most people, the real stench of Las Vegas came from the Mob. Organized crime had tainted it from the beginning. Long before Hughes arrived with his vision, Bugsy Siegel had a vision, and where there had been only a desert he built the first giant gambling casino on a highway to Los Angeles that became the Las Vegas Strip. Bugsy was long dead, rubbed out by his partners, but he had created Las Vegas in his own image and mobsters still set the tone of the town.

To Hughes, however, the Mob was just another form of contamination. And now Bugsy's creation, the Flamingo, was back in the news. One of Siegel's original partners, the underworld's financial wizard, Meyer Lansky, had been caught siphoning off millions. Hughes was outraged. He saw the scandal pulling his new purified, respectable, blue-chip Las Vegas back down into the gutter. It was time to clean out the Mob.

"Bob, the Flamingo has been accused of skimming," wrote the angry billionaire. "It is one more set-back in the reputation of the Strip. Now, I feel this kind of thing has gone too far.

"First there was Parvin and all their miserable dishonesty, then came the Circus, the Stardust and their personnel, then the Bonanza, and I failed to mention Caesar's and their junket of hoods.

"Bob, I moved heaven and earth to try and persuade you to do something about the mess. In spite of my pleas, however, each of these activities has been gradually swept under the carpet with absolutely no real effort by anyone to do anything about it.

"Now, finally, in the case of the Flamingo, I beg you from bended knee please to take some action, and urgently, immediately.

"The Flamingo, because of its position at the top or entrance of the Strip, has always represented and epitomized Nevada gambling. Many motion pictures have been made using the Flamingo as the example of the grandeur and the luxury of plush gambling on the Las Vegas Strip.

"I made one myself, called 'The Las Vegas Story,' using the Flamingo to represent all that is glamorous and exciting about Las Vegas.

"Anyway, the Flamingo has represented Las Vegas ever since its unfortunate beginning with Bugsy Siegel. And I assure you that, as a result of this incident, the Bugsy Siegel episode will get the full treatment again.

"Bob, you have got to take some action about it this time. I truly plead with you.

"Bob, I am sick and tired of being the Patsy of the entire Las Vegas area."

Hughes was sure he was the only honest man in town. He was certain that explained why all the unscrupulous rival casinos were piling up big profits, while his, against all odds, were losing money. "It goes without saying that you cannot have principles and high profits both," he wrote.

In fact, Hughes may have been far more of a "Patsy" than he ever realized. Las Vegas seemed to be changing hands, from the mobsters who created it, to Hughes; but the billionaire may have been only an unwitting front man for the Mob. His arrival could not have been more timely for organized crime. After two decades of lucrative skimming, the heat was on. A massive FBI wiretap operation had become public, revealing that the casinos were controlled by hidden owners who routinely took their profits off the top, shipping the hot cash down to Miami, where the mastermind Meyer Lansky counted the take in his condo on Collins Avenue and made the split for his Mafia cohorts across the country. Just when it looked like the jig was up, Hughes arrived. A mark with an unlimited bankroll.

It may have been a setup from the start. Maheu's Mafia pal John Roselli claimed the whole Desert Inn eviction crisis was a Syndicate scam. "We roped Hughes into buying the D.I.," Roselli reportedly told hit-man-turned-informer Jimmy "the Weasel" Fratianno. "Now it looks like he wants to buy the whole town, if we let him. He's just what we need, especially with Maheu running the show."

Clearly, Hughes was not running it. Apparently the Mob kept real control of his casinos, sold him their gambling emporiums at inflated prices, and kept right on picking his pocket, raking off millions. A secret IRS investigation would later conclude that Hughes had been the victim of a vast Mob skim, perhaps topping $50 million.

If that was true, Hughes was blissfully unaware of it, and for the moment seemed surprisingly untroubled by his casinos' puzzling losses. And while he saw the Mob as a dangerous contaminant, he also saw a way he could use their threat to get on with his Monopoly game.

He would save Las Vegas from the gangsters, and he would save it from the gangbusters as well. For a price.

"Today, the President is chaffing at the bit in his eagerness to get at Nevada with a massive crime crusade, in order to divert public attention away from his failure to improve the Vietnam situation," wrote Hughes.

"I think that you can argue with Gov. Laxalt that every day the situation continues brings with it an ever increasing risk of the entire beautiful castle of Nevada gaming coming crashing down in one overwhelming debacle which could be blown up to rival Tea Pot Dome.

"The President and his advisors would like nothing in this world so much as to find a basis under which he may attack Nevada gambling, because that is where the really big money is being made.

"He comes out against organized crime, but, in the absence of uncovering some huge underworld casino or some huge undercover brothel, which is not likely—in the absence of something like this, the President has no photos, no actual symbol, no example he can point to, in his efforts to attack crime.

"Bob, if he could just blacken Nevada gaming to the point where he could link it to organized crime, and make Nevada gaming the symbol of organized crime, then he could use all the figures, all the photos of Nevada casinos, all the pictures of Fremont Street with the flashing signs.

"All this would immediately become the vivid symbol of organized crime. Las Vegas would be pictured as Sin City.

"All the figures of gross gaming revenue, the figures of employment, the increased population, all this would be pictured to the public as one gigantic beehive of crime, a vast metropolis of sin, a vast factory for the industry of sin.

"I tell you, when the nation reaches a point where they need only say a man is 'linked to Nevada Gaming' to villify him beyond measure, and practically strap him in the electric chair, then I say it is time to worry about it."

Hughes was getting so carried away in his lurid presentation of the threat that he almost lost sight of his plot: to present himself as savior, as the man who could grant a stay of execution.

"So, I want you to convince the Governor that I will use every last dollar I have to prevent the President from using Nevada as his political football in his attack on organized crime," he continued, ready to buy a reprieve.

"I want you to convince Laxalt that he can count on me to prevent the President or anybody from damaging the reputation of Nevada Gaming, which I want to be treated like the New York Stock Exchange."

Right. And now for the hook.

"But, if I am to fulfill this promise, I must have the support of the Governor and his Gaming Commission.

"Bob, there will never be another opportunity like the one existing today to pick up an additional one or two casinos and to satisfy this crying drive inside of me against what I consider the many unfair competitive inroads—the competitive build up.

"It would only take the acquisition of a very few additional casinos plus the elimination of these same casinos from the competitive group— in other words, just a small tipping of the scales—a small addition to one side of the scale and a small elimination from the weight resting on the competitive side—just a small change in the balance, and I would be satisfied."

On April 30, 1968, Hughes got the support of the governor and his gaming commission. It approved the billionaire's purchase of the Silver Slipper and his planned purchase of the Stardust, granting him his fifth and sixth casino licenses, a small tipping of the scales that made him the undisputed king of gambling. He was not satisfied.

The vote was not unanimous. Two commissioners had dared to challenge his sovereignty. "It is obvious from the vote that there is considerable serious concern over the extent of your acquisitions," reported his lawyer, Richard Gray. "I do not believe we will be permitted to control so much of the economy of this state no matter what our intentions are."

Hughes was outraged. "I know God-damned well that people would not be making money around here as if they had a printing press if I had turned south out of Boston and gone to the Bahamas, as I almost did," he fumed. "They should have some gratitude for the fairy-godfather who pulled their chestnuts out of the fire, the same fairy-godfather who started the whole ball rolling."

If Hughes didn't quite see himself as the new Godfather of Las Vegas, he did feel that as its "fairy-godfather" he was entitled to own it all. The casinos. The hotels. The politicians. Everything.

He saw himself as bringing the best of American capitalism to what had been an underworld money-laundry, but in a real sense Hughes was less part of the established order, more hidden, than the Mob. And he was also more corrupt. The mobsters were content to run the casinos and skim the take, while Hughes demanded absolute control over the entire state, driven to purify Nevada by corrupting it completely.

His latest acquisition, the Silver Slipper, now became on odd fixture of Nevada politics. Its neon-lit high-heeled slipper revolving on top of a twenty-foot pole just across the Strip from the Desert Inn became a beacon for local statesmen. They flocked to the Hughes-owned casino next door, the Frontier, where his bagman Thomas Bell—law partner of the governor's brother—handed out hundred-dollar bills drawn from the cashier's cage at the Slipper.

Over the next three years, $858,500 passed from the gaming tables of the Silver Slipper to Nevada politicians, always in hundred-dollar bills, always in cash. There was hardly a political race Hughes didn't finance. He instructed Bell to support the likely winner, regardless of party or politics, and back both candidates if the race was too close to call. United States Senator Alan Bible got at least $50,000, his colleague Senator Howard Cannon got $70,000, Lieutenant Governor Harry Reid $10,000, Attorney General Robert List $9,500, District Attorney George Franklin $5,000, and twenty-seven state-legislature candidates trooped into Bell's office to collect a total of $56,000. Judges and sheriffs and assorted commissioners all came by and left with cash-filled envelopes.

From time to time, Governor Laxalt himself visited Bell to solicit contributions from the Silver Slipper slush fund. At Laxalt's request the state Republican chairman got $15,000, and the governor urged that Hughes go all out for his would-be successor, Edward Fike, who personally picked up his $55,000. Fike's Democratic opponent Mike O'Callaghan was more discreet. He sent an aide to get $25,000. The parade of office-holders and -seekers never stopped.

Nor did the demands from Hughes for a return on his investments. From his penthouse lair across the street, he ordered Bell to "advise him on every single bill introduced in the Nevada legislature . . . to encourage members of the legislature to adopt his views . . . to defeat bills authorizing dog racing . . . to stop the sales tax, the gasoline tax and the cigarette tax . . . to stop the Clark County school integration plan . . . to prohibit governmental agencies from realigning any streets without his personal views being first given . . . to do whatever was necessary to shield him from having to appear personally in any courts . . . to advise him on all ordinances or laws regarding obscenity and pornography . . . to take whatever action necessary to prohibit rock festivals in Clark County . . . to prevent any change of the rules of various gambling games, and in particular, roulette . . . to discourage state officials from permitting communist bloc entertainers from appearing in Las Vegas hotels."

In short, to control the life and laws of the entire state. The list was endless. Nothing escaped his attention. And although he almost always got his way, he was never satisfied.

"I feel we must go to work at once or the legislature will pass bills resulting in a Nevada I will not want to live in," wrote Hughes, eager to exercise his veto power. "Send me at once a *very brief* summary of all legislation of any consequence that is likely to pass. I would like to know if under *any circumstances* there is any chance at all of overturning them."

Hughes harbored a deep suspicion of all new laws. But he was especially opposed to new taxes.

"Please tell Gov. Laxalt that if he will follow my urgent appeal for avoidance of the increased sales tax, and if he will cut back a little bit in the unfair demands of the teachers, he may rely on me to assist in any fiscal emergency.

"With further reference to the tax bill, I think Laxalt knows I would not permit the State of Nevada to be in any really serious position of insolvency or poverty.

"However, I would very much rather make some contribution or take some simple action, such as bringing additional industry to Nevada, or to bring the Hughes Medical Institute to Nevada, which would at least bring me a little personal recognition. I would rather do something of this kind voluntarily, than to have the sales tax passed and then have some tax collector take it out of my pocket from now on, no matter what the circumstances may be. Day in and day out."

Given the free-spending ways of the local lawmakers, they would soon pick his pockets clean. Hughes had to watch them every minute.

"I just heard the most absurd thing on the news I ever heard—a $5,000,000 zoo!

"Bob, this is all we need—a zoo bigger than the one in San Diego! Please, please kill this one some way.

"It seems to me that these people in local government just dont have anything to do under the sun except dream up new ways to spend money."

In fact, Hughes didn't want the Nevada legislature to meet at all.

"There is a lot of pressure on Laxalt to call a special session," he noted with alarm. "Bob, for many important reasons I am violently opposed to this.

"Can't you get some of the other important political figures to come to his assistance and announce their strong support of his decision to keep this state out of financial chaos by resisting all the efforts to lay open the treasury of the state to the mass of blood thirsty vultures who are trying to remove all restraint and simply turn the sack upside down?

"Bob, if they have a special session in the present political climate, I assure you the state will emerge with the shirt stripped from its back and without five cents to buy a cup of coffee."

These vultures who were out to bankrupt his kingdom were, of course, the very same public servants who had sold their souls to Hughes at the Silver Slipper.

"In all fairness, Howard," Maheu reminded him, "the officials in Nevada have been most cooperative with us—at all levels."

"I do not claim one iota of credit for the foresight you had when you instructed me to make political contributions to 'worthy' public servants. I can assure you that it is paying dividends, and when I mentioned that Bell had been successful in killing the fair housing bill, please believe me that I had no intent to delete any of the credit which is due to your foresight. Without 'our friends' we would not have had a prayer."

Indeed, Hughes was doing quite well. He had blocked the zoo and defeated dog racing and killed fair housing. But he was not happy.

"I am not complaining about our treatment here," he explained. "I just say that, because of certain people's failure to keep accurately informed as to our desires, a large quantity of legislation which I consider highly undesirable is on the verge of being passed.

"So, I am proposing that you meet with the governor in Carson and try to reach an understanding under which he would assist in an all-out campaign to scuttle most of the remaining legislation that I consider undesirable.

"Assume the very strongest motivation for Gov. Laxalt, my question is: How much could he do?"

If Hughes was never quite content with his one-man rule of Nevada, others were impressed. And mystified. Even frightened. His unprecedented buying spree was by now a staple of nightclub acts, but the jokes tended to elicit only nervous laughter.

Johnny Carson greeted showroom audiences by saying: "Welcome to Las Vegas, Howard Hughes' Monopoly set. You ever get the feeling he's going to buy the whole damned place and shut it down?"

Even Frank Sinatra, himself a Las Vegas institution, picked up the theme.

"You're wondering why I don't have a drink in my hand," the singer joked with his audience one night at the Sands. "Howard Hughes bought it." Not long after, the billionaire also bought the Sands, and soon after that Sinatra stopped joking.

"For two successive nights into the wee hours of the morning Sinatra has made a damn fool of himself in the casino at the Sands," Maheu informed Hughes when the trouble began. "He moved around insulting people with vile language. Last night he drove a golf cart through a plate glass window and was disgustingly drunk. In an effort to protect him from himself Carl Cohen stopped his credit after he had obtained $30,000 plus in cash and had lost approximately $50,000. Sinatra blew his top and late this afternoon called me to tell me that he was walking away from the Sands and would not finish his engagement.

"One of the reasons that Cohen cut off his credit is that this SOB was running around the casino stating in a loud voice that you had plenty of money and that there was no reason why you should not share it with him since he had made the Sands the profitable institution it is."

The Sands had long been Sinatra's playground, the place he gathered with his "Rat Pack," where he and Dean Martin and Joey Bishop and Peter Lawford and Sammy Davis, Jr., put on legendary shows. Indeed, Sinatra had once owned a piece of the hotel but had been forced to give it up several years earlier when he was caught consorting with Chicago Mob boss Sam Giancana. But the singer still considered the Sands *his* domain, and a few days later he came back to confront casino manager Cohen.

Maheu sent Hughes a blow-by-blow description:

"At six A.M. today, Sinatra appeared at the Sands, made one hell of a scene and insisted on seeing Carl Cohen. He threatened to kill anyone who got in his way, used vile language, and said he would beat up the telephone operators if they did not connect him with Cohen, etc.

"In an effort to calm the situation, Carl agreed to meet him. Sinatra called Cohen every dirty name in the book, said he was going to kill him, pushed a table over on Carl, picked up a chair and attempted to hit Carl over the head. Carl ducked, took a pass at Sinatra and floored him. I understand Frank has a broken tooth."

Actually, it was two teeth. And Sinatra announced that he was quitting the Sands to sign with Caesar's Palace.

Hughes was upset. Not about losing Sinatra but about losing him to a rival hotel. He saw the entire brouhaha as a plot by the Caesar's crowd to steal his property.

"It seems to me that if they (Caesar's Palace) want what we have (Sinatra), they ought to deal with us in a decent and honorable way and buy it," he fumed. "Not try to take it for nothing.

"I dont intend to take this lying down. Sinatra made three pictures for me at RKO. I know him backward and frontward. All actors are a little crazy. But I dont intend the Caesar's group making us look weak and stupid."

Hughes of course had a plan.

"My script is something like this," he told Maheu. "Contact Sinatra now—before he gets too loaded. If he is asleep, give reasonable time only for recuperation. I urge you to tell him:

" 'Howard doesn't know if you remember the time when you were friends. But he remembers—it was back in the days when you were flying a Bonanza, one of the first ones on the coast. Anyway, he remembers, and when he heard of the recent events, he was distressed beyond measure. However, he was hesitant to inject himself between you and Cohen, since you had been close friends for such a very long time. He even remembers (or thinks he remembers) you introducing Sammy Davis Jr. to the public for the first time from the stage of the Sands.

" 'Anyway, returning to recent events, the story that was related to him was so fantastic it seemed as if it could only have occurred in a nightmare, not reality.'

"Please tell Frank that the only way I know to show that the recent events do not in any way reflect my feelings or wishes is to suggest that he visit the Sands or the Desert Inn and ask for $500,000 or $1,000,000 in chips and see what results he gets. I think he will find that he is not even asked to sign the marker."

Old Black and Blue Eyes disdained the offer. But the press treated the whole affair as if Sinatra had literally been kicked out of the Sands and suggested that he had been booted on Hughes's orders. There was some talk that it all had to do with lingering jealousies over Lana Turner, or perhaps Ava Gardner, but the favorite rumor had it that when Hughes was told of the fracas he just asked, "Frank who?"

In any event, it seemed symbolic of a revolution in Las Vegas. Sinatra and the old gang were out. Howard Hughes was in. Not only nightclub comedians noticed the change. Far from Las Vegas, others without a sense of humor also paid heed.

On June 28, 1968, just as Hughes was about to take control of the Stardust, U.S. Attorney General Ramsey Clark brought his Monopoly game to a sudden halt. Clark threatened that if Hughes closed the 30.5 million-dollar deal, he would haul him into court for violating antitrust laws.

Hughes was furious. He would not be intimidated. He would go right ahead with the Stardust deal. At first, he would not even consider a delay. He was certain that the entire country was as focused on the big showdown as he was. How would it look if he backed down?

"Why must we delay the closing?" he demanded.

"I am positive it is a mistake. It will focus the attention of the whole U.S. on this deal. The press, T.V., and Life Magazine will make an Irish Sweepstakes out of this. (They will even be booking bets on whether we will be able to take over or not.)

"The whole country will be focused on this deal, and they will all know that it was the Justice Dept. who caused it with a charge of anti-trust violation. And that has a nasty sound in itself. Also, somebody will dig up the fact that I am presently being sued by T.W.A. on an anti-trust violation, that is the biggest civil law suit in history. I can just see the editorials, like: 'Can't that man go anywhere without running afoul of those anti-trust laws??'

"Take my word, and I mean this, if we do not close now, this deal will never go through."

Maheu encouraged Hughes in his bravado.

"You can bet your life that the anti-trust division will live to regret their contemplated action," he boasted.

"Yesterday, they had 'first hand' evidence that we have many friends in Washington who *truly* believe in us. Today, they have received many inquiries—including one from the Chairman of the Judiciary Committee—and that is just the beginning.

"Howard Cannon called me this afternoon to inform me that he and Senator Bible have been told all day long—by fellow Senators—that they can depend on full support and assistance in sustaining their position that we obtain the Stardust.

"I've been in constant touch with George Franklin and Governor Laxalt, and they are both ready to challenge the Justice Department 'single-handedly.' "

Laxalt, in fact, made good on his pledge. He immediately shot off a letter to the attorney general, threatening to join forces with his hidden benefactor.

"If suit is instituted," warned the governor, "we would be faced with no alternative other than to intervene and oppose the action with all the resources of the State."

It was all to no avail. Ramsey Clark stood firm.

And Hughes was weakening. His ten-year battle over TWA had left him with a permanent fear of litigation, and he lived in dread of a subpoena.

"Suppose we take possession of the Stardust, and suppose we then notify Justice we want to talk," he wrote. "Suppose they say: 'Fine, let's talk!' So we talk, and while we are talking a story appears in the Sun that a U.S. Marshall is looking for me with a subpoena.

"Now, Bob, I dont have to tell you that this community is used to heroes who fall on their faces.

"Sinatra had the world in the palm of his hand during certain portions of his vivid, colorful life, only to fall off the pedestal and into horrible disrepute immediately afterward.

"So, as I say, this town is conditioned to the extremes of glorious success and failure to the criminal degree. Also, dont forget, Bob, that most people regard a subpoena or a court summons as equivalent to guilt and conviction. I assure you they dont bother to read the fine print.

"I repeat, they are used to seeing the guys on top fall off their thrones around here. So, when a story appears about me involving a subpoena, you can bet your life everybody in Clark County is going to have only one thought:

" 'Well, it had to happen sooner or later! Those big guys on top always wind up making some lousy little mistake, and then they get trapped with their hand in the cash register.'

"Dont forget, Bob, there is a crime crusade going on, and all of those loyal supporters of the Kennedies are just looking for somebody to nail to the wall."

Knocked off his throne and nailed to the wall. What an inglorious end to his grand adventure! No, Howard Hughes would not be denied his domain. He would expand it.

It was not enough to own Las Vegas. It was not enough to own Nevada. It was not enough to own Laxalt. Hughes would have to reach beyond his besieged kingdom and buy America.

He had been spying on it all the time—through television.

4 Network

It was Saturday night. Date night. Howard Hughes, alone with his television, stared blankly at the square of light.

"From Hollywood . . . the dating capital of the world . . . in color . . . it's 'The Dating Game'!" A fanfare of upbeat music. Wild applause. A half-enclosed round stage turned, coming full-circle to reveal the grinning host of the show. All teeth and double-knits, he stepped off the revolving disk as the music reached its crescendo, making his grand entrance through a superimposed heart.

"I feel I should have walked onstage with a *Band-Aid* across my mouth this evening because we have so many *secrets* up our sleeve," announced the game-show host, with a teasing pull at his cufflinks. "Why all the *mystery*?" he asked with a sinister chuckle. "*That's* a mystery, too!"

Hughes watched silently. The laughtrack tittered appreciatively, then roared, but the billionaire didn't even smile. Neither the TV show nor the wild incongruity of his listening to its fatuous emcee simper and smirk about secrets seemed to amuse him.

"I *can* tell you that game one brings to our 'Dating Game' stage one of television's brightest *young* actors," the announcer continued, drawing out the word *young* suggestively, now positively bursting with the secret to which he alone was privy. But he was not yet ready to divulge it. Instead, leering, he introduced a "swinging threesome" of starlets "designed to gladden any *young* bachelor's heart." Once more the stage turned, this time to bring into view the mystery bachelor's three potential "dates"—"an actress who loves to cook," a dancer (who also loved to cook), and a Playboy bunny.

Hughes watched the display impassively. Women no longer interested him. But now something happened that definitely seemed to pique his interest. From offstage—"we've kept him isolated in a soundproof booth"—came the "*young* bachelor," arriving to the rising laughter of the studio audience, finally let in on the big secret.

A small black child walked across the stage. Hughes stared at him in dismay.

The game-show host prattled on, enjoying the joke, never knowing the incredible impact that his secret would have on one viewer who had some secrets of his own, who at that very moment was deciding the fate of the TV announcer's entire network.

A network of his own. The idea had become an obsession.

Hughes watched television compulsively, around the clock, tuning in everything from "Sunrise Semester" (which he detested) to the "Late Show" (which he loved). He watched until the stations shut down, and even then often left his set on, falling asleep to the pictureless hum, waking up to test patterns.

Television was not only his sole source of entertainment but also his chief source of information. Hughes literally monitored the world through TV. It was as if he had a closed-circuit system spying on the feared outside, and virtually all he knew of the alien planet beyond his bedroom was the flickering images on the video glass.

The TV, always on and always at top volume, was his constant companion. He frequently wrote memos seeking to manipulate national policy or making multimillion-dollar deals while sitcoms or B-movies boomed in the background, sometimes making momentous decisions based solely on a chance encounter with a news broadcast, a commercial, even a game show.

Memo after memo would begin, "I just saw something on TV . . . ," to be followed by an order, a complaint, or a plan of action.

Sometimes it was merely a suggestion that others tune in an especially good program: "Ask Maheu to look at 13 on his set. This is the finest color television transmission I have ever seen. This looks like an oil painting. . . . Some of these scenes look almost as if they were paintings taken from one of the best known museums." (Not at all surprising, given the fact that Hughes was watching a special on Michelangelo.)

Other times it was to complain that he had to rely on television for his information: "Once more my nervous system is subjected to the strain of seeing a news item I am not prepared for . . . Bob, I

must be the least informed executive in the whole damned country
concerning his own business. I have to learn more from the news
media than anyone I know in a comparable position."

But once Hughes proposed selling a major segment of his empire—
the Hughes Aircraft Company, one of the nation's leading defense
contractors—to a firm he knew only from a TV commercial: "I saw
a broadcast today with some advertising for a company called AVCO,
and it seemed to me that they are in just about every business under
the sun except making toilet bowls. So, maybe AVCO would be a
good prospect."

And often the billionaire's viewing habits would have consequences far beyond his own domain. Seeing the world through television brought it down to manageable size, and Hughes was intent
on controlling the little people who paraded across his screen.

"I hear nothing but politics on TV," he wrote Maheu with childlike
petulance.

"You are in charge of all political activities for my companies and
me . . . yet I have had no single word from you as to which of the
many political aspirants is someone we want in office and which
is not.

"You promised I could pick the next governor.

"It seems to me that we should have had by now a hand picked
candidate in every one of these races—someone who would be loyal
to us."

Whether he was watching a political campaign, an assassination,
or the war in Vietnam, it was always with both the dispassionate
remove of a man long inured to the fate of characters in TV dramas
and the intense involvement of a contestant on "Let's Make a Deal."

"Did you see CBS News at 11:00 PM just completed?" he wrote
Maheu one evening. "If not, please get a summary of the portion
devoted to helicopters in Vietnam. More helicopters are being used
than was ever contemplated and more helicopters are being lost than
was estimated. CBS went on to say, over and over again, that this
is a helicopter war. . . .

"Bob, for you to have your Whitehouse relationship, while, at the
same time, our Aircraft Division sits empty-handed with the best
helicopter design in the world—the whole situation is just the damndest enigma I ever heard of.

"Cant you do something about it?"

Yet for all his efforts to control the world through television,
Hughes himself was ultimately held in thrall by the machine. He was

Bob –

I hear nothing but
politics on TV.

You are in charge
of all political activities
for my companies and me,
unless you have decided
to terminate the assign-
ment I gave you long
ago – "to handle all
political matters".

Yet I have had no
single word from you
as to which of the
many political aspirants
is someone we want in
office and which is not.

You promised I could
pick the next governor.

It seems to me that
we should have had by
now a hand picked
candidate in every one
of these races – some-
one who would be loyal
to us.

as trapped in its beam as in his penthouse prison, the true dimensions of his cell not the fifteen-by-seventeen-foot confines of the hotel room but the nineteen-inch diagonal of the TV screen.

Television was his other narcotic. Hughes needed it to blunt the pain of both his paranoid visions and his true conditions. Certainly his most central and deadening addiction, after money and power, was not the codeine he injected into his arms, legs, and groin, but the TV he shot into his brain in quantities sufficient to overwhelm even a well-balanced mind. Hughes clung to his TV set like an addict to his spike. Although he usually had several sets in reserve, the need to send one out for repair was almost more than he could bear:

"Let the TV man see if he can repair the Sylvania that just left my room, but only in compliance with the following:

"I dont want it placed anywhere near the number one Sylvania machine, and I want the TV man not to be working anywhere near or in the vicinity of the no. 1 machine.

"In other words, I dont want the man to be even within"—he started to write "twenty or thirty" then crossed it out—"40 or 50 feet of the no. 1 machine, because I dont want even the remotest, tiniest possibility of the TV man swinging an arm around, or backing up without realizing how close he is, and coming into contact with the no. 1 machine.

"If it should turn out to be impossible to repair the machine without taking it to his shop, then I will be willing for the TV man to take it (the no. 2 machine), provided he does not pass anywhere near the no. 1 machine, and provided the no. 1 machine is not touched in any slightest way and remains here in the hall or across the hall.

"In other words, provided the no. 1 machine is not disturbed in any way whatsoever, either by the TV man, the watchman, or any one else *whomsoever*."

Hughes's seeming reverence for the "no. 1 machine" would not last. Never fully satisfied, he was constantly changing sets, always wanting a sharper picture, better color, higher audio, and, especially, more remote control. With more money than anyone in the country, perhaps in the world, perhaps in all history, Hughes wanted no personal possessions, no luxuries, no worldly goods, nothing but a really good color TV. And still the perfect set eluded him. At times there was a veritable showroom of discarded RCAs, Zeniths, and Sylvanias—fallen idols gathering dust in and around his room. And still he'd send his aides in search of the ideal television.

"Lets get a brand-new very latest type portable," Hughes instructed the Mormons in one of an endless series of memos. "When we have a *really* perfect result lets get rid of all the miscellaneous sets we have here and across the hall. Leaving only 2 of the very latest. Lets see if we can get a set with remote contrast or brightness. I am forever wanting this. Also I understand they have an auto fine tuning adjustment now. They claimed the remote had more functions than any other.

"Lets really try to get the best.

"Before we close the deal," he added, in this as in all business affairs retaining final authority, "I want to know the price and the discount."

As it turned out, the price was $3.65 million. And there was no discount. But Hughes had a new "no. 1 machine."

"And now, ladies and gentlemen, welcome to the 'Swinging Shift'— programming until dawn for your late, late entertainment!"

Howard Hughes settled back to watch the show. He should have been happy. He finally had what he wanted. An all-night program he himself had created, introduced with an announcement he himself had written, presenting movies he himself chose, on a television station he himself owned.

KLAS-TV (channel 8) was his new "no. 1 machine." Hughes had been dickering to buy the local CBS affiliate almost from the moment he arrived in Las Vegas, and now it was his. No longer would the "Star-Spangled Banner" sign-off leave him alone with his dread at one A.M. No more would his Mormons have to beg for the westerns he wanted or the airplane pictures he loved. Never again would he have to face a blank screen.

Hughes was in control.

Not even Maheu would share that power. "This is one small corner of the kingdom that I expect to report directly to me," he informed attorney Dick Gray, his chosen instrument of communication with the station. "I want Maheu to have nothing at all to do with this department."

Still there were problems. Instead of a balky TV set, Hughes now found he had a balky TV station. Frantically, he tried to tune it in:

"Please contact the station manager of ch 8 and tell him the complaints of poor and unsatisfactory technical operation of the station have reached a point where they cannot be ignored any longer.

"1. Careless and unskilled operation of what would be equivalent to the projection machine in a movie theatre . . . almost as if the operator was momentarily engaged in some other duty or almost as if he were uncertain what film or tape was scheduled to be shown next, or as if he could not find the item next required.

"2. Consistent snapping in of the sound track of commercials at a sound level 10, 15, or even almost 20 db. above the sound level of the preceding film or tape. There must be twelve different commercials that blast in at a good 10 db above the normal entertainment level. . . .

"I am fully aware of the pressure from advertisers to keep the volume of their commercials up in order to blast through the many viewers who use their remote control to squelch the commercial. However, for every one viewer who squelches the volume at every commercial, there are ten or maybe fifty who do not carry the remoter around in their pocket and who are not so trigger-quick as to be able to squelch out a commercial like the Dunes that pops in with a blast that almost shatters your nerves."

Not quite quick enough on the trigger, his nerves shattered, Hughes could not even control the brightness and contrast on his own "Swinging Shift" movies:

"3. For the last three days, approximately, the transmission has been technically deficient in a manner that has resulted in the screen being periodically darker than any normal value. So dark in fact, that, in the Bette Davis film 'Stolen Life' and in the RKO film 'Half Breed' the screen was almost black throughout its entire area for long periods of time. . . .

"Now, also through a large part of 'Half Breed', the sound was way sub-standard, both in volume and also in quality.

"The dark picture was still noticeable this AM. . . ."

What made it all the worse was the humiliation of having *his* machine malfunction in public:

"I suggest you tell the station manager that the ownership of the station is publicly known to rest with the Hughes Tool Company, and that the Hughes Tool Company is known to have available to it the assistance of the Hughes Aircraft Company, probably the foremost organization engaged in advanced electronics in the entire world.

"Under these circumstances, it is just unacceptable that the quality of signal broadcast by Channel 8 be as far sub-standard as it is.

"So, if it is too much of a problem for ch 8 engineering personnel, the Hughes Tool Company will send a team of technicians to Las Vegas from Culver City, and they will damn well have this station operating satisfactorily."

But there were other problems not even the ultimate TV repairmen could solve, and Hughes grappled with them daily. Nothing escaped his attention. No detail was too small, as he had to contend now with distasteful commercials, then with "off-beat characters" delivering editorial opinion, even with "the programming slump which occurs from 6 to 6:30 AM."

Treating KLAS as if it were his private TV set, Hughes not only demanded final say on all shows but actually spent hours poring over lists detailing each episode of each series running on the station. A flurry of memos followed:

"Please determine whether the black and white Lucy Show has been the regular scheduled program for the 12:00 o'clock to 12:30 time period."

"Please ask Gray to ask Smith if it would not be better to use one of the remaining segments of 'Hawaiian Eye' instead of starting a new policy of running anything like 'Run for Your Life' which was in prime time only a week ago."

"OK, by all means use 'Hawaiian Eye.' But please ask Smith to hold onto both segments of 'Run for Your Life' and 'Man from Uncle' as long as he can, as I want to explore the possibility of showing these before they are shipped."

Time and again the beleaguered station manager had to await Hughes's decision on proposed new programs, which were routinely rejected without explanation, always at the last possible minute. A memo pleading "the manager urgently requests an answer as to whether or not he can include the show 'Playboy After Dark,' " would finally come back days later with Hughes's scrawl:

"Absolutely *NO*.

"But I want it handled very carefully. I want no trouble with the Playboy people."

Then there would be sudden outbursts from the penthouse, as when an enraged Hughes one evening discovered syndicated commentator Paul Harvey on the KLAS "Big News":

"We have never editorialized before, and when we do, I expect every word to come to me first.

"Pull the Paul Harvey show off the air. You have 10 days to try to sell it to someone (try Channel 5 first) before pulling it, but if you can't sell it then we will pull it anyway and pay for it. Maybe we could give someone the Merv Griffin show if they will take Paul Harvey."

And there were equally sudden fears: "I just heard something about an 84 hour telethon," wrote Hughes, dreading the marathon preemption. "I hope this is not planned for ch 8."

Nothing, however, quite so upset the recluse as commercials. In what was probably his one demonstration of populist spirit, Hughes saw himself representing aggrieved TV viewers everywhere as he declared all-out war on offensive ads.

"What about eliminating the Adjusta-Bed cure-all commercials?" demanded the bed-ridden billionaire, not about to put up with any hucksters. "Also, even after eliminating the undesirable Adjusta-Bed commercials, you want the Adjusta-Bed commercials reduced to about 1/8 of the present number and spotted in occasionally between other commercials.

"When a hard-sell, constant repetition campaign of this type is used, it may well be all right for the advertiser, but it drives the audience crazy."

His lawyers warned that he was "courting disaster by requiring the station manager to delete or ask customers to change commercials that do not violate the television code of ethics," but Hughes, who had his own code, was relentless.

In quick order, he banned a slew of "shabby, unworthy, misleading, untrue, distorted and fraudulent" real-estate promotions, then spotted a particularly offensive "onion-slicing machine" commercial that led him to issue a general edict:

"There should be no more presentations of food in the studio or an announcer trying to talk with food in his mouth. Any commercials including food are to be taped outside of the studio and are to be presented with good taste."

The real issue, however, was neither onion slicers nor Adjusta-Bed adjustments, but control. KLAS air time was *his* time, and Hughes's greatest wrath was reserved for the hapless station manager's onetime daring fling with charity.

It started innocently enough. A series of public-service spots promoting the sale of American flags, with the proceeds going to aid needy children. But the unapproved thirty-second ads drove Hughes into a blind fury:

"Please get me at once the real true explanation of what caused the manager of KLAS to give gratis the spot announcements on a broadcast station he does not own.

"I want to know by just what in the hell kind of a right does an employe involve a TV station in a charitable operation of this kind, which may, or may not be on the level.

"About half these charitable gimmicks turn out to be fraudulent or politically inspired, or motivated by some forces which are not disclosed.

"Also about half of them turn out to involve people who are left wingers or at least people with whom I dont want my name associated.

"I dont like this, and I want to know what induced the station manager to do this thing, and, if he wont give you a satisfactory answer, I want to have somebody investigate his activities and background."

Told that the suspicious charity was organized by the juvenile judge of the district court and staffed by a who's who of worthy local ladies, Hughes reluctantly allowed a sharply diminished number of flag ads to run for a short time. But when the commercials continued beyond the cutoff date, Hughes's anger exploded.

"TV time is no different from money," he fumed. "The principle business of the station consists of exchanging time for money.

"As I view it, the unauthorized giving of TV time (whether to a charitable entity or otherwise) is absolutely the same as reaching in the cash register and taking out a sum of money.

"Theft is theft—no matter what you do with the money after you steal it."

Various aides tried to calm him, to no avail.

"I do not believe that the station manager intentionally stole any money from you," wrote Maheu. "He is fully aware of the FCC regulations which provide specifically that certain announcements must be made gratis to support charitable projects."

Maheu's cavalier dismissal of the flag-ad theft was the last straw. Responding with Queeg-like zeal, Hughes ordered a sweeping investigation to find the missing strawberries:

"I believe he did it because he was pressured by somebody to do it. I am sure he knew he was sticking his neck out a mile, and he surely must have had a much stronger motive, to take a risk like this, than any of the casual, unimportant excuses which have been advanced. . . .

"I have been intending to ask you to make one of your usual thorough investigations of this matter before it is put aside.

"I personally dont think, when you dig into this thing, that you will find this contribution was made for the benefit of the FCC one damn bit.

"Bob, there are at least one hundred, by actual count, charitable funds, causes, drives, donations, etc., which rank equally high in point of importance, worthiness, validity, etc. So, why does the station manager select this one single entity out of all the others, and place the station in the posture of supporting this one cause so abundantly while neglecting all the other various causes, hospitals, Vietnam War Orphans, etc., etc.

"Only a careful investigation will disclose all the facts. Will you assume this task?"

Maheu apparently let the matter drop, and Hughes, forgetting about the flag-ad theft, once more became absorbed in his beloved "Swinging Shift."

Yet even into this special enclave of off-hour reverie came disconcerting problems. It was the cruelest of blows. These were Hughes's prime viewing hours—11:30 P.M. to six A.M.—when he could commune comfortably with his set, secure in the knowledge that he and he alone controlled television.

While nine floors below, beyond the blacked-out windows of his penthouse retreat, Las Vegas was alive with neon and nonstop action, the only light in his bedroom beamed from the overworked TV. But, like the swingers in the gambling halls, Hughes too was swinging—with his own "Swinging Shift." Every night, all night, three movies back to back, each his own selection.

Sometimes it would all be ruined by a tired KLAS announcer who flubbed the carefully phrased introduction. That at least could be corrected. One night, the announcer referred to the "first swinging shift," and Hughes quickly pounced:

"There should not be more than one Swinging Shift," he immediately scrawled on his bedside legal pad. "If it should be necessary to refer for any reason to the first picture, then it should be identified as the 'first movie on the Swinging Shift'—not the 'First Swinging Shift.' "

Other problems proved more intractable. Hughes insisted on personally clearing all movies in advance. But often he could not make up his mind until the last minute:

"Please ask Stoddard if he will be able, without too much difficulty, to substitute Las Vegas Story and Sealed Cargo in place of Gang War and Great Jewel Robbery. Please apologize for it being so late."

It became a nightly ritual: "If it will cause no confusion, it will be appreciated if he can substitute either Jeopardy or Inside the Mafia to replace Woman Obsessed at 4:30 AM."

"You and Roy failed to remind me in time about the movies for tonight, and now I am faced with the situation at the last minute," wrote Hughes on yet another occasion, this time blaming his Mormons for the lapse.

"Please ask Stoddard if, entirely without problems, he can substitute two pictures in place of the last two coming in the AM. Please say you will give him the names as soon as possible, and to assist in this, can he give you the synopsis on:

"Oklahoma Woman

"Fast and Furious

"Malta Story

"Great Diamond Robbery

"Also, principle cast, please."

The sudden changes caused some complaint. "Obviously, the problems which have arisen have been questions from viewers as to why one movie is listed in TV Guide or the newspapers and a different one is shown," explained the station manager. "If we continue to make unannounced changes certainly the questions are going to continue and eventually we could have a problem with the advertisers."

Hughes was understanding. "Re: the future," he replied two days later, "since the objectionable aspect of showing a program in conflict with the announcement was first called to my attention, I believe this is the one and only movie substituted at my request.

"I even permitted the showing of 'Mudlark', an absurd whimsy at 4 AM last nite, in preference to changing the program in conflict with the announcement.

"I will request as few changes as possible from now on."

It was a promise, however, that Hughes could not keep. There was a limit to how many *Mudlarks* he would suffer in silence. The billionaire, on the other hand, had a simple solution—in the future, titles of the late movies would not be given in the published TV listings at all.

But one recurring problem seemed to have no solution. KLAS could not manage to come up with three films a night that pleased its owner. Even after the station started sending Hughes multipage synopses of available movies a month in advance, the problem persisted.

"This list of pictures is just simply zero as far as I am concerned,"

Hughes complained. "Outside of 'Hired Gun' I dont see anything I would watch."

A new set of proposed shows was sent, to no avail. "There are simply no pictures on this list that I consider satisfactory," came the response from the penthouse. "I am familiar with every one of these movies—I even made quite a few of them—and there are not enough to fill out the package of 3 needed for tonight."

Still Hughes made plans to upgrade the show. Secret plans, of course. "It is my intention that Hughes Resort Hotels will sponsor the entire Swinging Shift program with no commercial interruptions, but I want this kept very secret for now. My first request is that this matter be held in complete confidence from *everybody* until I am ready to announce it in a big way."

Once ready to reveal his "big secret" to the station manager, Hughes insisted on tight security: "Ask him to go to an office where it is quiet, private, and where he will not be interrupted. You dont have to mention my name—just say at the beginning, 'I have a message for you and I am sure you will know whom it is from.' "

But before the secret plans could be executed, yet another blow was struck. The TV station, in violation of Hughes's direct orders, inserted a commercial between two of the movies one night.

"Now we are 4 min. over because I did not anticipate the commercial between Call of the West and Oregon Trail," Hughes fretted.

"Please explain to Stoddard, and ask if he doesn't think we can drop the 4 + minutes needed from the end of *Sunrise Semester* instead of cutting one of the movies."

The dreaded "Sunrise Semester" once again came full force into Hughes's consciousness. "I want to discontinue 'Semester' completely, anyway," he added, "as soon as it can be done without repercussions." The program had been plaguing Hughes for months, and he had already ordered it cut back to half an hour. But his lawyers warned that KLAS would certainly run afoul of the FCC if the educational series was canceled outright.

"Sunrise Semester" was his nemesis. Hughes never said why he so detested the show. But it came on at 6:30 every morning, just as the "Swinging Shift" ended, and to Hughes it seemed to represent something deeply antipathetic. Nonetheless he watched it—he was probably the only person in Las Vegas who did—as if compelled. At one point KLAS tried to move the show back to six A.M., and Hughes successfully resisted the change. But he could not get it off the air.

143

So, alone in his darkened room, Hughes had to face the end of his all-night movies and watch "Sunrise Semester" presage a new dawn on his TV screen. It was a daily agony.

Just as the perfect television set had eluded him, so now Hughes had come to recognize that owning a TV station was not the answer either. What did it profit him if he couldn't even get the movies he wanted and had to suffer "Sunrise Semester" as well? The quest must begin anew.

Locked in a struggle to control television itself—and thus to control his world—Hughes would have to reach still higher. He would need to buy an entire TV network.

"Do you realize I am going to be faced with making a $200,000,000 decision today?"

It was 6:30 Sunday morning, June 30, 1968. Howard Hughes squinted uneasily at the long string of zeros he had just scrawled on his yellow legal pad. He had not slept all weekend long, bedeviled by second thoughts and obsessed with last-minute details. The magnitude of the impending deal daunted even him.

Hughes was about to buy ABC.

No one had ever owned more than a small fraction of a major television network, but Hughes was determined to get a controlling interest. And to take it by surprise. He had been plotting the move for more than a year. ABC, then foundering in third place, far behind both CBS and NBC in the ratings and desperately short of cash, seemed the perfect target.

This time it was not late-night movies that interested the billionaire, but raw political power.

"I want to know confidentially and most accurately just how significant a position in the formulation of U.S. public opinion would be afforded us by the acquisition of ABC," he wrote to Maheu. "Anyway, my attitude is very simple. My objective is the ABC News Service and what can be done with it."

The ABC "Evening News" with Howard Hughes. Behind the scenes, of course. Even as he sought Maheu's reassurance, the billionaire had no real doubts that one-man control of a national television network—albeit the weakest of the three—could give him tremendous clout.

"Maybe you remember that the Los Angeles Daily News, when

it was still being published, was the most important news media by far, from the political standpoint, in the entire Sou. Calif. region," wrote Hughes, spelling out his strategy. "This despite the fact that the Times, Examiner, and the Herald were all far larger and better newspapers.

"The reason for this was explained very carefully to me. I was told it was because the News took a position pro or con on every political issue on the horizon and every candidate seeking office. The other, more conscientious newspapers usually refrained from taking a really strong position in any matter, merely because they did not want to be accused of being partial.

"Now, it seems logical to me, based upon the very wide public ownership of the two big networks, and the very small holdings of any one stockholder, that it would be almost impossible to obtain any really reliable assurance of strong support from either NBC or CBS. So, although ABC may be the weakest of the 3, if a really strong position could be achieved, permitting a predictable candidate attitude, this network might very likely turn out to be the balance of power."

The balance of power. With growing excitement, Hughes watched the price of ABC stock, saw it plummet, waited until it reached a record low. Then he pounced.

On Monday, July 1, 1968, just before the opening bell of the New York Stock Exchange sounded, Hughes announced his takeover bid, catching both ABC and Wall Street by surprise. That was vital. This was not to be a friendly business transaction but a sudden raid to seize control.

Hughes gave ABC stockholders two weeks to sell him two million shares at a price well above the market. If they did, he would own 43 percent of the network, more than enough to be in full command.

Stunned, ABC's board of directors met in a council of war, determined to block Hughes's bid. It was like wrestling with a phantom. They knew virtually nothing about the recluse or his intentions, except that he had not been seen for more than a decade. That, they decided, was their trump card. They would force Hughes to appear in public.

"WILL HUGHES RISK PRIVACY TO WIN ABC?" newspaper headlines asked. It seemed he would have no choice.

Ordinarily, anyone seeking to buy even a single television station— let alone an entire network—was required to make a personal appearance before the Federal Communications Commission. Hughes, however, had managed to obtain a license for KLAS while remaining hidden. Now he intended to do the same with ABC.

His attorneys insisted that would be impossible, but the billionaire disdained such advice. "This is no decision which a lawyer can make merely by looking in a book," he told Maheu. "It depends upon political strength and ability at your command *now*, since I am very sure this will be settled long before the new administration comes in.

"I have to take a business risk of large amount, and I can only make the decision so to do based upon my appraisal of your ability to accomplish a certain result with the FCC."

Fortunately, 1968 was an election year, and Hughes figured that he would soon have more than money to offer the candidates then running for president. With their help, he would have ABC.

"I dont see how I dare launch into [this] campaign unless I have some assurance of the FCC's support, without my personal appearance," he explained. "Now, I see only one way such support might be assumed, and that is in case one of the candidates or the white house on behalf of its favorite candidate wants the support of ABC. If such a trade could be made, it seems to me that we have the tools with which to make it. In other words, our present position plus white house or Humphries' full support would spell certain FCC approval in my book, and with that assurance, I would go full blast ahead. Now," he cautioned Maheu, "you really have to be careful how you approach this bag of hot potatoes."

Even Maheu was uncertain, however, that the plan was feasible. "The primary and election will have come and passed before we would be in a position to use ABC to our advantage," he replied. "There are other ways of making the candidates thoroughly devoted to us."

And, Maheu reassured Hughes, there were other ways of handling the FCC. "We still have time to condition the individual members of the board and at all levels below," he explained, promising that Washington's well-connected lawyer Edward Morgan would do the job. "Morgan happens to be an expert in the area of conditioning and will spend his time on this most important detail."

But while Morgan was conditioning the FCC, ABC moved on a new front. A week after the takeover bid had been announced, on July 9, the network filed suit in New York, seeking a federal-court injunction to block Hughes.

Ever since the TWA crisis, lawsuits had terrorized the recluse. He had surrendered control of his beloved airline rather than appear in court, and now he feared that the nightmare—"I was like a rat in a trap"—was about to engulf him again.

At four the next morning, a shaken Hughes roused his thousand-dollar-a-week Hollywood attorney, Greg Bautzer, to have a Mormon aide read him a memo over the telephone.

"I hate to awaken you," Hughes had written, "but I dont like the way this thing is turning out at all. Up to now there has been no real issue about my being personally called at all. But at the hearing today or tomorrow, ABC will demand my appearance. This will bring into sharp focus all the old rumors of my death, disability, etc., etc. And thereafter if, for any reason, the deal fails to materialize, people will say that the reason was my unwillingness to appear.

"Now, Greg, the minute this slant is put on things I am very likely to be sued for the losses that will no doubt be incurred by those individuals who bought stock when it was at its peak (in loyal support of their confidence in me) and then will be forced to take a loss if the deal fails to go thru.

"You see, normally, it would be held that any such losses would be simply the risk of the speculator. But here we have a man who, in the public's concept, could win this fight if he would just try, but he is too content to lean back on his billion dollar ass and enjoy life (at least most people think I do)."

As the sleepy lawyer listened long-distance, the aide continued to recite to him the miseries of the frightened financier:

"If I suffer a massive loss of face after two years of improving publicity. If I wind up sued by individuals who invested with me in my gamble. If my reputation as a successful businessman-financier-industrialist is shot to hell . . . if this is the result of my ABC attempt, you may be sure that it will have been one of the saddest mistakes I have ever made, and I have made quite a few."

Hughes was so terrified by the lawsuit that he was ready to abandon his network ambitions, if only ABC would promise to drop the litigation.

"Now, Greg, needless to say, this would be an awful disappointment to me. However, I did not muddle my way through 10 years of the TWA lawsuit only to wind up in another one that could easily last another 10 years.

"I dont like litigation, and there is no prize worth incurring more litigation for it."

Only an impassioned plea by Maheu, later that morning, persuaded Hughes to stay in the fight until at least the case was actually presented. "You have the image of being the only person to take on a Congressional Committee," he wrote, recalling Hughes's 1947 "Spruce Goose" hearing triumph, "of a rugged individualist, who is fearless and does not walk away from any battles."

That afternoon in court, it was a case of courage rewarded. The judge refused to grant ABC an injunction, two days later declined to order Hughes to testify, and then, in an unusual Saturday hearing just two days before the tender offer was due to expire, issued a final order backing the recluse's right to buy the network.

But there was no joy in the penthouse. For while the court battle proceeded, a new and unexpected adversary arose to bedevil the rugged individualist. And, once more, he cringed from battle.

From Washington came word that the Justice Department was concerned about the possible antitrust implications of the Hughes-ABC deal. His empire already included substantial cable television holdings, sold a wide range of electronics equipment, manufactured communications satellites, and, of course, there was also KLAS.

"It is beginning to look as if the name of the game is 'Justice Dept. Anti-Trust Pressure,' " Hughes fumed. "Without this factor, I think I know fairly well what to do. However, I dont care for the Justice Dept. questionaire. If the ABC affair is not only going to cost me what everyone seems to think is a fair price, but, in addition, is going to cost me submission to this program of harrassment from the Justice Dept., I am afraid I must bow out."

Yet even as he prepared to throw in the towel, Hughes was also deploying a growing platoon of lawyers, fixers, and bagmen. He considered engaging former Supreme Court Justice Arthur Goldberg to handle future legal conflicts in New York and, to deal with the antitrust threat, summoned from Austin, Texas, the president's own attorney—Johnson intimate Jake Jacobsen, a former White House adviser later to gain notoriety in the Watergate milk-fund scandal.

Now back in fighting trim, Hughes decided there was, perhaps, a solution after all to the "Justice Dept. vendetta." It was the kind of solution that had worked many times in the past.

"Bob," he wrote, "I think it is imperative that we make an alliance with Humphries, the White House, Nixon, or McCarthy and agree to supply all-out unlimited support in return for taking this Justice Dept. off my back but *now*!"

As he swung into the final days of his two-week crusade, Hughes devised a new array of stratagems to meet the stubborn obstacles that threatened to deprive him of his television network. One moment he proposed friendly negotiations with ABC president Leonard Goldenson, the next he threatened to dump all the stock he acquired and force a market collapse.

At one point he considered selling his ABC shares to rival Texas financier James J. Ling, if only as a ploy to convince network management he was the lesser of two evils:

"It seems to me the only hope lies in the remote possibility of persuading Goldenson that he really wont gain anything if he forces me, through threats of personal appearances, etc., to sell out to a Ling or somebody equally tough.

"In fact, if I were Goldenson, I would a damn sight rather cope with yours truly, who wants no part of the glamour that goes with the job—in fact does not really want the job at all—only wants a quiet working arrangement. I would a damned sight rather cope with a Hughes where I could always have a certain advantage in Hughes' desire not to be forced into public, than I would to cope with a Ling, or a dozen other younger, healthier, more active men who dont shun the spotlite at all—maybe even like it."

But with ABC still unexpectedly intransigent, the Justice threat unresolved, the FCC outcome uncertain, and yet another day in court ahead, Hughes wavered. Several times he decided to abandon the quest and plotted his extrication quite as feverishly as he had planned his coup. Then he would take heart all over again and scrawl new orders on his legal pad.

By Sunday, July 14, with only hours left before he would have to accept or reject the stock due the next day, Hughes remained mercurial. As Mormons working double-time scurried between typewriter and telephone, the billionaire sent a blizzard of contradictory memos from his penthouse command post, now resigned to defeat, then ready to "collar" the president of the United States. Yes, he would send either top Washington lawyer Tom Finney, a partner in Clark Clifford's firm, or better yet Larry O'Brien, right into the Oval Office.

"It seems to me, Bob, there is a comparatively easy way to get an immediate answer to the network decision," he wrote with renewed confidence. "I think such an answer should be obtainable by Mr. O'Brien or Mr. Finney marching in and collaring Johnson or Humphries and saying: 'Look, my friend, my client Mr. Hughes has initiated the machinery to acquire control of ABC. He has ridden out the first very controversial weeks and is in pretty good shape. He had no idea that there would be as much resistance from Mr. Goldenson. He thought that his interest in ABC would be greeted with cordiallity. . . .

" 'Mr. Hughes wants to spend his remaining years in productive accomplishment, not in protracted conflict,' " the script continued. " 'His only interest is to build the network up until it becomes an asset to this country—an asset of which the country can be justly proud. Mr. Hughes' only concern is that the FCC, being under intense influence and constant harrassment by ABC, will simply feel they have to be more thorough and more formal than they would be inclined to be if they were left alone.' "

And now the hook. How could it fail?

"Then I think O'Brien or Finney should work the conversation around to where he (our man) can gracefully say: 'What do you think Mr. Hughes should do? I think he would like your counsel.'

"Now, I dont know Humphries, but I can assure you Mr. Johnson would have picked up the ball long before the conversation ever got to this point.

"It seems to me," he concluded, "that such a meeting would certainly give us an indication of which way the wind blows across the White House lawn."

It would have been an interesting meeting, indeed. Because Lyndon Johnson, almost as obsessed with television as Hughes himself, with a three-set console in both his office and his bedroom, had come to decide that the TV networks were Communist-controlled. And he had been monitoring the Hughes-ABC deal closely, although avoiding any direct involvement due to his own controversial broadcast interests.

But Hughes, who had had dealings with the president before, never did learn the direction of the wind on the White House lawn. Maheu discouraged the plan. "We must remember," he argued, "that whatever the Pres. recommends—then we are bound *forever*. He is not, though, because his advice must be 'off the record.' He'll have an implied obligation but we must remember that he has had a lot of experience in the technique of 'sliding' away from implied obligations."

Hughes was not immediately convinced. What was there to lose?

"If we are going to cancel out tomorrow, I *urge* we put it right in Johnson's lap and offer him the opportunity to determine what we do. If we could get a real green light signal from Johnson, I simply dont think the FCC would hold us up in defiance of his wishes, and I doubt very much that Goldenson would pursue the issue in court if it became evident that we had the approval of the Whitehouse."

Still, Hughes's remote-control unit balked. Late Sunday evening, Maheu replied with the pessimism of a man who dealt with life's daily realities: "I know that you don't like to hear anything you don't want to hear. As you know, I was selling positive thinking before Peale ever thought of writing a book. But even affirmative thinking must have some foundation in the realm of realism. If you are prepared to tell me that, at a given point, you will make an appearance, I'll guarantee you that we'll deliver ABC to you on a silver platter."

Of course, that was the one thing Hughes could not bring himself to do.

As the three P.M. Monday deadline came near, it hardly seemed to matter. By midday less than 150,000 of the two million shares of ABC stock Hughes was seeking had been tendered.

The network's final court appeal, heard earlier that day, seemed beside the point. Then, at one P.M., a three-judge panel once more backed Hughes in his bid to buy ABC. And in the next two hours almost a million and a half shares flooded in to the billionaire's brokers.

When all the paper had been counted, Howard Hughes had 1.6 million shares, more than a third of all the outstanding stock in ABC. It was easily enough to control the network, and it would now be no problem to get more. A naked hermit, eager to mold mass opinion and manipulate national policy, had just been offered the most powerful position in broadcast history.

What made it all the more incredible was that Maheu, on Hughes's instructions, had been busily working behind the scenes to make sure that the two million shares Hughes was legally bound to buy would *not* be tendered. To the last, Hughes wanted to preserve his option to drop the deal.

Indeed, Maheu had gone so far in his efforts as to risk imprisonment. "Hell, Howard," he later boasted, "if some of the things which I did in order to extricate us from the ABC matter ever surfaced, I would be spending the rest of my life in jail."

But now Hughes was not at all certain he wanted to bail out. Everything was going his way. The stock had been tendered, the courts had backed him, and the FCC also seemed ready to approve his takeover. None of the commissioners even guessed at his true condition, or his true motives. All were ready to okay the acquisition.

There was only one catch: Hughes would have to appear in person to claim the license.

It was the one thing he would not, could not do. Informed Monday night that the FCC would definitely demand his appearance, Hughes immediately capitulated. Ready to pay $200 million, he would not emerge from his blacked-out bedroom.

"I am just not up to that," he explained.

Shortly after noon on July 16, 1968, a formal statement was issued. Hughes rejected the stock. And his bid to take over ABC—to have a network of his own—seemed to disappear as suddenly and mysteriously as it had been announced.

Hughes, however, had not abandoned his plans to control television. If he could not get one of the three existing networks without giving up his privacy, then he would create a new fourth network—a Hughes Network—and "chase ABC right out of business."

"My desire for a voice—for media—has not changed in the least," he emphasized from his ninth-floor retreat. "It seems to me that thru the alternatives of building a compact, wholly owned 4th Network, or a vast united complex of CATV systems, I might achieve the channel to the public at a lower price and with less bruises along the road."

The idea was not new. It had been in the back of his mind for years and had even come up several times while the ABC deal was still in progress. In one moment of despair, he had considered settling for a state-wide network in Nevada.

"I am absolutely sure my plans to acquire ABC will not bear fruit, so I am more anxious than ever to build the strongest network here in Nevada that anybody ever conceived. I will be very content with a really strong network in Nevada. I will be very unhappy if this blows up in addition to ABC."

But having come so close to a national outlet, Hughes could not now be content with a local system.

So he schemed to take over a major independent, like Storer or Metromedia, to string together every available cable TV station in the country, and to use the money that might have gone to ABC stockholders to make his new system a national contender.

Not long after walking away from ABC, Hughes actually did acquire a sports network, which he planned to augment with communications satellites his own company manufactured.

But soon he was finding the Hughes Sports Network as unsatisfactory as KLAS: "The broadcast looks like color television when it was first introduced twelve years ago. When something carries my name, as this network does, I dont propose to stand by and see these results."

And neither HSN nor any fledgling network offered the immediate power he craved: "Let's be realistic and admit that no such alternate could possibly be built up to the point of effectiveness in time to carry any weight in the forthcoming political contests—either primary or final."

The 1968 elections came and went, and still Hughes had no national "voice," no "channel to the public," certainly no "balance of power."

Maheu's report that the new president was interested in his plans— "Nixon, through his friend [Rebozo], has suggested the creation of a 4th Network as a means of elevating the standard of all TV broadcasting"—briefly buoyed the billionaire's spirits.

In the end, however, Hughes decided that a fourth network was not the answer.

"I dont say a fourth network cannot be built up," he explained. "I just say it wont happen without the back breaking, heart breaking kind of effort that went into the creation of the other networks. Even with the best of luck, it will take years for any fourth network to advance to the point where it could equal ABC."

Now, after nine months of toying with alternatives, Hughes was ready to return to his first love.

"I have finally decided to *go* on ABC," Hughes exulted in late March of 1969. It was, of course, a secret enthusiasm. "Now, if this is permitted to leak out, even a tiny bit, it will bounce the market up and I will have to cancel out. So I beg you to be careful whom we trust."

Secret or not, Hughes could hardly contain himself. It was technological ecstasy. With a passion he could feel for nothing human, Hughes now coveted the network he had so recently rejected.

"Bob," he wrote, "what appeals to me about ABC is its tremendous mechanical machine. There is an ABC outlet in almost every city in the US that has a CBS or NBC station.

"This tremendous giant of mechanical and technical perfection is just lying there going to waste. Being used daily for the transmission of the biggest pile of pure undiluted horse-shit that was ever assembled on one role of tape.

"Bob, ABC can only go one way, and that is up.

"I promise you that a 7 year old child could do a better job of running it than is being done today. That is what intrigues me—this huge slumbering giant of technical perfection that needs only to be waked up to come to life."

Lost for a moment in his dreams of arousing this genie, Hughes did not lose sight of the mission he had in mind for the "slumbering giant."

"Dont forget that every Whitehouse or congressional press conference will, by custom, require the issuance of an invitation to the ABC News correspondent in co-equal position," he concluded. "And also a co-equal position in reporting every election from now on—not after you build a network up, but right now."

The White House. Congress. Every election. A network of his own. Right now. With renewed and growing excitement, Hughes again began to plot his takeover of ABC.

This time, he would not try to seize control. That would only mean another round of trouble, new court fights, further demands for his appearance before the FCC. All of it unnecessary. With the right approach, Hughes was certain he could arrange a friendly business deal—"a completely non-hostile take-over with Goldenson's complete consent."

And if ABC, still in dire financial straits, would go along quietly, so might the FCC. There was a new administration. Nixon wanted an "elevating" Hughes network, and now he could have one. Besides, some of the commissioners were afraid that without an immediate infusion of capital, ABC, which had already been forced to cut back its programming, might actually go under.

Unfortunately, Hughes too was in something of a bind. With his Nevada business turning sour, the helicopter losses mounting, and a new TWA judgment for $137 million hanging over him, the besieged billionaire was no longer able to blithely consider a cash investment of $200 million.

But he wanted ABC, and he wanted it badly.

"We have got to dig up some money from somewhere," he wrote Maheu. Perhaps the TWA case could yet be salvaged. Perhaps the disastrous helicopter enterprise could be unloaded. But, if not, Hughes was still determined to get his television network.

Indeed, he wanted ABC so much he was willing to surrender his birthright. He would sell the Hughes Tool Company—the golden goose he had inherited, the foundation of his entire fortune—in order to control television once and for all.

Then, just a week after announcing his final decision to "*go* on ABC," Hughes suddenly changed his mind.

It was Saturday night. His penthouse retreat was filled with the sound of raucous laughter. Not that Hughes was happy. The laughter was booming from his TV set, tuned to the network he had decided to buy.

"Welcome back to 'The Dating Game'!" said the grinning host, his arm around the small black child standing beside him. "It's time for Marc to choose a delightful gal to share a 'dream date' with his dad! All right, Marc. Who will it be? Bachelorette number one? Bachelorette number two? Or bachelorette number three?"

The camera cut to the three starlets. The child considered his choice. "Sorry, there's the signal," announced the host. "That means 'time's up'!" The child picked bachelorette number two, the actress who loved to cook. She smiled for a close-up while the studio audience applauded.

Hughes watched it all in grim silence. By the time the show was over, he knew he had made a terrible mistake.

"That's it for tonight," declared the emcee, throwing a kiss. "Thank you, goodnight, and we hope *you* always get the date you want! Now make sure to stay tuned for 'The Newlywed Game,' next on ABC."

Hughes continued to stare at the screen. But as he watched the newlyweds bicker, his thoughts kept returning to the outrage he had just witnessed. He reached for his bedside legal pad.

"I just got through watching ABC's Dating Game and Newlywed Game," he wrote, "and my only reaction is let's forget all about ABC.

"Bob, I think all this attention directed toward violence in TV dramatic shows is certainly misplaced. These two game shows represent the largest single collection of poor taste I have ever seen."

But it was more than mere poor taste that riled the recluse into his sudden about-face. It was the horrendous immorality—the shocking violation—he had witnessed on "The Dating Game."

"The first show—'Dating Game' consisted of a small negro child selecting, sight unseen, one of three girls (adult girls) to make a sexually embellished trip to Rome with his father.

"Two of the girls were negro and one was a very beautiful and attractive white girl. The child chose the white girl, who then was introduced to the negro father of the child and informed that she (the white girl) was to make an all expense paid vacation trip to Rome on TWA."

Talk about adding insult to injury. Not only did they dare to arrange this sinful interracial assignation, but they were using—no, defiling, TWA—*his* airline—to boot.

"Bob, the entire handling of the show was, in every way carried out in a manner best calculated to titilate and arouse the sexual response of the audience. The whole show was of such a marginal character, sex-wise, that, if it had been presented as a motion picture to the governing body of the movie industry, its acceptance would have been very uncertain at best.

"But, let me explain that I make the above comment based upon the subject matter and the treatment of the show, without any consideration whatsoever of the racial issue.

"Then, on top of the very marginal show of miserable taste, which I have attempted to describe above, they have to compound the abuse of any conceivable moral standard by arranging a sexual rendezvous between a beautiful white girl and a negro man in Rome, which may even be in violation of the law.

"And all of this is done solely for one purpose: to shock and arouse the sexual response of the audience so as to obtain a higher rating from the TV polls for the benefit of the sponsors.

"Please consider this entire affair most carefully, Bob, to see if it gives you any ideas."

The two-hundred-million-dollar ABC deal was dead.

After months of frenzied effort, after all those sleepless nights, after plotting to collar a president and seize the balance of power, after planning to auction off the most profitable part of his empire, Howard Hughes had finally abandoned his grand quest for a national television network over a game show.

It was the collision of pure kitsch with pure power, a twilight-zone encounter between low camp and high finance.

Everything had come full circle. His struggle to control television, his dream of controlling the world through television, all came to nought because, in the end, Hughes was himself controlled by television.

It was as if the billionaire had finally entered the TV set he watched so compulsively, passing through its screen like Alice through the looking glass, the real "mystery bachelor" stepping out of his offstage

Bob —

I just got through watching ABC's Dating Game and Newlywed Game, and my only reaction is 'let's forget all about ABC'

Bob, I think all this attention directed toward violence in TV dramatic shows is certainly mis- placed. These two game shows represent the largest single collection of poor taste I have ever seen.

The first show — "Dating Game" consisted of a small negro child selecting, sight unseen, one of three 'girls' ('adult' girls) to make a sexually embellished trip to Rome with his father.

Two of the girls were negro and one was a very beautiful and attractive white girl. The child chose the white girl, who then was introduced to the negro father of the child and informed that she (the white girl) was to make an 'all expense paid vacation trip to Rome on TWA.

Bob, the entire handling of the 'show was, in every way carried out in a manner best calculated to titilate and arouse the sexual response of the audience. The whole show was of such a marginal character, sex-wise, that, ~~it had, I have been a doubtful~~ if it had been presented as a motion picture to the governing body of the movie industry, its acceptance would have been very uncertain at best.

But, let me explain that I make the above comment based upon the subject matter and the treatment of the show, without any consideration whatsoever of the racial issue.

Then, on top of ~~—~~ the very marginal show of miserable taste, which I have attempted to describe above, they have to compound the abuse of any conceivable moral standard by arranging a sexual rendezvous between a beautiful white girl and

a negro man in Rome,
which may even be in
violation of the law.

And all of this is done
solely for one purpose:
to shock and arouse the
sexual response of the audience
so as to obtain a higher
rating from the TV polls
for the benefit of the sponsors.

Please consider this
entire affair most carefully,
Bob, to see if it gives
you any ideas.

Many thanks,

Stoward

isolation booth to join "The Dating Game," only to discover that his chosen "dream date"—ABC—was soiled merchandise.

There was, however, one last twist, an irony that Hughes himself never discovered. Had he known, an entire network might well have fallen into his hands.

The "beautiful white girl" whose race-mixing Roman rendezvous so outraged Hughes was, in reality, a light-skinned black.

5 Fear and Loathing

The Bogeyman. Right there in his room.

A huge gargoyle of a blackamoor, horribly greased and dripping filth, a savage threatening unspeakable crimes, had violated his sanctum sanctorum, slipping past the locked doors, the armed sentry, and the phalanx of Mormons through the one unguarded opening.

Howard Hughes, sick with fear and revulsion, cried out in the night to Maheu.

"I hate to disturb you this late," he wrote in a shaken scrawl, "but I just saw something on TV that litterally and actually physically made me nauseated and I still am!

"I saw a show on NBC in which the biggest ugliest negro you ever saw in your life was covered—litterally covered from head to foot with vaseline almost $1/4$ of an inch thick. It made you sick just to look at this man.

"Bob, the producers must have deliberately tried to make this man as repulsive as possible. Anyway, he walked over next to an immaculately dressed white woman—sort of an English noblewoman type.

"Well, when this repulsive gob of grease came close to this clean carefully dressed white woman, all I could think was 'Jesus, don't let that woman touch him.' "

But it was too late. Not even Hughes could protect the purity of white womanhood from the potent forces of blackness.

"So, after a minute or two of talk this man grabbed this woman, opened his mouth as wide as possible and kissed this woman in a way that would have been cut out of any movie even if the people involved had both been of the same race."

His Mandingo complex fully aroused, the outraged Texan was

ready to call out a lynch mob. But no, the crime could not be punished.

"Bob, this show seems to be the presentation of the Broadway version of the Oscar, so I imagine the scene I described was a scene taken at random from the winning play. . . .

"I was all for making a protest to some congressional committee over this," continued Hughes, "but now that I see it is the Tony awards, I feel it is even more shocking, but I suppose one should approach it with caution."

Another great white hope unfulfilled. The "repulsive gob of grease" was, in fact, James Earl Jones playing prizefighter Jack Johnson in *The Great White Hope*, a segment of which was televised in the awards presentation. That realization did nothing to still the billionaire's sense of outrage.

"Bob," he concluded, "I dont care if this was the re-enactment of the Last Supper, that first scene is going to cause some comment."

Of all of Hughes's phobias and obsessions, few were more virulent than his fear and loathing of blacks. His was a classic racism straight out of plantation melodrama, often expressed in terms so outrageous that it seems a parody. But he was deadly serious, and his bigotry had very real consequences. He did, after all, own the plantation.

Hughes himself attributed his prejudice and paranoia to a traumatic event in his youth. "I was born and lived my first 20 years in Houston, Texas," he explained. "I lived right in the middle of one race riot in which the negroes committed attrocities to equal any in Vietnam."

In fact, when Hughes was only eleven there had been a dramatic explosion of black rage in his rigidly segregated hometown. On the night of August 23, 1917, more than one hundred soldiers from an all-black infantry battalion stationed near the city seized rifles and marched on Houston to avenge the beating of a black officer by white policemen. Sixteen whites were killed in the three-hour uprising. The Houston riot was a milestone in America's ongoing and, until then, rather one-sided race war—the first in which more whites were killed than blacks.

Undoubtedly that night did have a real impact on young Howard. However, now, half a century later, the well-guarded recluse was besieged not by armed mobs but by phantoms of his own creation. Consumed by a nameless dread, he projected his fears onto a variety of unseen enemies. Sometimes they paraded before him in blackface—a minstrel show of his subconscious mind.

Bob —

I hate to disturb you this late, but I just saw something on TV that litterally and actually physically made me nauseated and I still am!

I saw a show on NBC in which the biggest ugliest negro you ever saw in your life was covered — litterally covered from head to foot with vaseline almost $\frac{1}{4}$ of an inch thick. It made you sick just to look at this man.

Bob, the producers must have deliberately tried to make this man as repulsive as possible. Anyway, he walked over next to an immaculately dressed white woman — sort of an English noblewoman type.

Well, when this repulsive gob of grease came close to this clean carefully dressed white woman, all I could think was "Jesus, don't let that woman touch him."

So, after a minute or two

of talk this man grabbed this
woman, opened his mouth as wide
as possible and kissed this woman
in a way that would have been
cut out of any movie even if
the people involved had both
been of the same race.

Bob, this show seems to be
the presentation of the
Broadway version of the Oscar,
so I imagine the scene I
described was a scene taken at
random from the winning
play.

Bob, this must be shot in
a theatre with no air conditioning because every single
player is just covered
with a thick layer of
make up that is melting
and practically dripping off
onto the floor, just as the
layer of grease was melting
in the first scene I described
from the winning play.

I was all for making a
protest to some congressional
committee over this, but now
that I see it is the Tony
awards, I feel it is even
more shocking, but I
suppose one should approach
it with caution.

However, Bob, I dont care
if this was the re-enactment
of the ~~Last~~ Last Supper
that first scene is going to
cause some comment.

Best regards to you,

Howard

Actually, it was his terror of blacks that had driven Hughes to take a first decisive step into total seclusion. After their marriage, Hughes and Jean Peters lived in separate bungalows at the Beverly Hills Hotel, seeing each other only for marathon movie-watching trysts at night. They met each evening for their own "Late-Late Show" at Goldwyn Studios until Hughes discovered that his screening room there had been used to show rushes of *Porgy and Bess* to its all-black cast. He never set foot in that theater again.

Nor did he ever again invite Jean to watch movies. Instead, Hughes moved alone to Nosseck's Projection Studio on Sunset Boulevard, set up house there, kept his new location secret from his wife, and told her he was in the hospital with an "undiagnosed disease." It was half-true. For it was in the three months Hughes spent alone at Nosseck's that things first turned really weird.

At first he spent his time talking to bankers and lawyers about the TWA crisis, all the while compulsively cleaning the telephone with Kleenex or endlessly arranging and rearranging a half-dozen Kleenex boxes into various geometric designs. For several weeks he wore the same white shirt and tan slacks. Then one day he stripped off his rancid clothes, went about naked, stopped talking to bankers and lawyers, and ordered his aides to maintain strict silence.

Finally, Hughes issued a blanket decree: "Don't try to get me for anything. Wait until I call you. I don't want any messages handed to me."

Now he was set. He remained at the studio in silent seclusion until the late summer of 1958, when he suddenly moved back to his bungalow—and there had a complete nervous breakdown.

It probably would have happened even without *Porgy and Bess*. Blacks may have precipitated the move that cut him off from his wife and left him alone with his madness, but blacks were not the real threat. The real threat was "contamination."

It was not merely the purity of white womanhood that obsessed Hughes, it was the purity of his entire world. And that purity was endangered not merely by big ugly blacks but by innumerable other forms of "contamination."

The most dangerous was invisible. Germs.

Hughes set up bivouac in five pink bungalows at the Beverly Hills Hotel, and from his headquarters, bungalow 4, commanded his troops in the germ-warfare campaign.

With germs, as with blacks, there had been childhood traumas. Both his parents had died suddenly, unexpectedly, his mother when he was sixteen, his father when he was eighteen. But his long-standing terror of bacteria was by now irrational. And it dominated his entire life.

Hughes cut off all human contact—everyone was a dangerous carrier—except for his clean-living elite Mormon guard. And even they had to follow stringent rules designed to prevent the "backflow of germs."

The few who dealt with him personally, or handled anything he was to handle, first had to engage in a thirty-minute purification ritual called "processing"—"wash four distinct and separate times, using lots of lather each time from individual bars of soap"—and then don white cotton gloves.

Even that was not sufficient. Finally, Hughes demanded that everything his Mormons delivered to him with their gloved processed hands also had to be wrapped in Kleenex or Scott paper towels, "insulation" to protect him from "contamination."

But he was hardly yet safe from the invisible threat. Seated naked in a white leather chair in the "germ-free zone" of his darkened bungalow, its windows sealed shut with masking tape, the billionaire began to dictate a complete "Procedures Manual," a series of meticulously detailed memos codifying such rules as the number of layers of tissues required in handling particular items, such as the clothes he now almost never wore.

"Mr. Hughes would like you to bring a box of shirts, a box of trousers and a box of shoes," began one typical "Operating Memorandum" titled "Taking Clothing to HRH."

"He wants you to obtain a brand new knife, never used, to open a new box of kleenex using the knife to open the slot.

"After the box is open you are to take the little tag and the first piece of kleenex and destroy them; then using two fingers of the left hand and two fingers of the right hand take each piece of kleenex out of the box and place it on an unopened newspaper and repeat this until approximately 50 sheets are neatly stacked. You then have a paddle for one hand. You are then to make another for the other hand, making a total of two paddles of kleenex to use in handling these three boxes.

"Mr. Hughes wanted you to remember to keep your head at a 45 degree angle from the various things you would touch, such as the kleenex box itself, the knife, the kleenex paddles.

"The thing to be careful of during the operation is not to breath upon the various items."

And that was nothing to the precautions Hughes ordered in removing his hearing-aid cord from the bathroom cabinet:

"A. First use 6 or 8 thicknesses of Kleenex, pulled one at a time from the slot, in touching the doorknob to open the door to the bathroom.

"B. The same sheaf of Kleenex may be employed to turn on the spigots so as to obtain a good force of warm water. This Kleenex is then to be disposed of.

"C. A sheaf of 6 to 8 Kleenex is then to be used to open the cabinet containing the soap, and a fresh bar of soap that has never been opened is to be used. All Kleenex used up to this point is to be disposed of.

"D. The hands are to be washed with extreme care, far more thoroughly than they have ever been washed before, taking great pains that the hands do not touch the sides of the bowl, the spigots, or anything in the process. Great care should also be exercised when setting the soap down.

"E. A sheaf of 15 to 20 fresh Kleenex is then to be used to turn off the spigots and the Kleenex is then to be thrown away."

The really delicate part of the mission was yet to begin, removal of the hearing-aid cord, Step 2:

"A. The door to the cabinet is to be opened using a minimum of 15 Kleenexes. (Great care is to be exercised in opening and closing the doors. They are not to be slammed or swung hastily so as to raise any dust, and yet exceeding care is to be exercised against letting insects in.)

"B. Nothing inside the cabinet is to be touched—the inside of the doors, the top of the cabinet, the sides—no other objects inside the cabinet are to be touched in any way with the exception of the envelope to be removed."

The hearing-aid cord was carefully sealed inside an envelope, but not even the envelope could be touched:

"C. The envelope is to be removed using a minimum of 15 Kleenexes. If it is necessary to use both hands, then 15 Kleenexes are to be used for each hand. (It is to be understood that these 15 Kleenexes are to be sterile on both sides of each tissue with the exception of the very outermost edge of the tissue. The center of the tissue only should come into contact with the object being picked up.) If something is on top of the package to be removed, a sterile instrument is to be used to lift it off."

Hughes himself, of course, could never be touched. Not by naked or even gloved and scrubbed hands. On those rare occasions when contact was necessary, as with a wake-up ritual he devised, full insulation was required:

"Call Roy and have him come up to the house and awaken HRH at 10:15 AM sharp if HRH is not awake by that time. With 8 thicknesses of Kleenex he is to pinch HRH's toes until he awakens, increasing the pressure each time."

His Mormons, themselves reduced to sterile instruments, obediently followed every mad detail of their master's hygienic rituals, never questioning their missions even as they waded through the filth and debris of his bedroom, picking their way through the piles of newspapers and dirty Kleenex, treading carefully so as not to stir up the dust.

In terror of germs, Hughes lived in filth. Nothing that came from his own pure being, nothing in his own nimbus was "contamination." Indeed, he was fully as desperate to keep everything inside his bedroom from escaping as he was to keep everything outside from getting in.

He could not bear to part with anything that was his. Not his dust, not his junk, not his hair, not his fingernails, not his sweat, not his urine, not his feces. His hair and beard went uncut for years while highly paid barbers stood on standby; he stopped trimming his nails when he somehow "lost" his favorite clippers in the debris of his lair; soon he began to store his urine in capped jars kept first in his Bel Air garage and later in his Las Vegas bedroom; and he was so chronically constipated, so unable to let go of his bodily wastes, that he once spent twenty-six consecutive hours sitting on the toilet without results.

Nor could he let go of his wife. He kept Jean a safe distance away in bungalow 19, out of the combat zone, and barely saw her at all for three years. Still, he kept her under tight control, and safe from all contamination.

He tried to keep her from going anywhere, to trap her in her rooms, always finding reasons to delay her planned excursions. When he had to let her loose, his men always escorted her, following detailed written instructions in which Jean was often code-named "Major Bertrandez."

One such memo—"Handling Major Bertrandez for Theatre"— ordered: "If necessary to open the doors entering the threatre or closing the doors, do so with the feet, not the hands. If it is necessary or common procedure to enter the theatre with her to lower the seat for her, do so with kleenex."

Any sign that Jean was sick, that she had become contaminated, had to be reported immediately to Hughes, and she had to be prevented from seeing any doctors but his own, and never before he had been consulted:

"If the situation is critical enough, then it is permissible to let a doctor call her on the telephone. Under no circumstances should she be allowed to go see a doctor either at an office, a hospital or any place else, until HRH has talked to her first.

"The doctor will be cautioned to give her only such information that might be required for immediate relief of pain, or immediate medication, if required. This is to be done only if the immediate effect on the disease would be impaired by a delay. It is assumed that there will be some conversation over the telephone if all other efforts to delay EVERYTHING until HRH is available fail, but the doctor must be instructed, not told but instructed, to tell her nothing more than what medicine she should take to prevent further expansion of the ailment. The doctor should avoid giving her a diagnosis of any kind, or indicate the treatment required on an extended basis. Only the very immediate treatment should be offered."

Hughes himself would make the ultimate diagnosis and decide the course of treatment.

"HRH could use the fact that there is to be further treatment, or the fact that she doesn't know what the specific ailment is, as a basis of telling her something which might break her of the smoking habit, get her to eat more regularly, or any number of things that would be for her own good. This could not be accomplished if the doctor were to inform her completely.

"After the first contact between the doctor and Mrs. Hughes, you'll have to watch to see that she doesn't get the doctor back. If the doctor is at home, his wife should be asked to answer the telephone and say that the doctor is out.

"The doctor should report back the complete conversation between himself and Mrs. Hughes."

Even Jean's friends and associates had to be watched. Any that fell ill had to be placed in "isolation." When her former wardrobe mistress, Cissy Francombe, caught hepatitis, Hughes demanded a complete quarantine.

"Although the doctors are not sure whether this is the contagious type or not, I consider it to be highly contagious," explained the master physician. "Although we have had reason to put into effect a program of isolation before, I want this to be ten times as effective as any we have ever set up.

"With the present condition of my business affairs, if Jean, myself, or anyone else important in our organization were to acquire this disease, I just cannot even contemplate the seriousness of what the result may be.

"When Cary Grant got this disease in London some time back, he said that for six months he was totally and utterly unable to do anything other than just lie in bed and wish he was dead.

"I therefore want a system of isolation with respect to Cissy, the doctors attending her, nurses, or anyone in the past or future coming in contact with her, that is so effective and complete that anything we have done in the past will be nothing compared to it. I want this to go through the eighth or tenth generation, so to speak. Not only do I want this isolation to include personal contact, but also any items such as papers, clothing, flowers, TV sets, etc., that are transmitted to her, either direct or through the mails.

"Cut off every conceiveable channel of contact. Whether it be an object or thing, a letter or note, an invoice from a vendor, from the doctors at the hospital, no matter what it is it should not be permitted to come into our establishment. It will not be permitted to come into contact with any of our people, with any friends of our families, relatives or anyone else. See that absolutely no conceiveable avenue, channel or loophole is overlooked.

"I consider this the very most important item on the agenda, more important than our TWA crisis, our financial crisis, or any of our other problems."

Contaminated women had always been a special problem. Once, years earlier, Hughes had burned all his clothes, everything he owned—suits, shirts, ties, socks, overcoats, even all his towels and rugs—after he heard a rumor that an actress he once dated had a venereal disease.

Now he didn't have any clothes to burn, nor did he see any women. In fact, Hughes may well have gone into seclusion largely to escape his new wife. He began to withdraw almost as soon as they got married. Clearly he could not share his life, could not handle the intimacy. But it was more than that. Hughes actually seemed to be afraid of the woman he code-named "The Major." The troubles he had in a simultaneous affair with a teen-age mistress, more fetchingly code-named "The Party," suggests there was an even deeper reason.

All the while he courted Jean, Hughes was seeing his teen angel on the side. She was the last of the harem. Barely sixteen when he plucked her out of a local beauty contest, she remained on standby even after his marriage, stashed in a carefully decontaminated hideaway at Coldwater Canyon, under guard and under surveillance. Hughes brought her to his bungalows only once, to celebrate his fifty-third birthday on Christmas Eve 1958, his last extramarital fling.

It seems to have been less than a complete success. As months went by without another date, "The Party" cursed and browbeat Hughes unmercifully. The guards bugging her phone heard her tirades.

"You dirty old son of a bitch," she screamed. "You never come to see me. I'll bet you can't even get it up anymore, you impotent old slob!"

Impotent. The playboy hero of *The Carpetbaggers*, known for his string of starlets, may have been driven into seclusion by his fear of women, as desperate to escape his wife—and hide his impotence— as to escape the germs and the blacks and all his other nameless terrors. Soon he would flee her forever, move to Las Vegas alone, and spend the rest of his life surrounded by male nursemaids.

But he would never find sanctuary from "contamination."

In the past, Hughes himself had been the only victim of his fears. His ten-year battle against "contamination" had been waged within the confines of his blacked-out bedrooms. The fight had been to keep the outside world from getting in. A purely defensive struggle. Now he went on the offense. Now the same terrors that had driven him into seclusion also drove him to control the world outside.

He tried to decontaminate all Las Vegas, the fallen city he had come to purify. Its impure water quickly became an obsession.

"I maintain that you cannot build a resort of world-wide fame and lasting importance upon a basic foundation of pollution," he declared. "Nevada must not offer its tourists water from a polluted, actually stinking lake.

"I say the question goes beyond the matter of purity vs. impurity, on a basis of technical analysis. I say the real question is whether a sophisticated, thoroughly pampered tourist, a tourist who has been exposed to the careful treatment accorded him in the major, highly refined resorts of the world, I repeat the question is whether this tourist is going to feel comfortable in the confidence that the water which he is drinking, and in which he is bathing, is the pure mountain spring water pictured in the Coor's Beer advertisements, or whether, instead, he is going to have the uneasy, revolting feeling that the water he is forced to drink, the water used to make his drinks at the bar, and the water in which his food is cooked, that this water, in which he is also forced to bathe and wash his hands, that this water is, in truth, nothing more nor less than *sewage*, with the turds removed by a strainer so it can be pumped through a pipe.

"The name, quote Lake Mead Water unquote, means nothing more or less than *sewage!*"

Hughes was definitely one of those who had an "uneasy, revolting feeling." He never let up in his battle to scuttle the state's entire new eighty-million-dollar water system.

Indeed, all Las Vegas, all Nevada, finally all America fell victim to his endless runaway fears, as Hughes, from his penthouse, conducted search-and-destroy missions to protect himself from all imagined dangers. Among the prime targets were the state's thirty thousand blacks.

It was still blacks who instilled the most terror. They seemed the visible embodiment of all the invisible threats.

The Great White Hope trauma made that clear. Blacks were potent, mocking his impotence. Blacks were dark, brown, like the poison he could not release from his own bowels, like the sewage in the water. Blacks were not merely dirty. They were Giant Germs.

They had to be kept in "isolation."

Up in his penthouse, Hughes was seemingly safe from all outsiders, black or white. Yet even there he was constantly tormented by dark intruders. To make matters worse, they entered with the connivance of his own television station.

"Isn't there any safe way to get rid of this TV academic program on 'Black Heritage' which CBS is carrying every morning?" wrote Hughes, in obvious distress.

"As you know, this program was commenced without my permission.

"Since then I have been forced to squirm under the intense displeasure of watching this program every morning—I have to watch and listen every morning while the only academic program on KLAS pours out such propaganda as: 'Africa is the mother and the father of the world.' "

As with that other bane of his existence, "Sunrise Semester," Hughes apparently never considered the simple expedient of switching off his set. Actually, he had finally escaped the dreaded harbinger of dawn. "Sunrise Semester" was, at long last, off the air. It had been replaced in the 6:30 A.M. time slot by "Black Heritage." Squirming in displeasure, the billionaire fumed:

"Bob, if KLAS is to broadcast one single academic program and if this program is to be a study of history, why should not this be a program of U.S. history instead of a program of African history.

"If this is so, I cannot see why it should be necessary for a TV station to confine its academic programing to a policy of exclusive, sole negro representation."

Maheu sympathized, but warned that it might be dangerous to cancel the offensive show. "I, perhaps, am as vehement on this type of subtle propaganda as you are," he wrote in reply, "but I think we must be expedient in not buying unnecessary problems at this time. Sheriff [Ralph] Lamb and D.A. [George] Franklin have confided to me that we could potentially have a real 'hot summer' in Las Vegas this year. My humble recommendation, Howard, would be that we let this particular program run out its time, so that we do not give the black community any opportunity whatsoever to concentrate on us to any degree."

Hughes was not satisfied. He wanted no trouble, but he didn't want "Black Heritage" either. And he had a plan:

"Bob, I am wondering if a solution might lie in ceasing all academic programing for the summer months.

"After all, school is closed for the summer, and if the scholastic programing were abandoned, then maybe there would be less criticism for the abandonment of this particular program than if it were replaced by a white-oriented program."

While the two men continued, in a flurry of memos, to plot the demise of the TV show, Hughes received word of unexpected support: "Both the national and local NAACP has objected to the Black Heritage program. KLAS would like to cancel the show if they can get your approval."

That changed everything. Now Hughes was in no hurry to see the show go. It continued, in fact, until CBS pulled it off the air two months later.

The reprieve for "Black Heritage" did not apply, however, to other KLAS programs. Even the "Big News" was segregated. When racial tensions flared in local schools, the station went so far as to refuse its parent network film of the disorders for national coverage.

"It is the policy of KLAS to carry matters relating to the Afro problem which are favorable to Las Vegas and to play down that which is unfavorable," the station manager assured his unseen boss. "In this connection, there is a colored deaf mute who is one of the basketball stars at the University of Nevada. This boy is one of very high character and does not engage to any extent in the integration rabble rousing which is occurring. Therefore, his accomplishments are of nationwide interest to those who see the true reason for the integration problems and certainly would be beneficial to Las Vegas."

Hughes was unimpressed. Even this "credit-to-his-race" was unacceptable. "We do not want any programs involving negroes," came the reply from the penthouse. "If we have any other such programs, HRH wants to know of them."

Television was safe—for the moment at least—but Hughes was ever alert to new threats. Like Arthur Ashe.

The black tennis star had been invited to play in a tournament at the Desert Inn. Actually *asked* to come. And Maheu had secretly arranged it. It was the Davis Cup championship, a prize attraction, a real plum for Las Vegas. The night before the tournament began, however, Hughes discovered the plot and demanded that the match be canceled. He didn't want Ashe playing on his courts, fearing that he would lure "hordes of negroes" to his hideout.

Maheu tried to soothe him. "Howard, I am positive we have nothing to worry about. Tennis is not a game that appeals to his people and I am willing to wager that there will be less than a handful of them in the audience. The proportion will be considerably less than we have in our showrooms when some of them are performing here."

Ashe was accepted—reluctantly—but not Muhammad Ali. There was talk of staging a championship bout in Las Vegas. It was the Great White Hope all over again. Jack Johnson might have sneaked into town under cover of the Tony Awards telecast, but Hughes was not about to put up with his brash, draft-dodging reincarnation, Ali. As usual, he sent Maheu into the ring.

"Howard," Maheu wrote, "you do not have to spend any time trying to convince me how right you are in your feelings pertaining to Clay. If it is possible, perhaps I feel more deeply about these matters than you."

Maheu scored in the first round: "I moved on the Clay-Frazier fight and scuttled it to a fair-thee-well insofar as Las Vegas and Nevada are concerned. I personally believe it is incredible that there are those who even entertain the idea of having this no good bastard gain any amount of publicity at the expense of the State."

Hughes was not content simply to block the fight. He wanted Ali—then facing charges for refusing to fight in Vietnam—put in jail. "We shall do everything in our power," promised Maheu, "to assure that he ends up there."

The minstrel show was turning sour.

It would have been funny. Or merely pathetic. An addled old man sealed off from the world, desperately manning the barricades against Ashe and Ali, against propaganda in the morning and phantoms in the night.

But Hughes represented something very real and very ugly in America. Submerged fears. Hidden racism. Feelings no longer respectable to express but still pervasive. All across the country, ordinary people also cringed at shadows in the night. They too wanted blacks kept down or, at least, out of sight. George Wallace brought bigotry out of the closet, and they cheered him. Richard Nixon campaigned with code words like "law-and-order" and "crime in the streets," and they elected him.

And, all the while, America was burning.

It had started in Watts in 1965—the year before Hughes arrived in Las Vegas—and now it swept through city after city. Riots. Arson. Looting. Summer terror.

Then, at six P.M. on Thursday, April 4, 1968, Martin Luther King was assassinated. One moment he stood on the balcony of a Memphis motel, chatting with friends in the courtyard below. The next moment he was dead.

Black America took to the streets. White America watched the war on television.

And Howard Hughes saw all his fears come to life on the TV screen. It was the ultimate horror. Blacks were out of control. First in Washington, then in Baltimore, Detroit, Philadelphia, and Chicago, finally in more than one hundred cities grief turned to outrage and outrage to violence, a swelling firestorm of unprecedented fury that lasted a full week and claimed forty-six lives.

The images were overwhelming. Soldiers defending a nation from itself occupied charred ghettos, battling blacks on streets strewn with broken glass and stained with blood. Troops in full combat gear took up positions on the White House lawn. A machine-gun emplacement guarded the Capitol steps.

Alone in his penthouse, Hughes too rushed to reinforce the barricades. With not a mention of the martyred civil rights leader, with not a note of sorrow, with not a sober second thought, he poured out a diatribe of racist angst on his bedside legal pad:

"I have just finished watching CBS News on TV. The riots, looting, etc. in Washington, Chicago and other cities was terrible. I wonder how close we are to something like that here?"

Memories of Houston 1917 mixed with frontline footage of America 1968, bringing on nightmare visions of a Las Vegas torn by racial turmoil. It only stiffened his resistance to change.

"I know that is your responsibility and also your specialty," Hughes continued, taking some comfort in Maheu's FBI background, "but I also know there is tremendous pressure on the strip owners to adopt a more liberal attitude toward integration, open housing, and employment of more negroes.

"Now, Bob, I have never made my views known on this subject. And I certainly would not say these things in public. However, I can summarize my attitude about employing more negroes very simply— I think it is a wonderful idea for somebody else, somewhere else. I know this is not a very praise-worthy point of view, but I feel the negroes have already made enough progress to last the next 100 years, and there is such a thing as overdoing it.

"I just dont want to see you badgered into some concession, because once you do consent to some such concession, you can never cancel it and put things back the way they were.

"I know this is a hot potatoe," Hughes concluded, "and I am not asking you to form a new chapter of the K.K.K. I dont want to become known as a negroe-hater or anything like that. But I am not running for election and therefore we dont have to curry favor with the NAACP *either*."

Outside, far beyond the gaudy strip of gambling casinos and high-rise hotels, far removed from the make-believe world of glittering neon, fabulous showrooms, Olympic-sized swimming pools, hundred-dollar bills and fat cigars, there was another Las Vegas, housing the city's blacks. They had been kept in a ramshackle ghetto out on the edge of the desert—a grim American reality three miles distant from the great American dream—and that's where Hughes wanted them kept. In crumbling homes and segregated schools, with no jobs for one out of five adults, and nothing at all for the kids, the nearest recreation facilities being ten miles away.

By the late sixties it no longer seemed possible to ignore. Not even in Las Vegas. Federal courts ordered the classrooms integrated and bills were introduced in the state legislature to end discrimination in housing as well.

Hughes was aghast.

"Do you have any report from the people in Carson City re the civil rights or fair housing legislation?" he demanded. "I just heard one TV news report that stated the latest fair housing bill is the very most extreme anywhere in the U.S. That sounds pretty frightening."

His lobbyists in the state capital went to work, and two weeks later Maheu had good news: "Howard, Tom Bell was successful in knocking out the Fair Housing Bill in its entirety." But even Bell, law partner of the governor's brother and the billionaire's paymaster to Nevada lawmakers, could not so easily end the threat.

Within another two weeks, a new—albeit, far weaker—housing bill was introduced, this one ostensibly backed by Governor Laxalt himself. Hughes was both shocked and enraged:

"Bob, what is this about Laxalt's open housing bill? I thought he was a friend and I thought Bell had told him how I feel about that issue."

How could the governor so callously ignore the wishes of the state's leading citizen? Had Hughes not been generous? And just to take care of thirty thousand blacks, who probably never contributed a dime. Hughes fired off a second memo to Maheu, this time enclosing evidence of the governor's perfidy:

"Please read *all*—every word—of this article. This worries me. If Laxalt goes this far in his leaning toward benefits favoring the colored race, it may influence other legislation.

"What worries me most is that I am just hovering on the brink of further huge investments in Nevada, and Laxalt's friendship is an important part of this decision.

"If Laxalt knows I dont want this legislation, and he goes ahead and pushes it anyway, that is peculiar friendship.

"It says in this article that the bill would not pass except for Laxalt's urging.

"Please call him or ask Bell to contact him at once. It may be impossible to reach him in the AM and tomorrow may be too late. . . . I would like to go ahead with all my Nevada plans, but this worries me a great deal. . . ."

Just in case the governor was not moved by the promise of new investments, or the implied threat of not making them, Hughes now offered the real bait to bring the normally obliging statesman back to his senses:

"You may send Laxalt through Bell absolutely unlimited assurances of unlimited financial support. *He does not need the colored vote* and I want him to know this *loud* and *clear!*"

Apparently the message got through. Loud and clear. Maheu reported the victory to his boss later that day, April 16, 1969:

"Tom Bell just called to inform they have just definitely killed the open housing bill. He wanted you to know that Laxalt was very *'quietly'* helpful in accomplishing this. In other words Howard, he delivered to Tom the critical vote which enabled Bell to kill it in committee."

Very quietly indeed. The local press reported a far different story: "Governor Paul Laxalt's fair-housing bill was killed in the Senate Finance Committee Wednesday by a 4–3 vote. It was one of the first major defeats of Laxalt in the '69 legislature."

In the bitter debate that preceded the committee vote, one of the bill's supporters warned that Nevada was courting another Watts. State Senator James Slattery, one of the lawmakers who came to Hughes's rescue (and who had received $2,500 from the billionaire), responded: "If they'd had the guts to go in with machine guns and kill two or three hundred in Watts, you wouldn't have had it. They were breaking the law."

Apparently, Hughes himself also failed to heed the warning. A few months later he was once again trying to hold back the waves. This time by standing in the schoolhouse door.

"I just heard the ch 8 program re integration, and this is frightening," wrote the recluse.

"I understand the necessity of compliance (to the extent absolutely necessary) with the Supreme Court's decision, at least until such time as it may be modified.

"But I certainly am not very happy about this 800 thousand dollar loan the schools are seeking to make and the rest of the overboard more than necessary compliance with this far-out integration plan.

"Please tell me what can be done about it."

In fact, nothing could be done that the like-minded city fathers

Bob —

4-16-69

Please read all — every word —
of this article. This worries me.
If Laxalt goes this far in his
leaning toward benefits
favoring the colored race, it
may influence other legislation.

What worries me most is
that I am just hovering on
the brink of further huge
investments in Nevada, and
Laxalt's friendship is an important part of this decision.

If Laxalt knows I don't
want this legislation, and he
goes ahead and pushes it anyway, that is peculiar friendship.

It says in this article
that the bill would not pass
except for Laxalt's urging.

Please call him or ask
Bell to contact him at
once. It may be impossible
to reach him in the AM
and tomorrow may be too
late. Bob, I feel so much
better about the AEC situation
in view of the progress you
have made. I would like to
go ahead with all my Nevada
plans, but this worries me

a great deal. Please contact
him right away, and while
you have him please try to
get his support on the Racing
bill.

You may send Foxalt
through Bell absolutely unlimited assurances of un-
limited financial support.
He does not need the colored
vote and I want him to
know this loud and clear!

From: Maheu

Re: Open Housing

                          16 April 1969, 9:50 am

     Tom Bell just called to inform they have just definitely
killed the open housing bill. He wanted you to know that
Laxalt was very "quietly" helpful in accomplishing this. In
other words Howard, he delivered to Tom the critical vote
which enabled Bell to kill it in committee.

hadn't already done. A federal judge, explained Maheu, had ordered that $7 million be spent to integrate the schools. The local school district was holding the line at the $800,000 figure that Hughes found so outrageous. It was, Maheu assured his boss, "minimum compliance."

Two months later, the inevitable finally happened in Las Vegas.

It had been almost a year and a half since Hughes had worried in the aftermath of King's assassination, "I wonder how close we are to something like that here?"

Despite the horrible conditions, despite the callous indifference, Las Vegas had escaped the riots that raged through most of urban America.

But on Sunday night, October 5, 1969, the ghetto at the edge of the desert exploded. The rampage of looting and arson continued for three days. Two hundred blacks were arrested. Two men died.

The violence never threatened the Strip. In fact, it never went beyond the boundaries of the distant slum. But it left Hughes shaken.

6 Armageddon

It was already well into the evening of a very bad day when Howard Hughes finally reached for his afternoon newspaper, carefully extracting the middle copy from a pile of three, thus avoiding contamination from the two exposed editions.

Peering through his "peepstone," a battery-powered magnifying glass that lit up the page, Hughes prepared to scrutinize the paper, his deep-sunk eyes narrowed to catch every threatening nuance hidden in the small print.

The headline hit him without warning: "HISTORY'S MIGHTIEST A-BLAST NEAR VEGAS." It leaped into focus through his lens, the screaming mass of thirty-six-point type absurdly enlarged, and struck the stunned recluse with full megaton force.

"This is the last straw," he scribbled in a rush of fear and anger. "I just this minute read that they are going to shoot off the largest nuclear explosion ever detonated in the U.S. And right here at the Vegas Test Site.

"I want you to call the Gov. at once and the Senators and Congressman," Hughes ordered Maheu. "If they do not cancel this one extra large explosion, I am going direct to the President in a personal appeal and demand that the entire test program be moved. . . ."

It was war.

A massive hydrogen bomb with an explosive force greater than 1.2 million tons of TNT had been buried deep beneath the Nevada desert, just one hundred miles from Howard Hughes's bedroom. One hundred times more powerful than the atom bomb dropped on Hiroshima, big enough to shake four states, and practically right next door.

It was Tuesday, April 16, 1968. The bomb was set to be detonated in ten days. This was the moment Hughes had been dreading for more than a year, ever since the Atomic Energy Commission, with a malevolent sense of timing, launched a new series of major underground weapons tests just one month after he arrived in Las Vegas. The first, a megaton blast shortly before Christmas 1966, rattled the Desert Inn and left Hughes shaken. Since then, however, only low-yield devices had been fired, and the mollified recluse thought he had the AEC's promise that no future ground-shaking explosions would be conducted at the nearby Nevada Test Site.

Now, suddenly, this sneak attack.

In horrified disbelief, Hughes picked up his newspaper and reread the government's bland announcement: "Persons up to about 250 miles from the detonation may feel a slight earth tremor immediately following the explosion, *particularly if they are on upper stories of high buildings or other tall structures.*"

A message of doom clearly directed right at the penthouse. Ten days to zero and counting.

In his own kingdom, Howard Hughes was no longer the most powerful invisible force. The bomb was. Atomic fission—the ultimate in out-of-control power—was the ultimate terror to Hughes, who above all needed to be in absolute control.

He was determined, at all costs, to stop what he called "the bombing." It became his greatest obsession. He would carry his battle through every level of government and finally into the White House, offering bribes to presidents and presidential candidates, trying, in fact, to buy the government of the United States, all in a desperate effort to stave off nuclear devastation.

Hughes had finally found a menace worthy of his madness. He had spent years casting about for a danger to justify his dread, drifting from germs to blacks to impure water, and now his paranoia had become so finely tuned that it focused on the central horror of our age. A full decade ahead of the rest of the nation, he recognized the infinite threat of nuclear power, and seeing it alone was, of course, in mortal terror.

The bomb was not hidden to Hughes. Indeed, the nuclear tests were the only happenings in the world outside that he could actually feel, the only external force from which he could not hide. His ninth-floor aerie vibrated from the explosions, the entire building swayed, the chandelier in his attendants' office swung like a pendulum, the windowpanes in his own blacked-out room rattled behind the blinds, and the shock waves left him trembling in his suddenly unstable bed. All else beyond the penthouse was merely a TV show. This actually reached directly into his seclusion.

"When we came here, you will remember, it was a close decision between this area and one other," Hughes wrote, reminding Maheu that he had almost instead gone to the Bahamas. "I finally chose this one, oddly enough, to avoid the hurricanes. Well I promise you I did not come here to avoid hurricanes only to be molested by some stupid ass-holes making like earthquakes."

More threatening still was the unfelt, unseen, silent enemy—atomic radiation. Yet another form of contamination, it was all the more terrifying because, like the long-dreaded bacteria, invisible. There was no way to ward off the deadly rays, no possible "insulation." Kleenex and paper towels could protect him from germs. Isolation, armed guards, and loyal Mormons could protect him from people. But nothing could protect him from the radiation.

That same radiation, he was certain, was seeping through the underground strata, poisoning the earth beneath Las Vegas and polluting the water whose purity so obsessed him.

"The whole operation just makes me want to vomit," wrote Hughes, sickened by the thought. "I cannot for the life of me understand Laxalt permitting these bastards to dessicrate and lay forever waste, poisoned, and contaminated all of those miles and miles of beautiful virgin Nevada soil.

"I am not saying the bomb is unsafe in terms of leaving a crack in the middle of Fremont Street into which somebody might fall. I have said from the start that the real damage from these explosions was in the contamination of underground substances and the pollution of the very bowels of the earth on which we live."

In fact, Hughes was so afraid of the insidious atomic rays that he worried about aides he never saw or even spoke to becoming likewise contaminated.

"Please issue instructions to all of our people *not to go anywhere near that test site*," he ordered. "And, to the extent possible, to stay away from the AEC meetings and briefings."

A feared threat and a hated rival, the bomb was also bad for business. Hughes was certain it imperiled his entire two-hundred-million-dollar investment in Las Vegas.

"Who can possibly contest the fact that thousands upon thousands of tourists will be lost to Nevada if the testing continues and if Nevada becomes identified with the ghastly spectre of nuclear devastation?" he demanded.

"I have insisted from the start that any damage would be in the form of destruction to the attraction of this community as a peaceful paradise-like resort, at which people could get away from, and not be reminded of the gruesome, ever-present, over hanging threat of the ghastly image of the scarred and mutilated bodies which remained after the nuclear bombing of Hiroshima.

"As I say, the future image of this area should, hopefully, represent a vacation resort of the very ultimate quality—not a military experimental testing ground for exterminating devices."

While Hughes spoke of scaring off tourists, it was the billionaire himself who saw Las Vegas as Hiroshima. Although he often expressed his fears in terms of profit and loss, the lurid language of his memos and the shakiness of his scrawl betrayed a very real, very personal terror.

The fears were, in one sense, more than reasonable. Others may have learned to live with the bomb, or at least to ignore it after a 1963 treaty banned atmospheric explosions, the mushroom clouds disappeared, and the tests went underground. But Hughes, who well understood the potency of hidden power, was not beguiled.

"Nuclear explosions in the atmosphere were once considered entirely safe, and those who opposed them were laughed at," he argued.

"Now, nobody in the free world would consider exploding a nuclear bomb in the air or in the sea.

"Who is to say that, in the future, contaminating the earth upon which we live may not be frowned upon just as much."

Eventually a presidential panel would agree that the underground blasts posed grave risks. And ten years later, the forced release of suppressed documents would reveal an appalling truth: for a quarter-century the government had known its test program would condemn thousands of American citizens to disease and even slow death.

Ahead of his time, even prophetic in recognizing the dangers of nuclear experimentation, Hughes, however, was not opposed to nuclear weapons, nor was he really opposed to nuclear tests. He was opposed only to testing those weapons in his own neighborhood.

Indeed, the bomb was merely a focus for all his diffused fears. Nightmare visions of nuclear annihilation exploded in his mind. Time and time again Hughes would return to the "gaunt, ghastly horrors and tragedies of nuclear warfare with all its ghastly residue of burned,

I have ~~been~~ insisted
from the start that
any damage would
~~be to~~ be in the
form of destruction
to the ~~~~~~~~~~
attraction of this
community as a
peaceful paradise - like
resort, at which people
could get away from,
and not be reminded
of the gruesome, ever -
present, over hanging
threat of the ghastly
image of the scarred
and mutilated bodies

which remained after the nuclear bombing of ~~the~~ Hiroshima.

As I say, the future image of this area should, hopefully, represent a vacation resort of the very ultimate quality — not a military experimental testing ground for exterminating devices.

There are many people in the world who are violently opposed to everything ~~that~~ even remotely associated with war. I think this fact has been made more emphatically evident

recently, than ever before,
thru the many dem-
onstrations.

I am not one of
these people who feels
so strongly that this
~~realities~~ nation should
abandon its military
organizations and weapons
in this hostile world.

However, a large
segment of the world's
population does feel that
way, and the future
development of Las Vegas,
if it is to be fully
realized, must ~~be~~ be
designed to appeal to
everybody — not just the
hawks.

maimed, mutilated and scarred human flesh." Life in the penthouse became a never-ending scene from *On the Beach*.

And under that strain, Howard Hughes became a mad prophet of doom. He already looked the part, and had he been a man of equal madness, lesser means, and greater moral fervor, he might have taken to the streets, become a sidewalk savior, waving a placard, carrying to the masses his message of impending devastation.

Instead, he remained in hiding and scrawled his apocalyptic visions on his bedside legal pads.

"If the gigantic nuclear explosion is detonated," he warned, "then in the fraction of a second following the pressing of that fateful button, thousands and thousands, and hundreds of thousands of cubic yards of good potentially fertile Nevada soil and underlying water and minerals and other substances are forever poisoned beyond the most ghastly nightmare. A gigantic abyss too horrible to imagine filled with poisonous gases and debris will have been created just beneath the surface in terrain that may one day be the site of a city like Las Vegas.

"I say Nevada is no longer so desperate for mere existence that it has to accept and swallow with a smile poisonous, contaminated radio-active waste material more horrible than human excrement."

More horrible than human excrement. For the anally-fixated, chronically constipated billionaire, this was the ultimate imprecation.

Even before the impending test was announced, Hughes had had a premonition of doom. A month earlier, five thousand sheep had been killed in neighboring Utah when an Army biological-warfare experiment had gone awry. The frightened recluse instantly identified with the martyred flock. He took their slaughter as an omen, a clear sign that he too was in danger.

"I am sure that some expert somewhere must have pronounced as safe the bomb test in Utah," he reflected, "but that doesn't help the sheep lying there on the prairie."

Now, with the Sheep Omen revealed as a true prophecy, the fear-crazed seer, certain of his clairvoyance, conjured up images of future generations vindicating his judgment:

"Some day," he wrote, "guides will take tourists from here to Reno, and when they pass [the test site], the guide will say: 'And on your right is the ghastly grave-yard of atomic poison and polution, that is so dreadful no tourists are allowed to go near it for fear some child may wander away from its parents and step within the contaminated area.'

"Rome proudly displays its battlefields of historic fame, but this misserable blemish on God's creation, the earth, is such a tragedy nobody points to it or boasts about it, it means only one thing: 'Shame! ' "

Lost for a moment in his vision, Hughes suddenly remembered the impending blast only ten days distant and abruptly shifted his focus.

"Well," he concluded, once again the cold-eyed realist, "none of this is getting us any closer to stopping this shameful program. Now, how do we go about it?

"We must find a way to close them down."

From his penthouse command post, the naked general now prepared for Armageddon.

Firing off memo after memo to his field marshal Maheu, Hughes ordered him "to bring to bear on the AEC the very strongest, all-out concerted effort you can organize, in a final fight to the very last ditch.

"I want you to burn up all of your blue chip stamps, all the favors you have coming, and every other last little bit of pressure you can bring together in one intense, extreme, final drive," he continued.

"Bob, I want you to go all the way on this and spare no expense," Hughes stressed. "You know what we want to accomplish, and you know our resources are unlimited."

Meanwhile, one hundred miles to the north, on a barren desert flat called Pahute Mesa, enemy forces lowered a six-foot red-tipped cylinder into a 3,800-foot-deep shaft, unaware that the operation they code-named "Boxcar" was about to run into stiff opposition.

Nevada, with its vast stretches of arid terrain, had long been the nation's nuclear proving grounds. For almost two decades, the AEC had detonated its bombs on the 1,350-square-mile test site without significant protest.

But now the battle lines were drawn. It was Howard Hughes versus the United States. The richest man in America, the sole owner of one of the country's leading defense contractors, with almost a billion dollars a year in top-secret military work, ready to take on the Atomic Energy Commission, the Department of Defense, and, if necessary, the White House and the rest of the federal government in an all-out battle over the bomb.

Then, on the eve of war, came an unexpected breakthrough. Just one day after the "Boxcar" blast was announced, Maheu reported that peace was at hand. A cease-fire, at least a temporary truce, seemed imminent.

"We have gotten word to the Vice President and he will attempt to accomplish a 90 day delay," Maheu told his boss. Hubert Humphrey, soon to announce his candidacy for president and, as usual, short of funds, was only too happy to be of service. Moreover, Governor Laxalt was prepared to join Humphrey in calling for the moratorium.

"I have just completed an hour's conference here with the Governor," the field marshal explained. "He agrees with us 100%—particularly since you have made it clear that all the study and research could still continue in Nevada—with the exception of the blasts per se."

The peace terms were generous. All that Hughes would have to do was fund an independent team of scientists to determine the safety of the planned test during the cooling-off period.

"Bob, I leave this whole campaign in your hands," replied Hughes, already looking ahead to total victory. "I am sure you should *personally* go to the White House after we have obtained the 90-day delay and endeavor to sell the President on a permanent policy.

"I am sure H.H.H.," he continued, with a chummy reference to the cooperative vice-president, "would be glad to go with you and set up the appointment. You have gotten a lot of publicity as my *sole* representative in important matters and I definitely feel you would be more willingly accepted at the White House than anyone else I know of."

Yet even as he plotted an Oval Office parley, Hughes was shaken anew by visions of doom.

"The late TV news was startling," reported the recluse in a post-midnight memo that roused his would-be White House emissary. "They announced that while prior explosions may have been noticeable in the top floors of tall buildings, this explosion will be far more powerful (more powerful in fact than any prior explosion in the United States).

"They went on to say that this explosion will be accompanied by violent and prolonged and heavy longitudinal movement of the ground at the street level, that it may result in earth cracks and particularly in fractures and cracks in the pavement of city streets and highways.

"The news announcer went on to say that there was no doubt

whatsoever but that this explosion will far exceed anything ever set off around here.

"Bob, I think this is just *disgraceful*! Please let me hear from you if you are not too sleepy."

The awakened Maheu, accustomed to his commander's night fears and less awed by pronouncements from the video oracle, remained unruffled.

"We are quite confident that we will be successful in obtaining a 90 day delay," he reassured his boss, pledging eternal vigilance. "This whole situation is so damned important that I beg of you not to hesitate to call upon me further this morning. We can rest at a later date. As a matter of fact, Howard, please, and I sincerely mean it, *never* consider me as a guy who wants to sack out when there is business to be conducted. Fortunately the good Lord has blessed me with an unusual constitution."

Ready to stand watch in the night, Maheu was also busy by day, rounding up political allies while he assigned the resourceful John Meier to line up scientific support.

Meier, an inspired con artist who claimed two Ph.D.s but never actually got past high school, proved as adept at recruiting antibomb scientists as he was at swindling Hughes out of millions in bogus mining claims.

Nobel Prize laureate Linus Pauling soon joined the "Boxcar" protest, as did longtime nuclear foe Barry Commoner, whom Meier flew to Las Vegas to man the barricades from the comfort of a complimentary suite at a Hughes-owned hotel.

"We're making a lot of progress," Maheu reported to the penthouse. "Today the Vice-President requested data which is already on its way to his office. We have the State of Utah up in arms and their effects will be felt in Washington starting tomorrow. We are beginning to receive the data (wires from scientists) which Governor Laxalt requested. He now wants Governor Reagan to join in our efforts."

Hubert Humphrey, Ronald Reagan, Paul Laxalt. Linus Pauling and Barry Commoner. Progress indeed.

The sense of triumph, however, was short-lived.

Maheu, having gathered the support of thirty "prominent scientists," publicly announced his peace plan the next week. It drew an immediate and complete rebuff from the AEC.

"Boxcar," the government agency declared, was a "weapons-related experiment, designed to improve the nation's nuclear armament capacity"—specifically, to develop a warhead for the then-envisioned antiballistic missile system. A moratorium was out of the question.

"Any delay of the scheduled test," the AEC maintained, "would have an adverse effect on national defense."

Hughes was enraged. Not only had the peace been broken but his patriotism had been called into question.

"Where do they come off waving the American flag in my face and implying that I am some kind of bumbling idiot who, in his ignorance, might sabotage a one billion dollar defense installation?" he demanded.

"Me, who has done more for defense than the N.T.S. [Nevada Test Site] ever dreamed of. After all, only two nuclear weapons have ever been used, and the N.T.S. did not exist at that time. My equipment has been used extensively in World War #2 and in Korea and in Vietnam."

Moreover, Hughes was convinced that the AEC had lied. As an arsenal of democracy, he was not only privy to classified information but had actually helped develop the ABM.

"I am right on top of the entire anti-missile program for this country," he explained. "We have actively bid on these projects since the first one about seven years ago. Actually, we had a large part of the first system that proved at all successful."

The claim of national defense was, to his mind, entirely without foundation.

"Of course, we must be careful not to place ourselves in the position of disclosing military secrets," cautioned the billionaire. "But I can tell you, based on actual Defense Dept. technical information legally in my hands, that this last AEC statement is pure 99 proof unadulterated shit.

"If you want to know the plain blunt truth, it is that these explosions are not needed for anything," Hughes continued, now certain of his foe's malevolence. "The AEC is only making an issue out of this because, if they do not, and if they stop blasting, then it will be demonstrated for all to see that all of this destruction and damage and all of these violations of ordinary decent conduct were totally without purpose.

"You take it from me that these tests have no valid military purpose! This is not conjecture or supposition, this is *fact*! *I can even prove it!*"

At commission headquarters in Washington, AEC officials were equally suspicious about, but considerably less certain of the hidden Hughes motives. Rumors that he was plotting to block the "Boxcar" test had been filtering in for days, including one report that the mysterious recluse had readied "a fleet of aircraft to follow the radioactive cloud" if the bomb was detonated.

Already the agency had received an unprecedented rash of letters and telegrams inspired by the Hughes protest, and officials worried about moves he might make in the political arena. In a constant flow of confidential cables between Las Vegas and Washington, they traded tidbits of fact and speculative theories concerning their strange adversary.

One "eyes-only" report claimed that his agents had offered bribes to several scientists in return for antibomb statements, another lamented that "Hughes's fears concerning contamination and ground shock remain unpredictable," while a third suggested that Hughes might be "kept in an agitated state by people connected with the Hughes Biomedical Foundation in Florida, with the hope that Hughes would abandon his Las Vegas interests and consider moving to Miami."

All the while, the countdown at Pahute Mesa continued, as test-site workers began to cork the bomb shaft in final preparation for the big blast.

And now, after a week of illusory peace, with only four days left until the scheduled detonation, the battle of the bomb was finally joined in earnest.

Badly shaken by the rejection of his moratorium, Hughes resumed direct command of the campaign, forsaking sleep for the duration, ready to make any alliance, try any strategy, pay any price in his desperate bid to stave off nuclear attack.

His first instinct was to buy his way out of trouble. Despite his anger at the AEC, he would offer the agency a straightforward business deal.

If he couldn't get the test delayed for free, he would gladly pay for a postponement: "I am willing to supply any funds required for additional overtime or other expenses involved."

Would the delay set back the ABM project? Hughes would also finance a rush job "to achieve a completion of any weapons program based upon this test at the original target date for completion."

Finally, he had a true inspiration. He would simply cover whatever it might cost to move the bomb test elsewhere. Preferably to a new site then being built in Alaska.

"If cost is disturbing the AEC," wrote Hughes, "I feel so intensely about this thing, I will even pay the cost of moving this test to one of the other sites, *out of my own pocket*.

"I dont even know what the cost would be, and I would be at the complete mercy of the AEC, who would probably charge in everything under the sun, including the last three year's payroll. But I will still pay it to resolve this problem, which, if it is not solved, is going to change the entire course of the remainder of my life.

"They have plenty of time to set up the test in Alaska."

Yes, Alaska was the perfect place to banish the bomb. Moving expenses be damned. Indeed, Hughes had long been pushing the frozen wastes of the far north as an alternative test site, and he had gained some powerful allies.

Two months earlier he had personally called Governor Laxalt to propose the deportation. It was only their second phone conversation, and it left Laxalt shaken. Hughes was in a state of near-hysteria. He had just heard that the AEC was drilling an emplacement hole—the first early warning of an impending blast—and he wanted it stopped. Immediately. Hughes had gone on at some length about the hidden dangers of nuclear tests, about the contamination of earth, air, and water—especially the water—and about the invisible rays, telling the governor in great detail all about the rays.

Laxalt had seen the light. No sooner had he got off the phone with Hughes than he called the top man at the test site. Reached him at home with an urgent question.

"Why can't you move all your testing to Alaska?" demanded the governor, ready to drive his state's biggest employer out of Nevada, just to please one man.

Laxalt wasn't the only statesman suddenly seized by Klondike fever. Soon a United States senator would join him. That really caught the AEC by surprise. It was Mike Gravel, the senator from Alaska.

Flown to Las Vegas on a private Hughes jet, put up in style at a Hughes hotel, promised Hughes money for his next campaign, Gravel dropped in on the Nevada bomb range to suggest that the nation's entire nuclear test program be shipped north to his own state, then appeared on Hughes's TV station to make his surprise invitation public.

And still the AEC balked.

Hughes had done everything but provide the dog sleds, but the ungrateful bombers rejected out-of-hand his generous offer of an all-expense-paid trip to Alaska.

Rebuffed, the recluse issued an ultimatum.

Either the United States would negotiate a reasonable settlement with the Hughes empire or Hughes would force an end to the country's entire nuclear testing program.

"The way this fight lines up," he calculated, "the AEC will prevail and shoot 'Boxcar,' then given time, we will find a way to scuttle, but *completely*, their whole god-damned program.

"This is not what I want and not what they want. That is why I say they will deal.

"If they try to ride roughshod over me and go ahead with this explosion," he warned, "I will have absolutely nothing to discuss with them. They could not even get an appointment to get in the office, all the horses and tractors in Nevada could not get them through the door."

But Hughes was confident that the government, faced with his ultimatum, would capitulate. It was just a matter of arranging a face-saving compromise, one that would allow the test-site personnel to avoid a grim and ignominious exile.

"I am personally positive that the AEC by now is seeking only a graceful exit without getting their clothes torn off or worse," he explained. "They figure they will wind up on some god-forsaken Pacific island, and after becoming used to Las Vegas living, they are not about to swap it for some desert island."

Hughes, however, was not vindictive. He did not wish to impose a Carthaginian peace. Quite the opposite.

"Somebody should start negotiating with the AEC," he wrote, spelling out his strategy. "Just like buying a hotel. I want somebody to wheel and deal with the AEC and offer them a deal whereby they can continue to enjoy the pleasures of living in Las Vegas and more than ever offer them a graceful way they can give us the 90 day extension without injuring their position, without admitting defeat, without admitting by inference that the bomb they want to detonate would have endangered everyone in the community, and without embarassing themselves."

Should the peace talks fail, however, Hughes threatened to lead "a real lifetime crusade to stop all bomb explosions large or small anywhere in the U.S. or its possessions or mandates."

He was even willing to join the "peaceniks."

"If the AEC does not grant the extension and goes ahead with this blast," he declared, "I definitely will be forced to line up with the total anti-bomb faction throughout the U.S. This group has only been waiting for a strong leader and I am ready to dedicate the rest of my life and every cent I possess in a complete no quarter fight to outlaw all nuclear testing of every kind and everywhere.

"I prefer that we not be classified as Peaceniks, that is why I am reluctant to go the anti-war, anti-bomb route in the conventional sense.

"However, if that is the only way we can gather support for our cause, I will go to bed with the Devil himself."

Hughes had, indeed, already picked up some strange bedfellows. The Women's International League for Peace and Freedom joined the campaign and, in an unprecedented alliance of labor and capital, so did the maverick liberal United Auto Workers union chief Walter Reuther.

Reuther's enlistment inspired Hughes to open yet another front, quite literally to strike the enemy in its own camp.

"I understand the union that is striking the Bell Telephone System (200,000 men out) has jurisdiction over the Test Site," he wrote. "Maybe Reuther can persuade the head of the Communication Workers to strike that test site operation and I am informed all our troubles will be over. The phone operation, unhampered by a strike, is *absolutely necessary*."

Yet even as he conspired to cut the enemy's communication lines, his own campaign began to run into trouble. The AEC's national-defense claim had hurt Hughes with his more traditional allies, and only days before the scheduled blast vital political support disappeared.

First Nevada's two United States senators, Howard Cannon and Alan Bible, deserted. Finally, even Governor Laxalt announced his neutrality.

Nothing enraged Hughes quite so much as politicians who refused to stay bought. "I want you to meet with Laxalt, Bible and Cannon," he instructed Maheu. "They are going to have to make a difficult choice. They are going to have to support our stand in Washington or we will be forced to find someone else to represent us. And that is final.

"I want you to bear down on them immediately demanding that they take a position without another moments delay.

"Bob, when the time comes, and they begin crying on your

shoulder for support, and you come to me, and I say OK, as I have in the past, then once more, it will be the same story all over again: Unlimited support, and not one God Damned thing in return for it!''

It was an outrage. Still, perhaps they could be brought around. For the two wayward senators, the usual inducement might do: "Bob, cant you make a promise of support to Cannon and Bible—I mean *real* support beyond anything to date, and thereby obtain their absolutely undiluted sponsorship?''

As for the normally obliging Laxalt, "if we can truly convince the Governor that his future destiny lies with me," wrote Hughes, "then I am positive that, with a little coaching from me, he will have no difficulty in accomplishing our AEC objective.''

In fact, Hughes had already worked out a bold scheme for the governor. A plot to have Laxalt seize control of all federal land in Nevada, of course including the nuclear test site.

"Do you realize how much of this state is so-called 'owned' by the Fed. Gov.?" wrote Hughes. "Well, I think it requires only the slightest little effort by Laxalt to have all or nearly all of that land returned to the State.

"If we could persuade Laxalt to make such a request, it would not have to be linked by Laxalt to the bomb testing. We could get somebody else to focus attention on the Test Site, if we could only persuade Laxalt to ask the return of all land taken from the state by the Federal Gov.

"Now, Bob, lets face it, Laxalt is not going to do even this meager act of assistance unless we motivate him. I urge that, since he is not running for office this year, we ask him to designate a candidate he would like us to support in a big way—Nixon, or Senate or Congressional candidates.''

Obviously, however, Hughes could not wait around for Laxalt to perform that meager act, nor could he any longer depend on the other local politicians.

He would have to take his fight directly to the people.

"Anything the AEC can do in brain-washing, we can do better," he declared, plotting his public-opinion campaign. "The advantage always favors the one who is trying to create fear, over the one who is trying to erase it.

"Bob," he went on, "it is essential that we cast fears in the public's mind—real fears—as to water pollution, earthquakes, damage to the tourist trade.

"We must draw the public's attention to the plight of the sheep in Utah to destroy the simple all-out faith that people seem to have in any info released by the government.

"I dont give a damn how much it costs or what extremes must be resorted to."

Should the blast be detonated, all was lost. Having survived the holocaust, the populace would assume a stance of false bravado, ignorant of the real, hidden peril, ready to accept continued bombing without question. The whole awful scenario was all too clear:

"People love to be near danger and tell their friends about it, saying, 'Oh, it was nothing, really.'

"I can picture the local residents writing to friends in other cities, and saying: 'Well, we had another Nuclear test today, we are all beginning to get used to them now, so that we just take them in stride.'

"And Bob, when that attitude prevails, I assure you more and more people will be swung over to the N.T.S. supporters. Those people will lose confidence in us because we were unable to stop the blast. They will reason that it must be safe or the U.S. Government never would have allowed it."

There was only one answer. To stampede public opinion now and block the impending test. No approach was off limits, no conceivable ally was to be ignored.

"Bob, I see this as a proposition where all the peace seekers, beatniks, etc. could be carefully persuaded by a skillful publicity campaign, that this explosion would benefit only big business—the big corporations, the Establishment," wrote Hughes, willing now to denounce capitalism and consort with welfare mothers to end the bombing.

"The protestors are saying: 'If you have money enough to send men to the moon, how about taking care of the poor on earth.'

"Well, this same logic can be used, I believe, to generate a protest against the testing of nuclear weapons here in Nevada.

"In other words, all your efforts have been channeled toward the hazards of bomb testing in terms of earthquakes, pollution, etc.," he concluded. "But, maybe, without lessening in any slightest way your efforts in this direction, you can generate added protest against the nuclear tests here, on the basis that the expenditure of funds should be directed instead toward domestic anti-poverty causes."

Of course, no such high-minded appeal would reach the jaded

citizens of Las Vegas. For them, an entirely different approach was necessary.

"I think it will take a campaign that hits at the pocket book to carry any weight," lamented Hughes. "In this short-sighted community, where everybody lives for today, people are not very interested in morallity. They have been sold the bomb program on the basis that it provides jobs. I think that only by suggesting that the bomb is taking jobs away from Las Vegas will we make any headway."

That was it: he would announce that the bomb threat had caused him to abandon the "New Sands"—a one-hundred-and-fifty-million-dollar futuristic hotel complex he had long ago promised but never actually intended to build.

To this scheme, Maheu added his own inspiration. Perhaps they could convince archrival Kirk Kerkorian to join the antibomb campaign by halting construction of his International Hotel. It was a classic three-cushion billiard shot. Hughes had originally announced the "New Sands" only as a ploy to prevent Kerkorian from securing needed funds for the International.

"The more I think of your Kerkorian strategy, the more I like it!" the billionaire exclaimed. "I think the idea of telling him we postponed the 4000 room Sands because of the tests is terrific.

"Now, I think you should tell K I at no time announced to anyone that our reason for cancelling the hotel was related to the bomb tests," he continued. "However, now with the resumption of testing (and at an even greater level) I feel it is my firm duty to tell K the whole story."

Still, the primary appeal must be to gut fear. To arouse mass hysteria.

"We must make a real stink, and accuse the AEC of all kinds of perfidy and incompetence," wrote Hughes. "We must have some *headlines*. Let me see them right now, *please*!

"We must go further than you will want to go, Bob, but if we are to make headlines, we must make accusations—serious ones."

Maheu was wary. "To start hurling accusations at this time will necessarily cause the AEC, Dept. of Defense, and the Administration to join forces and really take us on—*but big*," he cautioned. "Howard, they simply have larger armies and we can end up being clobbered."

Clobbered? The Hughes empire? Never! "I dont agree that we

should back off into a state of inactivity, just because the government is big and rich," Hughes objected. "Bob, if we are going to be afraid to challenge [the government], on the theory that 'they have bigger armies than we have,' I just dont want to live in this country any longer."

Maheu's caution was well founded, however. Hughes was single-handedly reviving the nuclear protest movement, and with his success came a growing counterattack.

AEC Chairman Glenn Seaborg charged that the billionaire was "creating an atmosphere of harassment in our national security programs," and James Reeves, the director of the Nevada Test Site, appeared on local television to denounce the Hughes campaign.

"Did you see ch 13 at 10:30 tonight?" a worried Hughes asked Maheu. "Reeves really made us look terrible. I tell you Bob, in 30 min. tonite he wiped out everything you have so painstakingly accomplished toward giving me a new image. 18 months of effort shot down the drain by a bumbling, doddering old fart who looks so stupid you feel sorry for him.

"I tell you, when he shoots that blast off and no buildings fall down, then the wreckage of our little red wagon will be complete."

Finally the counterattack grew so intense that Hughes was threatened with a congressional subpoena.

"What is this I just saw on TV news where some ass-hole said that some congress committee might hold hearings and ask me to come to Washington and tell what I object to in the test program?" the recluse demanded.

Yet as terrified as he was of being forced out of hiding, Hughes remained defiantly determined to stand firm against the bomb.

"I dont agree with your fear that a strong campaign and embarassment of the AEC will lead to a subpeona," he told the fainthearted Maheu.

"I think the only way to win this battle is to discredit the AEC and emerge with public opinion on our side. I think it is defeat and loss of public favor that could lead to a subpeona. They dont want to force me to come to Washington if we are forging a successful campaign.

"Bob, where is your 'lead from strength' philosophy?"

"I didn't win the Senate hearing conflict by a defensive attitude," continued Hughes, recalling his "Spruce Goose" triumph twenty years earlier. "I did it by charging Sen. Brewster with corruption—with trying to bribe me in a room in a Washington hotel.

"Bob, if you dont take some measures to debunk the present attempt to reduce the issue to a simple question of whether to support the red white and blue, national defense, patriotism, etc., or whether to follow Mr. Hughes and be a traitor, I am sure we will not only lose the battle, but I will be subpeonaed.

"And if that subpeona is ever issued, all hell will not help me then. If we attempt to have the subpeona withdrawn in a red-hot controversy like this, I will lose every shred of stature that I may possess in this country, and everybody will charge that I bought the subpeona off.

"You are not the one who may be dragged out of bed and subjected to embarrassment, public disfavor, and disparagement.

"I want something done about this."

Maheu killed the subpoena threat in Washington, but he could do nothing to halt the relentless countdown in Nevada.

As his battle against the bomb entered its final days, the frantic recluse, sleepless in his penthouse bunker, wavered between fevered extremes, one moment gripped by visions of doom, the next worried that the explosion would prove anticlimactic.

"I am positive this blast is not going to leave any visible damage whatever," he fretted. "The dam is not going to break, and the movement of ground and buildings is bound to be less than people expect after all of the dire predictions we have been making.

"I can just see the newspaper interviews after the blast: 'Why, I hardly noticed it at all!' 'I stood there waiting for the earth to come to an end, and all of a sudden it was all over. I hardly felt it at all!'

"Then they will have pictures of the dam with a caption: 'The same old dam!' 'No cracks at all! Not even one little crack!' "

Those fools, those blind fools. The bombing would, of course, be awful. Every bit as horrible as Hughes had ever dreamed. It was just that it might not have the *visible* effects ordinary people could see, only the hidden impact apparent to him alone.

"I am afraid our stock is going to fall after that blast," wrote Hughes, now distraught over the anticipated dud. "We are going to look like the old lady alarmists of all time."

Precisely. It was a question of potency. Hughes had come to identify so completely with his feared rival, the bomb, that he could now no more accept a fizzle than a holocaust. If he failed to block the impending blast, not only would his fears be ridiculed—even as he suffered its unseen horrors—but his own invisible power would be deemed as feeble as the bomb's.

"If the explosion goes ahead, we will simply be chalked up as a failure," wrote Hughes. "It will simply be said that we do alright on small issues, but when the chips are really down, like the Bomb-test, then the hair on our balls is simply not long enough to accomplish a winning result.

"So, that makes it even more important than ever that we leave no stone unturned in our efforts to stop it."

With just forty-eight hours to go before the doomsday detonation, ambassadors from the Hughes empire descended on the nation's capital, talking tough with the AEC, conspiring with the vice-president, seeking an audience with the commander in chief.

"I suppose you know I have not been to sleep at all," scribbled the exhausted recluse. "So, I am going to wait up now until we hear something."

All day Wednesday and into the predawn hours of Thursday, Hughes continued his grim vigil, frantically maneuvering to block the blast still scheduled for Friday morning.

"I am no peacenik and I dont want to champion that cause," he wrote. "I just want to delay this blast long enough to bring some really heavy pressure to bear in Washington so we can obtain a 90 day delay in this one explosion. I dont care to scuttle the whole program, I only want the 90 days."

The news from Washington, however, was bleak. "There is no way we can get even a one day delay from the AEC," reported Maheu. "The only way this can be accomplished is at the White House. Now is the time to bring in another force."

Another force? Hughes was in no mood to find a new emissary, to send another hat-in-hand diplomat to Washington. He was through with go-betweens. He was through with peace talks. He would handle the final bomb offensive himself, and he would use his own ultimate weapon.

For the past nine days, Hughes had played many roles—mad prophet, naked general, movement leader—but here again he would deal with his bomb obsession the way he dealt with all other matters: by looking for someone to bribe.

"We must find a way to close them down," he wrote as the moment of doom neared.

"So, how do we acquire enough political strength to accomplish something like this? Well, there is only one way I know, and fortunately this is an election year."

He would not, like the peaceniks or the old ban-the-bomb crowd, reject America and take to the streets. He would embrace America and buy nuclear peace. Unique in the annals of corruption, Hughes would try to bribe the government to do what was *right*.

But now, just one day before the big blast, Hughes would make one last appeal to reason. At T-minus-24 and counting, he would personally take his plea to the man who had his finger on the button.

At the zero hour, it would be Howard Hughes and Lyndon Johnson alone at the summit.

7 Mr. President

"Mr. President," wrote Hughes. The time had come for direct action. Sovereign to sovereign.

It was in the odd predawn hours of Thursday, April 25, 1968. At first light the next day, the most powerful underground nuclear explosion in history was set to be detonated. One hundred miles from ground zero, "physically very ill and emotionally reduced to a nervous wreck," the exhausted billionaire remained determined to block the scheduled blast. He had just over twenty-four hours. And there was only one man who could still halt the relentless countdown.

So now, in sleepless terror, Howard Hughes drafted his letter to Lyndon Baines Johnson, the president of the United States.

"You may not remember it," he began, "but years ago when you were in the Senate, you and I were acquainted, not intimately, but enough so that you would have recognized my name."

Restrained. Dignified. Tactful. No need to mention the nature of their relationship. Johnson would remember.

"So, when you became President," Hughes continued, "I was strongly tempted to communicate with you, as one occasion after another developed in which I urgently needed your help. . . .

"However, I decided you were too busy for me to disturb you for anything with a purely selfish purpose."

Right. Put it all on a higher plane.

"Now, something has occurred that only you can alter from its present course.

"Based upon my personal promise that independent scientists and technicians have definite evidence, and can obtain more, demonstrating the risk and uncertainty to the health of the citizens of Southern Nevada, if the megaton-plus nuclear explosion is detonated tomorrow morning, will you grant even a brief postponement of this explosion to permit my representatives to come to Washington and lay before whomever you designate the urgent, impelling reasons why we feel a 90 day postponement is needed?"

A bit vague, perhaps, but surely there was no need to name the scientists or cite the evidence. Hughes was offering his "personal promise." And armed with an absolute certainty of the claimed danger—the "definite evidence" was in the pit of his stomach—the billionaire now barreled ahead.

"I am certainly no peacenik," he declared. "My feelings have been well known through the years to be far to the right of center.

"It is not my purpose to impede the defense program in any way, and I can positively prove that if my appeal is heeded"—he started to write "it will have no deleterious effect," then decided on a more positive approach—"the nuclear test program will proceed *more rapidly* than at present."

A nice touch. Now for a strong finish.

"If the A.E.C. technicians did not consider the nuclear explosions at the Las Vegas Test site to be of marginal safety, then why did they make a firm agreement with me, 11 months ago, to move the large explosions . . . to some more remote place?" Hughes demanded, reminding Johnson of the nonexistent broken treaty, assuming the stance of an outraged sovereign.

"I think Nevada has become a fully accredited state now and should no longer be treated like a barren wasteland that is only useful as a dumping place for poisonous, contaminated nuclear waste material, such as normally is carefully sealed up and dumped in the deepest part of the ocean.

"The A.E.C. technicians assure that there will be no harmful consequences, but I wonder where those technicians will be 10 or 20 years from now.

"There are some sheep lying dead in nearby Utah."

Ah, the martyred flock. It was the perfect clincher.

The four-page letter had taken Hughes all night and half the day to write and rewrite, and now, with the dreaded blast less than twenty-four hours away, there was no time to send it to the White House.

Instead, one of the Mormons dictated it over the telephone to Washington attorney Thomas Finney—law partner of Johnson's newly appointed Secretary of Defense Clark Clifford—who hand-delivered Hughes's impassioned plea to the president's office.

Lyndon Johnson had problems of his own. Less than a month earlier he had been forced to abdicate, solemnly telling a startled nation: "I shall not seek, and I will not accept the nomination of my party for another term as your President."

The withdrawal had brought him no real peace. It was not merely that Eugene McCarthy continued to sweep the primaries, or even that the hated Bobby Kennedy had announced his long-dreaded decision to claim his brother's throne. Everything, at home and abroad, seemed to be in disarray. The war in Vietnam had been shattered by the Tet offensive, the Great Society had been undermined by the cost of the war, the American economy was in danger, the world gold market was in collapse, the nation was torn by protest marches, campus upheavals, and race riots of unprecedented violence. The cowboy president, caught in a stampede, had been trampled.

Still, the outer Johnson remained intact. He did not remove all his clothes, let his hair, beard, and fingernails grow long, take to bed, and tape dark blinds over the Oval Office windows. But the inner man had crumbled. And the siege atmosphere in the White House now resembled the siege atmosphere in the penthouse.

By day the president would harangue his staff—now purged of all but loyal Texans—with shouted accusations of treason and whispered tales of conspiracy. Communists controlled the television networks. *New York Times* Washington correspondent James Reston was consorting with the Russian ambassador. Most of the press was in on it, and so were the professors. All were in league with the Kennedys, and together they had plotted his downfall.

By night Johnson would dream that he was paralyzed from the neck down, a helpless cripple unable even to protest as his most trusted aides fought to divide the remnants of his power. The nightmares were a secret, but the raging paranoia and wild suspicions, often punctuated by obscene outbursts and misplaced laughter, frightened his advisers and convinced several that the president had become dangerously unhinged.

So, if Hughes's letter was in one sense sovereign to sovereign, it was also bunker to bunker.

Johnson, keeping up appearances, had just returned from getting a haircut and was about to change into tails for a state dinner honoring the King of Norway, when the letter finally reached him early that evening. The president was in a foul mood. His day had been a disaster. Arthur Goldberg had suddenly quit as U.N. ambassador in a bitter confrontation over Johnson's war policy, no one else wanted the job, and George Ball had to be bludgeoned into accepting it. Hanoi was threatening to abandon the stalled peace talks, antiwar demonstrators were converging on New York for a march the next day, militant students had just seized several buildings at Columbia, top administration officials were defecting to support Bobby Kennedy, and with all these pressing problems, surrounded by traitors and turmoil, the president had to spend half his time playing host to King Olav, who arrived that morning for a state visit. ("He's the dumbest king I've ever met," complained LBJ, adding with sour impatience, "I didn't know they made kings that dumb.")

So when Johnson picked up the billionaire's letter, his first reaction was blind outrage. "Who the fuck does Howard Hughes think he is?!" the president bellowed, seeing the desperate plea to halt the bomb test as yet another challenge to his power.

It was, of course, a good question. Who, indeed, was Hughes? Neither Johnson nor anyone else at the White House really had the answer. Despite some past dealings, the president knew only what everybody knew—that Hughes was the richest man in the United States, a man of incalculable power whose secret empire seemed to reach everywhere, a mythic figure now in hiding who also happened to be the country's biggest private military contractor. That was enough.

Beleaguered as he was, Johnson did not ignore the bomb plea, nor did he take it lightly. In a move without precedent, he withheld approval of the scheduled blast, secretly alerting the AEC to await his final go-ahead.

The president's mood swing was dramatic. Although still more than a bit irritated that any private citizen would presume to dictate national defense policy, Johnson was also fascinated, even flattered by the hidden billionaire's direct approach. The letter seemed to make him feel more important. He proudly displayed it to several White House aides, more like a kid who had just obtained a celebrity's autograph than a president who had been petitioned to halt a nuclear test. In fact, Johnson was so intrigued by the personal contact from this mystery man that he falsely claimed Hughes had also telephoned, embroidering his tall tale with a detailed account of the conversation that had never taken place.

Moreover, the president was clearly impressed by what he considered the surprisingly logical and forceful case the reputedly eccentric financier had made.

"He may be wrong," Johnson told his chief speech writer Harry McPherson, "but he sure as hell isn't a loony."

Back at the penthouse, the naked recluse, while unaware that he had been officially certified sane, was nonetheless confident he had made the right move.

"My letter to the President was a masterpiece," he exulted. "Also when I started focusing my memory on the relationship I had about 8 years ago with Johnson, I came up with some very solid memories."

Solid memories. To Hughes that could mean only one thing: hard cash. And, indeed, the two Texans had once had what Hughes would later describe as a "hard cash, adult" relationship. Hughes had not only backed Johnson's first serious White House bid eight years earlier (when he had lost the Democratic nomination to their mutual enemy John F. Kennedy), but had secretly supported Johnson for at least two decades, right from the beginning of his rise to power as a freshman senator. The full extent of their dealings is unknown. In any event, it was a relatively small sum Hughes gave in the early days that now came most solidly to mind. He had once bought the man who was now president with pocket change, and if Johnson had since moved up in the world, to the billionaire he remained just another politician who had his price.

"I have done this kind of business with him before," explained Hughes. "So, he wears no awe-inspiring robe of virtue with me."

To what degree these past dealings now affected Johnson is less clear, but there is no question that the president had once been on the pad. In his leaner years as a raw-boned young congressman, Johnson was a regular visitor at the Houston headquarters of the Hughes Tool Company, where he befriended the absentee owner's top executive, Noah Dietrich. His big Stetson hat in hand, Johnson asked free use of company billboards for his first Senate race. Dietrich refused, preferring to use them to promote a Hughes sideline, Grand Prize Beer.

After an eighty-seven-vote victory in his second try for the Senate in 1948, however, "Landslide Lyndon" seemed a better investment. His triumph—marred by charges of ballot stuffing—happened to coincide with Hughes's first big plunge into buying national power, and Johnson soon joined numerous other politicians already on the Hughes payroll.

"Lyndon was taken care of annually," recalled Dietrich. "On the basis of contributing to the former campaign, the present campaign, and the anticipated campaign, why we could legally give him $5,000 a year."

Johnson was then a newly elected senator with no campaigns to run for another six years, but as his longtime aide Bobby Baker later noted, "he was always on the look-out for an odd nickel or dime." Hardly yet a national figure, as a member of the powerful Armed Services Committee he nonetheless soon became known for his uncanny ability to land military contracts for his defense-industry backers.

Hughes, although only three years older than Johnson, was already a national legend, but he was just then emerging as a major defense contractor. Tainted by the "Spruce Goose" hearings a year earlier, and in need of well-placed friends, he sent Johnson $5,000 a year for at least four years, at a time when a senator's salary was only $12,500.

The money came from a Canadian subsidiary of the Hughes Tool Company especially set up to bypass a ban on political contributions from domestic corporations.

Through the years there would be further contributions, and eventually Hughes would offer Johnson a million-dollar bribe. For the moment, however, he was confident his masterful bomb letter would carry the day. That, and the "solid memories."

The president clearly shared those memories, and apparently looked forward to future rewards. Certainly he must have savored the fact that Hughes was now the supplicant, that the man from whom he had once begged billboards was now begging him—the Leader of the Free World—to halt a nuclear blast.

In any event, he treated his erstwhile benefactor with unusual deference. Even before Hughes's letter arrived at the White House, Johnson had met privately with a Hughes emissary, Grant Sawyer, a former governor of Nevada now on Hughes's payroll. The meeting was arranged by Vice-President Humphrey, who had already tapped

Sawyer for a key position in his still unannounced presidential campaign. Sawyer would later deliver $50,000 in Hughes money to Humphrey's drive.

And a day earlier, another Hughes representative had called White House Chief of Staff Marvin Watson with an astounding offer: "Mr. Hughes has agreed to completely finance the pending campaign of Vice-President Hubert H. Humphrey to any extent necessary to match the funds expended by Senator Robert Kennedy." But only if Johnson delayed the scheduled nuclear test.

Watson later insisted he never even mentioned the call to either Humphrey or Johnson—perhaps because he was soon warned that "Drew Pearson has learned of Hughes's offer of money to HHH if the blast is held off"—and there is no evidence that Hughes himself authorized the payoff, although he would later order Maheu to make a similar deal directly with the vice-president.

Whatever Hughes, Johnson, and Humphrey knew, and when they knew it, Sawyer's Oval Office parley went quite well.

"Grant Sawyer has just left the President who sends his warmest personal regards," Maheu reported to the penthouse. "He told Grant that he had the highest respect for you and your ability and also was *very grateful for many favors of the past.* I am sure you know that in addition to what you may have done personally many years ago, we have been good supporters. You will recall that when he was Vice President you asked me to set up something with him whereby he could call upon us any time he had candidates in whom he had a personal interest. We have never let him down in that area among other things."

One of the candidates in whom Johnson had expressed a "personal interest" was his longtime crony John Connally, then running for governor of Texas. Maheu arranged a contribution to the Connally campaign through the Hughes Tool Company in Houston.

At the same time, Maheu had sought the then vice-president's advice on a well-connected law firm to represent Hughes in the TWA litigation that was just beginning. Johnson was pleased to oblige. He recommended Arnold, Fortas & Porter, where his old friend and business associate Abe Fortas was then a senior partner. Hughes, of course, retained the firm.

Now, Johnson, still grateful for past favors, seemed ready to help the billionaire battle the bomb.

"He continued by telling Grant that if you had concern about the pending blast that was sufficient enough for him to have concern also," Maheu reported, completing his account of the just-ended Oval Office parley. "In Grant's presence he summoned AEC Chairman Seaborg to the White House. He informed Grant that Seaborg would have to prove to him conclusively that the blast was safe in every detail."

At first elated, Hughes grew restive as the day wore on with no further word from the president. As evening approached, he became increasingly frantic, worried that Johnson would not read his letter, afraid that even if he did the AEC still might prevail.

"I wish you would call Sawyer and ask if he knows any way to find out if the President has actually read my letter and what his decision is and if he is going to do anything," wrote the impatient recluse, certain that his masterpiece would have more impact than the former governor's White House visit.

"The reason I ask is this: my letter contains a lot of material and data etc. which was not and is not known to Mr. Sawyer. On the other hand, when Sawyer arrived ahead of my letter and Johnson granted Sawyer an interview, he (Johnson) may have thought there was no need to read my letter since he had heard from Sawyer. We *must* find some way of persuading Johnson to read my letter *now*. It will do more for us than anybody can obtain through a meeting."

Yet even as he put his faith in the inspired words he had written, Hughes became alarmed at the thought that his foes might gain the ear of the president.

"I am positive that my letter was very very effective, but the AEC has had a rebuttal period since my letter was digested, and I have had no opportunity to answer any claims they may have made," he fretted.

"That is why I think we should discontinue being quite so bashful and risk the chance of finding we have made the first move," he continued, eager to counter the bombers' presumed backstairs lobbying.

"We *must* find out to whom this matter has been entrusted by the President. I am sure he has turned it over to one of his staff members. If we could make contact with such individual, I think we could make some exceedingly important suggestions: like how we dont seek glory of victory in this matter, and will be most happy to agree upon a press release (joint)."

In fact, Johnson had not delegated the matter to any single aide. Rather, he had taken personal charge of the bomb controversy and mobilized half the White House staff to deal with Hughes.

National Security Advisor Walt Rostow, AEC Chairman Glenn Seaborg, and the president's science director Donald Hornig were instructed to report on the substantive issues. Marvin Watson, his second-in-command Jim Jones, and Harry McPherson were assigned to coordinate the project and draft a reply to Hughes's letter.

It was a measure of Hughes's real power, the power of his myth, and perhaps the "solid memories" the two men shared, that his somewhat quirky last-minute appeal was taken so seriously by Johnson. But the president's top advisers were united in opposing any delay of the scheduled nuclear blast.

Johnson returned from the King Olav dinner shortly before midnight to find their reports waiting. He sent Lady Bird to bed alone, stripped off his formal attire, and sat awake for the next hour reading their replies to Hughes's protest.

Rostow, who had gained the president's confidence, now reassured Johnson that the planned bomb test was also entirely safe and under control.

"I see nothing in Hughes's letter that raises questions which the AEC has not confronted with as much responsibility as could be expected," Rostow declared. Hard-nosed as ever, he even dismissed the dead sheep. "Hughes raises the example of the Utah sheep," he noted. "If anything happened to the sheep, it arose not from AEC experiments, but from experiments for biological weapons in Utah."

Seaborg also called Hughes's fears unfounded, and warned that "without underground testing much of the dynamic nature of our weapons program would be lost and our strategic deterrent would erode."

Strong words. But when press aide Tom Johnson stopped upstairs to say goodnight, the president cast aside the Seaborg and Rostow reports and once more displayed the letter he had received from Hughes. It still intrigued him.

Of all the hundreds of papers that came across his desk that day— daily CIA briefings, daily National Security Council reports, daily body counts, war dispatches from Saigon and peace-talk news from Laos, an urgent memo on Chinese troop movements, FBI reports on the planned antiwar march, a message from Egypt's Nasser and another from the Shah of Iran—the one document that seized the president's attention and even now, well past midnight, still transfixed him, was the letter from Hughes.

Johnson showed the letter to his aide without mentioning the impending blast. It was not that Hughes was seeking a private test-ban treaty, it was not that Hughes might be right and his own advisers wrong, it was simply the name at the bottom—Howard Hughes.

And despite his experts' strong advice, Johnson went to sleep early Friday morning without making a final decision. The bomb test remained on hold.

Hughes, who had not slept in three nights, continued his vigil. Desperately awaiting word from the White House, he scribbled a note to his Mormons: "Please watch me carefully and dont let me go to sleep at all." Then, acutely conscious of the approaching megaton blast, he added a final plea: "But try not to startle me."

Finally, the recluse could no longer stand the tension and humiliation of waiting like a condemned man for an eleventh-hour presidential reprieve.

"I am sick of this continuous ass-kissing and subservient begging," he exploded. "Why dont we seek an injunction but immediately? We cannot wait to hear back from Johnson."

Hughes had toyed with the idea of court action earlier in his battle against the bomb and confidently concluded: "it is just a problem of finding the right judge." Before deciding on a personal appeal to the president, he was even ready to take his case to the Supreme Court: "They have some awfully left-wing characters on that court, and if we could just catch them when those men are attendant and not the others, it might slide through in about 20 minutes."

"Why are we hesitant?" the billionaire demanded. "The U.S. Supreme Court has issued injunctions many times on a thinner case than we have. I am sure the Supreme Court is out now because of the late hour, but lower courts have issued injunctive relief in the middle of the night many times."

Trying to calm his commander's rage, Maheu counseled that going to night court could not block a major atomic weapons test and cautioned that the attempt "would place the President in a position of having to fight us."

More resigned than convinced, Hughes reluctantly agreed to forgo a midnight legal maneuver. "If you dont want to seek an injunction until the President gives an answer, OK," he replied. "Since we have the 3 hour time spread, there is just a very microscopic chance the President might be persuaded to intervene.

"One thing is sure, we have nothing—but nothing to lose—so we dont have to pussy-foot around anymore," he added, with the reckless abandon of a man down to his final hours. "You know Johnson has just a few other things going, and if his cabinet does not want to see this favor granted, maybe we have to have somebody get into that White House and shake things up a little."

But who? Suddenly, from the depths of his desperation, came the answer. Hughes knew just the man for the job. He could certainly get into the White House, he would have no trouble shaking things up, and he was no stranger to Hughes.

"I just thought of something," he wrote excitedly. "Clark Clifford!!

"He was under retainer to me for 25 years and did practically nothing. And he needed the money."

Hughes had in fact been one of Clifford's first clients, having personally called him just a day or two after he had gone into private practice. Now Clifford was Johnson's Secretary of Defense, and his Washington law firm still represented Hughes. It was the perfect setup.

Just a month earlier, Clifford had persuaded the president to pull back from Vietnam, explaining that the war was bad for business. Obviously he could block a mere bomb test.

"Maybe we ought to have Long* see Clifford or Sawyer see him," suggested Hughes, "and point out that here is an ideal situation where he could be of assistance to me and have my truly undying devotion and gratitude, and where it will not cost the Defense Dept. one solitary cent.

"If our representative in Washington could make it clear to Clifford," he continued, "that although there is no monetary gain involved, this explosion is a matter of absolutely top importance to me, and that if Clifford will intervene in this affair, I will give him my most solemn pledge never, so long as he may be in office, to call upon him for assistance of any kind, if I make this kind of a promise, I think Clifford might take this on.

"It would only take one phone call for Clifford to pull the plug on the AEC's claim that this explosion is necessary for national defense."

Yes, Clark Clifford could do the job. How could he refuse so reasonable a request? Why, in the old days, Hughes had often spoken to him directly, sometimes calling at three or four A.M.

Over the years, Clifford had come through time and again. As

*Gillis Long, former congressman and new Hughes lobbyist.

Washington's premier lobbyist, a man with unique access to every national administration—indeed every president—since Truman, Clifford had once pushed through a Hughes land grab in Nevada vigorously opposed by the Interior Department. His firm had succeeded in blocking a 1966 congressional probe of the billionaire's Pentagon influence-buying. And, of course, it was Clifford's law partner, Finney, who had hand-carried Hughes's bomb plea to the president.

But neither their past telephone relationship nor their continuing business relationship now carried any weight.

Abandoned by his natural allies, Hughes now counted the dwindling hours, his last hope the letter he had sent to Lyndon Johnson. The yellow pages of his handwritten first draft lay beside him on the sweat-soaked bed.

Meanwhile, in the predawn blackness of the Nevada desert, a calmer countdown continued. Bad weather had briefly threatened a postponement, but by three A.M. the weather had cleared, and now test-site workers—ignorant of the Hughes-Johnson drama—made final preparations to explode the hydrogen bomb at sunrise. "Boxcar" was in the hole, stemmed, and ready to go.

At first light, a two-man team entered the red shack on ground zero, arming the thermonuclear device buried 3,800 feet below in a steel-lined, cement-filled shaft.

Alone in his bedroom, Hughes scrawled a final fevered memo in a desperate bid to reach the president and escape the impending holocaust.

"It is vital that somehow you prevail upon Mr. Johnson that this is an emergency and persuade him to read my letter," he begged. "There is about 20 minutes left."

Johnson, of course, had seen the letter almost as soon as it arrived at the White House, and was right now in his own bedroom, weighing the needs of national security against the words of Howard Hughes. Still undecided, he received a final bomb report from his top science adviser, Donald Hornig.

"There is still time to act in the next 15 or 20 minutes," Hornig informed the president. But, joining Rostow and Seaborg, he urged Johnson not to halt the scheduled blast.

"A complete cancellation seems inadvisable," his message read. "The test will furnish a calibration point for the ABM warhead, and is needed for that purpose and as a proof test for a Polaris warhead I recommend that we do not change the test plans."

That made it unanimous. The president could not, against the strongly worded advice of all his experts—against the entire national-defense establishment—cancel a major nuclear weapons test at the demand of one private citizen, even Hughes.

Johnson decided to detonate the bomb.

At precisely seven o'clock on Friday morning, April 26, 1968, a 1.2 megaton explosion roared through the Nevada desert and set the ground trembling in four states. It blew a gigantic dust cloud high above Pahute Mesa and vaporized the bedrock below, carving out a seven-hundred-foot-wide subterranean cavern with so much force that the shock waves registered on seismographs from New York to Alaska. At ground zero the earth bulged ominously, then slowly settled back until it finally collapsed, leaving another huge crater in the arid moonscape. One hundred miles away, hotels along the Las Vegas Strip shuddered, water splashed out of the swimming pools, and the carpeted floors of the gambling casinos vibrated, but the dice continued to roll without interruption.

Up in his penthouse, Howard Hughes gripped the sides of his suddenly unstable bed, bracing his wasted body against the blast.

A Mormon aide kept watch in the next room. "The motion I experienced lasted well over one minute," he reported to his shaken boss. "The first tremor was followed a few seconds later by a substantially stronger tremor, then gradually started to dampen out. The chandelier swayed well over four minutes."

Hughes himself waited half an hour for the aftershocks to subside, then reached for his yellow legal pad.

"You can take my word for it that this blast produced more than *twice* the yield [anticipated]," he wrote in a hand that still showed the full effects of the bombing. "They deliberately deceived us and everyone else about the size of the blast. This would explain Johnson's refusal and the terrific importance placed on this one shot."

Hughes's bedroom had actually swayed only a few centimeters, but for him the explosion itself was the shattering climax of a ten-day trauma. The countdown alone had left him in ruins.

"I just know I was physically very ill and emotionally reduced to a nervous wreck by the end of the week, and life is too short for that," he told Maheu, bleakly assessing the damage. "Now, Bob, I dont know how you reacted to the last week. You seem to be one hell of a lot better conditioned than I am, and you probably survived in much better shape than I did. All I can say to you, Bob, is that if I ever have to go thru another week like the last one, I simply will not take it, and this will mean an awful lot of work and planning shot down the drain. I am sorry, but that is the way I am.

"I would not repeat last week for all the money in the world."

Right down to the final minutes Hughes had hoped that his personal appeal to Johnson would save the day, but now it seemed clear that summit diplomacy had failed. The president had not even bothered to answer his letter.

Finally, two weeks later a double envelope, the inner one marked "Personal & Confidential to Mr. Hughes," arrived at the Desert Inn. Inside was a two-page message from Lyndon Johnson. It was hardly a welcome surprise.

"I received the letter from the President," Hughes noted bitterly, "and was it ever a disappointment!!

"He gloats over the fact that the explosion did not vent, there was no significant damage, and, in fact, the blast bore out the most minute forecasts of the AEC scientists, and satisfied the President, beyond any most microscopic doubts he might have had, that the AEC scientists have the atom under such complete control that they can make it turn a sommersault, jump thru a hoop, and say: 'Uncle!' any time they are of a mind to do so.

"Further, the AEC, with his complete support, is going right ahead full-steam to conduct their major high-yield explosions at Pahute Mesa in the N.T.S. [Nevada Test Site].

"Why would the President have gone out of his way to rub it in?" wondered Hughes, nearly as shaken by Johnson's reply as he had been by the blast. "I did not expect anything with a hint of future assistance. I realize this would have been too much to expect, but *Jesus!* he did not have to spend two full pages of deliberately hostile provocation."

In fact, the president's response, while formal and a bit distant, was hardly hostile. "I personally considered your letter and discussed it with my advisers, before coming to a final decision," it read in part. "I approved execution of this test only after considering its importance to our national security—and only after receiving the Atomic Energy Commission's assurances that extensive safety checks had clearly demonstrated that there was no cause for concern."

The entire tone was respectful and reassuring. And if Johnson also let Hughes know who was president, still he had gone to extraordinary lengths to deal with the billionaire's protest. Certainly few other private citizens, if any, could have caused the commander in chief to withhold until the last minute approval of a nuclear test deemed vital to national defense.

To Hughes, however, the president's letter was a deliberate slap in the face. Not only had Johnson failed to stop "Boxcar," not only had he refused to move all future blasts elsewhere, but he had kept Hughes waiting two weeks for a reply.

Perplexed and indignant, Hughes studied Johnson's response, reading and rereading it to find hidden meanings, his outrage mounting. By the next day he was certain his original interpretation had been correct.

"There was nothing in the President's letter to suggest any decision beyond the one taken when they went ahead with the last explosion," pronounced the frustrated exegete. "I read the letter with microscopic care. I looked minutely for some in-between-the-lines meaning. I could find none at all. Everything he said seemed to be an elaborate, over emphatic defense of his position. . . .

"Now, Bob, this entire affair is becoming more puzzling every day. . . .

"When I say 'puzzling' I mean this:

"He did not answer my letter until 2 weeks after he received it.

"This, above, coupled with the strange tone of his letter, suggests two things to me—Either (a.) that he waited the two weeks for me to contact him and work out a straight-forward 'deal' on this problem, and then became angry when I failed to respond and let me have the hostile letter, or (B.) that during the two week period he was negotiating with representatives of R.E.E.Co. or E. G. & G. [the test site's two private contractors] and finally made a deal with them. . . ."

Of course. It was all so obvious. How could he have missed it? The president had been expecting a bribe, and when the billionaire failed to come through, turned instead to the opposition for his graft.

Hughes's memo was a diatribe of lost innocence.

He had taken the high road in his letter to Johnson, offered a reasoned and restrained case pleading the dangers and uncertainties of unchecked nuclear testing. And the president had ignored his plea, dismissed him as a fool or a skinflint, and pocketed a payoff.

Well, no one would ever catch Howard Hughes napping again. No more romantic illusions for him. He had seen the light.

"You see, Bob, some people feel I have unlimited power and absolutely no scrupples," he explained to his veteran bagman and fixer. "You and I know this is not true, but they dont know it. . . ."

So be it. From now on, Hughes would do what was expected of him, and he would bring the bombing to an end.

"I urge what I have urged from the beginning: Down to earth, brass tacks, bargaining with the A.E.C. and the White House—in Washington, . . ." he wrote.

"I urge we get down off the soap box and quit trying to make over the morals of the world and focus on a bought and paid for compromise settlement of this issue.

"I feel we may find that, at a price we can afford, we can buy a settlement. . . ."

The president's perfidy had given Hughes some very definite ideas about where such a settlement could be bought.

"I think you should try to determine who is the real, honest-to-God, bagman at the White House," he urged Maheu. "And please dont be frightened away by the enormity of the thought. I have known for a number of years that the White House under this particular Democratic administration is just as crooked as it can be. Now, I dont know whom you have to approach, but there is somebody, take my word for it."

Finally, in a casual postscript to his somewhat chilling memo, Hughes took the true measure of the man he had tried to reach by honest reason.

"P.S. One thing I should have told you, in connection with my assumption that the Pres. may have waited the two weeks to hear from me on some kind of a hard-cash, adult, basis. I should tell you that I have done this kind of business with him before. So, he wears no awe-inspiring robe of virtue with me. I gave him some critically needed funds when he was in the Senate. He remembers this as he spoke of it to Finney. This is why he may very realistically have waited the two weeks for me to send somebody to him before he replied or took a stand. Anyway, I think this is one very plausible explanation of everything, including the hostillity when he did write. . . ."

Plausible or not, Hughes was now convinced that he must put his relationship with Johnson back on a "hard cash, adult, basis." After all the hope that Hughes had placed in his masterful letter, Johnson's rejection of his earnest appeal had a cataclysmic impact. It marked a turning point in Hughes's approach to politics and politicians in general. It removed his last remaining inhibitions to use his private wealth to buy public power. Eventually, it would convulse the entire nation.

"Now," concluded Hughes, in a classic expression of free-enterprise morality, "I think there is a market-place, somewhere, where the things we want can be bought or sold, and I urge that instead of spending any more time begging for a free hand-out, we find the right place, and the right people and buy what we want."

Hughes clearly believed that Johnson was one of the right people. As for the right place, it turned out to be not the White House but the LBJ Ranch. And the right amount, Hughes figured, was $1 million.

It was Maheu who first suggested the approach. Three months after the bomb test, in a memo to the penthouse, he inquired, "As long as I am going to be in Washington next week—what do you think of my calling on the President as your personal representative? It might buy us insurance on the AEC program as well as the Stardust. I could tell him that you are interested in his future plans and want to help him in any way possible. His answer might prove to be very interesting—indeed."

By the time Maheu proposed the parley, Hughes had become enmeshed in a battle with the Justice Department over his plans to acquire yet another major hotel-casino, the Stardust. Justice had moved to block the deal the same day the "Boxcar" blast was announced and despite pressure from Senate Judiciary Committee Chairman James Eastland, both of Nevada's senators, and Governor Laxalt, Attorney General Ramsey Clark refused to allow the recluse to continue his Las Vegas Monopoly game.

Now Maheu was heading to Washington for a showdown with antitrust chief Edwin Zimmerman and hoped to meet with the president as well—to buy some insurance. The trip was less than a complete success. Zimmerman curtly informed Maheu that the Stardust deal was "a cut-and-dried violation of the Clayton Act." As for getting to Johnson, he was ailing and had left the White House to recuperate at his Texas ranch.

"I strongly suggest we call off this caper and take another look at it six months hence—after the elections," a subdued Maheu counseled his master.

Hughes, however, was unwilling to wait. "Now, Bob, I realize

Bob —

5/14/68

There was nothing in the President's letter to suggest any decision beyond the one taken when they went ahead with the last explosion. I read the letter with microscopic care. I looked minutely for some in-between-the-lines meaning. I could find none at all. Everything he said seemed to be an elaborate, over emphatic defense of his position.

When I say "puzzling" I mean this:

He did not answer my letter until 2 weeks after he received it.

This, above, coupled with the strange ~~to~~ tone of his letter, suggests two things to me — Either (a.) that he waited the two weeks for

me to contact him and work out a straight-forward "deal" on this problem, and then became angry when I failed to respond and let me have the hostile letter, or (B.) that during the two week period, he was negotiating with representatives of R.E.Co. or E. G. & G. and finally made a deal with them.

You see, Bob, some people feel I have 'unlimited power and absolutely no scrupples. You and I know this is not true, but they dont know it.

Any way, you ask me what to do. I dont recommend hiring a firm to make a study. I urge what I have urged from the beginning: Down to earth, brass tacks bargaining with the A.E.C. and the White House — in Washington.

That is what I recommend, and that we do it right away. I think we ought to start by asking Long to ask the A.E.C. for a break down of aproximate costs and delays (if any) of performing the large blasts at another site. We may find this is the way to open the doors and start some effective negotiating toward a paid-for compromise.

At least if he is in daily talks with A.E.C. we will know their plans when the next blast etc.

In other words, I urge

we get down off the soap box
and quit trying to make over
the morals of the world and
focus on a bought and paid
for compromise settlement of
this issue.

I feel we may find that, at a
price we can afford, we can buy
a settlement and convince E.G.& G.
that under such settlement there
will be only one loser — me.
And that E. G. & G. will not lose
anything that will not be reimbursed
by me.

At least lets try it, and
quick, please!

Now simultaneously with
our efforts thru the A.E.C. or
E.G.& G., or both, I think you
should try to determine who
is the real, honest-to-God, bagman at the White House. And
please dont be frightened away by
the enormity of the thought. I
have known for a number of
years that the White House under
this particular Democratic administration is just as crooked as it
can be. Now, I dont know whom
you have to approach, but there
is somebody, take my word for
it. Now I dont say we should

count on this, but I certainly think we should explore it as another string to the bow.

I have more, but please let me have some assurance that we are at work on this program first. I feel we have hesitated a little during the last week, probably my fault, but I want to go full blast now, and I certainly would like to have, as I say, some confirmation of a take-off.

I wait to hear,

Howard

P.S. One thing I should have told you, in connection with my assumption that the Pres. may have waited the two weeks to hear from me on some kind of a hard-cash, adult, basis, I should tell you that I have done this kind of business with him before. So, he wears no awe-inspiring robe of virtue with me. I gave him some critically needed funds when he was in the Senate. He remembers this as he spoke of it to Finney. This is why he may very realistically have waited the two weeks for me to send somebody to him before he replied or took a stand. Anyway, I think this is one very plausible explanation of everything, including the hostility when he did write.

In any event, it all boils down to one point: We have been spending hours of mental toil and turmoil, and days of delay trying to force the A.E.C. to give us what we want free and, in addition, to take bread out of the mouths of E.G.&G. employes, figuratively speaking, and all free of charge to us.

Now, I think there is a market-place, somewhere, where the things we want can be bought or sold, and I urge that instead of spending any more time begging for a free hand-out, we find the right place and the right people and buy what we want.

Please let me know,

Howard

that if we emerge from the forthcoming election with the kind of political strength we anticipate, there will be no need for a negotiated settlement of this matter," he replied. "I dont question your ability to win this game on a political basis in an open contest. But I am afraid I will be a nervous wreck by the time it is over."

Fuming and boiling over the Stardust, in terror of the bomb, Hughes could not wait until Johnson had been replaced by a more pliable president.

And there was one other thing the billionaire wanted. He had already mentioned it in his letter to Johnson, although only as an example of one of the many urgent matters he had been too altruistic to call to the president's attention.

"The last of these," Hughes had told Johnson, "was when I undertook the manufacture of a small helicopter for use in Viet Nam. I lost in excess of $1/_5$ of everything I possess in the world on this one project, purely because the price was miscalculated.

"The loss was far greater than I have ever suffered in my lifetime. The price we collected for these machines was less than the bill of material alone."

It was true. The billionaire had taken a bath. The loss was not quite so great as he claimed, but it was close to $90 million. There was, however, one aspect of the debacle Hughes failed to mention. The price was not "miscalculated."

Hughes had intentionally submitted a ridiculously low bid in a plot to corner the market on helicopters vital to the war. But his scheme had backfired when he tried to triple the price and got caught in a messy congressional probe. Now he was stuck with the bill.

Like the war in Vietnam itself, the copter deal, born in deceit, was ending in disaster. Johnson should certainly sympathize.

Still, it was neither his staggering helicopter losses nor the antitrust blockade that really obsessed Hughes. It was the bomb. And having failed to persuade the president, Hughes was now determined to buy him.

Within two weeks of his failed White House mission, Maheu was on his way to the LBJ Ranch, flying there in a private Hughes jet, the full magnitude of his mission still a secret known only to his taciturn boss. "I'm not ready to tell you yet," said Hughes, sending Maheu off with no further explanation.

Johnson was completely in the dark. So great was the cachet of the name *Hughes* that the president had agreed to receive his emissary without even being told the purpose of his visit. In the previous two days Johnson had played host to Richard Nixon and Hubert Humphrey, and now, having seen his two potential successors, the president prepared to meet the representative of a third major power.

"Who is this Maheu, why does he get to see you, Mr. President?" asked White House Appointments Secretary Jim Jones.

"He's Howard Hughes's man," replied Johnson, as if that alone answered the question.

Maheu arrived in Texas the night before his scheduled rendezvous at the LBJ Ranch, checked into a motel, and called the penthouse. "I have an appointment with the President of the United States tomorrow morning," he reminded Hughes. "I wish you would tell me what you want me to discuss with him." Hughes again refused. "Call me in the morning just before you leave," he replied, "and in the meantime, just sleep comfortably."

If Maheu found that difficult, under the circumstances, so probably did the president. Johnson had met Maheu before, but not in the months since the president had bombed Hughes, and not in the year since he had finally learned the dirty secret that Hughes, Maheu, and the Central Intelligence Agency had long shared—the still hidden Castro assassination plot.

Maheu, of course, had played a pivotal part in that CIA-Mafia murder conspiracy. Hughes had been let in on the secret almost immediately and without a second thought. But the president had to learn about it six years later from Washington newspaper columnist Drew Pearson.

His belated discovery of the murder plot had sent Johnson into a rage. Convinced that the attempts on Castro's life had somehow caused John F. Kennedy's death, in fact certain that the CIA had a hand in Kennedy's assassination, Johnson—fearing that he too was in danger—had put the Secret Service on full alert and ordered a top-secret FBI investigation. He denounced the CIA as "a damn Murder Inc." and hauled spymaster Richard Helms into the Oval Office.

Johnson never got the full story, but he did learn of Maheu's central role in the bloody cabal.

So now the president knew that Hughes's ambassador had also been the CIA's top hit man, its link to the Mob in a failed contract to murder a chief of state. And in the early morning hours of August 12, 1968, as Maheu waited nervously in a Dallas motel for Hughes to call with final orders on his latest mission, the president was also left to ponder with some discomfort the reason for Maheu's impending visit. Finally, just minutes before Maheu's scheduled departure, the billionaire phoned his bagman.

"He wanted me to suggest to President Johnson," Maheu would later testify, "that he, Howard Hughes, was prepared to give him a million dollars after he left office, if he would stop the atomic testing before he left office."

It was one mission Maheu never carried out.

Johnson had been ailing again, but seemed in fine form when he returned from the hospital later that morning to find Maheu already at the LBJ Ranch. Still ignorant both of Hughes's orders and Maheu's intentions, the president betrayed no concern as he greeted his visitor.

He stepped easily from his helicopter, put his big arm around Maheu's shoulder, shook hands, and, pumping Maheu vigorously, guided him into the front seat of a waiting car, next to Lady Bird, for a half-hour tour of the Texas domain.

Johnson took the wheel of his white Lincoln Continental convertible and, gesturing broadly, kept up a nonstop monologue, showing off his spread, as he drove at breakneck speed across the rocky land, past the grazing Herefords, past the shack where his grandfather had lived, past the family cemetery with its low stone wall, finally stopping at the small cabin on the north bank of the Pedernales River where the president had been born.

The visit to his birthplace was mandatory. Unlike his fellow Texan, Hughes, Johnson had grown up dirt-poor, not in the oil-rich Texas personified by the billionaire's father, but in the rugged hill country near Austin, where his own father barely scraped by as a hardscrabble farmer. The president insisted that every visitor see his old home, and now he showed Maheu the humble cabin so that he too could be impressed by Johnson's hard climb to power.

Only then did the two men retire alone to the front yard of the big stone ranch house where Johnson now lived, and get down to business.

Maheu did not mention the million dollars. Instead, sitting next to the president on a padded lawn chair, in the shade of an old oak tree, Maheu noted that Hughes had a keen interest in Johnson's future and asked how the billionaire might be of assistance.

Finally, Johnson knew Maheu's mission. The ex-CIA hit man had come to offer him a friendly bribe. The president's reply seemed to invite that approach. Unaware of the potential stakes, however, he kept both his price and his promises discreetly low.

Johnson, Maheu later reported to the penthouse, said that "he is very much interested in dedicating all of his future years to a school of public affairs which will be run in conjunction with the Univ. of Texas adjacent to where the Johnson Library is being built" and "would very much appreciate some help with this program."

The LBJ School and Library increasingly obsessed Johnson in these waning months of his presidency. They would be his monuments to himself, the institutions that would secure his place in history, protect him from "the Harvards," the hostile Eastern professors who would otherwise write his epitaph. Johnson's pitch to Hughes, however, was somewhat more pointed.

"While discussing the purpose of the school and stating specifically his desire to have people become involved in politics and government," Maheu continued, "he stated 'so that we can avoid having jerks like this fellow Zimmerman who is running the anti-trust division of the Dept. of Justice.' He then asked me what the status was pertaining to our Stardust problem. I brought him up to date. He said 'well I am going to get into this and let's see what happens.' "

If the president was none too subtle in linking the library donation to the Stardust deal, he quickly made it clear that he was not willing to sell Hughes the bomb.

Before Maheu could even mention the nuclear tests, Johnson staged a preemptive strike. He recalled the billionaire's letter and deftly discouraged further discussion by saying "this was one document he would not place in the Johnson library, because it would prove embarrassing to Mr. Hughes if he did." Despite the put-down, however, Johnson did not entirely foreclose even that issue. Indeed, according to Maheu, he promised to "do everything in his power to stop future big blasts in Nevada."

Their business concluded, the president invited Maheu into his private office. There was no mention of the helicopter debacle. Despite his staggering losses, Hughes had merely instructed Maheu to find out when the war in Vietnam might end. Johnson would probably have paid a million himself for the answer, and the best he could now offer Maheu was a peek at some top-secret documents. While Maheu sat there trying to find light at the end of the tunnel, the president handled other matters of state. Ironically, among the papers he signed was an executive order allowing the displaced people of Bikini to return to their Pacific atoll. It was finally thought safe—

twenty-two years after the natives had been evicted to make way for America's first major atomic tests. (In fact, the island was later found to be dangerously radioactive, and is still uninhabited.)

After meeting privately with Hughes's ambassador for almost three hours, Johnson invited him to lunch with the First Family—a lunch also attended by Arthur Krim, finance chairman of the Democratic National Committee—and then personally drove Maheu back to his plane.

"I was at the ranch for a total of five hours and I could not have been treated more graciously and hospitably throughout the entire time," Maheu wrote Hughes, concluding his report. "Upon departure he asked me again to convey to you his highest respect and warmest regards."

It certainly seemed a friendly visit. Not long after Maheu flew off, however, Johnson told one aide quite a different story. Hughes's emissary, he confided with apparent dismay, had dared offer him money!

"I told him to stick it up his ass," the president declared, thrusting his arm upward with a vicious twist. Over the next few days word spread through the White House staff that Hughes had offered a big donation to the LBJ Library, and that Johnson had indignantly refused the offer, shocked that Maheu would even suggest such a thing.

Yet at their lunch with Maheu, the president had told his trusted fund-raiser Krim to follow up and get the Hughes money, and in fact later sent Krim to Las Vegas to press Maheu for the contribution.

The cover-up was unnecessary. Hughes had no interest in such side deals. Told that donations to the LBJ Library were limited to $25,000, he reportedly snapped, "Hell, I couldn't control that son of a bitch with $25,000," and never contributed a cent.

Johnson also failed to deliver. He never did bring the bombing to a halt, and if he intervened as promised on the Stardust deal, it had no effect on either the attorney general or his deputy, that "jerk" Zimmerman. Both the antitrust blockade and the dreaded blasts continued.

Circling each other like two wounded lions, neither sure of the other's true strength or intentions, Hughes and Johnson never came to terms. Soon the president would retire permanently to his ranch and himself become a virtual hermit, his failed encounter with Hughes a small part of his bitter memories.

For Hughes, however, it was a turning point. His failure first to persuade, then to buy, Johnson only left him more than ever determined to own the next president. In LBJ, Hughes saw a man he had once bought and was certain was still for sale, but who now refused to sell him what he wanted. Unable to recognize that he was trying to buy the one thing no president could sell—the Bomb—he began to search for a candidate with whom he could do business.

Hughes would pursue Johnson to his last days in office, but his focus had already shifted to another national leader who had proven himself far more cooperative.

8 Poor Hubert

"Here we are, the way politics ought to be in America, the politics of happiness, the politics of joy! And that's the way it's going to be, too, all the way from here on out!"

The voice, so overripe with good cheer, was unmistakable. Bobbing and weaving, flapping his arms, barely able to contain his own high spirits, Hubert Horatio Humphrey launched his presidential campaign. It was April 27, 1968. Almost a month had passed since Johnson's sudden abdication, and now the vice-president finally felt free to declare himself a candidate.

"And so my friends and fellow Americans," he told a national television audience and two thousand supporters jammed into the ballroom of a Washington hotel, "I shall seek the nomination—" Before he could finish, the crowd stood to cheer, shouting, "We Want Humphrey! We Want Humphrey!" the chant drowning him out, and Hubert, beaming, shouted back, "You have him!" and the crowd roared.

Always effusive, the Happy Warrior had never seemed quite so exuberant as now—with his band playing "The Minnesota Rouser" and his people waving their plastic Humphrey hats—he stood ready to enter the White House, proclaiming "the politics of happiness, the politics of joy."

It was a peculiarly inappropriate campaign theme in that wretched year of war, riots, and assassinations. And at that moment it could not have seemed more inappropriate to anyone than to the man who would soon become one of the vice-president's chief backers: Howard Hughes.

For there was no joy in the penthouse. Humphrey's announcement came bubbling over the billionaire's television set just one day after the "Boxcar" blast, and the shaken but determined recluse was plotting a very different kind of campaign.

The politics of money, the politics of graft.

"Bob," wrote Hughes, "we have to act fast or we will be right up against another deadline, making last-minute desperate attempts to abort another threatened blast. The A.E.C. is not going to let this thing rest.

"Now I am no political expert, but I can readily see that we have only one assett of really important value, and I dont have to spell that out, I am sure.

"So, it seems to me we have to lead off with our best shot. I think we must decide which candidate we intend to support and then support him till hell wont have it, but only if he will do something for us on the bomb.

"Now, if Humphries is the man, fine.

"Anyway, as I say, we have only one kind of markers to use in this game, and I think we should decide through whom, and how much, and then go to work."

Howard Hughes could never spell Hubert Humphrey's name correctly—he usually called him "Humphries"—but he had reason to place his bets on the vice-president.

Theirs was a curious relationship. The two men seemingly had nothing in common. Humphrey, the quintessential public man, loved a crowd, was outgoing, garrulous, almost embarrassingly emotional, a complete extrovert. Born in a room above the family drugstore, he grew up poor, had to drop out of college to return to work, and his political career had always been and still was plagued by a chronic lack of money. A classic old-line liberal, a farmer-labor populist, he had championed every social cause from civil rights to arms control to Medicare.

Only three weeks earlier, Hughes's reaction to the assassination of Martin Luther King had dramatized how different the two men were. Humphrey had first come to national prominence leading the fight for a strong civil rights plank at the 1948 Democratic convention, where he declared, "There are those who say, 'We are rushing this issue of civil rights.' I say we are 172 years late." Hughes seized the occasion of King's murder to declare "negroes have already made enough progress to last the next 100 years, and there is such a thing as overdoing it."

Yet now, in the spring of 1968, the Texas oligarch and the Min-

nesota populist forged an alliance. None of Humphrey's issues—
certainly not nuclear disarmament—had ever before been money-
makers. Now, suddenly, he struck gold. Hughes was determined to
stop the bombing at all costs, and the vice-president, who for a decade
had labored unpaid to limit atomic tests, readily enlisted in the billionaire's lucrative antibomb campaign.

Beyond the bomb they had no common bond. Except that Hughes
wanted a president who would be reliably indebted and Humphrey
desperately needed money to reach the White House.

Poor Hubert. Relentless in his pursuit of the presidency since 1952,
he entered the race in 1968 short of cash and haunted by memories
of past defeats, none more vivid than that of the night he sat helpless
in a stalled rented bus, flat-broke, shedding tears of anger and frustration as he heard the private Kennedy jet roar overhead, carrying
his well-heeled opponent to victory in the West Virginia primary, to
the 1960 nomination, to the White House.

This time it would be different. This time Humphrey was determined to go first-class. He would accept illegal corporate contributions from the milk lobby, he would take a questionable loan from
a Minnesota grain merchant, and he would make a deal with Howard
Hughes.

Still, he would be outspent four-to-one by Richard Nixon, would
not have enough money to buy a single national television spot until
the final weeks of his campaign, and would lose the election for want
of a few thousand votes that may well have been his for a few million
dollars.

The day after "Humphries" announced his candidacy, Hughes
pounced. "I read an article in the paper saying H.H.H. is sore-
pressed for solvency at the moment," he wrote. "Are we marching
through this obvious opening? I mean in a really big and definite
way?"

Within two weeks Maheu met privately with the vice-president.
The deal was struck. Before the campaign was over, Hubert Humphrey would receive $100,000—half of it in secret cash—from How-
ard Hughes.

Humphrey was not the only candidate to receive Hughes's support
that year, and it was not only the bombing that troubled Hughes.
As the 1968 election approached, he was faced with a number of
serious, unresolved problems.

His drive to buy up Las Vegas had been stalled by the threatened antitrust action. His once aborted but still cherished plan to acquire the ABC television network needed FCC approval. His move back into the airlines business, through the illegal Air West takeover, would require both CAB and White House clearance. His helicopter deal was ending in disaster, and any chance of salvaging it depended on a new government contract. His TWA legal battle, with $137 million at stake, would come before a Supreme Court reshaped by the new president. A major overhaul of the nation's tax laws loomed, imperiling the exempt status of his medical foundation. And there was always the Hughes Aircraft Company to consider, a billion-dollar-a-year business almost entirely dependent on defense, CIA, and space-agency contracts.

A man whose affairs were so intimately entwined with those of the federal government simply could not leave the selection of a new chief of state to chance.

"I think we should decide which Presidential candidate we are going to support, and then, I think we should go *all the way!*" wrote Hughes, completely nonpartisan, determined only to ride with a winner, even if it meant backing every man in the race.

"I feel that if we climb aboard in the all-out manner I have in mind, then either our candidate or the organization of his party will be able and willing to give us some important assistance. . . .

"For example, if we choose Kennedy or Humphries, then the Dem. party chairman and his associates should help us plenty thru the White House."

Among the Democrats, Humphrey was the obvious choice. For the moment, at least, Hughes saw Bobby Kennedy only as a card to be played in a cynical game that would further entrap the needy vice-president.

"Bob," wrote Hughes, spinning his scenario, "I am wondering if we should not sit down with Humphries and tell him I have been propositioned by Kennedy in the most all-out way."

It was not true. But the lie was certain to scare Humphrey, who did not have ready entree to many other billionaires.

"That I feel I can only sponsor one man in a truely important way," Hughes continued, feeding lines to his henchman to feed to the vice-president. "[T]hat I am willing to risk offending Kennedy and agree to give the most unlimited support to Humphries—not just in Nevada—but on a basis that should provide far more than he ever contemplated for the entire country."

Yes, that should do it. First spook Humphrey with the spectre of a Hughes-Kennedy alliance, then offer to underwrite his entire presidential campaign.

"Then," concluded the spider, finishing his web, "I think we have to tell him what we want. If he is indifferent, then I think we should go to work on Kennedy *without a moments delay.*"

Humphrey was not indifferent. Even before he had officially entered the race, the vice-president had been doing the billionaire's bidding. He arranged the preblast Sawyer-Johnson parley, also pressured a very reluctant AEC commissioner to meet with Hughes's emissary ("the request was so strongly put that he agreed to the meeting," noted an agency report), pushed for a ninety-day moratorium on "Boxcar" at Maheu's urging, and as early as 1967 had tried to plead the billionaire's bomb case with Johnson, only to be turned away by White House Chief of Staff Marvin Watson, who guarded the door to the Oval Office.

Hughes looked on the vice-president as his man in Johnson's White House and tried to influence the recalcitrant commander in chief through his more obliging lieutenant.

"The only way I can see to motivate Johnson," he declared before attempting to bribe the president directly, "would be through a meaningful offer of assistance to Humphries, who is, I understand, Johnson['s] designee."

"There is one man who can accomplish our objective thru Johnson—and that man is H.H.H.," wrote Hughes on another occasion. "Why dont we get word to him on a basis of absolute secrecy that is *really, really reliable* that we will give him immediately *full unlimited* support for his campaign to enter the White House if he will just take this one on for us?"

Hughes expected a return on his investment and was not always satisfied with Humphrey's performance. What the billionaire apparently did not know was that Johnson had only contempt for his vice-president, gave him no power, and in fact enjoyed tormenting him in the cruelest, crudest ways.

The pattern had been established early, in their Senate years. Johnson, then majority leader, would regularly grab Hubert by his lapels, give him his orders, and send him on his way by kicking him in the shins. Hard. Indeed, Humphrey still had scars on his legs, and they were nothing to the scars LBJ later inflicted.

Once he invited his vice-president down to his ranch, then decided that Humphrey should go horseback riding dressed up like a cowboy.

I am afraid there are only two people strong enough to face up to the A.E.C. They are Kennedy or Johnson.

I can see no way to motivate Kennedy except by a ~~truly~~ truly meaningful gesture of assistance.

The only way I can see to motivate Johnson would be through a meaningful offer of assistance to Humphries, who is, I understand, Johnson 'designee'.

So, Bob, I am wondering if we should not sit down with Humphries and tell him I have been propositioned by Kennedy in the most all-out way. That I feel I can only sponsor one man in a truly important way. that I am willing to risk offending Kennedy and agree to give the most unlimited support to Humphries — not just in Nevada — but on a basis that should provide far more than he ever contemplated for the entire country. Then, I think we have to tell him what we want.

If he is indifferent, then I think we should go to work on Kennedy without a moments delay.

He pulled out an outfit that dwarfed his sidekick, complete with a ten-gallon hat that fell over his ears, and put him on the meanest horse at the ranch. Finally, he called in the White House press corps to snap pictures of Hubert looking like a circus clown in mortal terror.

With Humphrey the heir apparent, Johnson continued the torment. Asked by a reporter for a comment on his candidate, LBJ replied, "He cries too much." Pressed further, Johnson snapped, "That's it—he cries too much."

And even now, as a presidential candidate, Humphrey remained quite firmly under LBJ's thumb.

At one point during the campaign, Maheu called Humphrey, and when an aide relayed his message, the vice-president exploded in impotent rage. "Goddamnit, tell Hughes to call the president of the United States, not me," the candidate stood up and shouted. "Just tell him this: right now I couldn't get a pothole fixed on Pennsylvania Avenue, much less have them stop atomic testing in the desert. Have him call Lyndon Johnson."

Still, Hughes continued to find missions for his man, often speaking of the vice-president as if he were just another employee. "I feel we must start a negotiation with the AEC, just as if we were negotiating a business deal," he wrote. "I think we can go thru Humphries. . . ."

"Please advise Humphries that the AEC shot off a 200 kilo test yesterday and did not even extend the courtesy of telling us about it," he complained on another occasion. "Under these circumstances I wish Humphries would try to get a statement from the AEC as to their future plans. . . ."

And when Hughes finally decided to contact Johnson directly, he considered using the vice-president as his messenger boy: "You know I am perfectly willing to write a short personal message to Johnson, which we could ask Humphries to deliver—hand deliver—to Johnson."

When LBJ rejected his bomb plea, the billionaire seemed to hold the hapless vice-president at least partly responsible.

"He should have more influence on the present administration than anyone else," wrote Hughes, still chafing over Johnson's two-week delay in replying to his letter. "But if he is doing anything at all for us, why should the President have gone out of his way to rub it in? This certainly does not sound as if Humphries or anybody has put in even a kind word."

Johnson's maddening intransigence, however, only intensified the billionaire's determination to replace him with a more pliable president.

Barely a week after Humphrey launched his campaign, Maheu launched the Hughes campaign. Soon the two drives would merge.

"The pros feel that the natural person to champion our cause is the Vice President, because of his present position and, more particularly, his candidacy," Maheu reported to the penthouse. "We feel it is important that he come to this conclusion 'on his own.' We, therefore, have the machinery in motion which we hope will cause him to invite me to Washington to plan the strategy.

"In the next 24–48 hours there will be suggestions made to the Vice President. If he reacts as I am hoping and takes the affirmative to work with us on this program, I really believe we will have come a long way."

It did not take Humphrey long to come to the right decision "on his own." The very next day he sent word that he was ready, indeed eager to join forces with Hughes. The news came through a member of his family who was already on board.

Robert Andrew Humphrey, one of the vice-president's three sons, had been hired by Maheu two years earlier as the "mid-western distributor" for Radiarc, Inc., an electronics firm Maheu had purchased as a private investment. The company was not part of the Hughes empire, but its most valuable asset, the junior Humphrey, most definitely seemed to be. He regularly acted as go-between in his father's dealings with Maheu.

"Bob Humphrey is his dad's favorite and a very competent young man," wrote Maheu in a memo on "political assistance" he sent to Hughes. "Any assignment given Bob Humphrey will automatically include the full support and effort of his father, as it has in the past."

Now the vice-president himself seemed ready to join the team. "Bob contacted me today to advise that his father was very anxious to meet with me concerning the future plans of the AEC," Maheu reported, adding a few days later that the Humphrey alliance would be cemented in Denver, Colorado.

"Today the Vice President sent word to me that he will be in Denver on this Thursday and would like to meet with me to discuss his strategy to *delay* and eventually *preclude* the necessity of the big blasts in Nevada."

On May 10, 1968, just two weeks after he entered the race, Hubert

Humphrey mortgaged his campaign to Howard Hughes. In a late-night meeting in the vice-president's suite at the Denver Hilton, Maheu would later testify, Humphrey agreed to battle the bomb in return for a promised one-hundred-thousand-dollar contribution, half of it to be paid in cash.

Deeming the joint venture too "candid" to reveal long-distance, Maheu submitted a written report to Hughes the next day: "The following reflects the suggestions and procedures set forth by the Vice-President. He feels we should have two objectives—(a) delay the future plans of these big blasts until (b) the propitious moment at which the Administration will urge that underground testing be added to the Ban Treaty. He pledges his support and that of the Administration."

This private nuclear-disarmament pact was a real bargain. It would cost Hughes just $400,000. A hundred grand for Humphrey, and $300,000 more to fund an "independent study" by six White House–approved scientists, all known critics of the bomb tests.

"During this program, the Vice-President will work with us very closely and confidentially," added Maheu. "He is anxious to get your reaction to the above-mentioned plan."

Hughes reacted with sour impatience. He expected results for his money—not studies—and he was willing to pay well.

"You say: 'What do you think of Humphries' program?' " he wrote. "Bob, I am no expert at these things. If I were, we would not have to go to Humphries to start with. Any program is as good or as bad as what he can produce with it—I am certainly nobody to evaluate.

"My position is very simple. You know what we want to accomplish and you know our resources are unlimited. You will have to take it from there. I thought you were satisfied with the results of your trip to Denver."

The disappointing Denver summit coincided with the opening of the Vietnam peace talks in Paris, which gave Hughes a new idea about how he might more profitably use the presidential candidate he had just acquired.

He would send Humphrey to Paris.

Obviously the vice-president could no longer be trusted to handle his own campaign strategy. Hughes would have to plot it from the penthouse. In fact, he had in mind a ploy so bold and complicated that Humphrey would have to be kept in the dark until after he had completed his assigned mission.

For the rest of the nation, the burning issue of the 1968 election was the war in Vietnam. For Hughes it was the nuclear blasts in Nevada. It was now his inspiration to subtly link the two issues. If all went well, the unwitting Humphrey would emerge a hero, and Hughes would have peace with honor.

"It is just beginning to filter through to me," Hughes wrote, "that now is the ideal moment for us to persuade Humphries or some other strong voice to come out and make a very inspiring tender of good wishes and felicitations to the just now convening delegates to the peace talks in Paris.

"In this first expression of the prayers of all mankind for the successful conclusion of the talks before the delegates and representatives now convening in Paris, I think it would be wise to omit any reference to the explosions in Nevada.

"However, the man we encourage to deliver this tender of good wishes and the prayers and hopes of all mankind, etc., etc., should be some one we can rely upon to deliver an impassioned plea for postponement of any explosion that may be scheduled. In other words, the man we select for this occasion should not know what we have in mind at all, and we should make sure he says nothing at this time to disclose what is being planned. However, it should be somebody we feel we control sufficiently so that, upon request a little later, he will be calculated to say what we may want him to say.

"This sounds more complicated than it is," Hughes assured Maheu. "I think you, knowing my devious mind, are pretty well aware [of] what I am thinking about."

Maheu knew very well what Hughes meant, but he still appeared to place more faith in the Denver plan his master had scorned. Humphrey did not embark for Paris. He seemed, however, to be doing quite well for Hughes in Washington.

So well, in fact, that the Atomic Energy Commission became increasingly alarmed that a Hughes panel of scientists, backed by the vice-president and packed with bomb-test foes, might well derail the agency's entire Nevada operation.

Soon top AEC officials were exchanging memorandums almost as frequently as Hughes and Maheu, trying to determine if the man who might soon be president of the United States had actually joined with its wealthiest private citizen in an antinuclear alliance.

"I called Col. Hunt in the Vice President's office to discuss with him rumors we had been hearing in Las Vegas as regards an agreement between the Vice President and the Hughes organization," reported the agency's director, Arnold Fritsch. "I indicated to him that while we had this only as a rumor, we were concerned since the high-yield test program involves some vital national security needs."

When the AEC discovered the rumors were indeed well founded, it first tried to abort the "independent" Hughes study, then, unable to block it, scrambled to remove the panel from the billionaire's control.

AEC Chairman Seaborg got word to the president. Johnson was angry. He had enough troubles without a new ban-the-bomb crusade to fuel antiwar feeling, and he did not appreciate Hughes's attempted end run. Besides, Humphrey was hardly being discreet about his dealings with the billionaire. Already it was common knowledge in the White House that the vice-president was getting campaign money from Hughes. Johnson was not merely angry. He was worried.

"Hubert had better keep his pants zipped," the president told an aide. "He's going to get caught with his pecker in Hughes's pocket."

Nervous about Humphrey's now open advocacy of the Hughes protest, Johnson took charge. He scuttled the Hughes-Humphrey plan by himself appointing a panel to investigate the bomb tests. But instead of Humphrey's half-dozen doves, Johnson picked a group of scientists more likely to call down tactical strikes on the Las Vegas Strip.

Still, Humphrey had forced the first official probe of nuclear hazards. And when the presidential panel made its report, its findings came as quite a shock. Hughes was right. The big blasts were dangerous. A blue-ribbon panel of conservative scientists hand-picked by the AEC, led by its own former research director and two top White House advisers, declared Hughes's fears well founded, warned that the megaton explosions could trigger major earthquakes, and called for a halt to the Nevada tests.

Humphrey had come through. Too late, however, to do either himself or his hidden benefactor any good. By the time the scientists convened in November, Humphrey had already lost the election. He was never even allowed to see their report, which first Johnson and then Nixon entirely ignored and completely suppressed. Despite the warnings of real and present danger, the bombing continued unabated.

Back at the penthouse, Hughes, always dubious about Humphrey's indirect approach, anticipated just such a debacle.

He had checked with his own scientists at the Hughes Aircraft Company, who warned that the government would simply reject any adverse findings: "They said, 'If you could bring Einstein back from the grave and let him make the study, it would not make one damned bit of difference.' They said, 'You are playing with a stacked deck, and surely you have been in Las Vegas long enough to know what a stacked deck is!' "

Indeed, Hughes knew precisely what a stacked deck was. He was using one, stacked in his favor, in the high-stakes game he was playing with candidate Humphrey.

As the AEC battle raged through the summer and into the fall of 1968, Hughes found new tasks for the vice-president. Still fighting the Justice Department on the antitrust front, and certain he was the victim of some unknown conspiracy, he expected his candidate to discover who was behind the vendetta.

"Here is what I dont understand," complained Hughes, speaking of Humphrey as if he were just another employee. "If we have notified H.H.H. of our responsiveness to his prior requests, then why dont we simply tell him we want to know who has instructed the Attorney General to threaten action against us in the S/dust matter. It is unrealistic to assume that Humphries does not know or cannot find out the real source of our trouble."

When Hughes was also hit with an antitrust threat regarding his attempt to seize control of ABC, he was no longer content to rely on Humphrey alone.

"The Justice Dept. is driving us crazy," he fumed.

"Bob, I think it is imperative that we make an alliance with Humphries, the White House, Nixon, or McCarthy and agree to supply all-out unlimited support in return for taking this Justice Dept. off my back but *now*!"

It was not the vice-president's willingness Hughes doubted so much as his ability. A bought man who could not deliver was hardly better than a man who could not be bought.

There was, of course, among the Democrats, no viable alternative to Humphrey, whatever his failings. And after June 6, 1968, there was no alternative at all.

Bobby Kennedy was dead. His assassination dramatically altered the presidential campaign, left the nation shaken, and even caused Howard Hughes to reassess his position. The political marketplace was in flux. It was no time to make a hasty purchase. He would wait a couple of days.

"Re. the next 48 hrs.," wrote Hughes, "I think we must decide whom we want to see nominated by each party, and then not wait for it to happen, but go out and do something about it.

"The last person I want to see nominated is Edward Kennedy. He would receive too much support from others. I want to see a candidate who needs us and wants our help. I still favor Humphries. But I urge against any further support until we feel his pulse. Only a couple of days—but I dont feel we should increase our investment in him in the meantime. Only until you get some kind of an indication of his attitude and his capabilities."

There was no need to rush to the bank. Humphrey would be waiting—still a candidate who needed and wanted Hughes's help—whenever the billionaire was ready.

Meanwhile, Maheu felt Humphrey's pulse and reported back to the penthouse. "We are continuing to move on all fronts on the AEC matter," he wrote. "The Vice President has been most cooperative in every instance and we continually, through him, are feeding most important data to the White House, the proper sources at the U.N., and even more importantly to those involved in very high level conferences with the Russians."

"I received a telephone call this morning from Bob Humphrey, the Vice President's son," Maheu told his boss in another of a steady stream of memos. "He informed me that his father was sending one of his top men to discuss with me the strategy for delaying any megaton tests until after the elections and then, hopefully, forever."

There was only one catch. Maheu intended to hold the big strategy talks out on his yacht. He was about to weigh anchor when Hughes got the message. As desperate as he was to stop the bombing, as anxious as he was to seduce Humphrey, he could not bear to let Maheu escape.

"Now, Bob, I dont have to remind you that I am just as disturbed about the AEC as you are," he wrote, catching the yacht just in time. "I am also just as aware of Humphries' importance. But I cannot believe that there is no way to service the VP properly except at the expense of punishing me.

"I will appreciate it very much, Bob, if you will delay your departure to Catalina until I communicate with you about several very important matters."

Neither Maheu nor the vice-president's aide ever left shore. Hughes kept his first mate on dry land all day, sending him an endless series

6/6/68

Bob -

Re. the next 48 hrs., I
think we must decide whom
we want to see nominated
by each party, and then not
wait for it to happen, but go
out and do something about it.

The last person I want
to see nominated is Edward
Kennedy. He would receive too
much support from others. I
want to see a candidate who
needs us and wants our help.
I still favor Humphries. But
I urge against any further
support until we feel his pulse.
Only a couple of days - but
I don't feel we should ~~be~~
~~increase~~ increase our
investment in him in the
meantime. Only until you get
some kind of an indication
of his attitude and his capabilities.

Please let me know
your recommendation on all
points. Many thanks,

Howard

of memos, all of course requiring his immediate attention. Still, Maheu managed to check Humphrey's pulse.

"Today we talked to Washington twice," Maheu reported from the Balboa Bay Yacht Club, "and I now believe that we will be instrumental in naming the next scientific advisor to the White House."

Next Maheu got word from Humphrey himself, who also wanted Hughes to help pick his running mate.

"Humphrey is going to be in L.A. Monday," Maheu wrote, "and, among other things, he wants to discuss with me the Vice Presidential candidate. He has asked if I would meet with him."

Humphrey's attitude was perfect. As for his capabilities, they would improve if he became president. And, with Kennedy dead, there was little doubt that Humphrey would soon be the Democratic nominee.

It was time to make the promised payoff.

On July 29, 1968, Robert Maheu checked into the Century Plaza Hotel in Los Angeles, carrying with him a manila envelope stuffed with $25,000 in hundred-dollar bills. He took a suite of rooms on the seventeenth floor and waited there for a courier to arrive from Las Vegas with an additional $25,000 in a black briefcase. Then he went downstairs to meet the candidate.

Humphrey had come to town a few days earlier and was winding up his campaign swing with a five-thousand-dollar-a-plate dinner for thirty select contributors in a conference room at the same hotel. Maheu greeted the vice-president at a cocktail reception, and toward the end of the evening arranged a private meeting through their mutual friend Lloyd Hand, former U.S. chief of protocol. Invited to accompany the candidate on a drive to the airport, Maheu left the dinner, went up to his suite, and returned with the black briefcase.

Humphrey's limousine was waiting. Satchel in hand, Maheu joined the vice-president in the rear compartment. They sat facing each other, Maheu on a jump seat, and chatted a few minutes about Hughes and the bomb tests. Then Maheu placed the cash-laden briefcase, now stuffed with the entire $50,000, at Humphrey's feet. The motorcade came to an unscheduled halt after traveling just five hundred yards, and Maheu, mission completed, stepped out.

"I had an excellent meeting," he wrote, reporting his conquest later that night, "and this man wants me to assure you that he will break his back in an effort to accomplish our needs."

Hubert Humphrey had lost his virginity in the classic American way—with a furtive quickie in the backseat of a car. It was a fittingly sad consummation of the Hughes-Humphrey relationship, the corruption of a candidate more to be pitied than scorned. He had simply surrendered to the sordid realities of politics in America.

Humphrey, who had opened his campaign proclaiming the "politics of joy," arrived in Chicago August 25 morose, with no one to greet him except a handful of paid party workers. There were no crowds lining the route from the airport to the hotel, no cheering supporters to welcome the candidate to his convention headquarters. Humphrey was relieved simply to get into his suite unmolested.

Chicago was in turmoil. Earlier that Sunday police had swept through Lincoln Park, clubbing antiwar demonstrators, beating youths blinded by tear gas. The mayhem mounted every day. Humphrey was nervous.

So was Maheu. The backseat payoff was his biggest bag job. Although he had handled Hughes's political money for years, he had never before passed $50,000 in secret cash to a vice-president of the United States.

"I know you think I may be overly cautious about having messages transmitted over the telephone which pertain to Humphrey and the convention," he wrote Hughes as the Democrats prepared to choose a presidential candidate.

"Personally, I would put nothing past the AEC and their attempt to curtail our efforts. If—they ever were in a position to show the extent to which we are helping this man—they would clobber us.

"I don't mind taking a calculated risk on Air West, L.A. Airways and many other projects in which we are involved—but—the Humphrey situation is one we should play real close to the vest."

And that's how they played it, all through the convention.

Closeted in their hotel command posts in Las Vegas and Chicago, both Hughes and Humphrey were feeling besieged. Neither really focused on the open warfare in the streets of Chicago but instead on hidden threats from rival powers.

First there was the president, Lyndon Johnson. For weeks he had been publicly ridiculing and privately tormenting his presumed heir, and now Humphrey feared something far worse. A coup. There were rumors that LBJ was about to board *Air Force One*, fly into Chicago, appear at the convention on his sixtieth birthday, and dramatically seize the nomination back from Humphrey.

"Howard, I dont think this will happen but it is a possibility which

I think we must bear in mind," Maheu cautioned Hughes. "When the President shows up at the Convention, it is conceiveable that the place may break up in pandemonium and that the delegates could insist on a draft. Obviously, if this takes place, the Vice President is in no position to fight it.

"I believe, therefore, that if it is your intention to pledge some support in helping the President with his new concept of a College of Public Affairs at the University of Texas, we should do so prior to the Convention being in full force."

Hughes, however, remained stubbornly unwilling to make the donation Johnson had requested in his secret meeting with Maheu at the LBJ Ranch two weeks earlier, and was instead preoccupied with the threat of a sudden boom for Teddy Kennedy.

"Needless to say, there is one hell of a drive on to draft Kennedy," Maheu told Hughes. "Our informants tell us, however, that, as of this morning, Mr. H. is in."

Hughes was not satisfied. "I dont want to see Ted Kennedy get the V.P. nomination," he scrawled, determined to keep Teddy off the ticket entirely. "Is there anything we can do about this?"

Maheu checked out the scene in Chicago and reported back to the penthouse. "Bob believes the Kennedy situation is under control," a Mormon aide told Hughes. "Bob's choice would be the Senator from Maine."

That senator, of course, was none other than Maheu's old pal Ed Muskie. In his hotel suite, Humphrey was about to make the same choice. After agonizing for hours, Humphrey finally turned to his campaign manager, Larry O'Brien, and asked, "Larry, if you had fifteen seconds to decide, who would it be?" O'Brien picked Muskie, and Hubert called in the big man from Maine.

"Howard, as I indicated to you yesterday, Muskie was definitely my No. 1 choice," wrote a triumphant Maheu. "He and his wife, my wife and I have been lifelong friends—all coming from the same small city in Maine. We have been supporting him since his first trip in the political arena, and he is truly one hell of a man. He was my personal attorney until he became a senator. As a matter of fact, he stopped here at the D.I. a few months ago to see me. The Vice President and Larry are fully aware of my closeness to Muskie."

All the while Hughes and Maheu and Humphrey and O'Brien were cutting backroom deals, the battle raged in the streets of Chicago. Finally, on the evening of Wednesday, August 28, just as the delegates prepared to cast their ballots in a convention hall surrounded by barbed wire and armored personnel vehicles, the violence outside peaked.

Out in front of the Conrad Hilton, right below Humphrey's window, in full view of the television cameras, the Chicago police suddenly attacked thousands of demonstrators marching on the amphitheatre. It was a bloodbath. Shooting tear gas, spraying Mace, waving their billy clubs, the helmeted cops converged from all sides, cutting through the crowd, chasing men and women, teenaged boys and girls, running them down, beating them with unrestrained fury, finally losing all control and attacking even middle-aged bystanders, pushing scores of them backward through the hotel's plate-glass window and charging in after them, swinging wildly, clubbing patrons sitting at the bar, eating in the restaurant, standing in the lobby.

"The whole world is watching!" chanted the demonstrators outside, but Mayor Daley and his police didn't seem to care.

Even inside the convention hall, Daley's security force attacked and dragged off dissident delegates, even went after Dan Rather, punching him in the belly and beating him to the floor live on national television, while a shocked Walter Cronkite called to him from the anchor booth in horror.

From the podium, Senator Abraham Ribicoff denounced "Gestapo tactics in the streets of Chicago," and Mayor Daley just below stood up enraged, shaking his fist at the senator, calling him a "fucking Jew bastard."

In that scene of violence and mass hysteria, Hubert Humphrey was nominated the Democrats' candidate for president of the United States.

So, at the end, it came down to that. After all the passion and hope and tragedy and turmoil of 1968, after McCarthy and his children's crusade, after New Hampshire and Johnson's abdication, after Bobby Kennedy and his assassination, after the riots and marches and demonstrations, after the siege of Chicago, it came down to that—a choice between the old Humphrey and the new Nixon.

Up in his penthouse, watching TV, Howard Hughes could not have been more pleased.

It was now a contest he could not lose.

"Rather than take the calculated risk of 'picking the winner' I think we should hedge our bets," wrote Maheu, plotting the final drive. "There is no doubt in my mind that if the election were tonight the Republicans would enjoy a glorious victory. There is equally no doubt in my mind that in the sanctimonious confines of the voting booth there will be many Democrats who will have a tremendous struggle with their conscience and make an instantaneous change in their thinking.

"I have taken the liberty of hedging our bets and sincerely hope that you will agree with my judgement. I also believe that we should do substantially more for each since we are playing for such big stakes."

Hughes agreed. He could hardly take his chances on sanctimonious voters acting out of conscience. Soon he would pass $50,000 to Nixon through Governor Laxalt and a second $50,000 to Humphrey through Dwayne Andreas, a longtime backer who had no official role in the campaign but handled the "sensitive" contributions.

"You may rest assured, Howard," reported Maheu, "that we have taken all necessary steps to be in a good posture, whichever way it goes."

It was not going well for Humphrey as he stepped to the podium in Chicago to accept his nomination on Thursday, August 29, the final night of the Democratic convention.

Indeed, poor Hubert had never looked worse than now, at his moment of greatest triumph. Weighed down by the war and LBJ and Mayor Daley, by all the dead in Vietnam and all the demonstrators beaten in Chicago, he seemed covered with blood, covered with shame, as irrevocably soiled as if he had had to crawl on his belly through the slime of the stockyards to get that nomination, and now that he finally had it, the prize seemed only to further befoul him.

Still he stood there with a frozen smile, slavishly thanked his cruel master Lyndon Johnson, and closed with words so obviously hollow they must have hurt: "I say to this great convention, and to this great nation of ours, I am ready to lead our country!"

It was past two in the morning by the time Humphrey made it back to his hotel. He was tired and battered but could not sleep. Obsessively immaculate and offended by dirt, he tidied up his room, busily emptying ashtrays and washing out half-empty glasses, as if by cleaning the suite he could also cleanse himself of the stain of Chicago. Then he sent a Secret Service agent to summon Larry O'Brien.

From three A.M. until past dawn Humphrey and O'Brien talked. The vice-president poured out his pain. He was desperate. He had no campaign money, he had no campaign plan, and now he also had no campaign manager. O'Brien had agreed to help Humphrey only through the convention. Now Hubert was on his own. O'Brien had other plans. He had never told Humphrey the details, but he had made it clear from the start that he was quitting politics to make some real money.

This was farewell. They sat together hour after hour in a room smelling of tear gas, with Humphrey, who cried easily anyway, close to tears, and all the while they could hear the angry shouts of demonstrators in the street below, even now in the middle of the night still chanting, "Dump the Hump! Dump the Hump!"

"Larry, do you hear those people down there?" wailed Humphrey, suddenly begging O'Brien to stay on and run his campaign. "Please, Larry, don't leave me naked."

O'Brien was not swayed. He was through with public service. He was through with the destitute Humphrey. He had a new job waiting. He was eager to cash in.

"For Christsake, Hubert," he exploded, "this is my private-sector move!"

Humphrey groveled. "Larry, I've just got to have you," he pleaded. "If I get them to agree to a delay, will that settle it?"

O'Brien relented. For the first time he told Humphrey the name of his new boss. It was a sickening final blow.

Now, at dawn on Friday, August 30, 1968, Hubert Humphrey, the vice-president of the United States, the man just nominated to be president, had to pick up his phone and call Robert Maheu, call the man who employed his son and had helped pick his running mate, call the man who had slipped him fifty grand in the backseat of a car, call and beg Maheu to allow O'Brien to remain his campaign manager.

Unknown to Humphrey until now, Larry O'Brien had already agreed to go to work for Howard Hughes.

9 Camelot

The old bastard.

That's who Howard Hughes thought of now, that's who he always thought of when he thought of the Kennedys. Not Jack. Not Bobby. Not Teddy. Not the glamorous sons but their cutthroat father. Old Joe. He was the real Kennedy, the one Hughes remembered. And despised.

"The Kennedy family and their money and influence have been a thorn that has been relentlessly shoved into my guts since the very beginning of my business activities," wrote the billionaire, bursting with a grudge he had held for forty years.

Right from the start Joseph P. Kennedy had been there to plague him. They had arrived together in Hollywood in the mid-1920s, the Boston Irishman and the Texas WASP invading an infant industry created by immigrant Jews. They both figured to take over the town.

Hughes had come to make movies. Not yet twenty, full of romantic visions, the tall, handsome tycoon left Houston in 1925 and took his inheritance to the Dream Capital. There, amid the palm trees and pink stucco palaces, former furriers and ragmen, many just off the boat, were shaping America's image of itself. But Hughes *was* the image they had created, and within a few years he was more than a top producer, he was a star.

Kennedy had come only to make money. He arrived less than a year after Hughes, at thirty-seven already an established, hard-bitten financier and in movieland strictly on business. "Look at that bunch of pants pressers in Hollywood making themselves millionaires," he told an associate as he set out for California. "I could take the whole damn business away from them."

He tried. Joe Kennedy was a ruthless operator, and he gave many men good reason to hate him. But what had he done to so irritate Hughes? It seemed to have something to do with RKO. Kennedy never made a movie of note, but he did found a movie studio, and Hughes seemed to hold that against him. "You see Joe Kennedy used to own the biggest part of RKO before I got into it," he explained, suggesting that the studio was somehow behind the big grudge.

Twenty years later Hughes himself would buy RKO. But not from Kennedy. Joe was long gone from Hollywood, in and out in his usual style, a quick raid for a quick profit, gone before Hughes had made his first big movie, gone before Hughes was anything more than a rich kid. They never had any dealings over RKO, they never dealt with each other at all.

So why the grudge? In his three years in Hollywood, Kennedy probably never even met Hughes--"Howard was just a kid," noted Joe's mistress Gloria Swanson. "We didn't move in the same circles"—and their paths would never cross again.

Joe moved on to banking, liquor, and land, always striking hard and fast, often skirting the law, building his fortune with whiskey deals that bordered on bootlegging and cynical stock-market manipulations, less a businessman than a predator on other men's businesses, a bold buccaneer who continued milking Wall Street right up to the moment he was named first chairman of the Securities and Exchange Commission, some said beyond. In short, a man much like Hughes himself would become, but less a romantic. He made many enemies, he crushed many rivals, he cheated his partners, but not once did he tangle with Hughes.

So what was the "thorn"? What terrible thing had old Joe done to young Howard that Hughes would hold so strong a grudge for forty years? Apparently nothing. Nothing at all.

All Howard Hughes held against the Kennedys was the simple fact that they too had money and power. That was the thorn shoved into his guts. Relentlessly.

In the beginning, they had more money. Now that he had far more money,* they had more power. They always seemed to have what Hughes wanted. Back in Hollywood, it was RKO. Later, it was the

*So much more that when *Fortune* magazine sized up the wealthy in 1968, the whole of the Kennedys' net worth—at most $300 million—was less than the margin of error in appraising Hughes.

White House. Old Joe had not only bought it for his son Jack, he had stolen it from Hughes. The billionaire had not forgotten or forgiven that either.

"You can see how cruel it was, after my all-out support of Nixon, to have Jack Kennedy achieve that very, *very* marginal so-called victory over my man," wrote Hughes, bitterly recalling the Kennedy gang's "theft" of the White House in 1960.

Both he and Joe had set out to buy America. Kennedy had succeeded. But it was more than that. Over the years there had been a strange reversal of roles. In their Hollywood days, Hughes had been the newsreel hero, Joe the cynical operator. Now the Kennedys had escaped the curse of their father to become royalty, while Hughes had taken his place as the troll under the bridge.

And now, in 1968, just as Hughes finally seemed to have it all in the bag, his drive to buy the government of the United States all but guaranteed, certain of victory, having bought both Humphrey and Nixon, old Joe was about to snatch it away again. With Bobby.

On Saturday, March 16, 1968, Robert F. Kennedy suddenly entered the race, announcing his bid to reclaim the throne from the same Senate room his brother had used to launch his campaign eight years earlier.

"I do not run for the presidency merely to oppose any man, but to propose new policies," he declared, looking very young and very vulnerable, his long hair falling across his forehead, his famous Kennedy voice halting and uncertain, yet striking fear into older, more powerful men. "I cannot stand aside from the contest that will decide our nation's future, and our children's future."

Neither could Hughes. Alone in his penthouse, with a fortune far greater than old Joe's but without an heir, the billionaire watched Bobby's televised speech, saw Joe about to put another son in the White House, and grabbed for his yellow legal pad.

"Re: Kennedy, I want him for President like I want the mumps," he wrote. "I can think of nothing worse than 8 years under his exalted leadership. God help us!

"However, lets face it. It could happen, so lets cover our bets both ways."

Hughes was not about to be denied the Oval Office. Not this time. He would own the next president even if he had to buy every candidate in the race, even if that meant backing Bobby. But how could he buy a Kennedy?

The question took on new urgency just one month later when the Atomic Energy Commission declared war. Facing the big blast, unable to move Lyndon Johnson, doubtful that Humphrey could block it, Hughes reviewed his strategy.

"I am afraid there are only two people strong enough to stand up to the AEC," he wrote. "They are Kennedy or Johnson.

"I can see no way to motivate Kennedy except by a truely meaningful gesture of assistance."

Reluctant to join forces with Kennedy and far from certain that Bobby could be bought, Hughes still saw a way he could use the Kennedy threat to end the nuclear threat. It was at this time that he sent word to Johnson that he would back Humphrey "to any extent necessary to match the funds expended by Kennedy." At the same time he ordered Maheu to throw a real scare into the needy vice-president: "sit down with Humphries and tell him I have been propositioned by Kennedy in the most all-out way."

It was a bare-faced lie. But less than two weeks later it came true.

Before Hughes could move to cover his bets, before Bobby had won his first primary, Kennedy sent an emissary to Hughes. Even Kennedy.

Maheu reported the contact: "Pierre Salinger called me asking if he could have a conference in Las Vegas immediately after the results of the Indiana Primary which is being held tomorrow. He stated that 'Bobby' agrees with our position of delaying these AEC tests and they want to confer with us before taking any 'overt' position.

"Howard, you and I both know that this is the overture to financial help for their campaign—and I would like some guidance from you as to how we play the music.

"If our only concern were of a 'political' nature, I would be tempted to forget about Kennedy—because I truly believe 'Hubert' has enough '*due bills*' from the political pros to assure him the Democratic nomination. However, we have other things at stake for the present and it might be wise to buy some 'insurance.' "

Hughes was not surprised by the approach. He had been expecting it. The overture might be from Camelot, but to him it was an old familiar tune.

"I dont know what it is that Sallinger and Kennedy want, but I have a pretty good idea what they will want before too long," replied Hughes, with the satisfaction of a cynic watching the last idol fall.

"I am not in favor, at the moment, of contributing any \$\$ unless he *can* and *will* make some kind of a half-assed promise to help us postpone or abort the bombing. Now, if he gets the nomination, then I think we are forced to contribute no matter what he does about the bomb.

"So, to summarize, until either some promise re: the bomb, or his nomination, I recommend a stalling operation inlaid with beautiful dialogue and all sorts of encouragement for the future, but involving no hard spending money.

"But, I repeat, I would try not to make an enemy of him."

Pierre Salinger came to Las Vegas early in May, just after Kennedy's first primary victory. He reminded Maheu that Bobby had called for an end to all nuclear tests in his maiden Senate speech three years earlier, assured him that Kennedy would now help Hughes battle the bomb, and asked for a contribution. Maheu stalled but promised to run it by his boss.

It was all quite friendly. Maheu and Salinger had known each other for years, and Maheu had even served as cochairman of Salinger's own 1964 Senate campaign in California.

Bobby Kennedy also knew of Maheu. From the Castro assassination plot. He had learned of that CIA-Mafia murder conspiracy in May 1962, when he was attorney general and his brother was president. The Agency had to tell him. There was no other way to block Maheu's prosecution for wiretapping comedian Dan Rowan, rival for the affections of singer Phyllis McGuire, girlfriend of Chicago Mob boss Sam Giancana. Kennedy was shocked. Not about the failed attempt to kill Castro, which he and his brother almost certainly approved in advance, but about the CIA's choice of hit men. Especially Giancana. Kennedy had to tell J. Edgar Hoover, knowing all the while that Hoover knew that brother Jack had only recently ended a White House affair with another of Giancana's mistresses, Judith Campbell.

And Maheu had been right in the middle of it all. Now Kennedy had to assume that Maheu—and therefore Hughes—knew the darkest secrets of Camelot, and had to wonder if Maheu knew something darker still: who killed his brother.

The possible connections between the Castro plot and Dallas had long anguished Kennedy. And just a year earlier the entire ugly story had started to surface with a column by Drew Pearson that virtually branded him with the mark of Cain.

"President Johnson is sitting on a political H-bomb," it began, "an unconfirmed report that Sen. Robert Kennedy may have approved an assassination plot which then possibly backfired against his late brother." It was Bobby's worst nightmare, the fear he confided to a few close friends that Castro or the Mafia or the CIA itself had ordered his brother's murder.

Lurking in the background of this tangled nightmare was Maheu's boss—the mysterious billionaire with a burning hatred of the entire Kennedy family.

Bobby could not have known the full extent of Hughes's hate, but he knew quite well the dangers of taking Hughes's money. He himself had singled out a scandal over funds Nixon received from Hughes as a decisive factor in his brother's 1960 victory, and later as attorney general secretly investigated the Hughes-Nixon dealings.

But now, in 1968, the need for campaign money was urgent, and Kennedy apparently solicited Hughes's contribution in the same spirit in which it would be given: business as usual.

Maheu called Salinger a couple of weeks after their Las Vegas meeting to say that Hughes would give Kennedy $25,000. Not a real investment, but a good hedge. Salinger, in Portland for the Oregon primary, said he would return to Las Vegas to pick up the cash right after the next contest, in California. It was only a week away. But by then it was too late.

At first the cheers drowned out the gunshots.

Bobby Kennedy had just won the big one. California. It looked like he might actually go all the way. In twelve incredible weeks he had helped force Lyndon Johnson to abdicate, he had beaten Hubert Humphrey in his home state, South Dakota, and now he had defeated his antiwar rival Eugene McCarthy in California. At midnight on Tuesday, June 4, 1968, he entered the packed ballroom of the Ambassador Hotel in Los Angeles to claim his victory.

Smiling and exuberant, Kennedy joked with his cheering supporters, flashed a V-sign and declared, "Now it's on to Chicago, and let's win there!" Then he left the podium, looking like the next president of the United States.

Minutes later he lay dying, shot through the head.

Howard Hughes watched it all. He saw it happen live and in color, and he stayed up through the night to watch the replays—the victory speech, the sound of gunfire, Bobby lying in a pool of blood—over and over again. He listened to the hospital bulletins, watched the random and collective scenes of shock and horror—people running, crying, screaming, kneeling silently to pray—he saw the Kennedy family gather for another grim deathwatch, and he kept his own TV vigil.

News reports and solemn commentary blared in his bedroom all night: "There was only one assailant . . . this was not a conspiracy . . . a sense of guilt for all Americans . . . it was clearly the act of one man . . . the crisis of violence in this country . . . just weeks after the King assassination . . . brother of the martyred president . . . there is no doubt, this was not a conspiracy. . . ."

While TV commentators once more rushed to reassure a shocked nation, Hughes began to conspire. He reached for his bedside legal pad and, while Kennedy's life still hung in the balance, wrote:

"It seems to me that this particular moment in the historical passage of time may be the very most ideal to launch our anti-anti-trust campaign.

"In other words, I cannot imagine another time, if we waited a year, when public sentiment will ever again be so violently and passionately focused on the need for measures to control crime.

"Surely this is the truely perfect background to support our appeal to the criminal division of Justice, pointing to what we have already done in clearing the atmosphere here, and the extreme disadvantage of permitting the Anti-Trust Division to jeopardize this unique opportunity, which in all likelyhood, will never again be available—that is to say, the opportunity, with the public aroused as it presently is, of eliminating completely force and violence as significant factors bearing on the way of life in this community.

"Bob, I urge you contact Justice *at once*. I just dont want you to miss the opportunity of mobilizing this intense feeling."

A golden opportunity to get on with his Monopoly game in Las Vegas. That was all the assassination meant to him. At first. But Hughes maintained his TV vigil for almost twenty-six hours while Kennedy clung to life, and by the time Bobby died he had come to see the deeper meaning of the tragedy.

He watched a dazed Frank Mankiewicz walk into the makeshift press room of the Good Samaritan Hospital one last time to tell the world that Bobby Kennedy was dead. It was the moment Hughes had been waiting for through two sleepless nights.

"I hate to be quick on the draw," he wrote, barely able to restrain himself, "but I see here an opportunity that may not happen again in a lifetime. I dont aspire to be President, but I do want political strength.

"I mean the kind of an organization so that we would never have to worry about a jerky little thing like this anti-trust problem—not in 100 years.

"And I mean the kind of a set up that, if we wanted to, could put Gov. Laxalt in the White House in 1972 or 76.

"Anyway, it seems to me that the very people we need have just fallen smack into our hands."

The suddenly leaderless Kennedy gang was up for grabs. He would hire the Kennedy machine and make it the Hughes machine. He would buy the Kennedy magic, and with it place a man of his own creation in the White House. A man like Paul Laxalt.

But Kennedy's murder had deeper meaning still. It had removed from the 1968 race the one candidate Hughes did not want and could not control. He had to move quickly to consolidate his gains.

Maheu was confused. The memos came at him so fast and furious in the middle of a night of national cataclysm, the missions proposed were so bold and outrageous, that not even Hughes's veteran bagman could immediately comprehend that his boss actually wanted him not only to pick the next president, but also to buy Camelot.

"I get the impression from your note that you want to confine this activity to someone within the 'Kennedy' people," Maheu replied. "I am sure my impression must be wrong because, naturally, to accomplish your purpose, we must think outside of this particular realm.

"Obviously Sen. Ted Kennedy will be their heir apparent. I expect to see some very strange alliances. In any event, Howard, will you please clarify my impression."

Strange alliances? Hughes was not interested in making any alliances, and certainly not with the Kennedys. What he had in mind was a simple business transaction.

"I want us to hire Bob Kennedy's entire organization," he explained with some impatience. "They are used to having the Kennedy money behind them and we can equal that. I dont want an alliance with the Kennedy group, I want to put them on the payroll."

Hughes fired all that off to Maheu within hours of Kennedy's death but was now so excited he could not sleep. Instead, he continued to watch the replays of the assassination and the film clips of Bobby's life, his eyes fixed on the TV screen until past dawn. Then, finally satisfied that he had seen the full meaning of the tragedy and all its opportunities, he went to sleep, just as most of the nation woke up in horror to discover that Bobby was dead.

Hughes himself arose Thursday afternoon still excited.

"I have just awakened," he immediately scrawled, dashing off another memo to Maheu. "I was up all night Monday and Tuesday nights.* I heard Mankiewicz make the fateful announcement and, since our ch 8 was still on the air, I stayed up all night to watch in amazement as we continued to achieve absolutely exclusive coverage of his death and obituary material etc."

Hughes was thrilled by the coup his own television station, the local CBS affiliate, had scored.

"The other two networks, ABC and NBC were not on the air in Sou. Nevada during the entire night. . . . ABC and NBC had just closed down their broadcasts from the hospital for the night and ch 13 and ch 3 had just gone dark for the night. This was understandable, as the doctors had just announced that there would be no more regular bulletins until morning.

"I believe it was sheer accident that CBS was still on the air when the bomb fell. Of course they (CBS) made the most of it, and I thought how lucky we were to have been on the air and achieved this historic news broadcast. . . .

"Anyway, Bob, please do not say anything to anybody about our achieving this TV exclusive," Hughes cautioned, suddenly serious, recognizing how unseemly and even dangerous it might be to boast about their small triumph when things so much more important were at stake. "It occurred to me you might mention it by way of gently needling your friends in ch 13. But please do not. I am very desirous that we retain the late night movie programing exclusively here in Sou. Nevada. I hope eventually to extend this into an all-night, every-night show, and I dont want any competition. I dont think the market can support 2 such shows."

My God! That would be a real tragedy. It could imperil his own private "Late-Late Show," his beloved "Swinging Shift." Having taken the necessary precautions on that vital front, Hughes moved on to other business.

"Returning to this morning, I am certain that you, at no time, really understood what I was urging you to do. Bob, it is true that

---

*Hughes was mistaken about the days—it was actually Tuesday and Wednesday nights.

I have discussed another project with you: The proposal to select one Repub. and one Demo. candidate and then to give that candidate full and all-out support. This project I still want carried out. Just as I still want the Reno TV project carried out. However, the item set forth in my first message of Thursday morning was something entirely different."

That was his plan to buy the Kennedy gang and place his own man in the White House. He had to make sure that Maheu understood the mission. Yet not even that megalomaniac vision could still his hatred of the Kennedys. It had been building all night while he watched TV chronicle their whole damn glorious and tragic saga. Now, on the day of Bobby's death, it all came boiling up out of Hughes, even as he continued to coldly calculate the opportunities presented by the assassination.

"I am mor[e] familiar than you realize with the history and the remaining entity of the Kennedy family," he wrote, thinking now of old Joe and letting loose his long-nurtured grudge. ". . . The Kennedy family and their money and influence have been a thorn that has been relentlessly shoved into my guts since the very beginning of my business activities. So you can see how cruel it was, after my all-out support of Nixon, to have Jack Kennedy achieve that very, *very* marginal so-called victory over my man.

"So, as I point out, thru this long-standing feeling of jealousy and personal enmity, I have become fairly well informed about the organization of people that sprung up, first around Jack, and then around Bob. Essentially the same group. They just moved over. But think of the experience they have had in the two campaigns combined!"

These were the men he needed, and now they were vulnerable. Hughes was not so blinded by hate as to miss the opportunity.

"Now, I am positive that all of these people (and dont forget the Convention and victory was virtually within their grasp) that all of these people, after they come-to following a 48 hour effort to drink themselves into oblivion, will feel awfully and terribly alone and frightened. Of course, they might make it again with Ted, but that is a long and uncertain road. Now, Bob, just try to visualize how it would feel," continued Hughes, imagining the horrible shock his own death would cause his gang. "I have a group of people who have remained loyal to me, or so I have chosen to believe, and I have worried sufficiently about them being faced with such a situation, that I have gone to extreme lengths in furnishing them protection against any such adversity. . . .

"Also, there is some similarity between the group who assisted the Kennedy brothers and my organization," he added, comparing the Irish Mafia to his strange crew of Mormons, "although, unfortunately, I do not have the lovable qualities of Jack and Bob that led to their famous popularity.

"Anyway, I do feel competant to judge the feelings of fear and lonliness which I am certain must have consumed the Kennedy group by now. I have experienced these emotions myself and I know how powerful they can be. So, I repeat that I am positive this is a once-in-a-lifetime opportunity to acquire a ready-made political organization, all trained and ready to go. . . ."

Hughes sensed that he had to move fast, before the Kennedy gang sobered up and found new patrons.

"So, Bob, . . . instead of waiting until somebody else grabs these people, let's move *first!*"

Bobby Kennedy was not yet buried as Hughes plotted to steal his legacy. His body lay in state at St. Patrick's Cathedral, where the men Hughes planned to hire formed an honor guard around his coffin, while tens of thousands of mourners filed past the bier in silent tribute.

At a solemn high-requiem mass that Saturday, Teddy Kennedy stood above the coffin to deliver his eulogy:

"My brother need not be idealized, or enlarged in death beyond what he was in life. He should be remembered simply as a good and decent man, who saw wrong and tried to right it, saw suffering and tried to heal it, saw war and tried to stop it.

"As he said many times, in many parts of this nation, to those he touched and who sought to touch him, 'Some men see things as they are and say why. I dream things that never were and say, why not?' "

And then Bobby Kennedy's body was carried out through the great bronze doors of the cathedral and placed aboard a train to Washington, for burial in Arlington National Cemetery.

Howard Hughes watched the funeral rites on television, also dreaming of things that never were. Yet even as he plotted to hire the Kennedy machine and with it seize national power, he could not resist one last jab at the sole surviving brother of the hated first family.

"I just saw Ted Kennedy campaigning from the tail end of the funeral train," wrote Hughes. "If that isn't the all time high in bad taste, I dont know what you may chose to call it. While I am all in

Bob —   6/6/68

I have just awakened. I was
up all night monday and Tuesday
nights. I heard Mankiewicz
make the fateful announcement
and, since our ch 8 was still
on the air, I stayed up all
night to watch in amazement
as we continued to achieve
absolutely exclusive coverage of
his death and obituary material
etc.

The other two networks, ABC
and NBC were not on the air
in Sou. Nevada during the entire
night until the following morning. I don't know if this
circumstance prevailed throughout
the US generally, or only in
Sou. Nevada. I do know that
ABC and NBC had just closed
down their broadcasts from the
hospital for the night and ch 13
and ch 3 had just gone dark
for the night. This was understandable, as the doctors had
just announced that there would
be no more regular bulletins
until morning.

I believe it was sheer
accident that CBS was still
on the air when the bomb
fell. Of course they (CBS)
made the most of it, and I

thought how lucky we were to have been on the air and achieved this historic news broadcast. However, I expected ABC and NBC to come back on and go crazy trying to recoup their position. But, to my amazement, the screens remained dark the whole night. Whether ABC and NBC were dark all night nationally, I do not know.

Anyway, Bob, please do not say anything to anybody about our achieving this TV exclusive. It occurred to me you might mention it by way of gently needling your friends in Ch 13. But please do not. I am very desirous that we retain the late night movie programming exclusively here in Sou. Nevada. I hope eventually to extend this into an all-night, every-night show, and I don't want any competition. I don't think the market can support 2 such shows.

Returning to this morning, I am certain that you, at no time, really understood what I was urging you to do. Bob, it is true that I have discussed another project with you: The,

proposal to select one Repub. and
one Demo. candidate and then to
give that candidate full and all-
out support. This project I
still want carried out. Just
as I still want the Reno TV
project carried out. However, the
item set forth in my first
message of Thursday morning
was something entirely different.

I am more familiar than
you realize with the history and
the remaining entity of the
Kennedy family. You see Joe
Kennedy used to own the biggest part of RKO studio before
I got into it. The Kennedy
family and their money and
influence have been a thorn
that has been relentlessly shoved
into my guts since the very
beginning of my business activities. So you can see how
cruel it was, after my all-out
support of Nixon, to have
Jack Kennedy achieve that
very very marginal so-called
victory over my man.

So, as I point out, thru
this long-standing feeling of
~~jealousy~~ and personal enmity,
I have become fairly well informed
about the organization of people that
sprung up, first around Jack, and then

around Bob. Essentially the same
group. They just moved over. But
think of the experience they have
had in the two campaigns combined!

Now, I am positive that
all of these people (and dont
forget the Convention and victory
was virtually within their grasp)
that all of these people, after they
come-to following a 48 hour effort
to drink themselves into oblivion,
will feel awfully and terribly
alone and frightened. Of course,
they might make it again with
Ted, but that is a long and
uncertain road. Now, Bob, just
try to visualize how it would feel.
I have a group of people who
have remained loyal to me, or
so I have chosen to believe, and
I have worried sufficiently about
them being faced with such a
situation, that I have gone to
extreme lengths in furnishing
them protection against any such
adversity. It was not easy,
because such protection, if it
places the person in the posture
of receiving a bequest under my
will, is worthless, and might do
more harm than good.

In any event, Bob, you
can see that I have given this
matter a great deal of thought.
Also, there is some similarity

between the group who assisted the Kennedy brothers and my organization, although, unfortunately, I do not have the lovable qualities of Jack and Bob that led to their famous popularity.

Anyway, I do feel competent to judge the feelings of fear and loneliness which I am certain must have consumed the Kennedy group by now. I have experienced these emotions myself and I know how powerful they can be. So, I repeat that I am positive this is a once-in-a-lifetime opportunity to acquire a ready-made political organization all trained and ready to go.

Now Bob, Mr. Gates, of the Gates Rubber Co. just stole from us the top prize winning designer of our helicopter and the top 7 or 8 technical men under him. It seems you might have warned me that this was a possibility. I am positive I could have persuaded him not to go - positive! So, Bob, this time, instead of waiting until somebody else grabs these people, let's move first!

favor of the effort to latch onto the Kennedy organization at this propitious moment, . . . I urge you not to do anything that might identify us as being in any way associated with Kennedy or his campaign. I am afraid that whoever has been acting as Mrs. Kennedy's guiding light since her husband's death has not been as shrewd or as clever as everybody anticipated. Personally, I think the entire funeral operation since the Good Samaritan has been one ghastly over-played, over-produced, and over-dramatized spectacle. I think that this whole deal is going to erupt into one horrible shambles. Mrs. Jack Kennedy was criticized badly for over-doing Pres. Kennedy's funeral activities and I think this operation is many times worse, if such a thing is possible."

Larry O'Brien was on that funeral train, feeling awfully alone and terribly frightened. He had quit Lyndon Johnson's cabinet to manage Robert Kennedy's campaign, as he had managed John Kennedy's eight years before, and now Bobby lay dead in a flag-draped coffin in the last of the twenty-one cars, en route to a grave beside his brother's.

At first O'Brien watched the crowds along the tracks, but as the crush of mourners blocked the way and the train slowed to a crawl on its eight-hour journey from New York to Washington, he just sat in a daze, recalling the nightmare flight of *Air Force One* that had brought another Kennedy back to the capital, from Dallas. The president's widow had been on that plane, her pink dress still splattered with blood, and now, pacing the aisle of the train, O'Brien again encountered Jacqueline Kennedy. "Oh, Larry," she said in a whisper, "isn't it terrible for us to be together again like this? It's unbelievable." Night had fallen by the time the train reached Washington. Finally, in the darkness of Arlington National Cemetery, O'Brien watched Bobby's casket being lowered into the ground next to the grave where he had seen Jack buried. And then, it was all over.

After sixteen years in service to the Kennedys, from Jack's first Senate race to Bobby's last campaign, Larry O'Brien was suddenly left without a job, without a patron, with no idea how to support his family or what to do next.

He was sitting home in Washington when Robert Maheu called.

"*Larry O'Brien*—He is coming here on Wednesday next for a conference as per our request after the assassination of Senator Ken-

6/8/68

Bob —

I just saw Ted Kennedy campaigning from the tail end of the funeral train. If that isn't the all time high in bad taste, I dont know what you may chose to call it. While I am all in favor of the effort to latch onto the Kennedy organization at this propitious moment, as I recommended yesterday, I urge you not to do anything that might identify us as being in any way associated with Kennedy or his campaign. I am afraid that whoever has been acting as ~~~~ Mrs. Kennedy's guiding light since her husband's death has not been as shrewd or as clever as everybody anticipated. Personally I think the entire funeral operation since the Good Samaritan has been one ghastly over-played, over-produced, and over-dramatized spectacle. I think that this whole deal is going to erupt into one horrible shambles. Mrs. Jack Kennedy was criticized badly for over-doing Pres. Kennedy's funeral activities and I think this operation is many times worse, if such a thing is possible.

I just wanted to let you know. We certainly have the best news service. I have been amazed.

nedy," Maheu reported to the penthouse. "He is prepared to talk employment and has received a commitment (without any obligation whatsoever) from the four or five key men in the Kennedy camp that they will not become obligated until they hear from him."

The leader of the Irish Mafia arrived in Las Vegas on the Fourth of July. He was put up in style at the Desert Inn and had the run of the town, compliments of Hughes, but he never met his would-be boss in the room upstairs. O'Brien had sat with presidents and moved in the highest circles of power. Jack Kennedy had personally recruited him, old Joe had welcomed him into his home, Lyndon Johnson had begged him to stay on at the White House, and Bobby had called to woo him away. But now O'Brien would have to settle for a surrogate. He never even got a peek at Howard Hughes.

"I've never met him myself," explained Maheu as the job negotiations got under way at his home next door to the hotel. Since that was hardly reassuring, Maheu reached into his desk and pulled out a memo handwritten on yellow legal-pad paper. "I don't want you to have any doubts that everything I'm saying comes directly from Hughes himself," he said, presenting his boss's sacred scrawl to O'Brien.

Incredibly, the proof Maheu offered was almost certainly Hughes's "thorn in my guts" diatribe. O'Brien's own account makes that clear. Except that instead of expressing hatred of the Kennedys, the memo— as O'Brien read it in his eagerness to take the job—was a heartfelt eulogy in which Hughes poured out his sorrow over Bobby's death and the continuing tragedy of the Kennedy family.

Maheu said nothing to disillusion his guest. Instead, he presented the job offer in a code both men understood. He told O'Brien that Hughes had a problem—he didn't think that his "good works" were sufficiently appreciated by the American people! O'Brien, one-upping his host, said he understood exactly what Maheu meant. Both Jack Kennedy and Lyndon Johnson had felt the same way.

It was a perfect meeting of the minds. Over the next two days Maheu mentioned some of the good works in which Hughes was now engaged. They were manifold. First, there was his stalled Monopoly game in Las Vegas. Then, his legal battle over TWA. And that very weekend, Hughes had extended his benevolence to a television network in financial distress and a struggling new airline. He hatched his plot to take over Air West and launched his sudden raid to seize control of ABC. That particular act of munificence required immediate attention.

As it happened, O'Brien was simultaneously dickering with the three television networks. They too felt unappreciated and wanted O'Brien to help improve their public image. In fact, it was James Hagerty, Eisenhower's former press secretary and now vice-president of ABC, who had proposed the deal. Since both Hughes and Hagerty were concerned only with good works, O'Brien apparently felt no conflict of interest.

And, according to Maheu, he was quite encouraging about the ABC raid. "He feels that we have no insoluble conditions before the FCC and/or the Dept. of Justice," Maheu reported to Hughes. "Whether or not we work out a deal with Larry O'Brien, I surely believe we should tap his brain before making 'the big move' in Washington."

Hughes was eager to put O'Brien right to work. Indeed, he wanted to send him right into the Oval Office. "It seems to me, Bob, there is a comparatively easy way to get an immediate answer to the network decision," he wrote. "I think such an answer should be obtainable by Mr. O'Brien marching in and collaring Johnson and saying: 'Look, my friend, my client Mr. Hughes has initiated the machinery to acquire control of ABC.'

"It seems to me that such a meeting would certainly give us an indication of which way the wind blows across the White House lawn."

Maheu had his doubts about collaring LBJ, but he was very high on O'Brien. "I don't know of one person to whom the President is more indebted and who could unravel this whole mess as quickly as he," replied Maheu. "I just happen to know that when O'Brien left the administration to become involved in the Kennedy campaign, he did so with the full blessing of the President. Furthermore, I know that the President and Humphrey are most anxious to get him involved in the Humphrey campaign."

In fact, when O'Brien returned to Washington he discovered that Humphrey had called while he was meeting with Maheu in Las Vegas. The vice-president had moved almost as quickly as Hughes to snare O'Brien, but just a bit too late. O'Brien had already more or less agreed to join the billionaire. With Maheu's approval, however, he put off the Hughes job to see Humphrey through the Democratic convention, and then, after forcing Humphrey personally to beg Maheu's permission, until after the November election.

But O'Brien never stopped his job negotiations with Hughes. He met with Maheu for a second round of talks in Washington at the end of July, just two days after Maheu delivered $50,000 to Humphrey in the backseat of a limousine. It was a busy weekend for the bagman. Now, in their meeting at the Madison Hotel, he gave O'Brien the $25,000 Hughes had promised Bobby Kennedy just before the assassination. O'Brien passed on the cash-filled manila envelope to Kennedy's brother-in-law Steve Smith, who gratefully accepted Hughes's unusual expression of condolences.

And at that same Washington meeting, Maheu and O'Brien came to terms. Howard Hughes would become a client of the newly formed O'Brien Associates, and its proprietor, Larry O'Brien, would get $15,000 a month, $500 a day, for at least two years, a $360,000 secret contract.

Hughes had done it. He had captured the leader of the Kennedy gang, hired its top gun.

Now the man who had managed the 1960 Kennedy campaign, the 1964 Johnson campaign, and Bobby's aborted 1968 race, the man who had just taken command of Humphrey's presidential drive, would also handle campaigns for Howard Hughes. Now the man who had lobbied Congress for the White House—for the New Frontier and the Great Society—would instead lobby Washington for the penthouse. Now the country's premier political operative would handle politics for a madman secretly determined to buy America.

Only the details remained to be worked out.

Right after the November election, O'Brien returned to Las Vegas to strike the final deal. By now he was also chairman of the Democratic National Committee. But that was no problem. He would simply serve simultaneously as unpaid leader of the Democratic party and as Hughes's very well paid Washington representative.

O'Brien was not scheduled to start work for Hughes until New Year's Day, but in fact he jumped right in. Even while he managed Humphrey's campaign, he was already secretly doing odd jobs for his new boss.

When Hughes announced his bid to take over Air West, plotting to swindle its stockholders—"This plan necessitates that the stock edge downward, and then that we come along with a spectacular offer"—Maheu conferred with O'Brien.

"I don't believe there is a living person who knows more about handling campaigns than Larry," he reported. "Although our present situation is not in the political arena, I look forward to receiving invaluable guidance from him in the motivation of stockholders to come our way."

When Hughes got hit with a judgment of $137 million on TWA, Maheu plotted with O'Brien to strike back at the bankers with a congressional investigation.

"The Establishment unfortunately does exist and, in fact, would make the Mafia look like a Sunday school picnic," he wrote his boss. "We happen to be victims of this group, and I sincerely believe we should not take all this lying down. In 30 days O'Brien will be available. I have discussed this entire situation with him and he can't wait to get going. We still have time to create a situation whereby these bums will come to us on bloody knees."

And when Hughes sent Maheu to offer Lyndon Johnson a million-dollar bribe to end the bomb tests, it was O'Brien who set up the big meeting at the LBJ Ranch. Although he succeeded, he was not the best go-between. Despite Maheu's assurances, Johnson was still bitter about O'Brien's defection to Bobby Kennedy.

"Poor Larry," the president told his appointments secretary Jim Jones. "First he jumps to Bobby, now to Hughes. He's making a big mistake. Hughes will just chew him up, then spit him out."

O'Brien had not even officially joined Hughes, however, when a threatened new bomb test set the stage for his first big mission.

It was December 12, 1968. The Atomic Energy Commission had just announced another megaton blast, the first since "Boxcar" started Hughes on his ban-the-bomb crusade eight months earlier. He had hoped to stave off the holocaust until a more pliant president took office. Now, with an unbought LBJ still in the White House and a bought Nixon elected but not yet sworn in, Hughes was faced with a real problem: he didn't know whom to bribe.

"Please press to reach Humphries, or let O'Brien take my offer to the Democratic chief of finance," wrote a frantic Hughes. "I implore that we pull out all the stops."

Once more Hughes demanded that Maheu offer a million dollars—to Johnson again, to the defeated Humphrey for his campaign deficit, to the depleted treasury of the Democratic party, to the victorious but still powerless Nixon—to anyone who could block the impending blast.

The AEC's sneak attack caught Maheu down in the Bahamas, hobnobbing with the Nixon gang. While he continued to work on the incoming administration, he called in his new recruit to pull out the stops in Washington.

"Larry O'Brien will meet with the top man tomorrow morning," Maheu reported to Hughes. "Howard, I have thought of going to

Washington but after serious consideration I cannot think of anything I could do there more effectively than O'Brien."

While O'Brien prepared to meet with Lyndon Johnson, the man he had helped make president, Maheu shuttled between Miami and the Bahamas in an effort to reach the president-elect, and also reached out to the still cooperative vice-president.

"I have a call in right now for Humphrey," he assured Hughes. "I really want to tap his brain in great depth before making any further moves, so please bear with me, Howard.

"On the other side, [Lee] DuBridge, who will be Nixon's top scientific advisor, is behind us but recommends very strongly to the new administration that they, definitely, take a hands off policy insofar as this particular blast is concerned.

"Nixon's closest advisors informed me that the president-elect in no way will stick his nose in this matter until, in fact, he has taken over.

"Howard," Maheu concluded, "this leaves us pretty much with the Democrats at this particular time, and that is the reason why it is so important for me to exhaust every possibility insofar as Humphrey and LBJ are concerned."

Up in his penthouse, sweating out another grim countdown, Hughes was dismayed by the failure of his henchmen to find a taker for his million-dollar payoff.

"I am heartbroken that you propose a hands off policy," he wailed, "and that we have not even come close thus far in delaying this test.

"You say we should accept this one because it will be successful. I dont question that it will be successful in terms of visible evidence.

"However, now I feel our prestige and entire public image will be most seriously damaged if we permit this one to proceed, or if we have not the political strength to stop it.

"I implore you to reverse your attitude and pull out all the stops. I have received no indication that my offer of support (20 times Humphries)* has ever been put to anyone who was in a position to accept it or negotiate.

"I agree with concentrating on the Democrats. My message of yesterday urged it."

*Humphrey received $100,000 from Hughes. It is unclear if the billionaire had forgotten the full amount or was counting only the $50,000 in secret cash handed directly to the vice-president when he now equated "20 times Humphries" with his proposed million-dollar bribe.

Maheu was quick to assure Hughes that he was not once more playing the reluctant bagman.

"I am continuing the battle to the fullest extent," he reported to the command post. "As to the offer, I am happy we did not proceed too quickly, because it is obvious that it would have done no good, for instance, to make it to the Republicans.

"I had a very long talk with Vice President Humphrey. He will make one more big try at delaying the blast, but admitted that he was not necessarily encouraged. He is most appreciative of our offer to help in the deficit, but would prefer not to accept it unless he is capable of causing the delay, or after we are fully convinced that his efforts will produce the necessary results as to future and bigger blasts."

Meanwhile, back in Washington, Larry O'Brien was also waging an uphill campaign. While Maheu confronted a Nixon gang not yet open for business and a vice-president too high-minded to accept payment for unfinished business, O'Brien was apparently getting the business from the man who had his finger on the button, Lyndon Johnson. He had made no headway at all.

"Howard," reported Maheu, "I just had a long talk with Larry O'Brien and we have decided to make one more pass at the President on the blast."

O'Brien continued to knock at the White House door but failed to gain entrance: "I have been in constant touch with Larry and as of 15 minutes ago he had not been successful in our mission, but he is continuing throughout the evening."

The dreaded blast was now less than two days away. Hughes had had it with O'Brien. As the zero-hour approached, he demanded that Maheu personally deal with the president.

"Howard, before I leave Larry wanted me to give you his thinking," Maheu replied from Miami. "He is convinced that this blast is a compromise to which LBJ is irrevocably committed. He is truly concerned that a request for an appointment for me could be misinterpreted by the President since he and Larry have been so close for many years, and it could be thought that we have no confidence in the President or Larry.

"He points out also that a personal contact between me and the White House at this critical time could not avoid public scrutiny."

This mission was getting dangerous. Both O'Brien and Maheu were eager to bail out. But Hughes was insistent. Again, he ordered Maheu to go see the president and make the big payoff. So far

Maheu had not brought O'Brien in on the bribery plot. Now, however, with Hughes demanding that he once more personally offer Johnson a million dollars, Maheu apparently spelled it all out for his cohort.

"Via a pre-established code I was able to convey to Larry the extent to which we are willing to go," he reported.

Perhaps for the first time O'Brien had to realize exactly what he was getting into, just what kind of a man he had signed on to work for. It must have been a chilling moment. He was not about to bribe a president. But neither was he so shocked as to quit his new job.

"He thought this should be reconsidered," continued Maheu, reporting O'Brien's reaction, "because he feels it is too late for LBJ to change his mind, and, in fact, it could eventually be used to our detriment. He is willing to stake his business career with us (which starts officially on Jan. 1, 1969) that he will accomplish our principal goal."

If O'Brien himself was not willing to bribe Johnson, he apparently was still ready to arrange for his new partner to make the payoff.

"Howard, as you know I am prepared to do anything you request," concluded Maheu, "and Larry, of course, will set up the appointment."

Only Lyndon Johnson's continued intransigence prevented the White House parley. Whether because Hughes had failed to make the library donation, or because Johnson was never made aware of the potential rewards, or simply because he remained unwilling to sell Hughes the bomb, the president refused to meet Maheu.

The megaton-plus blast went off as scheduled on Thursday, December 19, 1968. It triggered a violent artificial earthquake that shook Las Vegas and sent out tremors powerful enough to register on seismographs around the world. Alone in his bunker, Hughes gripped the sides of his bed, once again foiled in his plot to buy nuclear peace.

But his battle against the bomb was not over. And neither was his obsession with the Kennedys. Having bought O'Brien, Hughes never gave up hope that the last surviving Kennedy brother could himself be persuaded to sell out.

"Ted Kennedy is going to make a speech here, and I authorize you to offer him the sky and the moon and unlimited support for his campaign for the presidency if he will use our material and take the

AEC apart in his speech here," wrote Hughes, making his big move to snare the last pretender to the throne.

"Bob, if he mentions the sheep in Utah, I tell you he will bring the house down," Hughes continued, again invoking the martyred flock, and the five thousand sacrificial lambs killed in a biological-warfare test gone awry. "He must know this, and surely he does not hesitate to embarass the Nixon administration if he has the opportunity."

It was April 25, 1969. Teddy Kennedy was coming to Las Vegas to keynote a hundred-dollar-a-plate testimonial dinner for his Senate colleague, Nevada's Howard Cannon. It was the perfect opportunity for Hughes to cement his new Camelot connection and at the same time to score a real blow against the bombers.

That battle had by now escalated to the point that Hughes was threatened with a congressional subpoena. He needed powerful allies. He wanted Teddy Kennedy.

"Do you have any word from Kennedy?" he asked Maheu, growing restless as speech time neared.

"And also, please tell me what it is we want him to mention, I have forgotten," added Hughes, either so far gone on codeine and Valium that the bomb had actually slipped his mind, or more likely just testing his lieutenant, making sure that he had not forgotten the Teddy-AEC-sheep scenario. But now he was suddenly seized by another obsession.

"Incidentally," he added, "I think you should have somebody explain most carefully our position on the water system to Kennedy, otherwise he is sure to say something suggesting his support of the lake system in his speech."

The reminder reached Maheu at the Sands, where he was throwing a predinner private cocktail party for two hundred select invitees to the big Cannon bash. The guest of honor was Teddy Kennedy.

Whatever Maheu may have said to the senator at his little soiree, Teddy did not savage the AEC, or blast the bombing, or eulogize the dead sheep in his speech that night. And he never got the sky or the moon or any of Hughes's money.

But Kennedy did get a showgirl.

The assignation was arranged by Jack Entratter, Hughes's entertainment director at the Sands. The onetime bouncer at the Stork Club met with Kennedy at midnight and took him upstairs to a suite on the eighteenth floor. Teddy spent the night there—although he was registered at another hotel—and so did the showgirl.

When the publisher of a local scandal sheet got wise and threatened to reveal all the racy details, Maheu tried to buy him out to suppress the story. When the feisty muckraker, Colin McKinlay, refused to sell, Maheu had to tell Hughes.

"Until several hours ago Bell was convinced that he had McKinlay under control," reported the worried fixer.

"McKinlay, however, informed Bell that he had a 'hot story' pertaining to Senator Kennedy's recent trip to Las Vegas when he appeared to make a speech on behalf of Senator Cannon. McKinlay claims that upon the completion of the festivities that evening, Senator Kennedy went to the Sands Hotel and spent the evening with a 'broad' which was furnished to him by Jack Entratter.

"Today McKinlay made the statement that he is going to bury Kennedy and you and me by publishing this story in his next News Letter. In an attempt to prove that when important people appear in Las Vegas all provisions for their satisfaction are made available through the Hughes interests.

"Unfortunately, Howard, there is substance to the story, although Entratter had not cleared any of the details with me," concluded Maheu, admitting the worst. "We are still making every effort to make sure that this next scandal sheet will not be printed and distributed."

It was futile. The story ran. But without Maheu's secret admission of its truth, the report was virtually ignored—although it told of a "bosomy blonde" who answered the door at Kennedy's suite when a bellhop arrived with liquor that night, who was still there when room service brought up breakfast—and although by the time the story appeared, Kennedy's womanizing had become front-page news.

It was July 1969. Mary Jo Kopechne was dead. And Teddy Kennedy was preparing to go on national television to explain Chappaquiddick.

"What is the most educated guess as to what is going to happen about the Kennedy situation?" Hughes inquired on the evening before Teddy emerged from a week of seclusion following the accident.

"I just heard a newscast saying Kennedy is planning a statement tomorrow. Do you have any idea what it is likely to say?

"I only want to know what, if anything you already know. Please do not become in any way involved in this, and please do not permit O'Brien to become entangled in it.

"I heard that all the Kennedy hiarchy was gathered today at Hiannisport Mass. I hoped OBrien was not included, but I realize it could be very dangerous if it should filter back to Kennedy that any such request was made of O'Brien.

"So, tread very carefully in this entire affair."

Larry O'Brien was not actually working for Hughes at the time the billionaire sought to shield him from the taint of Chappaquiddick.

Just as O'Brien had been about to go on the payroll, he backed out. It was not a moral decision, no sudden pangs of conscience. At the last minute, he simply got a better offer from Wall Street. He never broke off his relationship with Hughes, however. He kept in touch with Maheu and persuaded Hughes to hire two close associates, Joe Napolitan, a media consultant who had worked with O'Brien in both the Kennedy and Humphrey campaigns, and Claude DeSautels, a top Washington lobbyist who had been O'Brien's deputy in both the Kennedy and Johnson administrations. Both Napolitan and DeSautels received $5,000 a month, and both regularly consulted with O'Brien on Hughes business.

"Although O'Brien took the position with the investment company," reported Maheu, explaining the setup to Hughes, "he has continued to make himself available to us and has kept his basic team intact. Larry continues to be of great help, and there are many things he can do which he could not if he were an employee."

Indeed, all the while O'Brien labored on Wall Street, Maheu reported his Hughes missions to the penthouse.

"Re: CAB, Howard, things are progressing unbelievably well," wrote Maheu, as he maneuvered to get federal approval of the Air West takeover. "It is obvious that Larry O'Brien and his people had done a good job prior to the meeting." Of his own CAB testimony, Maheu later added, "I think I did a reasonably good job at keeping perjury to a minimum."

As Hughes continued to battle TWA, O'Brien tried to roll back the mammoth default judgment. "As a result of having accomodated a few select people in Washington," Maheu noted, "O'Brien and Long reported just last night that we have a 50-50 chance of tagging a provision to pending legislation that will make it impossible to secure treble damages."

And for the big battle against the bomb, the O'Brien team lined up reliable allies in Congress: "O'Brien and his people have carefully deleted from opponents of the tests those which have any tinge of liberalism. They are working very closely with the solid group, and

7-24-69 R

Bob-

What is the most educated guess as to what is going to happen about the Kennedy situation?

I just heard a newscast saying Kennedy is planning a statement tomorrow. Do you have any idea what it is likely to ~~so~~ say?

I only want to know what, if anything, you already know. please do not become in any way involved in this, and please do not permit O'Brien to become entangled in it.

I heard that all the Kennedy hierarchy was gathered today at Hiannisport mass. I hoped O'Brien was not included, but I realize it could be very dangerous if it should filter back to Kennedy that any such request was made of O'Brien.

So, tread very ~~so~~ carefully in this entire affair.

Howard

they will launch programs of their own which will not be traceable to us."

Hughes, however, was not satisfied. He didn't want O'Brien's team, and he didn't want O'Brien's unofficial help. He wanted O'Brien.

"I was very impressed with the line up of political talent you mentioned," he wrote Maheu, approving his roster of operatives. "However, Bob, I want a political oriented executive to be available full time."

Hughes had already hired Richard Danner, a longtime Nixon associate who handled dealings between the penthouse and the White House through the new president's closest friend, Bebe Rebozo. That took care of the Republicans.

"What I would like best would be to have both O'Brien *and* Danner," continued Hughes, seeking control of both parties.

"Do you think O'Brien can be persuaded, on any reasonable basis, to change his mind and come back?

"I realize he is limited with Republicans, but that does not disturb me particularly."

No, not with the Democrats in control of both houses of Congress and most of the federal regulatory agencies. He was not disturbed at all. And, as it turned out, O'Brien needed no persuading. His Wall Street firm had gone bankrupt, he was saddled with worthless stock options, and he had plunged deeply into debt. In mid-August 1969, Larry O'Brien returned to Las Vegas, eager to join up with Howard Hughes.

O'Brien Associates opened for business October 1, just in time to help rewrite national tax legislation for its chief client, Howard Hughes.

The Tax Reform Act of 1969 was the most sweeping overhaul of the country's revenue system in history, and it posed a real problem for Hughes. It was not that the richest man in America had paid no personal income tax for seventeen consecutive years, until his windfall profit on TWA finally forced him to ante up. It was not that the holding company for his entire empire, Hughes Tool, had paid no corporate income taxes for the three years its sole owner had been hiding out in Las Vegas. No, the big problem was the billionaire's big charity—the Howard Hughes Medical Institute.

Like the other great philanthropists—Ford, Rockefeller, Carnegie—Hughes had discovered a way to get great public acclaim for hoarding his wealth and evading his taxes. He created a foundation.

Hughes, however, almost seemed intent on exposing the entire racket by making his foundation an outrageous parody.

In his sole act of philanthropy, he had turned over all the stock of the Hughes Aircraft Company to the Hughes Medical Institute, thereby making his billion-dollar-a-year weapons factory a tax-exempt charitable organization. He named his personal physician, Verne Mason—the Hollywood doctor who had long been his codeine connection—director of medical research. But Hughes himself remained president of the defense plant and became sole trustee of the new foundation, retaining absolute control over both. He had generously given all his stock to himself. And now that incredible act of benevolence was about to be undone.

It was Wright Patman who started all the trouble. For years the Texas populist had been using his power as chairman of the House Banking Committee to push a congressional investigation of the foundation game. His probe had uncovered hundreds of self-styled charities that were nothing more than fronts used by the wealthy to amass vast fortunes tax-free. And now, in 1969, Patman was zeroing in on the most blatant fraud of all—a top-ten defense contractor, a manufacturer of missiles and spy satellites, masquerading as a charity devoted to medical research "for the benefit of all mankind."

In fact, Patman discovered, the Howard Hughes Medical Institute had only one real beneficiary: Howard Hughes. In the fifteen years since its founding, the institute had given only $6 million to medical researchers and kicked back almost $24 million to the billionaire. During those same years, Hughes Aircraft piled up accumulated profits of $134 million but never paid a dividend to the charity that owned it and donated just $2 million to good works. Under a complex double-lease arrangement with Hughes Tool, the foundation received another $20 million, but most of that went to pay Hughes himself interest on a loan. Nearly a million dollars every year to the shylock trustee. And every penny Hughes-the-Benevolent gave to his foundation—including all the money he took back—was tacked onto the bills Hughes-the-Defense-Contractor presented to the Pentagon, so that other taxpayers picked up the entire tab for his philanthropy. Indeed, he turned a profit. By 1969 the medical institute, however, was flat broke. It had to borrow a million from a bank. Not to make research grants, but to pay the interest it owed its generous founder.

"This sounds more like high finance to me than charity," complained Patman. And another member of his committee, in grilling a foundation director, sharply ridiculed the whole setup: "You mean Mr. Hughes, the trustee, has never felt that Mr. Hughes, the chief executive, ought to be hamstrung in paying Mr. Hughes the money Mr. Hughes owes Mr. Hughes?"

Dangerous talk. Into the breach stepped Larry O'Brien.

"I am thoroughly knowledgable of the affinity which has existed for years between Patman and O'Brien," Maheu reported to the penthouse philanthropist. "In addition, I accidently found out last night that Dick Danner and Patman have been close friends for many years. Unless you advise me to the contrary, it is my intention to coordinate among Danner and O'Brien a program which perhaps could get Patman off our backs."

But Wright Patman could not be stopped. He was on a crusade, and his revelations were finally forcing Congress to impose strict controls on all tax-exempt private foundations.

Except one. Larry O'Brien was seeing to that.

"It was Larry O'Brien's people who called to my attention the deficiencies in the pending Tax Reform Bill," Maheu told Hughes. "O'Brien and his people detected deficiencies which could be devastating to HHMI and Hughes Aircraft."

Devastating indeed. Under the bill passed by the House, the medical institute would actually have to become a charity. It would be forced to spend at least $10 million each year on good works—probably two or three times that amount—far more than what it had paid out in the past fifteen years combined. Worse yet, the new law would prohibit "self-dealing." Hughes would have to pay a 200 percent tax penalty on all the kickbacks he received from his foundation. And worst of all, he would have to surrender control of Hughes Aircraft, sell off 80 percent of his stock within ten years.

O'Brien had his work cut out for him. But he also had powerful allies. In addition to Nixon's pal Danner, Hughes deployed a team of lobbyists that included Gillis Long, a former congressman from Louisiana who just happened to be a cousin of Russell Long, chairman of the Senate Finance Committee—next stop for the Tax Reform Act.

By the time the tax bill emerged from that Senate committee, it had a special loophole. One tailored just for Hughes. Now hidden in the 225-page law was a single sentence that exempted "medical research organizations"—namely the Hughes Institute.

Maheu flashed the good news to the penthouse: "In meetings today and yesterday, the Senate Finance Committee adopted all the amendments we were pressing on behalf of HHMI."

The revised bill still had to survive a House-Senate conference and a final vote of the full Congress, but mainly it had to get past one man—Wilbur Mills, chairman of the House Ways and Means Committee. O'Brien took his old friend Mills out to lunch. For two hours they discussed the impact of the new tax law on foundations, and while O'Brien later insisted he never even mentioned Hughes, Wilbur Mills became a fervent advocate of the Hughes loophole.

Maheu was ecstatic. "Howard, we have secured a group of highly qualified men to handle our Washington problems," he crowed. "Thanks to your foresightedness, the availability of O'Brien is perhaps the coup of the century. I am sure that we have no situation pending which O'Brien, Long and Danner cannot handle to your satisfaction."

But Hughes was not satisfied. A secret exemption for his charity was not enough. He wanted a major part of the whole tax law entirely rewritten.

"I am horrified," he wrote.

"You assured me the new tax bill was not going to be unacceptable to me, and that you were not needed in Washington during these critical days because everything was under control.

"I have just heard on the news that the capital gains tax will be increased, and very substantially. I am afraid your refusal to make an all out effort has resulted in a tragedy."

Maheu took it all in stride. With his new team of fixers, nothing was impossible.

"I am so happy that you called to my attention your interest in the capital gains portion of the Tax Reform Bill," he replied. "We were able to hold meetings with O'Brien, Long, Danner, Morgan and I present. We studied in depth the House version and the Senate version. Fortunately, among the five of us, we have excellent entrees to every member of the Committees involved.

"We do not intend to leave one stone unturned. We also intend to call to the attention of the President how unpopular this particular portion of the Bill would be to those who undoubtedly account for perhaps 80% of the political contributions needed for a national campaign."

Richard Nixon had problems of his own. He too was against the capital gains hike, but the Democratic-controlled Congress was in open rebellion, and that was the least of his problems with the new tax law. The president's real concern was quite personal. Like Hughes, Nixon was preoccupied with his own private philanthropy.

While Congress debated a complete overhaul of the country's revenue code, the president focused on one minor provision—the repeal of charitable deductions for donations of documents. Nixon had been planning to make a gift of his prepresidential papers to the National Archives. In return for a half-million-dollar tax break. Now he had a real dilemma. Throughout the fall the effective date of the repeal fluctuated. Not knowing what the final cutoff date would be, Nixon withheld his gift until he was sure he could claim his deduction, while his chief White House lobbyist, Bryce Harlow, pushed Congress to leave the loophole open, at least long enough for the president to slip through.

In his strategy sessions with Harlow, Nixon kept raising another concern: the Hughes-O'Brien alliance. The president had learned about it a year earlier from his pal Rebozo, who had heard it from Danner, who had heard it from Maheu, just months after O'Brien first journeyed to Las Vegas. Larry O'Brien and Howard Hughes! The connection would never be far from Nixon's mind in the years that followed, an obsession that grew throughout his presidency. And now O'Brien, the leader of the Kennedy gang, the former chairman of the Democratic National Committee, was actually out there lobbying Congress for Howard Hughes.

Nixon wanted all the details, all the dirt. Harlow kept bumping into O'Brien's operatives, and every time he huddled with the president, Nixon kept asking him about O'Brien and Hughes.

"We discussed it as a matter of surprise and interest," Harlow recalled. "I used to meet with the president every morning and in the evening, along with Haldeman and Ehrlichman and sometimes Kissinger. We'd sit there and chew the fat about whatever was going on, and from time to time that would pop up: 'I wonder how Larry's getting along with Howard Hughes.' It seemed to us very odd that that arrangement existed and was acceptable to the Democratic party."

Of course, Nixon also kept pressing Harlow to buy time for his papers, to save his big tax break. It was the president's top legislative priority, but the issue remained unresolved as the tax bill headed for the final House-Senate conference.

Up in his penthouse, Hughes also sweated out the last crucial round. The capital gains tax had been cut, but not sufficiently, and his big charity loophole was still at risk.

"We have had our people in Washington practically sleeping on the Hill, watching every move that is being made," Maheu assured his boss, but warned that he could expect no help from Nixon.

"The President continues to evidence his inability to control Congress insofar as the tax reform bill is concerned. Fortunately, we are not in an unfavorable position with that particular group because of your foresightedness in getting the O'Brien team aboard.

"I talked to O'Brien an hour ago and he has no fear about being able to incorporate language which is beneficial to us when this whole matter goes to conference."

On December 22, 1969, the House-Senate conferees emerged from five days and nights of intense negotiations with a compromise version of the Tax Reform Act. It was swiftly approved by the full Congress the same day.

Larry O'Brien had come through. Howard Hughes had won an incredible victory. The historic new law would affect virtually every American taxpayer, every business, every corporation. Even the long-sacred oil-depletion allowance was cut. And more than thirty thousand tax-exempt organizations came under strict new controls. The Ford Foundation, the Rockefeller Foundation, and the Carnegie Endowment were all brought under the law. But not the Howard Hughes Medical Institute. It was completely exempt, thanks to Larry O'Brien.

Hughes did not thank him though. The philanthropist did not celebrate his great victory, did not appreciate the secret deal that saved him tens of millions of dollars, saved his control of Hughes Aircraft, saved all his kickbacks, saved his entire tax dodge.

"I am naturally gratified that the changes in the language of the tax bill (as it relates to foundations) will make it unnecessary to revise the by-laws of HHMI," wrote Hughes, grudgingly.

"This is nice, Bob, and it is a convenience I appreciate.

"However, I hope you realize how totally insignificant this piece of news becomes, if it is accompanied by the report of an increase in the capital gains rate.

"I have pointed out at great length and with great emphasis that the affairs and funds of HHMI lie on the other side of the great wall, as far as I am concerned.

"I further explained that HHMI has plenty of resources, is well provided with money for its future activities," he continued, casually dismissing the threadbare charity he had milked dry, "and therefore that a dollar in the treasury of HHMI did not have a value to me approaching anywhere near the value of a dollar in the treasury of Hughes Tool Company or a dollar of my personal funds.

"Therefore, you can readily appreciate that the present plans to increase the capital gains tax strike right at the very heart of the only area from which I have any hope of obtaining any profit of any consequence at any time from now on.

"So, Bob, please put this project at the top of the list, where it should have been all along," he pleaded, once more demanding that the tax law be rewritten—but not selfishly, not for him alone.

"It is also the only source of substantial income for any other moderately wealthy man, whether he is a corporation executive, a broker, investor, financier, or what have you.

"It appears to me that the bill would be devastating to almost everybody in the nation, except those in the very lowest income brackets.

"Please report at once, Bob, I am more worried about this than about anything else that has happened at any time during the entire period of our relationship."

Hughes need not have worried. The new capital gains rate would hardly affect him at all. Hughes Tool had already slipped through its own special loophole, designed to benefit struggling small businesses—corporations with ten or fewer shareholders. That of course included Hughes Tool, which had only one. From now on, his holding company would pay no capital gains, indeed no corporate tax at all.

Half his empire was now a tax-exempt "charity," while the other half was a tax-exempt "small business." Only Hughes himself would have to pay taxes. For the first year under the new law he paid $20,012.64. This was the kind of tax reform the billionaire had in mind. O'Brien Associates had done well on its first official assignment.

Richard Nixon had not done quite so well. The president lost his battle with Congress. On December 30, 1969, after threatening a veto, he bitterly signed into law a tax reform act that eliminated the deduction for his private papers. The repeal was retroactive to July. Nixon had missed the cutoff date. He had blown the chance for his big tax break. Or so it seemed.

But on April 10, 1970, there was another signing ceremony in the Oval Office. On that day, the president signed his 1969 income tax returns. He claimed a charitable deduction of $576,000 for his papers and attached a deed showing that they had been donated to the National Archives in March 1969, four months before the new deadline. That whopping write-off allowed Nixon to escape virtually all of his taxes while he was president. In 1970 he paid $792.81. In 1971 he paid $873.03. In 1972 he paid $4,298. There was only one problem. It was all a fraud, one his own lawyers would later call "the Presidential Papers Caper." Nixon had backdated the deed on his papers, cheated on his taxes, and evaded $467,000 he owed the IRS while he sat in the White House.

By the time the president backdated his deed, Larry O'Brien had once more become chairman of the Democratic National Committee. For the next year he would serve Howard Hughes and the Democrats simultaneously, and Nixon's concern about the Hughes-O'Brien relationship would become an absolute obsession.

O'Brien was not merely a figurehead party chairman but the real leader of the opposition. With Johnson in exile, Humphrey in defeat, and Teddy Kennedy in disgrace, he was perhaps the most prominent Democrat in the country, the point man for his party in the 1970 congressional elections. With the financial freedom afforded him by the huge retainer he received from his hidden boss, Howard Hughes, O'Brien toured the country attacking Nixon.

Hughes and O'Brien! The leader of the Democratic party a secret Hughes lobbyist, getting $500 a day from the billionaire, $15,000 every month, $180,000 per year while he served two masters—and getting away with it! O'Brien, the leader of the Kennedy gang, getting away with it, just like the Kennedys always got away with everything. Nixon was determined to nail O'Brien, to get proof of his Hughes connection, to find out just what he was doing for all that secret money.

The president would have been surprised had he known. Certainly he never even guessed at O'Brien's role in the big "Bold Ones" mission.

It began one night when Hughes was watching television. What he saw was so shocking that he wanted O'Brien put right on the job, even though it came up at the very height of the great tax-bill battle.

"Message to be given to Bob when he first wakes up," Hughes dictated to one of his Mormons while he sat in the bathroom darkly brooding.

"Sun. night on television was a program entitled 'The Bold Ones' which portrayed an almost identical sequence of events as the Apollo

12 flight," the aide scribbled down as his boss grunted in the background. "This one had one colored man and two white men in it, however HRH is not objecting because of the colored man.

"HRH thinks this type of show is detrimental to the welfare of the U.S. by showing scenes that would indicate that some things happened which could have been prevented, etc. In the program it showed the colored man getting sick and later one of the other men got sick and passed out and the problem had to be diagnosed by a doctor on the ground at Houston with the colored man's wife sitting beside the control center.

"HRH thinks you, through your connections in Washington, should register a violent protest about such a program being permitted to run. HRH thinks it is unpatriotic and puts the US space program in a bad light.

"HRH thinks perhaps Larry O'Brien might handle such an assignment. However, HRH does not want this protest to be traced back to us."

There were other top-secret Hughes-O'Brien missions, some of them directly involving Nixon himself. Oblivious to the president's obsession, completely unaware of Nixon's fear and hatred of O'Brien, Hughes regularly suggested sending O'Brien right into the White House.

"Suppose you have our top contact with Nixon (maybe O'Brien) go to the administration and offer to assist them in satisfying the southern Nevada public with an alternative water system which would be privately financed and require no government funding," Hughes suggested, ready to pay any price to assure the purity of fluids.

And when he feared that the president was getting in bed with the bombers, Hughes again proposed that O'Brien make contact: "The very most urgent matter right now is, by all odds, the Nixon-AEC alliance, which I think is absolutely terrible, and must be untied somehow. Can't you put O'Brien on this and *pull out all the stops?*"

Indeed, Maheu and O'Brien hatched a plot to help Nixon get Senate approval of a Supreme Court nomination in return for a bombing halt.

"I have been in touch with O'Brien and some of his people," reported Maheu, "and they are going to make an attempt over the weekend to swap votes for Carswell in exchange for a postponement of the blast. You may rest assured that we are handling this one with extreme caution. But O'Brien thinks it's at least worth a try."

Nixon, however, never learned of any of these missions. And the president grew ever more obsessed with discovering exactly what O'Brien was up to. He called in Haldeman—"We're going to nail O'Brien on this, one way or another," he told his chief of staff. He called in Ehrlichman, he called in Colson, he called in Dean, he called in the IRS, he called in his pal Rebozo and had Rebozo pump Danner and Maheu. He called in his private gumshoes, and finally he called in his attorney general, and Mitchell called in Liddy, and Liddy called in McCord and Hunt, and Hunt called in the Cubans, and they all got caught in Larry O'Brien's office at the Watergate.

All in a desperate effort to get to the bottom of the Hughes-O'Brien connection.

"I thought it would be a pleasant—and newsworthy—irony," Nixon later explained in his memoirs, "that after all the years in which Howard Hughes had been portrayed as my financial angel, the Chairman of the Democratic National Committee was in fact the one profiting from a lucrative position on Hughes's payroll."

But there was another factor in Nixon's obsession, one he did not mention in his memoirs.

The president was also on the pad.

10 Nixon: The Payoff

The blood dripped slowly from a suspended pint bag, trickling red down a clear plastic tube, flowing through a hypodermic needle into the emaciated arm of the cadaverous old man.

Howard Hughes, near death, was coming back to life.

He had been losing blood for months, apparently from his ruptured hemorrhoids, a now critical anemia compounded by chronic malnutrition. His hemoglobin count had dropped below four grams, a 75-percent blood loss that left him as leeched as a week-old corpse.

Unwilling to be hospitalized—he would not leave his lair, he dared not face the daylight—Hughes instead sent his henchmen in search of uncontaminated blood. It was no simple mission. Hughes insisted on knowing the precise origin of each pint, requiring a thorough investigation of every potential donor, rejecting some for their dietary habits, others for their sexual activity, and all who had ever given blood in the past, before he finally selected several clean-living Salt Lake City Mormons to be bled for him alone.

And now, after getting his first taste of pure Mormon blood— blood the billionaire came to like so much that he would later demand transfusions he did not need—Hughes watched television and waited for news that would satisfy an older craving.

It was Tuesday, November 5, 1968. Election night.

". . . and it's a very tight election indeed," boomed the absurdly amplified voice of Walter Cronkite. "A seesaw race right across the country. Nothing like the presidential countdown that had been anticipated. . . ."

The same report echoed, at a considerably lower volume, in another grim hotel room three thousand miles away. There, men as yet unknown but soon to be notorious monitored the returns for Richard Nixon.

Nixon himself, secluded in a separate room on the thirty-fifth floor of the Waldorf Towers in New York, would not allow even a TV to share his solitude. Hour after hour he sat alone, hunched over his yellow legal pads, analyzing the vote pattern, shut off from his family down the hall, withdrawn from his closest aides in the adjacent suite.

Nixon had been losing ground to Humphrey for weeks, had seen his once overwhelming lead shrivel day by day, and now, alone in the gloom of his secret room, knew that his political survival was in serious doubt. "You could almost feel the mood changing as the darkness came over the land," his aide Leonard Garment later recalled. "We knew there was this hemorrhage of votes, this dreadful phenomenon, like a strange disease." All night and into the early morning, Nixon watched his vote count waver.

Precisely at the stroke of three A.M., he suddenly emerged in an old rumpled suit, haggard from the ordeal, and announced he was ready to claim victory. The outcome was still uncertain, but Nixon savored the moment. It was at the same hour eight years earlier that he had conceded defeat to John F. Kennedy.

Beaten in 1960, buried in 1962, he had delivered his own obituary—"You won't have Nixon to kick around any more"—in the famous "last press conference." But now he was back, risen from the grave and ready to enter the White House.

In Nixon, Hughes had at last what he had always wanted—a debtor in the Oval Office.

"I am determined to elect a president of our choosing this year and one who will be deeply indebted, and who will recognize his indebtedness," he had declared early in the 1968 campaign.

"Since I am willing to go beyond all limitations on this, I think we should be able to select a candidate and a party who knows the facts of political life."

"If we select Nixon," he later wrote, "then he, I know for sure knows the facts of life."

Theirs was a special relationship. It stretched back more than two decades, had survived multiple crises, and still endured. Hughes, of course, flirted with other politicians, but with the others it was often hard to tell how far he could go, and he always came back to Nixon, who appreciated a big spender, and would always go all the way.

I am determined to elect a president of our choosing this year and one who will be deeply indebted, and who will recognize his indebtedness.

Since I am willing to go beyond all limitations on this, I think we should be able to select a candidate and a party who knows the facts of political life.

If we select Nixon then he, I know for sure, knows the facts of life.

Hughes had supported Nixon in every bid for office since his first congressional race in 1946 and would continue to back him to the end. In addition to campaign funds, he provided large sums for the personal use of the president and his family. The known bequests—the few made openly and the hidden payoffs later discovered—eventually totaled more than half a million dollars.

More than a financial angel, Hughes was a virtual fairy godfather in Nixon's faltering rise to power. In 1956, when Eisenhower was ready to find a new running mate, Hughes ordered a covert operation to crush the "Dump Nixon" movement, sending Maheu to infiltrate the enemy camp and concoct a spurious pro-Nixon poll. Whether the problem was hanging on to Ike's coattails or flying a planeload of dignitaries to a testimonial dinner or saving a relative from financial ruin, Hughes always seemed to materialize when Nixon was in need. Then, suddenly, the spell was broken.

The billionaire's largesse may have cost Nixon his first bid for the presidency when a scandal erupted in the closing days of the 1960 campaign over a never-repaid $205,000 Hughes "loan."

Nixon had personally requested the money four years earlier, shortly after he was reelected vice-president, ostensibly to bail out his brother Donald's failing business—a chain of restaurants featuring "Nixonburgers." The cash came from a Canadian subsidiary of the Hughes Tool Company, was transferred through a cutout to the vice-president's aged mother, Hannah, who passed it on to her bankrupt son. The name *Hughes* appeared nowhere on the loan agreement, and none of the Nixons was responsible for repayment. Their only collateral was a vacant lot in Whittier, California, once the site of the Nixon family home. It had an assessed value of $13,000.

Hughes was pleased to play the friendly pawnbroker. "I want the Nixons to have the money," he told his reluctant business manager, Noah Dietrich. "Let 'em have it."

Nonetheless uneasy about the secret deal, Dietrich flew to Washington in a futile attempt to dissuade the vice-president. "About the loan to Donald," he cautioned Nixon, "Hughes has authorized it, and Donald can have it, but if this becomes public it could mean the end of your political career."

Nixon, unfazed, responded self-righteously. "Mr. Dietrich," he reportedly said, "I have to put my relatives ahead of my career."

Donald's fast-food enterprise soon collapsed despite the easy credit, and Hughes never did get back his money. Still, he apparently came out well ahead. Less than three months after he so generously aided the needy Nixons, the Internal Revenue Service officially recognized his philanthropic status. It declared the Howard Hughes Medical Institute a tax-exempt charity. Twice before the IRS had refused to certify the foundation, calling it "merely a device for siphoning off otherwise taxable income." Nothing had changed. Indeed the institute had thus far kicked back more than $9 million to Hughes, and spent only $404,372 on good works. Yet, suddenly, the IRS reversed itself. Records of the abrupt about-face remain hidden even today, but Hughes's timely benevolence to the vice-president was not so well concealed.

The "Hughes Loan Scandal" hit the headlines in the final weeks of the closely contested 1960 election. Maheu took time off from plotting to kill Castro and tried instead to kill the story. Nixon, however, panicked. He put out a preemptive report that never even mentioned Hughes, and promptly got caught in his lies.

"I was successful, during the presidential campaign, in killing a story which was about to break in the St. Louis Post Dispatch and later in the New York Times," Maheu told Hughes, recalling the failed cover-up. "It was only the complexities involved originally in setting up the loan which caused the Nixon forces to panic days before the election because some small-time accountant, who never should have been cut in, was terribly hungry and playing with the Kennedy forces.

"If a simple loan had been made to brother Don with the Whittier property as collateral, the very simple loan may not have become as complicated," continued Maheu. "Two weeks before he died, Drew Pearson told me for perhaps the tenth time, that he never would have broken the story if he had not been suspicious of the incredible steps which were taken in the origin to conceal the fact that the loan had been made."

Although only a hint of his full relationship with Hughes, the revelation ruined Nixon. He lied, denying that either he or Hughes had been involved in the transaction. Confronted with contrary evidence, he lied again, claiming that his widowed mother had "satisfied" the $205,000 loan by turning over "half her life savings," namely the thirteen-thousand-dollar vacant lot. Nixon never stopped lying, but there was no escape.

At a rally in San Francisco's Chinatown, he posed with children carrying a huge banner, its message inscrutable but seemingly supportive. Translated, it read: "WHAT ABOUT THE HUGHES LOAN?" Later, at a post-rally luncheon, every fortune cookie contained the same suggestion: "Ask him about the Hughes loan." The scandal dogged Nixon down to the wire.

He was certain it cost him the presidency, blaming his "poor damn dumb brother" rather than himself or Hughes for his narrow loss to Kennedy.

The "all-out support" Hughes gave Nixon in 1960—a still unknown number of hundred-dollar bills secretly passed through the same bagman who handled the loan transaction—never became public. But the loan scandal would not die. It resurfaced full force when Nixon ran for governor of California two years later, and once more he was sure it caused his humiliating defeat. "I must have answered questions about the Hughes loan at least a hundred times," he complained. "The media loved the story and played it up big—because it was so damaging to me."

Hughes had become a haunting symbol of Nixon's greed and corruption, apparently driving him out of politics forever. Yet neither could now break off the fatal attraction both had done their best to conceal.

Now, in 1968, Richard Nixon was staging a startling comeback. And both he and Hughes were ready to deal again.

"I want you to go see Nixon as my special confidential emissary," Hughes instructed Maheu just two days after the presidential race opened with the primary in New Hampshire. While the rest of the nation focused on McCarthy's upset of Johnson, Hughes immediately recognized that the real victor was Nixon, not only back from oblivion but also facing a badly split Democratic party.

"I feel there is a really valid possibility of a Republican victory this year," Hughes continued. "If that could be realized under our sponsorship and supervision every inch of the way," he added, so confident of Nixon's corruption that he was already plotting the succession, "then we would be ready to follow with Laxalt as our next candidate."

Nixon was indeed eager to renew their ill-fated relationship. Even before Maheu could get to Nixon, Nixon reached out to Hughes.

Of course, Nixon could not reach Hughes directly. Nobody could. In fact, despite their long relationship, the two men had never actually met. Their dealings had always been through intermediaries, and this time Nixon wanted as much insulation as possible.

At one of a series of meetings in Washington and Florida in the spring of 1968, Nixon huddled with his closest friend, Bebe Rebozo, and the man who had introduced them to each other twenty years earlier, Richard Danner. Nixon and Rebozo ran through an apparently well-rehearsed script, designed to maneuver their old pal Danner into handling the dangerous contact with Hughes.

"The discussion was generally did I know or did I have any contacts that I could use to raise money," Danner would later testify. "And the people I knew, of course, they knew equally well or better. The question arose as to what would be the best way of contacting Mr. Hughes. . . . And at that time Mr. Nixon and Mr. Rebozo asked me to attempt to contact someone in the Hughes organization relative to a contribution."

Nixon was as clear in his instructions to Danner as Hughes had been in his orders to Maheu: "The question was, 'Would he contribute, and if so, how much?' "

Yet the connection quickly became a tangled affair. Unable to resist each other but unwilling to meet, Hughes and Nixon groped toward each other through a profusion of go-betweens. Even the middlemen required middlemen. The clear purpose of the principals was lost. Only their paranoia remained. And the middlemen finally came together months later in an atmosphere of mutual suspicion.

The scene was Duke Zeibert's, gathering spot for Washington power brokers. Three men were seated around a table in the front room reserved for the real movers and shakers—Bebe Rebozo, Richard Danner, and Edward Morgan. They were there to exchange money for power on behalf of two men who were not there—Richard Nixon and Howard Hughes.

Rebozo was there as Nixon's surrogate. The Cuban had long been his closest confidant, the perfect companion for a self-absorbed loner like Nixon, willing to sit in silence for hours and listen to his monologues or to sit for hours in mutual silence and just brood with him. Nixon spent more time alone with Rebozo than he did with his wife, and some White House aides would later make suggestive jokes about their strange intimacy. But the real key to their relationship was money. A millionaire bank president who had helped make Nixon himself a millionaire, Rebozo was now putting together a secret slush fund for the president that would eventually total at least several hundred thousand dollars. He was at Duke Zeibert's to collect a bundle of cash from Hughes.

Danner was at the table because Nixon had personally asked him to find out if the Hughes money was available. A tall, thin former

FBI agent from Miami who was now a Washington lawyer, Danner had known both Nixon and Rebozo longer than they had known each other. In fact, they first met when Nixon came down to Florida to recuperate from his first Senate race, and Danner took him fishing on Bebe's boat. Danner had no connection to Hughes, but he was trusted, and he did know the third man at the table, Ed Morgan.

Morgan had the Hughes connection. Another former G-man now practicing law, he was an intimate of Robert Maheu's, and had parlayed their friendship into a lucrative position as prime go-between for Hughes and the likes of Moe Dalitz, collecting six-figure "finder's fees" from the billionaire's Las Vegas acquisitions. A classic Washington operator who specialized in handling sensitive deals for people who could not afford to deal openly with each other, he represented Teamster boss Jimmy Hoffa, Maheu's Mafia partner in the Castro plot, Johnny Roselli, and several other top mobsters, yet still managed also to traffic with leading politicians in both parties. As Maheu would later tell Hughes, in recommending that Morgan be put on a regular retainer, "You can check him out with anybody from Moe Dalitz to the President of the United States."

Now, over breakfast, the three middlemen got down to business. Morgan had taken Danner's request from Nixon and Rebozo to Maheu, and Maheu had taken it to Hughes. Everything was set. Hughes had approved a $100,000 contribution—$50,000 for the campaign, $50,000 for the candidate. Maheu had secured the cash. Morgan was prepared to make the transfer. Rebozo was ready to take delivery. Yet the meeting at Duke Zeibert's ended unresolved. No money changed hands.

What followed was a clash of fear and greed, a comic opera of missed connections, with confused intermediaries stumbling over each other while the two prime movers remained offstage.

Rebozo instinctively backed away from Morgan. The more he reflected on their encounter and the more he recalled the impact of the earlier Hughes loan scandal, the more concerned he became about Morgan's ties to Drew Pearson and Jack Anderson, the very men who had exposed that transaction and kept Nixon out of the White House in 1960. No, Rebozo would not deal with Morgan, and he was having some second thoughts about Hughes.

Morgan, meanwhile, had also decided he wanted no part of this deal. Willing to play the bagman, he was not about to be left holding the bag. All through their meeting, he kept pressing Rebozo for some formal acknowledgment of the transaction. Rebozo instead kept assuring Morgan that he was extremely close to Nixon. An operator whose clients had a tendency to turn up dead in oil drums or disappear into trash compactors must have a sharp instinct for self-preservation. That instinct told Morgan it would be unwise to pass a wad of cash from a man like Hughes to a man like Nixon without getting a receipt. It was the kind of deal that could go sour.

With Morgan out of the picture, Maheu moved to reassure Rebozo that all the old skeletons would remain in the closet. "I can assure you that right now both candidates are very happy with us," he reported to Hughes. "In addition to material support, we were able last week to kill a recurrence of publicity pertaining to the Don Nixon loan. Humphrey himself issued the instructions to his people not to use this matter and Nixon knows that Humphrey did so at my request."

But whatever soothing effect Maheu's coup accomplished was blown when the ubiquitous John Meier appeared with Donald Nixon in tow and announced that they would pass the Hughes money to Rebozo. Called out from a New York meeting with Danner and John Mitchell to take Meier's call, Rebozo came back apoplectic. Donald was under strict orders to steer clear of campaign money period, not to mention Hughes money. And to make matters worse, Rebozo confused John Meier with Johnny Meyer, the Hughes fixer from an earlier era who became notorious in the "Spruce Goose" Senate hearings.

The potential for another dangerous Hughes scandal seemed to be growing geometrically. Rebozo felt himself surrounded by skeletons. He decided on the spot to wash his hands of the deal.

Maheu was now left with a bundle of cash, but no one to pass it and no one to receive it. He decided to cut through all the confusion and deliver the money himself, directly to Richard Nixon.

He had already made a formal contribution to Nixon's campaign, $50,000 in checks passed openly through Governor Laxalt a few weeks before the November election. Now, with the election over, Nixon victorious, and the promised secret cash still undelivered, Maheu once more turned to Laxalt. Early in December they flew together in a private Hughes jet to Palm Springs, where Nixon was due to attend a Republican governors' conference. Laxalt, however, failed to arrange a meeting with the president-elect. Nixon, apparently still nervous about accepting Hughes's money, at least about accepting it personally, sent word that his schedule prohibited a meeting with Maheu.

One week later, Maheu was down in the Bahamas, conferring with representatives of the incoming administration, and there are indications that he at least tried to pass the money again. A cashier at the Sands casino noted on a fifty-thousand-dollar withdrawal slip dated December 5, 1968: "The money was given to Bob Maheu. I was told he was to give this to President Nixon on Maheu's trip to the Bahamas."

So much money was gathered from so many sources—$50,000 from Hughes's personal bank account early in September, another $50,000 from the account "for Nixon's deficit" in December, the disputed $50,000 from the Sands a few days later, yet another $50,000 from Hughes's account in June 1969, and $50,000 more from the cashier's cage at the Silver Slipper in October 1970—that it is impossible to determine how much money actually reached Nixon.

But it is certain that $100,000 in secret cash, two bundles of hundred-dollar bills from Howard Hughes—still undelivered by the November election, still undelivered by the January inauguration—finally found its way to Bebe Rebozo's safe-deposit box. Where it came to haunt Richard Nixon.

It was the terrible guilty secret whose feared discovery would drive him to self-destruction—the tell-tale heart of Watergate.

———

Richard Nixon entered the White House on January 20, 1969, in broad daylight to the cheers of thousands, the duly elected and sworn president of the United States. But trusting no one, fearing everyone, he immediately retreated into isolation behind his palace guard and tried to run the nation like Hughes ran his empire—secretly, from hiding, through a small group of henchmen instilled with the same siege mentality.

It was a government Howard Hughes himself could have created, and one with which he could certainly do business.

"I want to see just how much water we really draw with this Administration after so many years of all-out effort to achieve it," the billionaire wrote Maheu shortly after the inauguration, eagerly anticipating a good return on his investment.

Even before Nixon actually took office, Maheu began flashing news of early triumphs to the penthouse.

"Nixon has decided on his law partner, John Mitchell, to be Attorney General," Maheu reported from the Bahamas, where he was hobnobbing with members of the new administration during the transition. "Mitchell is thoroughly acceptable and we have excellent entrees to him, particularly through Bebe Rebozo.

"We have a definite promise that it will not be [Herbert] Brownell or anyone on whom Brownell can exert any influence," he added, referring to the attorney general under Eisenhower who was now special master in the TWA case and had recently slapped Hughes with the one-hundred-thirty-seven-million-dollar default judgment.

Later, in Washington for the inauguration, Maheu had more good news to report. Things were shaping up quite well at Justice, which for months had blocked Hughes's bid to buy the rest of Las Vegas. "I am most happy with the new head of the anti-trust division," Maheu told his boss. "He was our #1 choice from among several very highly qualified candidates whose names were submitted to me well in advance of the appointment."

The early signs were good, and within a year Hughes would get nearly everything he wanted from Nixon: a green light for his Las Vegas Monopoly game, approval of his illegal reentry into the airline business, a vast increase in his already great cost-plus no-competitive-bidding business with the Pentagon, even an end to federal financing for the dreaded Nevada water project.

But still Hughes was not satisfied.

First there was the Wally Hickel problem. "I sent word to you a couple of days ago that the confirmation of Hickel as Sec. of the Interior would not be consistent with the best interests of my various entities," Hughes complained to Maheu, although there was no apparent reason for his objection to the former Alaska governor. "I was therefore certainly surprised to note today that he was confirmed."

In fact, Hughes was displeased with the entire cabinet selection process. "Not one of the Nixon appointees was given to me for consideration and none such nominee was made in my behalf with my approval," he continued. "I consider this shocking in view of my involvement and dependency upon this Administration. Now to top it off, a new AEC Commissioner has been appointed without any information to me in advance."

As if that was not sufficiently outrageous, the president was about to reshape the Supreme Court, again without consulting Hughes. "[T]he new Supreme Court Justice to replace Fortas could be the most urgent item before us with the TWA suit coming up," Hughes wrote Maheu. "You know I have been disappointed in the very meager voice I have had in the consideration of various opointees for cabinet and other lesser administrative posts. . . .

"You remember I told you the sky was the limit in campaign contributions and I really expected, as the result, to have some small chance to propose a few people for consideration for these positions in government, all of which were re-selected as a part of the new incoming administration.

"So, please, please, Bob, let us have some small voice in the selection of the new justice."

Nixon's failure to clear his government with Hughes should have prepared the recluse for the next blow, but it caught him by surprise.

"Jesus what next!" he wrote in a fevered scrawl. "The news just announced that now Nixon is going to buy $10,000,000,000 (billion) worth of long range conventional manned bombers.

"Bob, that means Boeing, McDonnell-Douglas, Lockheed, or Convair—nothing for us at all."

Part of the new military budget was going to someone other than Hughes, and while he became a top-ten defense contractor for the first time under Nixon, having to share the Pentagon with other corporations left him shaken.

"When Nixon ran for President I told you I wanted to go just as far as necessary to have some voice in the new administration," he concluded in bleak despair, "but I just have no assurance at all as to what the future holds."

The new president was turning out to be something of a disappointment. And the real shock was yet to come.

Hughes, in fact, had grown quite disillusioned with Nixon long before most of the nation. Not over Cambodia or Kent State, not over Vietnam or the Christmas bombing, certainly not because he knew that Nixon was, of course, a crook. No, Howard Hughes was appalled by Nixon's first major act of statesmanship.

In March 1969, less than two months after the inauguration, Hughes expressed his pained disappointment in the new president.

"The news just reported that Nixon will go ahead with the ABM," he wrote Maheu, full of dismay. "Bob, this is an awful mistake. It would perhaps be to my best interest selfishly to do nothing and let the system proceed, but it is a ghastly mistake for the country and for Nixon, whom I want to grow in stature."

Hughes voiced his sad disillusion in the high moral tones of a James Reston or a Walter Lippmann, without mentioning his true objection to the antiballistic missile system.

5-12-69

Bob –

Can't you do something about the Parvin situation? It goes back on the board in the face of Parvin being identified with Justice Douglas in some kind of corruption deal. Please advise, ~~urgent~~.

Next, the new Supreme Court justice to replace Fortas could be the most urgent item before us with the TWA suit coming up. You know I have been disappointed in the very meagre voice I have had in the consideration of various opointees for cabinet and other lesser administrative posts. So, please take this opportunity to salvage this situation.

You remember I told you the sky was the limit in campaign contributions and I really expected, as the result, to have some small chance to propose a few people for consideration for these positions in government, all of which were re-selected ~~yet~~ as a part of the new incoming administration.

So, please, please, Bob, let us have some small voice in the selection of the new justice.

most sincerely, Howard

Building the ABM meant big money for Hughes the defense contractor, but it also meant more big bomb blasts in Nevada, the nuclear nightmare Hughes thought had ended with the election of a man who "knows the facts of life."

One month later, Hughes's disappointment turned to shocked outrage when White House communications director Herb Klein made a speech in Las Vegas backing the nuclear tests.

"Who is this bastard Klein?" Hughes demanded. "I am really seriously worried about the Nixon administration's apparent intention of turning loose all the expensive forces of the government publicity machine to bring public opinion into an attitude favoring the test program.

"This is shocking, Bob," he continued. "I always have assumed that you had the Nixon administration committed to our side. It is *urgent* that something be done to bring this Nixon Nuclear Test Campaign to your well known screeching halt."

Hughes, in fact, was so shocked that he could hardly believe Nixon's ingratitude:

"Sometimes I wonder if Nixon is aware of the donation, which I hope was made, or did somebody possibly forget to make it?"

No one had forgotten. Even as Hughes wrote his pained memo, Bebe Rebozo and Richard Danner were finally arranging the long-delayed $100,000 donation to Nixon's private slush fund.

Danner was now working for Hughes, hired on shortly after the inauguration to be his Nixon connection. Danner was in regular contact with Rebozo, who was now quite comfortably handling his role as the president's Hughes connection. Several times a month, Danner visited his old friend in Key Biscayne or Washington, and Rebozo often flew into Las Vegas, sometimes on a private Hughes jet.

"On several occasions we transported Rebozo when the White House did not want a record of his movements," Maheu reported, making clear Nixon's continued fears of being publicly linked to Hughes.

But if fear had overcome greed before the election, greed overcame all as Nixon settled in at the Oval Office. By the spring of 1969, Rebozo was needling Danner about Hughes's apparent favoritism toward the Democrats. Somehow the president had learned of the

$100,000 Hughes had given Hubert Humphrey, and Rebozo wondered why there had been no contribution to Nixon.

Maheu sent a reminder of the $50,000 donated to Nixon campaign committees, but Rebozo dismissed that money, and said it was "not comparable" to what Hughes had done for Humphrey.

Maheu, who had delivered $50,000 in cash to Humphrey in the backseat of a limousine, understood. He immediately offered Rebozo the $50,000 that had been similarly earmarked for Nixon but never actually passed. Rebozo turned it down.

But he kept right on needling Danner about the Humphrey money, softening him up before finally asking for the Hughes cash he had twice spurned. Not the $50,000 originally discussed, but twice that amount, $100,000.

Everyone called it a "campaign contribution," but there was no campaign, and Rebozo made it clear that the contribution should be delivered directly to him—in cash—rather than to any campaign committee.

The request for $100,000 came to Hughes as he was battling Nixon over the ABM, fighting the president for votes in a closely divided Senate. It was the first major congressional battle of the new administration, and one that pitted Nixon against his hated foe Teddy Kennedy, who was leading the opposition.

So Nixon coupled his request for the money with a plea that Hughes back off from the ABM fight. "The President sent an emissary to ask me if we could relent some of the pressures on the ABM program," Maheu informed his boss, shortly after Rebozo visited Las Vegas late in May.

Hughes replied in kind. He readily approved the payoff, sending word of his benevolence along with a twelve-page meticulously drafted and closely reasoned appeal to Nixon that he drop his support of the ABM. The memo would help the president to recognize his "ghastly mistake," but if Nixon failed to "grow in stature," surely he was still a man who knew "the facts of life."

"Bob," wrote Hughes, "you asked me recently if I had any thought as to what reply might be given to Mr. Nixon on the ABM question.

"Bob, I want you to tell Pres. Nixon this: I am aware of the many, many conflicting viewpoints that have been pressed through to him from right and from left. However, there is one very important difference between a message from me on this subject and the many persuasive inputs which I am sure he is receiving constantly from others.

"This is the difference:

"1. My technical information is absolutely accurate.

"2. My personal monetary selfish interest would be benefited in every way by an immediate, definite, final ABM go-ahead, with no further after-thoughts."

Having established his credentials and his altruism, Hughes presented his arguments—very similar to views Nixon had already secretly received from former President Eisenhower.

"I do not argue in any slightest degree the wisdom or imprudence of spending X billion dollars for an increased defense capability," wrote Hughes. "I argue only that the proposed ABM is not the way to obtain the maximum defense for the X billion.

"It is logical to assume that if the U.S. builds an ABM, then the enemy will do likewise. . . . Any ICBM's saved from destruction by the ABM would not be completely effective, since they would have to run the gauntlet of enemy ABM's before they could reach their targets.

"Now, on the other hand, if the same X billion dollars were expended for an increased fleet of Polaris Submarines, it would be an expenditure for a known and proven product, instead of an experimental, unproven, completely unpredictable weapon system of fantastic complexity.

"The U.S. will never know, really, whether the ABM will work until a real, true enemy missile is actually launched and in flight on its deadly course through the upper regions of space headed for its target in the U.S.

"No matter how it is tested, it will never really be known whether or not it is going to work."

Hughes concluded his ABM memo without mentioning the $100,000, but he had Danner deliver it to Rebozo with word that $50,000 was available immediately and that a like bundle of cash would soon follow.

"Danner is meeting with his friend Rebozo on the ABM situation in Washington, D.C. on Monday," Maheu reported late in June. "Depending on the results of that meeting, we may decide, subject to your approval, to have a personal meeting with the President."

In fact, it was not until June 26 that Danner finally caught up with Rebozo in Miami. The next day Maheu withdrew $50,000 from Hughes's personal bank account for "nondeductible contributions," the code word he used to cover political payoffs.

The deal went down on the Fourth of July.

The president had spent that morning reviewing a parade in Key Biscayne, performing his public duty with obvious discomfort, sweating profusely in a heavy suit on a sweltering hot day, telling parade spectators they were "proof that the great majority of people haven't lost faith in this country."

Then Nixon boarded a helicopter and flew off with Rebozo to a private island in the Bahamas owned by his other millionaire crony, Robert Abplanalp, celebrating this weekend, as he did so many others, drinking martinis with his two old pals. Finally alone, having escaped his wife, having escaped the press, having escaped even Haldeman and Ehrlichman, the president got down to private business.

Rebozo gave Nixon the Hughes memo, undoubtedly also brightening the festivities with word that the long-sought payoff had finally been arranged. Then the Cuban placed a call to Las Vegas.

"Howard, Rebozo has transmitted your message on the ABM to the President," Maheu reported that same day to the penthouse. "He was very appreciative but Rebozo could not tell from the reaction whether or not the President was ready to countermand the position of his Secretary of Defense."

Nixon, however, was prepared to immediately show his appreciation to Hughes in another way.

"Howard," Maheu added in the same report, "our present intelligence indicates that the President's approval of Air West and that of the CAB will come down next week."

Hughes was, at long last, back in the airline business. Air West was not, of course, TWA. But it was an airline, and Hughes, who had first gained fame as an aviation pioneer, very much wanted to own one again. He had been plotting to take over the struggling little carrier for a year.

"This plan necessitates that the stock edge downward," he had written at the outset, outlining his scheme to swindle the stockholders, "and then that we come along with a spectacular offer."

At first it had gone according to plan. When the stock had tumbled to sixteen dollars a share, depressed by a spate of adverse news stories secretly orchestrated by Hughes publicists, the recluse made his offer—twenty-two dollars a share. More than half of the stockholders voted to accept.

But then a stubborn Air West board of directors voted 13–11 to reject Hughes's bid. "I do not think these selfish bastards are ready to change their position," Maheu reported. But he had a plan, a phony stockholders' lawsuit against the directors leading the opposition and a plot to have three front men dump tens of thousands of Air West shares on the market, setting off a panic.

Maheu reported the entire illegal scheme to Hughes:

"As I am sure you know the derivative actions were filed today in Deleware. Tomorrow there will be further actions filed against the 13 Directors in Federal court in New York. The unions will serve notice tomorrow reflecting their complete disgust, and certain machinery has been put into motion to depress the stock so that the Directors who voted against the deal will recognize their individual obligations to the fullest extent."

The campaign of stock fraud and intimidation was a complete success. The opposition capitulated. And when Hughes finally closed the deal, a loophole in the agreement allowed him to pay not the twenty-two dollars a share promised, but only $8.75.

He had cheated the Air West stockholders of nearly $60 million. And now the airline was finally his, courtesy of Richard Nixon. (As promised July 4 in the message from Rebozo, the CAB approved the takeover July 15, and the president made it final July 21.)

Almost two weeks went by, however, with no response from Nixon on the ABM. Hughes was getting impatient.

"I am disappointed because, since I have no report of the President's reaction to the paper I wrote, I can only assume he did not ask anybody to read it," Hughes complained, hardly satisfied with an airline.

"Bob, I have given you unlimited resources financially with which to operate, and I have given you absolute freedom to choose anybody under the sun you might wish to assist you.

"Since I consider I have given you carte blanche, financially, executively, and every other way, I think I am entitled to receive some kind of a report, setting forth in specific terms just what has happened and by whom it was done, and what is being attempted at this time and what is expected to result from same.

"I didn't spend about 6 hours on that paper just to have it wind up in somebody's waste basket. If the President could not be bothered to consider this matter, it seems to me it should have been pursued thru somebody else."

But the president had not forgotten about Hughes. He had asked somebody to read the ABM memo—Henry Kissinger. On July 16, 1969, the same day that the Apollo 11 astronauts blasted off for man's first walk on the moon, Nixon huddled with his national security adviser. That morning in the Oval Office, just before they shared the historic moment watching the launch together on television, the president told Kissinger to go see Hughes.

Kissinger returned to his White House basement office angry and incredulous. He told his deputy, Alexander Haig, that Nixon had just ordered him to give the billionaire a private top-secret briefing, not only on the ABM but also on the general strategic threat, on the balance of nuclear power—and, as a final outrage, to solicit Hughes's own views on defense policy.

Although he regularly briefed his own patron, Nelson Rockefeller (who secretly slipped him $50,000 just before he joined the White House staff), Kissinger always bristled at having to service Nixon's patrons, and he had never before been asked to do anything remotely like this. The Hughes mission really had Kissinger fuming.

"Henry was not particularly impressed with the thought of it," Haig later recalled. "He was rather cynical about it, somewhat skeptical, wondered whether this sort of activity was the right thing to do." Others who overheard Kissinger's tirade say he questioned both the president's motives and his mental health.

"He's out of his mind," yelled Kissinger. "He can't sell *this*! I can't hold private peace talks with Howard Hughes."

Haig himself seemed to find it all amusing. He emerged from Kissinger's office waving the Hughes memo in his hand, and told Larry Lynn, a senior aide who handled the ABM, "Guess what's up now—Howard Hughes is in the act!"

Maheu meanwhile immediately flashed word from Nixon to Rebozo to Danner to the penthouse.

"Howard, we have just been informed that the President will be writing you a letter in the next several days to thank you for your comments on the ABM in your memorandum delivered by Rebozo.

"More importantly, however, is the fact that the President chose to discuss said memo with Dr. Kissinger, his number one technical advisor. Kissinger was very much impressed and admitted that you had covered some concepts which had not come to their attention previously.

"As a result, the President would like to know if he could send Kissinger to Las Vegas to brief you on some new developments and to get the benefit of your thinking.

"As you know, Howard," added Maheu, dealing delicately with a sensitive point, "because of the direct line from my home to your office (which is 100% secure) such a briefing could take place without the necessity of your having a personal confrontation with Kissinger."

It was shuttle diplomacy of a new order. Nixon dealing with Hughes as if negotiating nuclear policy with a sovereign power. But the prospect of Kissinger's visit terrified Hughes. He simply could not deal with an outsider, not even Kissinger, not even by telephone.

"Re the ABM," he scrawled to Maheu. "I urge you thank the president profusely for his offer to send Kissinger, but tell him I do not consider that this is necessary and I do not think it would advance the situation.

"Bob, to have this man here could only embarass me.

"It would place me in the position of refusing to see an envoy of the president, and, no matter how you try to dress it up, this is the way the president will view it.

"Please, regardless of how you do it, *kill off this trip in some way.*"

The offer that Nixon must have assumed would so flatter Hughes that it would ensure the payoff—and end his opposition to the ABM as well—instead left the recluse shaken.

As yet unaware of the debacle, but taking no chances on the $100,000, half an hour later the president sent further evidence of his good faith. All through July Nixon and Kissinger had been considering final plans for a series of mammoth nuclear blasts, designed to test the ABM warhead. No official decision had yet been reached. But now, on July 16, the commander in chief sent advance word to his hidden benefactor.

"Howard," Maheu flashed to Hughes, "we are reliably informed that the AEC has finally given up the battle and will have all tests of a megaton or more held in Alaska. We are also informed that, for security reasons, they cannot, at this time, make any public announcement confirming their capitulation."

Howard Hughes had won his desperate battle to ban the bomb. Or so it seemed. Richard Nixon, after all, was growing in stature.

It was time to celebrate.

Bob—

Re the ABM. I urge you
thank the president profusely
for his offer to send Kissinger,
but tell him I do not consider that this is necessary
and I do not think it would
advance the situation.

Bob, to have this man here
could only embarass me.

It would place me in the
position of refusing to see an
envoy of the president; and,
no matter how you try to dress
it up, this is the way the president will view it.

Please, regardless of how you
do it, kill off this trip in some
way.

All I ask for, re the ABM,
is a simple, brief, explanation
of why he cannot consider the
plan I proposed; if, in fact,
it is his decision to reject it.

Also, and more important,
I want to know whose assistance,
other than the president, you
intend to seek. In other words,
what course of action do you
intend to pursue, now that the

president obviously has turned
it down.

What about the senate leaders
of the faction opposing the ABM,
do you want to consider going to
them?

Please advise,
                    Howard

11 Howard Throws a Party

It was to be the greatest party Las Vegas had ever seen, and Las Vegas had seen a lot of great parties. But this party was going to be thrown by Howard Hughes.

All through the spring and summer months of 1969, as Hughes and Nixon moved to close their big deal, the billionaire was planning a party. It was tentatively scheduled for the same Fourth of July weekend that the hundred-thousand-dollar payoff was finally arranged. Indeed, Hughes was far more preoccupied with the big party than with the big payoff.

The occasion was the opening of the Landmark, his latest hotel acquisition, and the first of his purchases to break the antitrust blockade—approved by a suddenly cooperative Justice Department three days before Nixon moved into the White House.

But it was more than that. It was a celebration of the triumph of the Hughes-Maheu partnership. Nothing could stop them now.

And yet that party would open a wound between them that never healed, one that festered for months. There would be other wounds—wounds terminal for Hughes, for Maheu, and for Nixon—but it was the explosion over the Landmark party that marked the beginning of the end.

The Landmark was the ugliest hotel in town, an ungainly bubble-top tower with an interior decor that struggled to combine outer-space murals, ancient Incan wood panels, and Italian marble statues of other famous "landmarks": the Eiffel Tower, the Colosseum, Big Ben.

There was something strangely off-key about the entire place. A thirty-one-story haunted house, it had stood empty for eight years until Hughes bought it for $17.3 million from its bankrupt owners. With an air-conditioning system that never really worked and a constantly malfunctioning glass-walled elevator that crawled uncertainly up an outside wall of the tower, the Landmark had a permanent air of impending catastrophe. It seemed more like the setting for a disaster movie than the stage for a grand party.

But to Robert Maheu it looked beautiful in the spring of 1969.

"Howard, if you ever decide to leave the Penthouse, you will be flabbergasted at the sight from the top of this bubble," he wrote, so carried away with his enthusiasm that he actually sought to lure Hughes from his lair. "It is magnificent during the day and unbelievably beautiful after dark. You get the feeling that this edifice was constructed at the very dead center of the valley, and that all the mountains surrounding the valley are in equidistant position."

It was an uncharacteristic burst of poetic sentiment. However, within weeks, this beautiful vision had degenerated into an ugly brawl, one that would last for months.

"Instead of you and I clawing each others' eyes out over the Landmark," Hughes wrote Maheu as the planning for the grand party began to strain their marriage, "why dont you collaborate with me in endeavoring to find a formula for the opening that will satisfy both of us."

Like all their big fights, this one was over something trivial, but in this case both the triviality and the fight were taken to operatic extremes. Perhaps the very notion of an "opening" was frightening to Hughes, a man whose life was devoted to keeping things closed. This would be his first party since arriving in Las Vegas, indeed the first since he had drifted into seclusion more than a decade ago. And while Hughes himself would not, of course, be at the party, still he was in some sense going public.

But there was more to this particular opening. It was Hughes going mano-a-mano with his arch-rival Kirk Kerkorian. Right across the street from the Landmark stood Kerkorian's International, the biggest hotel in Las Vegas, taller than the Landmark, and it was scheduled to open the same week in July. The key issue was which day to hold the opening, whether to throw their party before or after Kerkorian's. What Hughes wanted was a real blast that would blow Kerkorian right out of the water.

"The public can definitely be persuaded to believe that the opening of the Landmark will be the greatest event since the Last Supper," wrote Hughes.

"On the other hand, to actually accomplish a fantastic opening of a brand-new hotel-casino with all of its complexities and all the things that may go wrong on opening night—that is something far more difficult.

"And, it only takes one incident in which one stupid dealer accidently insults just one of the many, many newspaper writers which you and I will no doubt decide should be brought out here from New York, Washington, London, Paris, etc., and then the fat will be in the fire.

"So, I say it is possible to control what people will expect the Landmark to be," he concluded, "but I feel it is impossible to control with any certainty the outcome of the actual opening night."

Quite a dilemma. Hughes, however, had a solution. He would not approve any date for the opening.

"Re the date of the opening, why dont you leave that open," he told Maheu. "If the show and all other elements shape up very rapidly, fine, but I urge that a July 1st date not be committed any further in any publicity or word of mouth. I just dont want it to be embarrassing if the opening should be a little later.

"With my reputation for unreliability in the keeping of engagements, I dont want this event announced until the date is *absolutely firmly* established."

Maheu was concerned. It was difficult to plan a Las Vegas gala and yet keep it secret; it was impossible to plan without knowing when it would take place.

"If we are not going to open on July 1, we would very much appreciate your giving us a fixed date (whenever)," he replied, gently urging Hughes toward a decision. "We truly believe that July 1 is a good target. If on the other hand you have a reason why July 1 bothers you, you need not give us that reason, but we beg you to give us a fixed date."

Hughes had a reason, and he was pleased to give it. What he would not give Maheu was the date.

"I would hate to see the Landmark open on the 1st of July and then watch the International open a few days later and make the Landmark opening look like small potatoes by comparison," explained Hughes. "Also, I would hate to see the International open with Barbara Streisand while the Landmark has no name on the marquee.

"So, please string along with me on an open date," he insisted, relieved to have found a reason to avoid making the decision. "If you will go along with the above, then may I persuade you to help me try to find the very strongest name that can be made available by any conceivable device?"

Unwilling to set a date, Hughes was more than willing to throw himself into planning the party. Down to the smallest detail. The big question, however, was who would entertain.

There were pipe dreams. Bob Hope. Hope *and* Crosby. But neither had ever performed in Las Vegas. How about Dean Martin? He used to work at the Sands, but left soon after Sinatra stormed out. Now Martin was under exclusive contract to another hotel, indeed was part-owner, but Hughes wanted him. By any conceivable device.

"Before I try to obtain somebody from my Hollywood contacts," he schemed, "do you think there is any slightest possibility of getting Dean Martin by the following strategy:

"I think Martin can be motivated by one of three factors, or all three:

"1. Money—a capital gain on some asset he no doubt owns.

"2. An agreement to finance some picture he would like to make. (Bob, there is not an actor alive who does not have some pet idea he would like to make into a movie. If Dean Martin does not have such a pet idea, he will be the first movie star I have ever heard of in my entire life who does not.)

"3. I think Martin can be persuaded that my friendship may, in one way or another, be important to him sometime. I also think he can, very carefully, be persuaded I have a deep hurt from the lousy way he acted, and I think he can be motivated to repair the damage. . . ."

The idea of getting Martin, of enticing him away from the "Rat Pack," of stealing him back from his reputed mobster partners, began to really excite Hughes.

"Can you imagine the nationwide publicity possibilities of Martin performing at the Landmark when he owns part of the Riviera?" Hughes added in a P.S.

"I can see some smart reporter, with the proper encouragement, taking this thing and writing a complete dime novel out of the behind the scenes 'True Story.' Dont you see the possibilities of creating a plot out of that situation: Las Vegas moguls fight battle under the glittering surface. First Sinatra, then Martin walks out—then, the axe falls.

"I know one thing," added Hughes, concocting his own dime novel, "if I were a newspaper reporter, and my editor told me to take that story and make the most of it, I would have everybody from Sinatra to Martin to Moe Dalitz, the Justice Department, and two hired guns in it before I got through."

Maheu, also excited about getting Martin, offered an even grander vision. They would reunite the entire old "Rat Pack" on the stage of the Landmark, a coup that would truly leave its mark on Las Vegas history. Maheu took it one step further. They would call the whole dazzling assemblage of talent the "Hughes Parade of Stars."

The concept disturbed Hughes. He was not ready to step out on the stage.

"First, Bob, I dont think my name should be used in connection with a theatrical production at the Landmark," he wrote, instantly deflating Maheu's dream. "I am fearful that the critics will consider that I have moved into the theatrical realm and have thereby placed myself in their target range. If it were used, it would give the critics the opportunity to hack away at my name at will."

The fear of being personally reviewed rekindled all of Hughes's fears of going public, prompting him to reopen the still unresolved question of the opening date.

"Now, regarding the opening date," he added, "I humbly beg you not to permit anything to leak out in confirmation of any July 1st date. Just as determined as you are to beat K to the punch with an earlier opening than the International, I am equally convinced it is a mistake.

"In two nearly simultaneous dates such as this, the later one is always the climax, and the one remembered. Also, the entity opening second is always the newest, and the first one is as old as yesterday's newspaper.

"I urge that no further statement be made or word leaked about the date until further along."

Maheu was getting upset. It was not Kerkorian who worried him. It was Hughes. It was not the date of the opening that concerned him. It was the fact that Hughes refused to pick any date.

"I sincerely hope that you understand the truly unbelievable position in which I am placed when I still cannot commit a day of opening," he wrote. "Howard, we are not the least bit stubborn on July 1 per se. If you prefer that we do it a few days after the International, please give us a fixed date and we will proceed accordingly.

"But darn it, Howard, if you care about what happens to the Landmark you simply cannot hold this decision in abeyance any longer."

Hughes was not about to be outflanked. If Maheu would not be drawn into a debate over the merits of throwing their party before or after Kerkorian's, the naked impresario had a new excuse to leave the opening date open. Another rival event, bigger than the International.

"I just had a rude awakening," he wrote in mock alarm. "The moon landing is planned for July!

"Now, what disturbs me equally is the fact that there may be another event scheduled for one of the dates under consideration, either locally or elsewhere, which may dilute the publicity impact of the Landmark.

"So, Bob, please review the calendar, both locally and nationally, and report to me all events of publicity import which are scheduled for July. Then, I will do my best not to delay the selection of the Landmark date."

By mid-June, however, Hughes had still failed to approve a definite date for the opening, still tentatively set for July 1. Maheu was climbing the walls. It had gone beyond the party. His entire public image in Las Vegas was at stake. He was one of the most powerful men in town, and now he was being shown up as a flunky who did not even have the power to pick the date of a party. Finally, he could no longer stand the humiliation.

"Here I am on the front line talking to Dean Martin, Danny Thomas, the Astronauts, the public, the Governor, and I don't know what in the hell I am talking about because you still have not given us a date," a frantic Maheu wrote Hughes.

"I am getting to a point where I frankly don't know what in the hell to tell them when they ask the very simple question—when are we going to open?

"Honest to God, Howard, if this question is not resolved forthwith, I am simply going to have to get the hell out of town because I just simply cannot continue facing all these people any further."

Hughes refused to answer the question of the opening date. Instead, he responded to Maheu's frantic plea by calling their whole partnership into question.

"Bob, you have done a good job for me and I appreciate it," the billionaire wrote with heavy solemnity. "I also appreciate your several statements to me that you have a low flash point and that I should learn to accept this in its proper relevance.

"However, Bob, there are some things in life becide money and success," he lectured his underling, taking the broader view.

"I am afraid I have reached the point where I have a greater reserve allowable tolerance in my money-success column, than I have in my health-and-remaining-years column.

"If, under these circumstances, you think my failure to give you a specific date has placed you in a position of embarrassment under which you dont want to be in Las Vegas, I think maybe the time has come when, for my health's sake, a somewhat less efficient and less successful man, but one who would not find it so difficult to put up with my, admittedly less-than-perfect operation, should perhaps be the resident managing executive here in Las Vegas.

"Re: the Landmark opening, I have told you repeatedly that I dont want the Landmark to open until after the International.

"Bob, I say this only in the interest of harmony.

"If I were indifferent to your barbs and inferences, it would be no problem," he concluded, "but I am not indifferent, and some of your implications get under my skin and my blood pressure goes higher than [the] Landmark Tower, which is not good."

Hughes had called Maheu's bluff and raised him the limit. Suddenly, it was not merely Maheu's public image, but his five-hundred-thousand-dollar-a-year job that was at stake. He quickly backed off, left the opening date open, and gently urged his boss toward the next order of business: the guest list.

Planning for the Mad Hatter's Tea Party now proceeded in its own lunatic fashion. Hughes threw himself into the debate over who would attend with a frenzied delight born of the knowledge that at last he had found a device that could forever delay the opening. Obviously there could be no party if there were no guests.

Maheu tried to impress upon Hughes the urgency of assembling a guest list by raising the specter of Kerkorian.

"I just received an exquisite invitation for the opening of the International," he wrote. "While we are talking, he is moving. Howard, I really believe that any further delay on the list of potential invitees for the Landmark will place us in an embarassing position."

It made no impact. Hughes refused even to consider the list Maheu had painstakingly compiled until a week before the still tentative date of the opening, and then rejected the entire list out-of-hand. He presented this rejection as an act of pure reason, suggesting that Maheu simply prepare a new list according to certain scientific specifications.

"I understand your anxiety to get started on the list of invites," the billionaire wrote Maheu solicitously.

"However, the only lasting damage will come from failure to invite certain important people while inviting others, about whom said important people will no doubt learn.

"Now, Bob, I simply dont have the man-hours, and you dont want to wait for me to go thru this list name by name," he continued, maintaining his pose of sweet reasonableness and complete cooperation as he cast aside all of Maheu's invitations.

"You will just have to appoint somebody to make a new list using this concept:

"Categorize the people you want, and where you invite one such person, invite likewise the others in the same category who have equal merit, who are equal friends, etc., unless they have done something to be disqualified, or unless they should be disqualified because of simple lack of stature, or disloyalty, or such-like.

"For example, if you intend to invite actors and actresses, as you evidently do, I think somebody should go thru the Central Casting Directory, or the Academy lists and pick out all the actors or actresses above a certain level of importance, unless they are ruled out for some reason such as I have suggested above.

"I only ask that it be based upon some consistency," Hughes insisted, as he continued to unfold his mad scheme.

"For example, in view of some of the people included, such as the head of Reynolds Electric, I certainly think you should include all the very top people at Lockheed, and this may make it necessary to include the heads of other aircraft companies, and this immediately brings up the question of the heads of the airlines whom I know well."

The inclusion of one local businessman suddenly seemed to require invitations to all the executives in two entire industries and also raised the thorny issue of what to do about Hughes's old friends. Earlier he had decided to bring in the entire old gang for the big bash. Now he was having second thoughts.

"This is one most important question, Bob. If you ask too many people who are good friends of mine, then you must consider how many of these may be disappointed if I do not see them. Also, you must consider how many others may unavoidably be forgotten and who will be deeply hurt for this reason.

"When you boil it down, Bob, I think, for a number of reasons, it would be a mistake to invite anybody just because he is a friend of mine," he concluded, relieved to have headed off the clamoring hordes he pictured pounding at his door.

"I think you should divide the list into categories," he reiterated, "and try to be *consistant* in inviting all people in each category who are *equally qualified*."

What could be more reasonable? Maheu, however, recoiled from the task. Afraid to challenge the theoretical construct Hughes had so passionately presented, he was also wary of trying to apply it to the billionaire's satisfaction. He suggested that Hughes himself compose the new guest list.

"Bob, I do not have the facilities to compile a list," the master host replied. "You will have to make the list."

Clearly that was Maheu's job. Hughes's job was to approve it, a task he attacked with relish as soon as the new completely categorized and carefully calibrated list arrived at the penthouse.

"I am starting on the businessmen," reported Hughes, plunging right in. "I dont expect it to take long.

"Your first name is an automobile dealer," he noted. And got stuck right there. At the first name.

"I know there are a number of prominent car dealers in this area," he mused. "I recognize that, if you attempt to include all the businessmen in the area, it would be a completely impractical number of people. I only want to know what ground rules and formula was used in selecting these names.

"In other words, if some auto dealer should complain that he was not invited, I would like to know what satisfactory explanation could be given.

"I am not suggesting that it is likely Fletcher Jones or Pete Finley, etc., are likely to give anybody an opportunity to explain," continued Hughes, conjuring up the image of sullen car salesmen to impress upon Maheu the need for rigorous analysis of the invitations. "I am just thinking that, in the event you should hear a rumor that one of these dealers is unhappy, then it would be helpful for you and for me to feel that there was a sound valid reason for such dealer not being included, based upon the list being prepared in compliance with some clearly understood formula or set of ground rules which you and I fully approve.

"So, Bob, if you will just explain the basis of the establishment of this list, I will give you immediate action in clearing it."

Obviously there was no point in reviewing the rest of the businessmen until the question of the auto dealers was resolved, and that would require a great deal more information. Awaiting Maheu's annotations, Hughes moved on to the next category. Actors and actresses. Again, there were problems.

"I am well aware of the time element on the invitations and do not need to be reminded," Hughes began impatiently, annoyed by Maheu's hurried approach to this complex undertaking.

"Bob, re your list, you have really left out a lot of people who will be awfully offended—for example, you have included Rita Hayworth, Sidney Poitier and Connie Stevens, but omitted Darryl Zanuck and the heads of all the major studios, plus many other important stars. Susan Hayward for example. Dont you remember my comments on this?"

Clearly Maheu had failed to consult either the Central Casting directory or the Academy rolls, had made no real effort to include all *equally qualified* candidates. And what was Connie Stevens doing on this list, anyway? Hughes decided to check that out personally, secretly contacting his Hollywood lawyer Greg Bautzer for 'solid intelligence.

Meanwhile, he plowed in to the next batch of invitations. Once more, there were unanswered questions.

"Re the list of invitees from the news media," he inquired, "do you think the list should be slightly expanded?

"I dont know. I am just asking.

"I see you have nobody from the radio stations. I am not criticizing. Only asking."

It went on like that for days, the guest list ballooning to embrace everybody as qualified as those already included, until Maheu finally suggested two separate parties to accommodate all the proposed guests, a pre-opening preview to be followed by the big opening gala.

Hughes, however, had not yet actually approved *any* invitations. And now he started to move in reverse, questioning every name on the list, eliminating entire categories.

"I have reviewed carefully the new integrated complete lists," he advised Maheu. "I suggest you make new lists as follows:

"Why dont you eliminate all out-of-towners plus as many locals as you feel would not be harmful.

"Studio Execs—all out of town, so understand will be eliminated.

"Union Officials—urge you review with objective of shortening slightly and eliminating any questionables.

"Local Business Men—I urge that you, Bob, personally go thru this list. I would like to see it slightly shorter if it can be done without hurting too many feelings.

"Airline and Aircraft Industries—I feel all of these can be eliminated.

"Hotel Industry—this seems an awful long list, Bob."

For the third time in three days, Maheu revised the guest list for the still unscheduled party. Hughes was not satisfied. He demanded the same absolute consistency in excluding guests as he had in including them, dropping all who were equally unqualified, and the once swollen list was now shrinking at an alarming rate.

"These will be my final comments on the invitation lists," Hughes assured his harried underling, as he started to prune the undesirables, slashing away with wild abandon.

"Do you really think so many hotel executives should be included?" he asked dubiously. "If I am going to eliminate all of my friends in the movie business and in the aircraft business, such as my friends at Lockheed, then I just wonder about such names as those I have noted."

Having decided not to invite his old friends for fear they would insist on seeing him, having eliminated all out-of-towners to cover their exclusion, Hughes now questioned every name still on the list. Why invite a bunch of strangers, if not his friends?

"Please give me your views," he encouraged Maheu, not at all close-minded, "but bear in mind that I am not inviting about 500 highly qualified candidates of mine in Los Angeles, New York, Washington, and Houston.

"You may say: 'Go ahead and invite them.'

"But we have discussed that and agreed that there are many disadvantages.

"I just feel that if all of my out-of-town friends are going to be excluded, it will be easier for me to explain if the list is confined to the people who would normally be included under almost any kind of analysis.

"This surely includes Laxalt, Baring, Bible, etc.," he continued, citing the governor, Nevada's only congressman, and one of its two senators.

"Whether it includes a man, because he is the biggest meat packer in town, or not—I just really dont know, Bob, and that is why I solicit your advice.

"Please feel free to resubmit to me a reccomendation for rein-statement of any of the names," Hughes concluded generously, "to-gether with an explanation of what specific qualifications you desire to use as the controlling guidelines in reinstating them."

Maheu had reached his limit. He had been filing an endless series of reports, justifying his proposed lists, explaining the qualifications of each proposed guest, quickly agreeing to drop those Hughes chal-lenged, to add those he suggested, to drop the names added as the billionaire suddenly questioned invitations he had just insisted upon, submitting revised lists and revising the revisions.

It was all futile.

Every name added and every name deleted called into question all the other names, causing Hughes to re-analyze the entire list. Over and over again.

"I am certain that one submission back to me of the revised and shortened lists I have proposed will be sufficient," he once more assured Maheu. "I am hoping to give you a green lite within an hour after you re-submit the lists.

"Re the opening date, etc., I urge you count the number after the revisions. It looks to me as tho the number, in total, after the revisions I have requested, will be small enough to permit one event only, *which I strongly recommend.*"

Hughes's demand for yet another revised guest list came just after midnight, three days before the still tentative date of the grand Land-mark party. He had lopped so many names off the list that the big gala could now fit comfortably in the hotel's constantly malfunction-ing elevator. He had not yet approved a single invitation. And he had stubbornly kept the opening date open.

Maheu finally lost control.

"Howard," he exploded, "we don't have a revised guest list be-cause, as of right now, we don't know whether we're going to have one group or two groups—or any group. If we don't have any invitees at all, then it becomes moot to furnish a guest list.

"I have given you the schedule of events about ten times now," he raved at Hughes, who all along had been peppering him with questions about details of the still unscheduled party, especially about food for the still uninvited guests, which he refused to allow Maheu to order.

"Unfortunately, I have been so busy with this and many other of your problems, that I have no idea about the menu, except that, as I indicated to you in a previous memorandum, it will cost us about $10 per head to feed the beasts.

"At this point," Maheu concluded, "I couldn't care less whether we have an affair on the 30th, on the 1st, or whether we ever open up the damned joint. My recommendation to you, Howard, seriously, is that we put this whole caper aside, not take advantage of the fact that we can make the International look foolish, let them make us look foolish instead, and wait until you are satisfied that you have capable people around you to have your opening, at which time I wish you the greatest success."

Hughes absorbed the diatribe with uncharacteristic calm. Having waited so patiently for Maheu to bite, he did not want to try to hook him too soon. Also, Hughes was himself hooked on the guest list. He was not willing to be diverted. Not quite yet.

"Bob, I dont think I have been unreasonable about this invitation list," he wrote, replying with elaborate patience to his aide's intemperate outburst.

"I honestly feel, Bob, that if I can bear to devote the time to go through this list, you should be willing likewise to do so.

"I am sure there will be another occasion like this some time, and if this list can be refined and analyzed to the end of the line, all this work will be done and not necessary to be repeated."

With that, Hughes was off again, refining and analyzing with undiminished zeal, urging Maheu to go the last mile, not for the sake of this party alone, but for the Eternal List.

"Please consider the remaining names," he continued. "I would appreciate the facts supporting invitations of these people, and I would also appreciate the names and qualifications of any other people you think should be added in the event these names are returned to the list.

"In other words, if these real estate men and contractors are restored, aren't there other people in the same line of work whom, in all propriety, should be included?

"Re Morrie Friedman, please tell me the story on him.

"Also, Bob, I am awaiting a list of other auto dealers who perhaps should be included, in view of the fact that I have returned Ackerman to the list."

Ackerman. The first name on Maheu's first list. The one that had stopped Hughes right off. Ackerman had finally made it back onto the list. But the larger issue raised by his inclusion—what to do about the rest of the automobile dealers—still preoccupied the would-be host.

It remained a troubling inconsistency. Hughes, however, had promised Maheu a green light within an hour after receiving the latest revised guest list. Now, at 7:40 A.M. on June 28, twenty minutes ahead of schedule, Hughes, true to his word, gave the big go-ahead.

"Here, finally, is the first installment of names for the invitation list," Hughes announced triumphantly.

"I have marked 3 of the names OK.

"I give my complete blessing to your going ahead and phoning these men.

"What time do you desire to ask them to arrive?

"As I understand it, there will be no written invitations. That is important."

Three names. And one small problem. Hughes had still not told Maheu the opening date. He could not even invite the three guests Hughes had grudgingly approved.

Three. Maheu had been working day and night for weeks to put together the big party, having to call on all his skills as a clandestine operative to pull it off despite Hughes's best efforts at sabotage. He had again gone without sleep to prepare the final revised guest list and humor his mad boss. Here was his reward. Three guests. No food. No opening date.

Maheu finally snapped.

"Howard, I really don't know what you are trying to do to me," he wrote more in pain than in anger, "but if your desire is to place me in a state of complete depression you are succeeding.

"Howard, I don't mind making myself available to you every moment of the day, 24 hours a day. It is a hell of a sacrafice to do so, but your staff can verify that in the last 2½ years they have never spent but a few moments to locate me. I feel, however, that all of my efforts to cooperate with you in this matter are becoming an exercise of complete futility.

"Now, Howard, I am getting pretty damned disturbed about what seems to be developing into a compulsive need to give Bob hell," he added, his anger rising. "I find it very depressing to pick up the telephone and, practically in each instance of the recent past, I am catching hell for what I did, or what I did not do. I am being second-guessed at each corner."

The longer Maheu went on, the angrier he got. Finally, the scheming Jesuit lost all control, forgot his cold calculations, stopped caring about the consequences, and, as if this absurd party were what really counted, allowed himself to get drawn fully into the Landmark brawl.

"Now, Howard, this may come to you as a shock, but we are soon entering the realm of not being believable.

"All I know is that we have an opening taking place in a few days. Everyone seems prepared for it, except you. There have been many hours of sweat and blood poured into this project, and all we need is evidence of confidence from you. After all, Howard, in the last analysis, only you have something to gain or lose. In my present state of mind, I couldn't care less if it takes place or not."

But Maheu did care. Cared deeply. This was his party. It was his sweat and blood that had gone into planning it. And it was he, not Hughes, who was going to be up there in that bubble when the whole thing blew up.

"Howard, all I can tell you in conclusion, is that I have no desire to be identified with a fiasco. But if you are so hell-bent on being the author of one, I am afraid that there is nothing else I can do to prevent you from accomplishing just that.

"If this whole thing means nothing to you, why in the hell should I be concerned about it?

"The opening, if we have one, is now only a few days away, and, as much as I want to help you, we have almost, already, run out of time.

"It is becoming urgent that we announce a definite date.

"If, on the other hand, Howard, you would prefer that I not be involved at all in the Landmark caper, just simply tell me, and you will never live long enough to see how quickly this Frenchman can make the disappearing act thru the nearest escape hatch."

This was the moment Hughes had been waiting for. Maheu had finally taken the bait. Now it was time to reel him in.

"I am sorry," Hughes wrote with a heavy heart that barely concealed his secret satisfaction, "but I cannot give a go-ahead on the Landmark until the situation of disaccord which has developed between us is put in better condition."

It was all working out so well. Not only had he succeeded in drawing Maheu fully into the fight, but now the fight itself was a perfect excuse to keep the opening date open. Better yet, it was clearly Maheu's own fault. And beyond all else, he had finally flushed out his partner's true feelings, all the anger he feared, all the passion he desired.

"You keep telling me that I am imagining things when I speak of misunderstandings between us and that none exists except in my mind," continued Hughes. "Then a time comes like this morning and you take the wraps off and expose a pent-up condition of resentment that is just boiling over.

"I do not agree with anything in your message—not anything at all," he added.

"I think today is fortunate, in a way, because you have finally taken the wraps off and said what is on your mind, and what is at the root of all our troubles.

"It does no good to gloss over these things and pretend they dont exist," Hughes went on, warming to his role as marriage counselor in his own stormy marriage. "If we dont lay them on the table in front of us, they will never be resolved.

"I assure you that, if you feel even half of what you said in your message, it has to be straightened out to the point where you look at the situation entirely differently.

"It is just absurd for two people in the position we are in, where each depends as completely on the other as we do, to have the compressed, bursting package of bitterness and resentment, bottled up inside one of us as you disclosed this morning.

"And, I assure you, Bob, it is not a one-way street," Hughes continued, abandoning his even-handed approach, "because for every feeling of injustice, or whatever it is that is bugging you, I feel just as strongly in the opposite direction.

"Just as convinced as you appear to be that I am wrong and that you are getting the bad end of the deal, etc., just as convinced as you appear to be that you are mistreated, and that you have to take some kind of revenge, just as firmly convinced of this as you seem to be, you may rest assured I feel equally strongly that you are 100% wrong.

"So, I am sure this walled-up bitterness must not be permitted to continue between us," he concluded, having laid things on the table with a vengeance. He now turned back to the matter at hand.

"Meantime, Bob, please do not allow us to have a further misunderstanding about the Landmark.

"I am asking you, for the record, not to give a go-ahead on the basis of any specific date, and not to make any preparations for the opening. Also, I implore you, Bob, not to permit some rumor to leak out about a July 1st opening, or anything else in connection with this matter, until we get these issues settled."

Finally, to really nail down an open date, Hughes added a stern P.S.: "Bob, the above is really important if we are to have any chance at all of healing this breach between us."

Maheu didn't know what had hit him. The CIA tough guy was flat on his back, crying for mercy.

"Even a person who professes to be as rough and strong as I do will eventually hit the canvas when he is consistently clobbered on all parts of his body and head," wrote the outmatched challenger, throwing in the towel. "He is bound to become punch-drunk. Then to find himself on the canvas and to be kicked in the groin too, I don't think he is entirely unreasonable if he eeks out: 'Ouch, this hurts.'

"As to the Landmark, Howard, I am sure you realize that the logistics involved in an opening are many. If we are not going to open on July 1, we would very much appreciate your giving us a fixed date."

With Maheu on the ropes, Hughes now shifted his tactics. There was no need to beat his sparring partner bloody. A TKO was sufficient. Besides, why let Maheu claim all the sympathy? Hughes too was in pain. Deep pain.

The terror over the opening, which had brought their marital strife to a head, had also forced Howard Hughes to look inward, to examine his life, to search his soul. He began the long journey with a brief but seemingly heartfelt review.

"Sixty-four years of my life have been devoted to hard work," he wrote, somewhat sadly. "What I have to show for this consists of assets, liabilities, and a small amount of cash.

"If the above items will not purchase a certain amount of freedom for me, then my 64 years of effort have been wasted.

"If I am not permitted to use such funds and resources as I have to purchase a little more time prior to the Landmark opening, in order to remove the weight and pressure on me which would result from an attempt to meet a July 1st deadline, then I must assume that my 64 years of effort has been wasted.

"I do not say it cannot be done on July 1st, I just say I dont want the July 1st date committed or promised."

July 1 was less than three days away. Maheu was in a state of panic. Hughes had just told him that his entire life was meaningless if he could not keep the opening date open, but Maheu desperately needed a decision.

"Any decision is better than none from this point on," he urged his boss. "Howard, the impression is being gained in certain quarters that we are not very well organized."

It was the ultimate understatement. Hughes, however, took it as the ultimate insult, one that called into question not only the Landmark party, not only his entire Las Vegas adventure, not only his troubled relationship with Maheu, but his entire life. Indeed, he now reviewed the whole of it in detail, all in another attempt to justify leaving the opening date open.

"I am very grateful to you for the many contributions you have made toward the success of the various activities I have assigned to you," wrote Hughes.

"However, Bob, there comes a time when the success of a man's business endeavors are not as important as his peace of mind and the condition of his health.

"Bob, I have worked as hard, and devoted myself as completely to my work as anybody I know.

"So, I now wind up a supposedly successful business man who has wrecked his health and consumed the best part of his life in the process," he continued, seeming for the first time to glimpse his own sad reality.

"Bob, I have tried to be scrupulously honest, and I have tried to give, for charitable purposes, a sum in relationship to my earnings in excess of what is considered fair," he went on, seeking salvation by a spurious statement of his good works.

"When the newspapers print stories of the unbelievable increase in business revenues in this area and the incredible increase in population, I can't help but feel I must have given something to this community.

"Yet, somehow, this supposed success story does not seem to be enough for you, Bob," he complained, as if to an unflattering mirror.

"Your messages, every so often, disclose a resentment lying beneath the surface. Sometimes it is only a few words, sometimes it is more.

"I got the impression from you that the purchase of the Landmark constituted an important contribution to the community.

"But now, you tell me that I dont have enough reserve of good will on deposit with the Governor and our other friends to permit a moderate delay in the announcement of the opening date of the Landmark.

"Bob, I think the most disturbing feature of your message is the statement that I should reconcile myself to the fact that the appear-

Bob –

I am very grateful to you for the many contributions you have made toward the success of the various activities I have assigned to you.

However, Bob, there comes a time when the success of a man's business endeavors are not as important as his peace of mind and the condition of his health.

Bob, I have worked as hard, and devoted myself as completely to my work as anybody I know.

So, I now wind up a supposedly successful business man who has wrecked his health and consumed the best part of his life in the process,

ance is being gained in 'certain quarters' that we are not very well organized.

"The shocking part of this whole thing, in my opinion, Bob, lies in the fact that you and I dont have enough good will stored up to bridge over a delay of a few days in an announcement of this kind as if it were nothing.

"So, Bob, my point is that, if, after all the contributions to the community, which have led to unprecedented income and growth, if, after all this, I cannot tell you ~~that I will give you this opening~~ date in a few days without being warned that the Governor, etc. are going to lose faith and think the entire operation is 'not very well organized,' then I say my life is drawing too short for this kind of pressure."

Not very well organized. He certainly would not sit still for that kind of slander. And all this pressure, where was it coming from? Maheu.

"Bob," he continued, "you are one of the most high powered units of manpower I have ever come across. But, like most extremely competant people, you have enough pride in your work to resent any interference at all.

"I am convinced that you will not ever be happy in an organizational set-up such as we have. I think you will only be truly content when you are in a position comparable to working for yourself.

"I am sure you can see that, so long as you are in the position of administering all of the details and loose ends that go to make up my every-day life, complete independance free of any interference is just not possible.

"So, I am going to make a suggestion, Bob.

"I suggest, Bob, that you assign this Las Vegas job to any of your men you select.

"On this basis, Bob, I would be happy for you to spend the entire summer in Newport, and on your boat as much of the time as you wish.

"I think you subconsciously blame me for every week-end you are not on your boat, and it would be my hope that this plan would end that."

It would also end Maheu's power. No party was worth that. In a desperate bid to avoid being put out to sea, Maheu tried to soothe Hughes with abject deference and nostalgic praise.

"Howard," he wrote, "I am familiar with the story of your movie 'The Outlaw' and how you decided to delay releasing it against the advice of all the experts. I am also familiar with the fact that in 1947 in your testimony before the Brewster committee—after having listened to all of the inputs—you negated them all and handled Brewster in your own way.

"I would not want to deprive you of being right once more as to the opening of the Landmark. After all, Howard, it is one thing to argue and for me to make known all of my thinking, but there can be only one Captain."

The invocation of past glories had a magical effect. Captain Hughes finally picked a date for the party. Or rather a whole series of dates— July 3, July 4, July 5, July 24, agonizing over each, analyzing all of them quite carefully both in absolute terms and in relation to every rival event from the moon landing to the opening of the International, even considering a three-month delay—before he finally settled on July 1, after all.

"I dont mind yielding to your wishes as to the Landmark opening, both as to the time and as to the nature of the show," he wrote Maheu grudgingly, with the big party now only two days away. "I only want to ask that the record show I want the opening delayed."

The momentous decision caused Hughes immediate anxiety. His approval of the opening date opened the floodgates of his fears. His melancholy deepened. He could not sleep.

"I have been doing some very heavy soul-searching all night," he solemnly informed Maheu at dawn on June 30, one day before the dreaded event.

"Now that I feel all decisions concerning the opening of the Landmark are in sight (I will have the invitation lists in your hands this morning. I dont want you to start calling until then, but there will be no problem. The changes I want are very simple.) I want to make some very important decisions concerning the future.

"Bob, I want to lay it on the line with you. I simply am not happy under present circumstances. And I dont have such an abundance of years remaining that I can afford to continue on with a pattern of life which seems to fall such a long way short of what I really want."

Hughes was not talking about his grim seclusion, his bizarre lifestyle, or his wretched condition. He was talking about the terrible frustration of not having things entirely his way in Nevada, a feeling apparently intensified by the impending Landmark party. And he was thinking of leaving.

"I have a number of very important new projects and investments that I want to commence at once," he continued. "If it is to be in Nevada, fine.

"On the other hand, if a program to sell the hotels is going to be attempted, then naturally I want to commence the new projects at a new location to be selected either in Baja or in the Bahamas.

"Bob, I have been in this frustrated position for a number of months. This has left me in an uncertain, faltering frame of mind which, combined with a tendency to be overcautious anyway, has resulted in sort of throwing me off balance.

"Well, all these months I have been fuming and boiling here in a state of intense frustration," he concluded, tired of playing Hamlet in his penthouse.

"I want either to go ahead in a big way, or I want out—and *now*! *Please*.

"Please reply, Bob, on a most urgent basis.

"I am working on the invitation lists right now."

Hughes was, indeed, hard at work on the invitation lists even as he searched his soul, still poring over the lists one name at a time, still seeking that elusive consistency.

"I have now returned all the names to the list of business men, except only Scott and Tiberti and the two men from REECo. and EG&G," he proudly informed Maheu.

"I will think about REECo. and EG&G. I would like you to think carefully and analyze the pros and cons of Scott and Tiberti and report fully to me."

Yes, that should just about wrap it all up. Except for one nagging problem.

"P.S., I still need to look at sometime tonite the list of any added automobile dealers you may feel should be included."

Of course. The auto dealers. Now that Ackerman had been returned to the list. One day before the big party, Hughes was still hung up on the auto dealers, as he had been from the beginning, from the first name on the first list.

With one day to go, Hughes had actually approved only forty-four invitations. He was still refusing to allow Maheu to order any food. He was still questioning every detail of the party, still withholding his consent. And while he had finally approved the opening, he had still not approved the closing. Almost forgotten in the frantic planning for the party was the salient fact that Hughes did not yet actually *own* the Landmark. He simply refused to close the deal.

"It appears that the only two people in Clark County who do not know when we are going to close our purchase of the Landmark are you and I," complained a frazzled Maheu, suddenly gripped by the realization that the five P.M. deadline was only hours away.

"I have already given you authority to close the Landmark deal at such time as you consider most favorable," Hughes replied impatiently.

"What I am not willing to accept is the closure today being rushed thru in the next few hours merely to avoid the inconvenience of obtaining a 24 hr. extension."

In fact, any delay would be more than a small inconvenience. It would require a series of complex renegotiations with at least fifteen separate creditors to the hotel's bankrupt owners. It could take days. It might never be resolved. Hughes, of course, knew that quite well.

"I simply dont want to see benefits sacrificed," he blithely continued, "merely to accomodate a rushed closing scheduled to avoid the inconvenience of obtaining a simple extension on the 15 open claims which would become void if the Landmark is closed in the morning instead of tonite."

No guests, no food, and suddenly no guarantee that Hughes would even own the Landmark in time to celebrate its opening. Early on the morning of June 30—after listening to the billionaire search his soul and re-analyze the guest list, but refuse to buy the hotel—Maheu flipped out all over again.

"Howard," he raged, "here it is 7:00 AM and I am still left dangling.

"With the present posture of our opening at the Landmark, you might as well be the first to know that if you want to find me during the 'festivities' at the Landmark, on the evening of July 1, you might tell your men to start looking for me at the CIRCUS CIRCUS."

Maheu was looking for trouble. The Circus-Circus was a particularly hated rival, a new casino Hughes had tried desperately to block, fearing that it would lower the tone of Las Vegas, give it a cheap, honky-tonk, carnival atmosphere. Maheu knew that, but, in a reckless mood, he went on.

"You see, Howard, I have not yet had any time to spare to visit the CIRCUS CIRCUS *once,* but I am beginning to believe that since I'll have nothing better to do on July 1, perhaps I should take advantage of the occassion."

The calculated provocation left Hughes seething. He would not, however, give his underling the satisfaction of triggering an uncontrolled outburst. Instead he replied with a restrained fury that hissed more ominously for being kept under control.

"I know that you have said in the past that you are a free spoken person who cannot keep things bottled up, etc., and that, when you have to let off steam, I should just take it in stride," wrote Hughes.

"I usually can. But this situation wherein you seem to think you have to resort to making threats of dire consequences is just more than my nervous system can handle.

"Suppose you set forth the minimum formalities that will satisfy you for the 36 hours starting now and ending after the hotel is operational.

"Suppose you do this with no further drama than necessary. I will agree to a program that is satisfactory to you, provided you do your best to outline a program which you believe to be as near as possible to what you think I want.

"I will then tell you what I propose for the remainder of our relationship after the Landmark is opened."

Neither Hughes nor Maheu was in a festive mood. By July 1, the day of the big party, their marriage was so strained they were barely talking and there was more than a hint of separation in the air. What had been planned as a celebration of their partnership was looking like a prelude to their divorce.

Hughes, however, was still busily revising the guest list, too dedicated to be diverted by his unsettled domestic situation. Unfortunately, he was running out of time.

"Please consider very carefully the matter of a delay," he urged his estranged helpmate first thing that morning. "I have now gone thru the lists and could give you a go-ahead within a matter of hours.

"I personally have always favored a delay," he continued, "but know this would not rest well with you and others in your organization.

"Anyway, please do not announce anything until further consultation."

The consultations went on all day. Hughes and Maheu were civil with each other, but no more. Under the circumstances, that was a considerable achievement. It was too late for Hughes to block the party, having foolishly approved the closing the night before, but he kept on kibitzing right up to the end, besieged by last-minute fears.

"There is one thing I have been meaning to take up with you," he suddenly inquired. "How many people are you permitted to have up in the bubble of the Landmark at any one time?"

A few minutes later came a more elaborate paranoid vision, this one straight out of a disaster movie:

"One more thing. Are you really sure it is going to be cool enough in that bubble with hundreds of people present? You know a crowd dissipates a lot of heat.

"To my knowledge there has never been a crowd in that tower and, you will remember, one of my first questions re Landmark was about the air conditioning."

The image of partygoers packed into the bubble, trapped inside without air conditioning in the blast-furnace heat of a Las Vegas summer, got fixed in his fevered mind.

"I dont suggest a dry run," added Hughes. "I just urge somebody make careful calculations adding in the necessary correction to compensate for the crowd. I think you might also investigate alternate machinery and alternate power source, in case of a failure of some kind.

"Boy, oh Boy, would some people laugh if something like that were to happen on the opening night."

With the opening only hours away, Maheu had more immediate problems on his mind. It was not that Hughes had authorized only forty-four invitations and seemed unable to find any more equally qualified guests. Maheu had taken care of that. He had secretly invited another 440 people to the party, enough to fill the small Landmark showroom.

No, Maheu's big problem was the food. Hughes would not let him order it. Finally, at five P.M., two hours before the big gala, Hughes relented.

"I will not ask you further to withhold the procurement of food for tonight's dinner at the Landmark," he wrote, even now adding a caveat.

"However, I will be very grateful if you will keep such procurement to the bare minimum, until I am able to discuss with you, in considerable length, some of my views relative to the procurement of food."

Shortly before seven P.M., as the first arrivals drifted into the bizarre Landmark lobby for a VIP cocktail reception, one final message arrived from the penthouse.

Maheu was already at the hotel when Hughes's memo reached him, greeting guests with his usual aplomb, flashing his big gold cuff links, confidently standing in for his unseen boss. And although something was obviously askew about this grand opening, although there was a bit of a buzz about the last-minute telephoned invitations, none of the guests could have imagined what Maheu had been through, and none would have grasped the unintentional black humor in the two sentences scrawled on the sheet of yellow legal-pad paper that Maheu now removed from its sealed manila envelope.

"Bob—You and your people have my wishes for good luck tonight, in every way," Howard Hughes had written from the safety of his seclusion.

"Is there anything further I can do to be helpful?"

12 Nixon: The Betrayal

Three thousand miles from Las Vegas, someone else was planning a party. It was to be the greatest party the *world* had ever seen. A lavish state dinner in honor of the first men to walk on the moon. The host was Richard Nixon.

Although he hated playing host, Nixon threw himself into planning this affair, driving everyone crazy, from his top White House staff to his wife to the waiters, getting personally involved in the smallest details, picking the menus, making the seating arrangements, even choosing the party favors. And, of course, approving the guest list.

There were 1,440 invitations to this August 1969 dinner, the most prestigious state dinner in history, and Nixon went through them several times, name by name, simultaneously compiling a list of the people he didn't want invited, his first "enemies list." Nixon was still making final revisions the day before the big party.

There were governors and senators and Supreme Court justices, Hollywood celebrities, business and religious leaders, fifty astronauts, diplomats from ninety nations, luminaries from every walk of life. But most important were the special honored guests, aviation and space pioneers like Charles Lindbergh and Wernher von Braun—and Howard Hughes.

Hughes was puzzled by the invitation. "Re the President's party, what is it you actually need from me?" he asked Maheu, uncertain how to R.S.V.P. "In other words, Bob, I will not be able to attend. But I am sure you already knew this."

The invitation also puzzled White House aides. Nixon rarely discussed Hughes with even his closest advisers—and never disclosed his dealings with the billionaire to anyone except Rebozo—but all his top men were aware of the old loan scandal, knew that it still touched a raw nerve. And Hughes was feared in Nixon's White House, an unspoken yet palpable fear that emanated from the Oval Office.

Now, with the hundred-thousand-dollar payoff finally arranged and about to be delivered, the president's submerged fears started to surface. As the secret deal went down in the weeks before the party, Nixon initiated a series of stealthy inquiries about his hidden benefactor, working through the back channels of the federal bureaucracy.

He had already ordered the Secret Service to bug and tail his brother, worried that Donald's bumbling deals with John Meier would revive the loan scandal and blow his own bigger dealings with Hughes. Rebozo was constantly on the phone with Danner, demanding that Meier be kept away from Donald. "The President is truly concerned about wheeling and dealing involving these two characters," Maheu informed the penthouse. "We are reliably informed that they have opened an office in Geneva, are involved in very precarious oil leases in Alaska, and God knows what all else.

"The President and Rebozo have confided in us that brother Don is, by far, one of the biggest threats to the future of the President's political career," Maheu added. "They are fearful in Washington that the combination of Don throwing his brother's name around, and Meier throwing yours, will eventually cause serious embarrassment to both you and the President."

Late in June the Secret Service wiretap had overheard Donald trying to finagle a "finder's fee" for Hughes's acquisition of Air West, just as the president was preparing to approve that illegal takeover, and early in July, as Nixon moved to consummate the big payoff, the Donald problem had come to a head.

On July 8, the president's brother was caught at a secret airport meeting with Meier and a known organized crime figure, Anthony Hatsis, and the three men were photographed together by Secret Service agents. Donald had always denied his connection with Meier, but now the White House had undeniable proof. Back at the Oval Office, Nixon spent a long time studying the evidence, and it couldn't have made him comfortable about his own Hughes connection.

While he continued to keep tabs on his brother, Nixon had tried to improve his intelligence on Hughes, seeking help from the federal agency that seemed to know the most about him, the Atomic Energy Commission.

Late in July, Will Kreigsman, a White House staffer whom Nixon would later name to the AEC, made an unusual and very confidential inquiry. He wanted all available information on the "Howard Hughes Matter." An "eyes only" AEC report to the chairman noted, "Higher levels have requested that he be fully informed on this.

"He requested that we conduct an investigation, in the most discreet manner possible, of the background of Hughes organization staff members, emphasizing the obtaining of information from AEC-Nevada people who are in close contact with the Hughes staff."

Nixon was not only trying to figure out why Hughes was so opposed to the nuclear tests—very much a mystery to the president, because he couldn't see the profit in it—but he was also clearly seeking some solid facts about Hughes himself and the true nature of his shadowy empire.

What the president got was a detailed eighteen-page report on the billionaire's ban-the-bomb campaign but little insight into his motivations, which were also very much a mystery to the AEC. One claim in the report would soon boomerang on Nixon, a false assurance that "Hughes will not object to the current test program as long as detonations do not exceed a megaton." And there was nothing about the phantom himself.

Nixon was determined to get the inside story on the Vegas recluse.

So now as he planned his moon-walk dinner, the president plotted a more daring and devious maneuver. He invited Hughes to the party—knowing full well that the billionaire had not appeared in public for more than a decade—and used that invitation as a pretext to run a routine "name check" on his hidden benefactor through the FBI.

J. Edgar Hoover personally reported back to the president on August 13, the day of the big dinner. His report was truly astounding.

Howard Hughes, said the FBI director, was "a ruthless, unscrupulous individual who at times acted like a 'screwball paranoiac' to the extent that he, Hughes, might be capable of anything, including murder."

Including murder. It was an alarming description of a man with whom the president was about to make a dangerous deal, especially since Nixon had no way of knowing that the incredible characterization was based solely on the claims of a disgruntled Hughes executive who had turned informer almost twenty years earlier. The report had Hoover's imprimatur, and Nixon was both in fear and awe of the director ("He's got files on *everybody,* God damn it!").

In any event, the intelligence didn't stop Nixon. He went right ahead conspiring with Rebozo to collect the promised hundred-thousand-dollar payoff.

Still, the FBI report had to come as something of a shock to the president. But it was nothing compared to the shock about to hit Howard Hughes.

On September 10, 1969, Maheu, now in exile for his own unauthorized attendance at the moon dinner, called Hughes from Vancouver with disturbing news—the AEC was about to announce a new Nevada blast, and a big one.

Maheu tried to put the best face on the first major nuclear test of the Nixon administration. It was less than a megaton, and the really big bombs would be exploded in Alaska, just as the president had promised.

Hughes was not appeased. "I am very disturbed about the blast you mention," he wrote, in a memo to be read long-distance to his banished lieutenant. "I have told you many times that there is nothing magic about the megaton measure.

"I am truly worried about what you tell me today," he continued, not yet aware of the true magnitude of the impending explosion.

"I note what you say about the importance of being on the ground, 'at the scene of activity,' as you put it," he told Maheu, who was attempting to use the bomb threat as his ticket back to Las Vegas. "Well, Bob, until we pull out every last stop in trying to block this explosion, I am sure Washington is the scene of activity, and I wish you would depart for there tonite, staging a campaign to marshall every last organization or individual opposed to these explosions, and to bring to bear on the AEC the very strongest, all-out, concerted effort you can possibly organize, in a final fight to the very last ditch.

"I want you to burn up all of your blue chip stamps, all the favors you have coming, and every last little bit of pressure you can bring together in one intense, extreme, final drive to determine, once and for all, whether I make any further investments in Nevada or not.

"Bob, I want you to go all the way on this and spare no expense."

Maheu was reluctant to go to the brink. Nixon had already granted Hughes a private test-ban treaty, this new blast did not violate its terms, and it seemed futile to press for further concessions in national nuclear policy.

"Howard, we have made every conceiveable appeal to the Vice-

President and to the President," replied Maheu, urging restraint.

"One of the reasons that the President was so anxious to establish direct contact between you and Kissinger relative to the ABM was so that the doctor could reveal to you top security information reflecting the necessity of detonating a few more blasts under the megaton range, and also to explain that the megaton plus blasts would not be continued in Nevada as a result of your efforts.

"We have never lost sight of the ultimate goal of complete stoppage, but in the meantime, Howard, it becomes a pretty difficult task to tell the President of the United States and the Vice-President, that they are lying when they tell us that, although they have honored many of our requests, this specific test is mandatory to the national security of our country.

"I am afraid that if we push them they might well proceed gung ho, even with megaton plus shots," warned Maheu. "After all, Howard, I am sure that in the last analysis, they couldn't care less whether we make one more investment in Nevada or divest ourselves of those already made."

Hughes, however, was hardly ready to back down. Eyeball to eyeball with Nixon, he would not blink, although for the moment he seemed more eager to battle his own chief of staff.

"You have not given me any explanation of the need for this explosion," Hughes complained. "I know nothing of all the reasons why the test is necessary to the defense of the country. Why haven't you given me this info which you obviously received thru your White House contacts?

"Bob," he continued, his anger mounting, "I am not stupid enough to think Nixon gives a damn about my plans in Nevada, and, if you have any desire to see a better relationship between you and me, I would sincerely appreciate you restraining your periodic impulse to voice some sarcastic, salty comment such as this one. . . .

"I dont think you are so far from the mark as to believe seriously that I am dumb enough to think the President would care what I do here, so Bob, I can only assume you have some other purpose in making such an insulting remark.

"So, it must have been in an effort to irritate me. If that was the purpose, you succeeded."

Having vented his spleen, Hughes got back to the bomb, and once more ordered Maheu to Washington.

"Anyway, Bob, whatever is done, and I have not asked you to tell anybody he was a lyar, whatever is done, I will feel better about it if you do it from Washington," he insisted. "Please proceed there without delay."

Further resistance was futile. Maheu had Danner contact Rebozo, who suggested that they work things out at the ambassadorial level, inviting the Hughes emissaries to the compound he shared with the president in Key Biscayne.

By the next morning, as Maheu prepared to leave for the Florida White House, Hughes had discovered the full dimensions of his nuclear peril. This was not merely another blast but a full-blown holocaust.

"Bob," he wrote in a wildly shaken scrawl, "I have been up all nite and am very anxious to know that you are on the way before I go to sleep.

"This test is a megaton for all practical purposes," he continued in words writ large with fear, anger, and exhaustion, "so I cannot see how you can view this test as being other than a complete defeat and a complete waste of all your efforts.

"The difference between 900,000 and a million is so slight it simply falls under the heading of the degree of pregnancy. I just cannot see any difference."

Maheu left Vancouver, stopping in Las Vegas to pick up Danner, and they flew out to Miami together in a private Hughes jet. Danner had with him a zippered case. Inside was a manila envelope, containing $50,000, ten bundles of hundred-dollar bills he had retrieved from the cashier's cage at the Frontier casino earlier that morning. It was the money Maheu had secured for Nixon back in 1968, now finally to be delivered as the first half of the $100,000 Hughes had promised the president.

Early on the evening of September 11, the two envoys arrived in Miami. Before driving out to Key Biscayne, Maheu checked in with the penthouse. Hughes was in a frenzy.

"I am more grateful than I can tell you that you are there," he wrote in a memo for his Mormons to read to Maheu.

"Bob, I dont think you have any idea how I feel about this thing," he continued in a scrawl that made it quite clear.

"When you first told me about it [the blast], God knows I felt bad enough, but I naturally assumed it was in the so-called 'Low intermediate yield' range.

"I had no faintest idea that this bomb was a huge unit comparable in every way to the first two large explosions we fought so bitterly.

"I just cannot understand how under the sun the AEC could have imagined that we would be so utterly stupid and naive as to consider this explosion as being within the limits we had requested to be followed, merely because it may technically be under one full megaton."

The treaty had been broken. And the president was responsible. Hughes wanted that message delivered in no uncertain terms.

"I wish you would tell Mr. Nixon thru Mr. Rebozo that this is the most outrageous and shocking breach of faith and attempted deception I ever heard of any highly reputed government like the United States attempting to perpetrate against one of their own citizens," he wrote, furious now that the full extent of Nixon's betrayal hit him.

"If this is the way the U.S. pays off one of its own citizens, who has given a lifetime of service toward the betterment of the defense system, and contributed countless important advances, plus a half billion dollars in taxes, then how can anyone expect foreign governments to believe our promises.

"I have much more to say," Hughes concluded, "but will let you get started."

Maheu absorbed the diatribe, then went directly with Danner to see Rebozo. The president's friend gave his two guests a guided tour of his newly remodeled ranch house, especially eager to show off an ice-making machine that spewed cubes from the refrigerator door.

Danner handed Rebozo the manila envelope, saying, "Here's the $50,000, first installment." The Cuban opened the envelope, shook out the bundles of cash, and counted them. He marked "HH" on a corner of the envelope, then took the money into another room. When he returned, the three men went out to dinner.

Whether Hughes knew that his money had gone to Rebozo, whether he was hoping that it would buy him a nuclear accord with Nixon and approved the delivery despite his anger, is unclear. But he contacted Maheu at the crack of dawn the next day, expecting to get word to the White House.

"What is the plan today?" he demanded. "I just heard the announcement of the President's planned defense meeting. When do you expect to endeavor to penetrate thru to him in this matter? I am anxious to know in order that I may have as much time as possible in preparation of my material."

While the billionaire plotted the antibomb campaign on his bedside legal pads in Las Vegas, and Rebozo stashed the Hughes money in

Bob — 9-11-61 @ 6:30 PM
I am more grateful than I can tell you that you are there.

Bob, I don't think you have any idea how ~~I feel~~ I feel about this thing.

When you first told me about it, God knows I felt bad enough, but I naturally assumed it was in the/ so-called " Low intermediate yield " range.

I had no faintest idea that this bomb was a huge unit comparable in every way to the first two large explosions we fought so bitterly.

I just cannot understand how under the sun the AEC could have imagined that we would be so utterly stupid and naive, as to consider this explosion as being within the limits we had requested to be followed, merely because it may technically be under one full megaton.

I wish you would tell
Mr. Nixon thru Mr.
Rebozo that this is
the most outrageous and
mocking breach of faith
and attempted deception
I ever heard of any
highly reputed govern-
ment like the United
States attempting to
perpetrate against one
of their own citizens.

If this is the way
the U.S. pays off one
of its own citizens,
who has given a
lifetime of service
toward the betterment
of the defense system,
and contributed countless
important advances,
plus a half billion
dollars in taxes,
then how can anyone

expect foreign govern-
ments to believe our
promises.

I have much more
to say; but will let
you get started.

Deep thanks,

Howard

a safe-deposit box at the bank he owned in Key Biscayne, Richard Nixon convened his top advisers in Washington for a major review of the war in Vietnam.

The president was frantic, perhaps as frantic as Hughes. He had been elected on a pledge to end the war but had failed to bring peace. Now Nixon huddled with Kissinger secretly plotting a major escalation, a "savage, punishing blow" against North Vietnam, while the same antiwar movement that had toppled Lyndon Johnson threatened to bring Nixon down, massing for a nationwide protest that would culminate with the moratorium march on Washington in October.

Nixon had from the outset of his administration felt himself encircled by enemies; now, as he himself would later put it, he was "reeling under siege."

Yet even at the peak of crisis, the president did not ignore the billionaire's bomb protest. Once more, he offered to send Henry Kissinger to Howard Hughes. Maheu transmitted this offer to the penthouse, along with Nixon's pledge that the scheduled nuclear test posed no danger.

"In all sincerity, Howard," he wrote, "I truly believe that this is one hell of a concession for the President of the United States to make, since we were given the definite indication that you would become knowledgable of certain top secret information available only to a handful of people in this entire world."

Again, Maheu assured his boss that the negotiations with Kissinger could be handled by telephone, sparing the recluse a personal confrontation; but the secret peace talks had to be held directly with Hughes.

"I cannot find it within myself to be presumptuous enough to insist that this information be made available to me when it is you to whom they want to talk," added Maheu. "I am thoroughly convinced that Nixon has a deep-seated respect for you which won't quit. And also that there are certain things which he cannot entrust to any of your subordinates, unfortunately including me."

Hughes was not impressed. Again he spurned shuttle diplomacy, once more refusing to receive Kissinger, and this time not in fear but anger.

"I am surprised that you would accept without some resistance the statement of this explosion's so-called 'safety,' " he shot back at Maheu, rejecting the president's assurances.

"As to my listening to Kissinger, the statement that he has things to tell me which cannot be entrusted to your knowledge is an insult, and simply not true.

"As to the contention that this explosion is in some way necessary to maintain our strategic negotiating position, or our military security in respect to Russia, this kind of an argument is just a plain insult to my intelligence."

Hughes had had it with intermediaries. No more envoys: he would not receive Kissinger, and he did not want Maheu to deal with Rebozo. It was time to go straight to the top.

"Bob, I want you to go all the way on this," he ordered at dawn the next day, with the dreaded blast now only three days off. "I have written some very carefully drafted comments, and I want this argument made to the President in the very most forceful way.

"I dont want to write a letter as I did to President Johnson, and have it discarded into some dead file," he noted, bitterly recalling the rejection of his last bomb plea.

"Bob, I want you to request a personal meeting with the President just as quickly as he will grant it.

"I will give you the full text of what I hope you will say before you go into the meeting."

Having stayed awake all night to plot this bold move, however, Hughes could not wait to begin scripting Maheu for his big White House scene.

"You might tell him," he added, spinning out lines for delivery to Nixon, "I am deeply, deeply sorry for the shortness of time, but that . . . I had made my feelings known concerning the testing of large bombs in this area.

"And now, as a complete farce, they plan a test here at Las Vegas which is supposed not to violate the implied agreement they made with you, because it is marginally under one megaton.

"I hope you can find some way of showing this disgraceful trickery to the President as the fraudulent effort to deceive that it really is.

"Bob, I have given a full lifespan of service to this country, and taken very little for my personal pleasure or glorification.

"If I dont rate better than this shoddy treatment, it is pretty sad."

Maheu accepted the script but rejected the part. It was not that he didn't like the lines, only that he didn't think they would play well at the White House. He knew that it was futile to see Nixon. He had known it from the start. But it was pointless to tell that to the frenzied scenarist up in the penthouse. Instead, Maheu insisted that Rebozo was the man to play this part.

Hughes was not convinced. "I am fully confident of Rebozo's position with the President," he replied. "I just am fearful he cannot convey the entire story, simply because he does not know it all."

With that, Hughes was off again, giving Maheu his lines, determined to write, direct, and produce this melodrama as he saw fit.

"If you were with the President," he told his alter ego, "you could tell him about the 200 million dollar loss I am swallowing on the helicopter, due to my patriotic zealousness in accepting a contract at a price that did not even pay for the bill of material," presenting as noble his bungled bid to corner the market for the war in Vietnam.

"Also, you could convince the President that, had it not been for his personal identification with the Air West order by the CAB, I would have extricated myself from that unfortunate involvement 100% by now, instead of finalizing the deal," he continued, also claiming altruism for the illegal takeover he had just paid Nixon to approve.

"I think you could convince him that our arrival here in Nevada was an event of great good fortune to the state, as evidenced by the fact that Nevada has become a true oasis in the sea of campus disorders, race riots, poverty, etc.," he added, claiming credit for the tranquility as if it had resulted from his Monopoly game.

"So, Bob, to summarize, I think what I am asking, in relationship to what I feel we have contributed, is God-damned little.

"And, if cost is disturbing the AEC," he concluded, as final proof of his selflessness, "I feel so intensely about this thing, I will even pay the cost of moving this test to Alaska, out of my own pocket."

The script had a shameless audacity worthy of Nixon himself, but the president would never hear it delivered. Maheu left Key Biscayne for Washington to mollify his boss, but before going he filed a discouraging report.

"Howard, I have just completed a long conference with Rebozo," he told Hughes. "It is his humble opinion (and we must remember that he understands the top man, perhaps better than the rest of the world put together) that it would be a very serious mistake in strategy to try and see the President without going through Kissinger first.

"He recommends, therefore, that we make immediate plans for Kissinger to fly to Las Vegas and have a meeting with you in order to afford you the opportunity to convince them that what they are doing is wrong."

Henry Kissinger was a power second only to Nixon himself. There was no door closed to him anywhere in the world. Except on the ninth floor of the Desert Inn in Las Vegas. Even in his final day of desperation, Hughes would not receive him.

Instead, as the relentless countdown continued, the sleepless recluse pushed frantically to reach Richard Nixon, calling Maheu all night and into the predawn hours with pleas to stave off nuclear devastation.

"Please give me some idea of what you plan to do in a last minute attempt to obtain some kind of a temporary reprieve in order to permit a direct request from me to the President asking for an audience to be granted you," he scribbled at four A.M. on the morning of the scheduled blast.

"It seems to me that, after 64 years of devotion to this country, I should be entitled to a 10 minute audience before the President."

At 4:45 A.M., Hughes sent Maheu another message for Nixon.

"I wish you would tell the man that in 64 years as a citizen of this country I have not ever once asked the President to do or not do anything whatsoever," he wrote, apparently forgetting that just in the last few months he had asked Nixon to scuttle the ABM, submit his cabinet appointments for approval, and move all bomb tests to Alaska.

"I have not even ever sent a message of any kind to any President, except the one plea to Pres. Johnson to stop the other blast here.

"Please say a three day delay will satisfy me, and forget the personal audience. It seems to me that if he grants this and I am satisfied, it would be 3 days well spent. If he will grant the 3 days and his answer is still 'no', I will not resist further, and will feel that I have been treated right."

At 5:15 A.M., in a final appeal, Hughes scrawled numbered points for Maheu to make to Nixon:

"1—Cheap price to pay to satisfy me.

"2—I will be content with the delay, even tho the decision thereafter is still go.

"3—I cannot believe the pres. would be criticized for granting this plea even if it should be established at some later date that the purpose was solely to satisfy one important local citizen and avoid causing him to move elsewhere and destroy all of his extensive plans.

"4—Certainly there can be no real deficit from a few days delay except a small increment of cost which I will gladly bear."

It was all in vain. None of the desperate pleas Hughes scribbled through the night ever reached Nixon. It is unlikely that the president had any real concept of the billionaire's terror and outrage, much less that to Hughes the bomb test was *the* test of their entire relationship.

At 7:30 on the morning of September 16, 1969, the blast went off on schedule. Three distinct shock waves rippled through Las Vegas. The penthouse swayed for a full minute. But the real impact of the explosion would not be felt for years. And then it would shake the entire nation.

Its immediate impact was quite evident as Hughes grabbed his yellow legal pad half an hour later.

"This test produced more ground motion than either of the other two," he wrote in a hand that still showed the full effect of the blast.

"I want you to contact Nixon-thru-Rebozo and say that I am really disappointed in this matter because I feel I was misled.

"Anyway, Bob, I have had it. I want you to try today, while we are still in the position of having been turned down, to make an all-out effort to get an agreement that they will not test any more megaton, or 'in name only' bombs of the same general magnitude.

"If they reject this, I am going to announce publicly my withdrawal from Nevada, and the abandonment of all my future plans here. I am going to state my extreme regret and explain why."

At the bottom of the page Hughes scrawled, "Rebozo for Nix only." It was a cryptic warning that the president and his confidant would not comprehend. Not until it was too late.

In the months that followed, Howard Hughes, assured by Maheu that the nuclear nightmare was now over, settled down to the routine business of buying the rest of Las Vegas.

His Monopoly game had been stalled for almost two years, ever since Lyndon Johnson's attorney general Ramsey Clark blocked the Stardust deal in April 1968, threatening antitrust action. Hughes had tried to run that blockade several times, then relented, waiting for a more friendly administration to take power.

"If we emerge from the forthcoming election with the kind of strength we anticipate," Hughes had confidently predicted during the 1968 campaign, "there will be no need for a negotiated settlement of this matter."

Maheu had concurred: "I strongly suggest we call off this caper and take another look at it six months hence—after the elections."

And, indeed, on January 17, 1969, as Richard Nixon prepared to move into the White House, the Justice Department did allow Hughes to acquire a sixth Las Vegas hotel, the Landmark. But the Landmark was a special case. Hughes was allowed to buy it only to save it from bankruptcy.

Otherwise, the antitrust blockade remained in force.

Now, early in 1970, Hughes prepared to test the new administration. He was eyeing the Dunes Hotel and Casino, a major resort on the Las Vegas Strip.

His own lawyer, Richard Gray, warned him it was a dangerous move. "While the Republican Attorney General might have a different view than his predecessor," he wrote, "it is my humble opinion that the acquisition of any additional hotel would make us a prime target for antitrust action."

Hughes decided to take the risk. Maheu had assured him that John Mitchell was an ally who could be reached through Rebozo, and that the new head of the antitrust division, Richard McLaren, was "our #1 choice."

In January 1970, Richard Danner, who knew John Mitchell well from Nixon's 1968 campaign, initiated a series of secret meetings with the new attorney general.

Neither McLaren nor anybody else from the antitrust division was invited. The Dunes deal would be handled informally, just between friends.

By February 26, after his second session with Mitchell, Danner had good news. Maheu relayed it to the penthouse. "Howard," he wrote, "you will be pleased to know that Danner had a very pleasant and friendly meeting with the Attorney General who sends you his gratitude for all of your cooperation. He indicated that he could see no reason why we should not move forward with the purchase of the Dunes."

A few days later, on March 9, the news was even better. "Howard," reported Maheu, "it is our move to make on the Dunes. Danner had a long talk today with the Attorney General. He all but gave final approval today, but he wants the last say to emanate from the anti-trust division."

Mitchell called in McLaren for the first time on March 12. He told his deputy he was "inclined to go along with Hughes's purchase of the Dunes." McLaren was not so inclined. He immediately informed Mitchell that it would violate antitrust laws, that approval of the deal would be "entirely inconsistent with the Justice Department's earlier refusal to approve Hughes's purchase of the Stardust."

That kind of contrary attitude would eventually incur Nixon's wrath.

"I want something clearly understood," the president later raged in a taped conversation. "And if it's not understood, McLaren's ass is to be out within one hour. I do not want him to run around prosecuting people, raising hell about conglomerates, stirring things up. Is that clear? I'd rather have him out anyway. I don't like the son of a bitch."

In the Hughes case, however, Nixon's rage was not required. John Mitchell simply ignored his antitrust chief.

Just after noon on March 19, the attorney general again met secretly with Danner. He gave Hughes a green light on the Dunes deal. "We see no problem," Mitchell told Hughes's emissary. "Why don't you go ahead." There were no records kept. It was just a handshake deal.

The approval was a signal victory for Hughes. He had won a complete reversal of Justice policy, he had broken the antitrust blockade, he was finally free to expand his Nevada empire, to buy the rest of Las Vegas.

But the triumph meant nothing to Hughes. Nothing at all. It came just as a new megaton blast was announced in Nevada.

An atmosphere of terminal crisis gripped both the penthouse and the White House during Holy Week in 1970.

Howard Hughes learned of the impending blast on the same day in March that Richard Nixon got news of a coup in Cambodia. That coup, and the simultaneous failure of peace talks with Hanoi, started the president on a bloody course that led to the invasion of Cambodia, the murders at Kent State, and the Christmas bombing of North Vietnam, events that shocked the nation.

But it was the Easter bombing of Nevada that shocked Hughes and sealed Nixon's fate. Oddly enough, instead it almost brought them together.

Robert Maheu was in New York City, when news of the blast first hit Hughes, meeting with the executive committee of Air West to finally close that fraudulent deal.

"Howard," he wrote, "I am firmly convinced that only the President of the United States can stop this next blast."

Hughes's response was immediate.

He called Maheu out from the New York meeting and had him call back the penthouse from a pay phone. Then Hughes gave Maheu his mission: he was to proceed directly to Key Biscayne and there offer Bebe Rebozo one million dollars for Richard Nixon—if the president would halt the bomb test.

Maheu flew down to Washington, picked up Richard Danner (who had just closed the Dunes deal with John Mitchell), and the two went together to the Florida White House.

Maheu would later claim that he never offered the million-dollar bribe, which he and Hughes code-named the "Big Caper" in their telephone conversations that week.

If Maheu and Hughes had their "Big Caper," Nixon had long been enamored of the "Big Play," a bold move that he often used to cut through some tangled crisis.

While Maheu held back on the bribe, Rebozo tried out Nixon's "Big Play" in his first meeting with Hughes's emissaries on March 21. It was a three-option plan, one alternative being a Camp David summit meeting between Howard Hughes and the president.

Maheu reported the dramatic offer to the penthouse.

"Danner and I have just left our friend after 8 hours of solid and serious conference with innumerable phone calls back to the east," he informed the billionaire, apparently referring to calls between Rebozo and Nixon.

"Now, Howard, we have three alternatives which have been offered to us and it is imperative time-wise that we choose one of the three:

"1—Kissinger is prepared to fly to Las Vegas and have a similar meeting as that which they were hoping would take place many, many months ago.

"2—Although the President does not feel that he should go to Las Vegas at this particular time, he is prepared to meet with you at a moment's notice, preferably at some place like Camp David.

"3—They will guarantee that this one is very definitely the last big one."

Hughes was no more willing to see the president than he was to see Kissinger. Instead he pushed Maheu to make the million-dollar bribe.

Maheu resisted for three days. Finally, he at least pretended to give in and reported a failed attempt to buy nuclear peace.

"Howard, under very relaxed and comfortable conditions, I tried on the 'Big Caper' per our telephonic conversation of yesterday," he told Hughes. "There is no doubt as to the trust and confidence which was clearly enunciated, however it was made very clear that because of the national defense aspects, which they so wanted to explain to you, it was categorically impossible to do anything in this particular instance."

Hughes was devastated.

"Please pull out every last stop to delay or cancel this test," he pleaded.

"I do not trust their promises so the commitment that this would be the last test is not too important.

"Please push the Holy Week aspect and every other similar angle in every way," he continued, now reduced to trading on religious sentiment.

"I am relying on you. This is truly an all-out, end of the road necessity."

Rebozo kept pressing Hughes to meet with Nixon.

"He suggests a conference which could be set up so that you and the President, backed up by Kissinger, and you by your scientists, take place immediately, because of the shortage of time before the scheduled blast," Maheu urged.

"Howard, you have to believe that it becomes increasingly difficult for Rebozo, the President, and even Kissinger to understand the impossibility of having a personal interview with you.

"They truly cannot understand why you will not meet with the President himself."

But Hughes could not leave his penthouse seclusion.

Perhaps if Howard Hughes and Richard Nixon had been able to meet they could have worked out the president's "Big Play" and the billionaire's "Big Caper," made the big deal their agents could not make for them. Perhaps they could have consummated their long, arm's-length affair, thus avoiding national cataclysm.

But it was not to be. The Camp David summit died stillborn, and with it the million-dollar deal.

At eleven A.M. on Thursday, March 26, 1970, the day before Good Friday, the Easter bombing went forward, the six hundredth nuclear explosion since the beginning of the atomic age, and one of the biggest. Once more the tremors rippled through Las Vegas and shook the naked old man whose hidden dealings with the president were to be the real fallout of the blast.

Once again Hughes grabbed a yellow legal pad and, in one last futile gesture, scrawled a threat to leave the country, taking all his assets with him.

"Bob," he wrote, "I dont know where to begin.

"You said the president couldnt care less whether I remain in Nevada.

"This may well be true in the literal sense.

"However, bear in mind that, if I pull up stakes here, I am not going to some neighboring state.

"I am going to move the largest part of all of my activities to some location which will not be in the U.S.

"The president already has the young, the black, and the poor against him. Maybe he will be indifferent if the richest man in the country also finds the situation in the U.S. un-livable, and because of the country's intense preoccupation with the military.

"I know one thing:

"There is at present a violent feeling in this country against all the experimental activities of the military. . . .

"So, I just don't know how the public would react to a frank statement by the wealthiest man in the U.S. that he, also, considered he was being elbowed aside by the military.

"I know one thing: It would, or, at least, it *could* be a hell of a newspaper story."

Before the year was out, Hughes would make good on his threat. He would leave the United States forever. And his departure would set in motion a chain of events that would, indeed, become a hell of a newspaper story. One that came under the headline "WATER-GATE."

Richard Nixon, in bombing Howard Hughes, had unwittingly brought about his own destruction as surely as if the White House had been ground zero.

While you have access
to Rebozo, I want you
to concentrate on him.

Bob, I dont know where
to begin.
You said the president
couldnt care less whether
I remain in nevada.
This may well be true
in the literal sense.
However, bear in mind
that, if I pull up stakes
here, I am not going
to some neighboring state.
I am going to move
the largest part of all of
my activities to some
location which will not
be in the U.S.
The president already
has the young, the blacks,
and the poor against him.

maybe he will be in-
different if the richest man
in the country also finds
the situation in ~~the~~ U.S.
~~intolerable~~ un-livable, and because
of the country's intense
preoccupation with the
military.

~~I know one thing, and~~
~~that is that the fact~~
~~that the~~ .

I know one thing:
There is at present a
violent feeling in this
country against all the
experimental activities of
the military — starting
with the sheep in Utah,
the shipment of the
poison gas, the explosion
of the bomb train in
Nevada, the horrible
costs of the C5A and
other military purchases,

this fantastic spending on
defense while the Ghettos
go untended, etc., etc.,
the sinking of the destroyer
Evans, the countless con-
troversial items in Viet-
nam, etc., etc.

So, I just don't know
how the public would
react to a frank state-
ment by the wealthiest
man in the U.S. that
~~he wouldn't aside the~~
~~opposition of the military~~
      also,
he, considered he was
being shoved aside by
the military.

I know one thing; It
would; or, at least, it
could be a hell of a
newspaper story.

13 Exodus

This was not just another move. It was going to be, it had to be, the Great Escape.

Alone in his darkened bedroom, Howard Hughes plotted each step as if he were about to break out of the most tightly guarded cellblock on Alcatraz rather than his own penthouse at the Desert Inn.

Once more he reread the "Exit Plan."

"The exit plan is to divert the penthouse security guard, enter the elevator and, by using a key, proceed non-stop to the first floor," his Mormons had written, refining days of tense scheming to a one-page master plan.

"At a signal from us about 20–30 min. before leaving this floor, Hooper's men will place a screen across the path that leads from the elevators to the front desk-casino area. We make a left-hand turn and proceed to the side door of the building."

So far so good. Out of his cell, past the guard, down the elevator, and out the door before anybody suspected a thing. Now for the big getaway.

"We then pass through the side door, walk 50 feet or so towards the west and a limousine or conveyance will be waiting for us there," the Exit Plan continued. "This is the point at which we have little control over people who are walking from hotel to hotel or are walking from the parking lot to the hotel or from people just window-shopping in front of this building."

Wait. What was this? Suddenly exposed to the outside world, for fifty unpredictable feet, with "little control." All the warning signs started to flash as Hughes pictured himself caught in the Yard, frozen in the searchlight, halfway between the Big House and the Wall.

"We should enter the car at 11:30 PM," he read on, finishing the escape plan, but already certain it was dangerously flawed. "Hooper's Cadillac could be used, as it is less conspicuous than a limousine. However, you will have to enter any car without the use of the stretcher."

Without the stretcher? This entire harebrained scheme would have to be scrapped. Howard Hughes was determined to leave Las Vegas the same way he arrived: unseen and carried on a stretcher.

There would be other plans, urgent plans day-by-day as Hughes continued feverishly to plot his escape, never letting up until he finally did sneak out of town—more than a year later.

It all began in September 1969.

The utopian dream that had brought Hughes to Las Vegas was crumbling, the dream that he could remake Nevada, indeed America, to his own perfect vision. It had been crumbling for years. Now the first Nixon bomb blast exploded it completely. His kingdom was no longer even safe.

"Bob," wrote Hughes in the grip of nuclear terror, "my future plans are in a state of complete chaos, as a result of what is happening.

"I have things I want you to do in both New York and Washington, and thereafter, unless something surprising occurs, I will want you to come here to Las Vegas to supervise a massive sale of practically all of my Nevada assets."

It was time to go, and take all his assets with him. Whether he should also take Maheu was a whole other question.

"I am sorry you dont apparently view this matter as the total defeat I consider it to be," Hughes continued, blaming Maheu for allowing the bombing.

"As far as I am concerned, the AEC and the bomb test program has been the #1 item on our list of projects. It has stood at the very top of the list ever since our arrival.

"AEC—number one

"Pollution of the lake—number two.

"That is why I am at a loss to understand why you seem to view this situation with such coolness.

"Anyway, unless something unforeseen happens, there will be much to do."

Hughes had come to Nevada to create a world he could control completely. That was his vision of paradise—a world free of contamination and competition, a world where he would not only rule, but which he would not even have to share. A world where only he existed.

"Ever since our arrival, I have felt certain uneasy foreboding qualms about the future," he explained, revealing a deep dissatisfaction with Nevada that went far beyond the bomb. "These qualms have centered around the AEC, the water situation, and lately a mass of miscellaneous problems which mainly seem to be the product of sharing the state with a number of other people.

"In other words, the unions, the minorities, the threat of overabundant competition . . ." The list just went on and on.

It was time to escape from the complications, the contamination, the competition, to flee Nevada, to find a new Eden.

"I am prepared to invest almost every cent I can scrape together in the development of an entire new community and way of life in some location where some of the restraints, incumbrances, and competition of this area are not present.

"I want to make this new development the last and, I hope, most important project of my life."

Having failed to buy the government of the United States—what better proof of that than the Nixon bombing—Hughes was determined to achieve "Empire Status" elsewhere, to leave the country and make some other nation a "captive entity."

Hughes gazed at the globe, surveyed the imperfect world for a safe haven, for some unfallen paradise. First he ruled out the entire continental United States and all of Europe.

Next he turned his gaze south of the border, taking Maheu on a tour of prospective paradises.

"I cannot think of any location worthy of consideration except Mexico and the Bahamas," wrote Hughes imperiously. "Of course, Onassis had the really ideal set up with Monaco. However, I prefer a location close enough to the U.S. so that the U.S. would never permit any hostile intervention by outsiders. I feel both Mexico and the Bahamas qualify in this respect.

"So, lets, for the moment, compare those two. Which government do you think would be the most reliable and lasting?

"It seems to me that the Bahamian situation is very unpredictable due to the recent change in the complexion of the government," he continued, his racist fears aroused by the blacks' ouster of minority white rule there.

"I think the Mexican government is more stable, but I have less confidence in our ability to occupy a position of sufficient influence and privilege with the Mexicans.

"In other words," he concluded, still undecided, already fearing trouble in paradise, "I have pretty well assumed that you felt confident of a very favorable position with the new Bahamian government, whereas, I do not somehow gain that impression in respect to Mexico."

Hughes continued his Godlike review of the globe, ranging over the map in his search for some suitable refuge, endlessly re-analyzing the possibilities, finding fault with all. He kept coming back to the Bahamas, the last place he had visited before drifting into seclusion.

"In the light of everything we know," he wrote, "this is the most hopeful and very most realistic possible site for the location of the projects I have planned.

"However, there are many other powerful entities located in the Florida, Bahama, Carribean area, and they present a deeply entrenched powerful force that may not take kindly to my entry into that area. There is no way I can estimate the strength of these competitive entities since we must keep my plans the most religiously guarded secret, or everything will really be screwed up completely."

Hughes was not up to a clash of the Titans. He was looking for virgin territory he could just walk into and take right over.

"I do know that Baja has been much, much less invaded by rich American projects than the Florida-Bahamas area," he mused, returning to the invitingly undeveloped Mexican peninsula.

"I want to consider a development in Baja that would be similar to the all-inclusive arrangement Onassis had in Monte Carlo. I dont mean that I aspire to take over the Mexican government as he did Monaco. I mean that I want to make a deal with the Mexicans which would be somewhat similar to the deal [Daniel K.] Ludwig made with the Bahamian government when Freeport was established.

"Please consider the problems in obtaining 'Empire Status,' " he instructed his henchman.

"It has been my hope that we could approach this project, since it is so much more important than even you realize, with a basis of three strings to the bow—the Bahama location, Baja, and Puerta Rico.

"I put Puerto Rico last," he added, explaining his new addition, "only because it is a little far away for the headquarters location I am seeking, but please dont encourage anyone else to move in that direction because I want to keep it as an ace in the hole."

Having narrowed the field to three, Hughes reiterated the absolute need for absolute one-man control.

"It just does not work out to have more than one tiger to each hill in a situation like this," he concluded. "In Las Vegas, everything was fine until the place was invaded by Kerkorian, Parvin-Dohrman, and a few others."

While Hughes juggled travel plans, he also juggled travel agents. It seemed as if everyone were in on it. He was reaching out to all his key executives, advisers, attorneys, and aides, all of them eager to control the move and thus control Hughes. It finally shaped up into a battle of Maheu versus the Mormons.

Maheu did not want Hughes to leave at all, but if there was going to be a move, he wanted to be at his boss's side, calling the shots.

First he tried to scare Hughes into staying. Did he really want to go to the Bahamas, where blacks were in control—and out of control?

He sent Hughes a twelve-page confidential report, code-named "Down-hill Racer" to appeal to Hughes's love of cloak-and-dagger intrigue. "Blood—*white* blood—will run in the streets of Nassau," the report warned. "When the axe falls, it will take an army to protect a white man in the Bahamas."

Hughes betrayed no fear to Maheu. He saw the chaos Maheu had described as a challenge, an opportunity:

"If this report is even partially accurate, boy, they need a saviour down there like the poor bastards in the Middle East never needed when they were in trouble."

While Maheu tried to arouse Hughes's fear of blacks, the Mormons tried to arouse his fears of Maheu.

"It seems to me," one of his nursemaids suggested, "that asking Bob about leaving here is like a bird asking how to get out of his cage so he can fly away."

Hughes hardly needed the warning. When the planning for the exodus began, Robert Maheu was already in exile. He did not know why he was in exile. Hughes would not tell him.

He had kept Maheu away from Las Vegas ever since his unauthorized attendance at the Nixon dinner in August by giving him one mission after another that took him from Seattle to Vancouver to Dallas to Washington to New York to Los Angeles. Hughes did not try to conceal his own travel plans. In fact, he conferred with Maheu about the getaway by long-distance all the while. What Hughes did not reveal was that he intended to keep Maheu out of town until after he had made his escape.

After more than a month of this mysterious exile, more than a bit worried about what plot Hughes might be hatching, Maheu threatened to return. With or without Hughes's permission.

"Howard, now that all the reasons for which I must stay away from Las Vegas have faded into the dust of oblivion, will you please let me return," he pleaded. "There is an occasion taking place involving my immediate family which makes my presence mandatory. I intend to be there whatever the consequences may be, and however disastrously it may affect my career. It would make it so much more pleasant, therefore, for me to be there with your approval."

Maheu's threatened insubordination forced Hughes to take off the wraps. He finally told Maheu why he was in exile. He had been banished before he could wrest control of the empire from Hughes.

"I am very sure you are well aware of the fact that my reason for asking you to remain away from Las Vegas at this time is in some way related to the position of over-powering dominance to which you have climbed in the organizational structure of my business affairs," he wrote.

"Bob, I have no way of knowing, or even estimating accurately the extent to which you have dominated just about everybody associated with me.

"You have succeeded in achieving a position of such strength that I just dont know how many of my people are afraid to disclose information to me or how much information is being withheld."

Hughes had long feared that Maheu was secretly seizing control. Now, encouraged in his paranoia by the whispering Mormons, he was certain that Maheu had in fact taken over completely and was actually planning a coup.

"You have built an 'organization-within-an-organization' here in Nevada," he continued, hurling the ultimate accusation, "the very thing you have so vehemently denied, and the very thing that Dietrich did to me, and which you, yourself, so violently criticized.

"In fact, I have been told that the 'blueprints have already been cut' for a mass exodus of the guts of this organization exactly along the lines followed by Ramo and Wooldridge."

Once more his trusted alter ego was about to betray him, as Dietrich had. Once more his key men were about to defect, to set up a rival operation, as had the top scientists of the Hughes Aircraft Company. It was the same story all over again—treachery by trusted insiders, undermining him from within.

"Bob, this capsulized organization-within-an-organization, being easily removable and capable of setting up shop elsewhere, this is a terrifying thing, and it worries me a great deal," added Hughes with a sick sense of déjà vu.

"I dont say you did it deliberately. I dont even say you were aware of its subtle growth.

"I dont know exactly to what extent it exists. But whatever that extent may be, it is very dangerous to me.

"Under these circumstances, your statement that you intend to be here tomorrow evening for a social engagement, whether I like it or not, and even if it means a severance of our business relationship of twenty years standing, this comes as a pretty severe shock.

"Frankly this scares the hell out of me, Bob," he concluded, despite his dark suspicions not yet ready to make the final break. "I am fearful that one of these disagreements we have may one day reach a dead end."

If Hughes was afraid that his relationship with Maheu was coming to a dangerous dead end, the Mormon aides who encouraged those fears were afraid that Maheu would discover their whispering campaign.

"We hope you will consider our security as seriously as we consider yours," the frightened attendants wrote their boss from the room next door. "The thing that really bothers us is that we gave you a confidential message about the organization that Bob has built up and you immediately pass the entire message on to Bob, and in even stronger language.

"Bob is a smart guy and would be able to figure out in a second where this information came from. They have things locked up real tight here and if they know where an open gate is, they will soon close it. We would just as soon remain personna grata with the entire organization. We will be more useful to you and it will be safer for us.

"You must remember that so long as you live we come under the mantle of your protection, but if anything should happen to you, we would be at the mercy of somebody," added the conspiring nurse-maids, less than sanguine about the long-term prospects of their bedridden boss.

"You have assured us that we have nothing to worry about, and we don't—as long as you are healthy enough to function, but after that what?"

The atmosphere of double-dealing and dangerous intrigue grew more intense just one week later when Hughes discovered that Maheu had secretly slipped back into Nevada, and was hiding out at his country retreat in nearby Mt. Charleston. Far worse, he had used one of the loyal Mormons to deceive Hughes into thinking he was still in obedient exile.

Hughes flew into a jealous rage. Maheu had violated his harem, his polygamous immediate family, and Hughes was even more angered by the seduction than by Maheu's defiant homecoming.

First he turned on the hapless Mormon.

"Roy," he wrote, "there is no use of us fencing or manoeuvering about this any longer.

"For Maheu and his people to be evasive with me and cover up for one another is serious enough. But when this practice penetrates into my own, personal, most trusted staff, it is a great deal worse.

"Roy," he continued, lecturing the faithless aide, "my relationship with you and your group must be on a basis of such complete trust that I do not ever have to pause, consider, reflect, or wonder—not even for a fraction of a second—not ever—and not about anything.

"If I cannot have this kind of 'Stock Exchange' trust with my own top echelon inner sanctum, how can I ever hope to have loyalty from more remote executives?"

Next Hughes turned on Maheu. His secret return, his penetration of the palace guard was final proof of his clandestine takeover.

"Re your whereabouts—I dont want to debate this until I get settled at my destination," wrote Hughes, still frantically plotting his escape, now desperate to move his headquarters out from under Maheu before Maheu could steal the empire out from under him.

"I only hope everybody accords my forthcoming trip the same security and secrecy that was given your movement to Charleston Peak.

"Bob, I dont say you intentionally fail to inform me of things, I just say you have created such a spirit of loyalty to you and your group of people that it simply amounts to an 'organization-within-an-organization.'

"I perhaps could live with this. You have said you must inspire loyalty to get the job done.

"But when my immediate, personal group of five very most trusted senior executives, men who have been with me for many, many years, who have been granted by me authority to place my signature to commitments involving hundreds of millions of dollars—I say when these men are so fearful of being in the posture of disclosing some scrap of information which might displease you—to the extent that I virtually had to cross-examine Roy and drive him into a corner to bring out the fact that you had returned, I feel this is going too far.

"Nobody wants to be in the unpleasant position of being an informer," concluded Hughes, who was now constantly hearing whispered tales of Maheu's treachery from the very Mormons he feared had been seduced, "but the conscious feeling of tension that my close friends and associates feel when the conversation touches on you or anything concerning you, is so evident that I cannot help but be aware of it."

Now, more than ever, Hughes had to escape Las Vegas. He had to escape Maheu as well.

All this time, while his relationship with Maheu was falling apart and the tensions within his empire growing, Howard Hughes had been making urgent plans to bust out of his penthouse, getting conflicting advice from the rival courtiers and driving all of them crazy with his constant alerts and endless delays.

He was afraid to go, afraid to stay.

Day after day Hughes tried to make good his getaway, but each step was terrifying. For three years he had not left his blacked-out bedroom, had not once even looked out his window, and by now the entire world outside was a dangerous unknown. He could hardly bear to think about the perils, much less actually walk out into them.

Day after day Hughes found one reason after another to put off the trip, but never let the planning or the stand-by alert flag for a minute.

His greatest fear was of being seen. But the billionaire had a plan. He would announce that he had already left, then sneak out sometime later.

"I want to consider very seriously the immediate issuance of a brief statement announcing that I have forthcoming plans which will be announced in due course," he wrote, "and that in the meantime I have left on a long overdue trip abroad in connection with certain interests I have overseas."

Maheu was dubious.

"Howard, I am fearful that such a statement would cause your exit without being seen to be an impossibility. I can just visualize a 24 hour coverage of the Desert Inn by reporters, free-lance photographers and what have you. The logistics could be handled much more advantageously if such an announcement were made shortly after you have in fact departed."

Despite his fears of Maheu, Hughes still depended on the ex-FBI and CIA agent for security, so even as he plotted to escape his protector he continued to rely on his expertise. Still, he would not easily give up his plan.

"It seems to me the go-but-not-be-detected deal would be more difficult to accomplish," he reasoned, "because if your principal were seen, just for one second, getting out of an automobile, or such-like, the success of the project would be destroyed.

"On the situation we are discussing, nobody sees anybody except for one small group of highly trusted men."

It was hard to argue against that. As long as Hughes remained in his lair, no outsider would see him. The plan, however, had one serious flaw. It would work only so long as Hughes stayed up in his penthouse.

"I guess a whole new plan is indicated," he reluctantly conceded, and once more threw himself into the planning.

Each day he made a definite decision to leave the next day, or certainly the day after, but there were so many important details to work out, so many dangers to consider.

"Only one feature of this trip causes me to hold off until Monday," he informed his Mormons after weeks of delay.

"I want someone to make the trip from the D.I. to the point where the airplane will be parked here, and someone else to make the movement from an airplane to the door of the apartment at the destination, and both take along some kind of an air temperature measuring device, and both men to report maximum temp. encountered during the entire transition process, and duration of any high temperature encountered.

"Also, freedom from insects at destination *without* using spray.

"Also, same measurement to be made in apartment at destination without our man spending any time therein other than the momentary period in the region just inside the front door necessary to measure temperature and check absence of insects.

"I definitely want to leave no later than Tuesday," added Hughes, quite confident now that he had scouted ahead for bugs and bad weather, "and prefer Monday in order to have a day of leeway in the event of some unforeseen circumstances."

But the circumstances he had not foreseen always required more leeway than he had anticipated. And no wonder. The world outside seemed like one vast conspiracy aimed at preventing his getaway.

"Please give this message careful consideration, as I am on the verge of making a decision concerning our departure," he wrote days later, ready to go but sensing real danger.

"It seems to me the most important issue is the event scheduled for Wednesday. There is going to be a huge anti-Vietnam affair next week, and if the far left crowd should get wind of the fact I am in transit on this trip at that particular time, they might attempt some kind of public demonstration to protest, due to my symbolic representation of the military-industrial complex, etc.

"It seems to me it would be highly desirable for us to arrive before this affair," he continued, not at all eager to head smack into a mass of angry demonstrators.

"If we are en route, it could add to the problem should the press learn that I am on the way and where we are going. I can just visualize some bitter publicity by the leftist factions pointing to our destination and suggesting that it is a pleasure trip—which it is *not*, but I am sure they would use that approach.

"So I want you to please weigh carefully advantages of an earlier arrival," he concluded, analyzing the calendar like an astrologer looking for the propitious day, "and balance that against the disadvantages of the Friday night departure versus the Sunday night departure, and give me your opinion based on all these conflicting considerations as to which is the better choice, and please describe carefully the various factors which lead you to make such decision."

When the report came, however, Hughes was not at all happy with the chosen day.

"Have you taken into account the fact that Sunday night is a time when the news gathering people come back to work after the weekend and start searching about for something to fill the Monday newspapers?" he inquired, alert to all hidden dangers.

"I admit the hotel is more crowded over the weekend. However, it is not the public or the crowds who pose a problem for us, it is the press, the columnists, newscasters, publicity men and related people who would be the threat to maintenance of this trip in an unnoticed state.

"One thing is certain, I do not want a situation where the press is going to learn I am en route and descend on the train en masse at the end of the trip and insist on seeing me. This could develop to a point where they might demand to see me and really press the issue."

Trapped in his penthouse, trying to summon up the courage to make his daring getaway, Hughes could only picture himself trapped in his private railroad car, surrounded by swarming insects, angry antiwar demonstrators and hordes of reporters ready to expose him to the entire hostile world.

And it was hostile. He could see that even from his blacked-out bedroom, watching warily through his TV screen.

"Every news broadcast seems to suggest increasing fear over the risk of prominent Americans being molested while travelling," he noted with alarm.

"Today, for the first time, reference was made to the potential kidnapping and execution of tourists as well as diplomats.

"I know the easiest thing for you to do is to say to me, 'Well, lets play it safe and forget the trip.'

"But this is not what I want," added Hughes, although he made no move to go.

"What I want is the very most careful and dilligent all-out effort to advise me of the extent of the risk and what can be done about it, and all this without discussing it with anyone whomsoever, *and I mean this in the very strongest terms.*

"The surest way to encourage somebody to dream up some wierd plot like this would be for even the slightest trace of a hint to leak out, suggesting that we have been talking about this or that I might be concerned."

Hughes was, of course, concerned. Yet even as he sat naked on his unmade bed compiling a catalog of the dangers outside his closed world, he continued just as feverishly to plan his escape from the dangers within.

By now he had a vast array of getaway vehicles on stand-by. Chartered jet planes under special guard at remote airfields. Private railroad cars pulling in to obscure junctions. Yachts being appraised at distant ports. Mobile homes being outfitted for cross-country travel.

Whole fleets of unmarked cars and limousines and customized vans waiting for his "go" signal.

Train schedules and flight-condition reports, weather reports and road maps littered his bedroom.

And his loyal Mormons stood on alert, packed to go ever since Hughes first decided to make his escape.

But the billionaire would not, could not budge.

August 1970. Howard Hughes lay sprawled on his bed watching the eleven-o'clock news when the utter and complete desperation of his sorry situation suddenly crystallized on the TV screen. Hit him as it never had before.

Almost a year had passed since Hughes first planned his big get-away, month after month of frantic stop-and-go preparations, but at last he was actually ready to escape Nevada and set off for paradise—Paradise Island, in the Bahamas.

Not one, but two entire floors in two different hotels were reserved, sealed, under guard, and awaiting his arrival. Hughes was, in fact, about to close a deal to buy the whole enchanted island.

But now, late on the evening of Friday, August 7, right there on his television, came the shocking news. Nerve gas! Sixty-six tons of lethal nerve gas, one-ninth of the Pentagon's entire poisonous stock-pile, 12,500 decomposing old M-55 rockets encased in concrete "coffins," all being loaded onto trains at army depots in Kentucky and Alabama, hoisted by derricks into open freight cars guarded by soldiers wearing gas masks, trains headed for U.S. Navy ships in North Carolina, ships that would carry the thousands of leaking canisters south and dump the entire deadly cargo into the Atlantic Ocean, sink it all right off the coast of the Bahamas—just 150 miles from Paradise Island.

Hughes watched the incredible spectacle in stunned horror. What he saw was beyond his worst paranoid vision.

Tons of GB and VX gas—the same gas that had killed the sheep!—gas so lethal that a few pounds could kill thousands in minutes, gas so deadly that one-ten-thousandth of an ounce could destroy the central nervous system, simply dissolve the enzymes that transmit nerve impulses, leave a man twitching horribly and choking for air until he just stopped breathing and died, all that gas was right now headed straight for his secret safe haven.

The one place fit for his exile was about to be irrevocably poisoned by another invisible plague. A plague fully as terrifying as atomic radiation, indeed somehow even more insidious, more threatening to a man obsessed with the purity of fluids.

Hughes grabbed his bedside legal pad and scrawled an urgent all-points bulletin to all his key aides and executives.

"Bob—

"Chester—

"Roy—

"George—

"John—

"& Bill Gay in Los Angeles

"I want this to be an all, all out effort beyond anything we have ever mounted before on anything, and putting aside all considerations of expense," he wrote, mobilizing his Mormons and their leader, Bill Gay, calling in his chief counsel, Chester Davis, no longer willing to rely on Maheu alone, Maheu who had failed him on the bomb.

"I want you to hire one of those Washington or N.Y. public relations firms that specializes in single difficult emergency political problems such as this, . . ." Hughes continued, mapping out his antigas campaign.

"I want every available avenue of effort to be pursued, but I think the most effective is to persuade the Bahamian Govt. to lodge a *really strong* demand.

"I know they have already complained, but not to any-where near the extent that can be done.

"If we have even 1/10th the amount of influence with the Bahamian Govt. that you have assured me we have, then a really strong new complaint can be lodged and somehow a way must be found to publicize this to the high heavens.

"I assure you that if hundreds of TV stations all over the world, starting right now during the weekend can be induced to start in ballyhooing this issue and playing up the black vs. white aspect of it, I think there is a real chance of success.

"Nixon, with his well-publicized attitude toward the black race, is a natural target for this kind of a campaign," he continued, zeroing in on his unlikely nemesis, the ingrate he had so generously supported all these years, the man he had chosen to be president.

Nixon was calling down strikes on all his positions. Bombing him in Nevada. Gassing him in the Bahamas. Forcing him out of his kingdom. Now cutting off his escape route. It was time to strike back.

"I can just see a cartoon of the Bahama Islands with a carricature of a thick-lipped black boy, of the typical Calypso-singing variety, and Mr. Nixon descending on him with his bulging container of nerve-gas," wrote Hughes, relishing his counterattack on the treacherous commander in chief.

"I am positive Nixon will be more responsive to a plea from another government, particularly a negro government than he ever would be to pressures from within.

"I beg you to move like lightning on this. I am sure you agree that the most difficult problem we face is *time*."

Those trains had to be stopped.

Rather than launch a covert operation against the president, Maheu tried to reach Nixon through the regular channels, using the established Danner-Rebozo connection.

Just a month earlier Danner had visited Rebozo at the western White House in San Clemente and there delivered to him another $50,000, the second installment of the promised $100,000 from Hughes to Nixon. It was over the Fourth of July weekend that the two had last met, sorcerer's apprentices still acting under an old spell. Hughes had soured on Nixon long before, but Maheu was counting on Rebozo to arrange a settlement with TWA, a coup that might save Hughes a large chunk of the default judgment and get Maheu back in the billionaire's good graces.

So, on July 3, 1970, Danner had gathered up another wad of hundred-dollar bills from one of Hughes's Las Vegas casinos, stuffed them into a manila envelope, and handed the secret cash to Rebozo in the Cuban's guest cottage at Nixon's California home. Rebozo, as he had done before, slid the money out of the envelope, laid the bundles on his bed, and counted them. Ten bundles, each bound in a Las Vegas bank wrapper, $50,000 in all. Rebozo put the cash in his handbag, then took Danner on a tour of the estate, strolled with him around the private golf course, and finally dropped in on the president at his office.

The three men chatted amiably for ten or fifteen minutes, none apparently so gauche as to mention the just completed transaction. Nixon instead bemoaned the problems of finding suitable entertainment for the White House, noted how difficult it was to get movies that were not "a little too raw," and asked Danner about the shows in Las Vegas.

Bob –
Chester –
Roy –
George –
John –
& Bill Gay in Los Angeles

I want this to be an all, all out effort beyond anything we have ever mounted before on anything, and putting aside all considerations of expense.

I want you to hire one of those Washington or N.Y. public relations firms that specializes in single difficult emergency political problems such as this.

In addition, not in place of the above, I want you to use Carl Byoir without a moment's delay.

I want every available avenue of effort to be pursued, but I think the most effective is to persuade the Bahamian Govt. to lodge a really strong demand.

I know they have

already complained, but
not to anywhere near
the extent that can be
done.

If we have even
$\frac{1}{10}$ th the amount of
influence with the Baham-
ian gov't. that you have
assured me we have, then
a really strong new com-
plaint can the lodged
and somehow a way must
be found to publicize this
to the high heavens.

I assure you that
if hundreds of TV stations
all over the world starting
right now during the week
end can be induced to
start in ~~right~~ ~~now~~ ~~during~~
~~the weekend~~ ballyhooing
this issue and playing
up the black vs. white
aspect of it I think there
is a real chance of
success.

Nixon with his well-
publicized attitude toward
the black race, is a
natural target for this
kind of a campaign.

I can just see a cartoon of the Bahama Islands with a caricature of a thick-lipped black boy of the typical Calypso-singing variety, and Mr. Nixon descending on him with his bulging container of nerve-gas.

I am positive Nixon will be more responsive to a plea from another government, particularly a negro government, than he ever would be to pressures from within.

I beg you to move like lightning on this. I am sure you agree that the most difficult problem we face is time.

All that had happened a month ago. The second half of the Hughes payoff was now safely stashed away in Bebe Rebozo's Key Biscayne bank, another cash-filled manila envelope with "HH" marked discreetly on one corner, clipped to the first envelope delivered back in September 1969, both now locked in safe-deposit box #224, $100,000 for the president's personal use.

Now, in August, Danner was desperate to make contact again. He finally reached Rebozo through the White House switchboard and relayed Hughes's fears about the impending nerve-gas attack.

By the time Rebozo got word to Nixon the trains were already rolling, carrying their deadly freight on a slow trip to the sea. The president was surprised by Hughes's protest. He had no idea that his hidden benefactor was planning to move to the Bahamas, much less that he was going there to escape the bomb tests. As for the nerve gas, Nixon had decided to dump it in the ocean just to appease Howard Hughes. The original plan had been to blow it up in Nevada.

"Howard, the 'top man' has asked that the following information be imparted to you," reported Maheu with no hint of irony. "In deference to you he rejected, out of hand, the suggestion that the gas be exploded by the AEC in Nevada. The decision to dump the gas at the designated location was made because the area is restricted by virtue of Cape Kennedy activity, and continuously monitored.

"I was also asked to tell you that you would not believe the pressures (particularly from the South and East) which they withstood in order to avoid the necessity of bringing the load to Nevada," he continued, unfolding a tale that could have been written by O. Henry. "The man said that he *truly* believed he was cooperating with you to the fullest in this matter.

"We have just received a telephone call asking if you have any alternative means for the disposition of this gas, and we are assured that if you do it will be considered very seriously."

Hughes was not appeased. He no longer trusted Nixon, who first took his money, then bombed him, and was now about to gas him. But the billionaire did have an alternative to suggest.

"If the Administration can be persuaded to dump the gas at a location further away from the Bahamas than the presently selected location, I would be very grateful," he wrote.

"In such event, I would like to study the situation before suggesting a location.

"My desire is to see a location selected as far as possible from the

Bahamas," he reiterated. "Preferably near the Arctic Circle, or as far North as they can possibly take it."

Yes, the North Pole would be excellent. No need to study the situation after all. Meanwhile, distrustful of Nixon, Hughes pressed for his covert operation, the plan that would pit the president against the calypso boy.

Maheu wanted no part of it.

"Since I feel Danner and I are primarily responsible for any White House intervention, it would be absolutely irresponsible for us to be identified with a caper which could end up embarrassing the White House," he advised Hughes. "Therefore, I think it is important that the 'tiger hunt' designed to embarrass the President should not be identified with Danner and me.

"Since Davis and Gay took over responsibility for the Bahamian situation a year ago," he added, revealing some pique over his rivals' role in the escape plans, "I am awaiting a report from them pertaining to the situation there before Danner and I can make our next move with the White House."

Seizing the chance to gain on Maheu, Bill Gay and Chester Davis immediately set out on the tiger hunt their rival had refused to join.

They first went to work on a Bahamian government eager to lure Hughes and his millions down to the islands and within days had inspired the cabinet to meet in emergency session and issue a "strong protest" against the threatened nerve-gas dumping, the first formal complaint it had ever lodged against another nation.

Meanwhile, Gay made his own move on the White House. He contacted an obscure bureaucrat in the Department of Transportation, a fellow Mormon named Robert Foster Bennett, whose father happened to be a United States senator and, like Gay himself, a leader of the Church of Jesus Christ of Latter-Day Saints.

Gay knew that the younger Bennett also had a White House connection, Nixon's bullyboy Chuck Colson. Gay asked Bennett two questions. Could he, through Colson, block the gas dumping? And would Maheu really be able to do it through his Danner-Rebozo connection?

Nothing could stop the nerve gas, Bennett reported back. Not him. Not Colson. Not Maheu. No one.

While Gay made his secret move on the White House through his mysterious Mormon connection, Chester Davis was having more success with a clandestine court action.

Working entirely behind the scenes, never letting the name Hughes surface in public, Davis had a longtime legal associate, Lola Lea, file suit in federal court to enjoin the nerve-gas pollution, ostensibly on behalf of a group of concerned citizens, the Environmental Defense Fund. He also managed to get Florida's governor, Claude Kirk, a Republican feuding with Nixon, to join in the lawsuit.

At first, the surreptitious legal maneuver triumphed. Just as the army finished off-loading the gas from its trains to the waiting ship, a federal judge issued a temporary injunction, ordering the gas-laden old freighter not to set sail with its deadly cargo. The victory, however, was short-lived. After further hearings the next day, the judge lifted her injunction despite "serious misgivings" about the dump site. It was not its proximity to the Bahamas that troubled the judge, but her fears that sinking the nerve gas three miles deep would subject it to water pressure so great that all of the concrete coffins would get crushed at once, releasing all of the lethal poison simultaneously. Freeing the military to dump the gas, she suggested that it be done in shallower water.

Up in his penthouse, a distraught Hughes received the news with alarm. It was not the legal setback that most upset him but the change in depth.

"What has me worried the most now is all this talk about selecting a location where the water will be shallower," he wrote in an urgent scrawl.

"I think this is dynamite, because the search for such a site could easily lead to a location even less desirable than the one presently selected," he added, envisioning a dump practically on the beach of his intended island refuge.

"I have no concern about the depth of the water. In fact, I think *the deeper the better.*"

On Saturday night, the unstoppable Lola Lea, still posing as an attorney for the Environmental Defense Fund, reached Chief Justice Warren Burger at his home and managed to persuade the Nixon appointee to once more block the dumping. It was only a temporary reprieve. At high noon Sunday the military won the final showdown in the court of appeals, and the gas-laden ship immediately left port on its two-day voyage to the Bahamas.

With the collapse of his clandestine court battle, Hughes turned frantically back to Maheu and Nixon. There was no more talk of calypso-boy cartoons. The billionaire had been reduced to another desperate eleventh-hour plea. Only the president could save him now.

Maheu confidently stepped back in, dropping code names, presenting himself to the penthouse as the only operative with the real connections.

"Our 'friend from Florida' has just returned after spending the entire weekend with the 'top man,' " he wrote, after making contact with Rebozo, just back from Camp David.

"In spite of our participation in the injunction, which they very quickly identified, they are thoroughly convinced that Danner and me were not involved in that particular operation," added Maheu, unable to resist an I-told-you-so slur on the failed Gay-Davis initiative.

"There was much time spent considering alternate sites, but additional scientific inputs bolstered the conviction that the proper site had been chosen. Our friend stated that the 'top man' presumably did not reiterate his request that you have faith and confidence in him, since that message had been delivered previously.

"Again, however, they are prepared to give you a full scientific briefing, either in person or on the telephone, which they are convinced would satisfy all your apprehensions," he concluded, for all his big connections able to offer only blind faith and another briefing. "Our friend stated again that the 'top man' had categorically refused to listen to any suggestion about disposition here in Nevada, thinking very seriously that he was cooperating with us to the fullest."

Hughes didn't want a briefing, and he didn't want to hear another word about Nixon's good intentions. He wanted the nerve gas shipped to the North Pole. And now, on Tuesday morning, as it instead neared the Bahamas, the billionaire demanded that Maheu stop fooling with Rebozo and go see the president.

It was too late. By the time Hughes sent Maheu on his White House mission, the deadly convoy had already reached the dump site. By the time Maheu could get to Washington, the nerve gas would be deep-sixed. But the resourceful Maheu had a plan.

"Howard, bearing in mind that when we reach the 'top man' the scheduled dumping will be literally minutes away, I wonder if we should not consider the following action," the never-say-die lieutenant wrote. "I happen to know that at San Clemente they are geared with a permanent installation of scramblers which permit the President to communicate comfortably anywhere in the world where comparable scramblers are located.

"It is conceivable, therefore, that I should fly immediately to San Clemente so as to communicate whatever message I have within a period of an hour rather than the 5 or 6 hours it would take to go to Washington," he suggested to Hughes, who was furiously composing a still undisclosed secret message to Nixon.

"The decision which the Army has made, and which obviously the White House has backed 100% is being watched by the whole world to its final conclusion. It would be a lot easier for the President to explain a delay of an hour than one of six.

"I think we should be doubly careful that we do not make one false move and that in no way do we lose the confidence of the Administration. There is no doubt, Howard, that the man's nose was out of joint when he detected our 'Italian hand' in the injunction," added Maheu, even now at the zero hour taking another shot at Chester Davis, born Caesar Simon in Rome, Italy.

"Howard, I hope I am not being too verbose because time is of great urgency and I truly know what this particular matter means to you," concluded Maheu, his sharp tactical analysis turning into a windy exposition as the minutes ticked away.

While Maheu discussed tactics with Hughes, a crack team of navy frogmen opened flood valves deep in the holds of the *LeBaron Russell Briggs,* and the old World War II liberty ship, weighed down by tons of nerve gas, began to sink slowly into the Atlantic 150 miles from Paradise Island.

Unaware that the gas ship had already been scuttled, Hughes finally made a command decision. No phone calls. No San Clemente. He insisted that Maheu meet personally with the president.

"Howard, there is no problem in getting the appointment," a glum Maheu replied in a classic good-news/bad-news memo. "Unfortunately, however, the sinking started some time ago, and they are now at the point of no return."

At 12:53 P.M. on Tuesday, August 18, 1970, after taking on water for four hours, the half-submerged death ship with its cargo of nerve gas suddenly took a huge gulp and disappeared beneath the waves. Within eight minutes it had hit bottom.

So had Howard Hughes. Once more he was totally immobilized. Trapped in his penthouse. Without a refuge. Afraid to go, afraid to stay.

While Hughes brooded about the nerve gas dumped in the Atlantic, a top-secret task force at the Central Intelligence Agency was trying to figure out how to raise a sunken Russian submarine from the bottom of the Pacific.

The CIA had been grappling with the problem for a full year, the same year that Hughes had been desperately trying to make good his escape. Now, just as all of Hughes's plans were foiled again, the CIA finally came up with a plan it was sure would work.

It would build a three-hundred-and-fifty-million-dollar ship, longer than two football fields, with a two-hundred-foot-tall derrick in the center that straddled a well in the hold, and towered over a hull that could open to reel out more than three miles of steel pipe and lower a giant claw that would just reach down and snatch the Soviet sub from the sea floor. Without anybody being the wiser.

Of course, the Agency would need a good cover story. It would claim the fantastic ship was a futuristic deep-sea mining vessel designed to scoop up the oceans' vast untapped mineral wealth.

Now all the CIA needed was a plausible front man. It decided on Howard Hughes.

Thus began the *Glomar Explorer* project, a bizarre caper that for the next five years would have the whole world believing Hughes had once more embarked on an incredible pioneering business adventure—and then, when the true mission of the *Glomar* became public, that Hughes was a full-time partner of the CIA.

But not even the CIA knew that it had made a naked madman privy to its biggest national security secret.

In any event, the most immediate victim of the *Glomar* deal was neither the Russians nor the CIA nor any of the great powers in the world beyond, but Howard Hughes's own right-hand man, Robert Maheu.

Late in August 1970, just days after the nerve-gas fiasco came to its terrible end, the CIA reached out to Hughes. It first tried to contact him directly but had no more success than Richard Nixon or Henry Kissinger.

Casting about for a suitable go-between, the Agency settled not on Maheu, its erstwhile partner in the Castro assassination plot, but instead on his rivals, Bill Gay and Chester Davis, and their new ally in Houston, Hughes Tool Company chief Raymond Holliday.

Maheu was frozen out completely. He was now considered unreliable, a bad risk, a man who knew too much and drank too much, an embarrassment and a danger, far too close to his Castro plot cohort John Roselli and their mutual lawyer Ed Morgan, who had already leaked the story of the failed murder conspiracy to columnist Jack Anderson.

To make contact with Hughes, the CIA turned instead to a discreet businessman, Raymond Holliday.

Holliday held the purse-strings and he held the title of chief executive in the Hughes empire, but he had not seen his boss for fifteen years and had spoken to him by telephone only once since the billionaire arrived in Las Vegas. That was when the Mormons wanted a raise and Holliday had refused to approve it without direct word from Hughes. To reach him again with the CIA's big secret, Holliday would first have to get past the nursemaids.

To do that, he would need to bring in their boss, Bill Gay. And before he presented the CIA's sensitive proposal to Hughes, he would also need a legal reading from Chester Davis. The shared secret helped forge a new alliance.

When Holliday finally presented the *Glomar* project to Hughes, the recluse was more than enthusiastic.

His empire already had strong ties to the CIA through the Hughes Aircraft Company, but Hughes himself had no contact with that operation and he had long wanted a more personal alliance with the Agency. In fact, he had been pressing Maheu for years to make just such an intimate partnership.

Now Hughes gave Holliday his full blessing.

"Give them my assurance that I will do my utmost to help them in their mission," he instructed his man from Houston, "and anytime they don't receive the cooperation they think they ought to, be in touch with me and I'll see that they get it."

Hughes was impressed with the *Glomar* project. It had both the bizarre grandiosity and the cloak-and-dagger spirit that complemented his own self-image. And he was impressed with the men who had brought it to him.

The new team had succeeded where Maheu had failed. Suddenly Maheu did not seem quite so well connected, quite so omnipotent. It was Holliday, Gay, and Davis who really had the big connections that Maheu only claimed. The more Hughes considered it all, the clearer it became. Maheu had failed him as a protector, failed him as a fixer, and if the others had also failed him over the nerve gas, at least they had not balked, had not lectured him about "tiger hunts."

Late in August, shortly after the *Glomar* contact, Hughes let it drop to his Mormons that he was preparing a proxy that would give Gay, Davis, and Holliday authority over all his Nevada operations.

The plan for Maheu's ouster began to take shape.

Emboldened by the apparent Hughes-Maheu split, sensing that their once impregnable rival was now vulnerable, the other powers joined forces to make their move against him.

Gay flew to Washington to meet secretly with Robert Peloquin, president of International Intelligence, Inc., a private cloak-and-dagger firm better known as Intertel that happened to be a subsidiary of the same company that owned Paradise Island. Gay told Peloquin that Hughes wanted to retain the spy-for-hire outfit to conduct a secret audit of his Las Vegas casinos.

Not long afterward, Peloquin flew to Los Angeles to confer with Chester Davis. The gruff lawyer took the plot a big step further. He asked the man from Intertel to draw up a detailed plan "for a change of management in Nevada."

Meanwhile, Raymond Holliday was feeding Hughes's growing fears of financial ruin and suggesting that Maheu was largely to blame.

There were indeed real problems, and Hughes himself had presented the grim picture to Maheu months earlier: "I can boil it down to one fact—three years ago there was 650 million dollars in cash in the till. Now, after three years, this year is scheduled to finish with a hundred million dollars shortage of funds which have to be borrowed."

Now the problems were even worse. Hughes had been hit with a final default judgment of $145 million on TWA. His disastrous helicopter enterprise was headed for a loss of $90 million. He was not yet even aware that John Meier had swindled him out of $20 million for phony mining claims. And his two-hundred-million-dollar Nevada investment had, against all odds, lost money every year.

But most of all, Hughes was worried about his image.

"At the present time when I am having a little trouble making both ends meet," he wrote, "I am sure there is a large army of people waiting in expectant, hushed silence for the first indication of a slide backward in my financial resources.

"There is only one thing worse than being broke, and that is to have everybody know that you are broke.

"In most cases, and at normal times, I am quite content to be referred to merely as an industrialist without a price tag," continued Hughes, upset by a local newspaper story that had referred to him as a "millionaire," a story based on a press release issued by his own p.r. firm.

"However, at present, in my highly critical situation, I think it is a bad time for us to put out publicity referring to me as a mere millionaire. There are several hundred millionaires on the horizon now, and since I have been referred to as a Billionaire ever since we became established in Las Vegas, I am fearful that some enemy of mine will pick up this small deviation and make a story about it— you know, something like: 'Well, well, has he finally gotten to the bottom of his bankroll? Etc., etc.'

"I think that kind of a report with attendant jokes could be very bad right now."

Playing on those fears, Holliday now sent Hughes a bleak accounting of financial conditions in his crumbling empire. It was no laughing matter. He had $111 million cash on hand, of which $75 million had to be kept as a bond on the TWA judgment, with another $16.5 million pledged as collateral on a bank loan. That left only $19.5 million for operating funds, in a year that would require at least $30 million.

Holliday followed the cold figures with a slashing attack on Maheu: "You will note that no provision is made for a dividend to you, and you will certainly require at least $2 million by year-end," he wrote Hughes. "However, provision is made for payment to Maheu of his $10,000 per week basic compensation, but without provision for his expenses that will surely be considerable. In other words, no provision is made for the purchase or use of a right-hand or left-hand ass-wiping machine that he may require.

"The long and short of our position," added Holliday, "is that we are in trouble, and very serious trouble."

Hughes needed no persuading. He had long been convinced that Maheu was profligate, worse yet that he spent Hughes's money without Hughes's permission.

"I have given up all hope of controlling unauthorized expenditures at this end of the line," Hughes morosely informed Holliday. "Since Bob is not inclined toward economy measures, I want you to take the steps necessary to prevent expenses I have not approved."

Holliday needed no further encouragement. He quickly sent another financial report to the penthouse, this time zeroing in on the Nevada books. They were dripping red ink. Maheu's operations had never turned a profit. They lost nearly $700,000 in 1967, more than

$3 million in 1968, almost $8.5 million in 1969, and halfway through 1970 close to $7 million, with projected losses for the full year headed for a whopping $14 million.

"The Nevada operations," noted Holliday with a businessman's icy scorn, "are not profit-oriented or cost-conscious."

Hughes, encouraged in his suspicions by the whispering Mormons, drew a darker conclusion. He became increasingly convinced that Maheu was, in fact, stealing him blind.

He never confronted Maheu directly with the accusation, but their pen-pal relationship was now becoming more of a poison-pen relationship, and as the bitterness reached a dangerous breaking point the whispering Mormons made their big move. They cut Maheu's communication lines to the penthouse.

First the Mormons convinced Hughes that Maheu should, like all other executives, transmit his messages exclusively through them.

"Bob," wrote the billionaire to his estranged henchman, "I've decided not to ask you to write me any more messages in longhand and sealed envelopes. I know this is time consuming for you, and my men think I dont trust them. So, in the future, except in rare instances, I prefer you dictate your reply to my messages via telephone to whichever of my men happens to be on duty.

"I shall continue to send you most of my messages in writing, simply because it is much quicker and more accurate."

It was not long, however, before the Mormons also persuaded Hughes that Maheu could not be trusted to receive, much less keep, the billionaire's own handwritten memos. Without warning, Hughes suddenly dispatched one of his attendants to retrieve from Maheu all the old correspondence.

Maheu, who was still unaware of the larger forces moving against him, instantly recognized the dangers of losing direct contact with Hughes and lashed out bitterly in a futile effort to restore his unique access.

"If, for some reasons known only to you, I cannot be trusted as the depository of these reference documents, then I categorically tell you that as far as I am concerned, you and your entire program in Nevada can go to hell," he angrily told Hughes, risking a complete break in his desperation to regain lost ground.

"Howard, I am so hurt and so mad that you may never be able to make amends. I beg of you to release me of my obligations, because I have a belly-full of the chicken-shit operation within which I am living and from which I would like to get released.

"Howard, whether you realize it or not, you cut and cut deep. I want out.

"Will you please do me a great favor. Will you kindly relieve me of my obligations and appoint someone else to be your top man in this area."

It was the kind of bluff that had worked before. Maheu was certain that Hughes could not get along without him. But this time around Hughes would not be bullied.

"If you want to be relieved of your present assignment, then, regretfully, I will not object," he coolly replied.

"If, on the other hand, it is your intention to march out of here taking the entire upper echelon of executives along with you in a grand-scale industrial executive strike, then you will have to face up to this sweeping gesture of disloyalty and treachery in your own conscience, but without my slightest consent thereto.

"If you intend to convert this into a power-play of some kind, aimed not at a considerate plan of separation designed to impose the minimum hardship upon me, but instead aimed at a carefully devised strategy calculated to pose a threat over my head sufficient to extract an apology and humble pleading for reconciliation, if this is your objective, please be frank. You, yourself, have said that we should not play games.

"Something has struck me phony about this requested abrogation from the beginning."

Maheu stood his ground. He saw the fear behind Hughes's rage and did his best to encourage it.

"You must have a very low estimate of my capability if you interpret anything that I have been saying as a power play on my part," he replied with some swagger. "I don't need any more power than I now have, but if I had the least desire to make such a play, I can assure you that it would take place much more suddenly, and in so many areas, that it would be unbelieveable.

"I could not find it within myself to indulge in such activity," he continued, easing off now that he had made clear his threat, "and strange as it may seem to you, I have no fear of my ability to earn a living, with or without Howard Hughes.

"I have no devious intentions, there are no hidden gimmicks, and I have told you repeatedly that *no one* could ever cause me to hurt you in any way whatsoever, and I would go out of my way to clobber anyone who might try to cause you any damage.

"Now, Howard," concluded Maheu, once more positioning himself as the billionaire's faithful if short-tempered protector, "please tell me wherein I am being unfair and also what in the hell you expect from me."

Hughes, either mollified by Maheu's loyalty even *in extremis,* or frightened by his implied threat, moved to heal the breach. He was still not ready for the painful, and quite possibly dangerous, final break.

"If I can be sure that you and I have reached the end of our unfortunate period of doubts and suspicions each about the other, then I have a couple of projects that are so staggering in their enormity and huge in over all expanse that they will absolutely leave you breathless," wrote Hughes, dangling visions of new glory before his regent even as he secretly plotted to replace him with his rivals.

"I dont have to tell you, Bob, that I am a person who is capable of manifesting extreme suspicion if encouraged," he added, perhaps intentionally hinting at the coup now in progress, perhaps once more doubting his Mormons' whispers.

"How many times have I asked you to check out various telephone lines in the past to ascertain if they were secure?

"So, to summarize, Bob, I have trusted you with the very most confidential, almost sacred information as to my very innermost activities," he went on, obviously more than a bit concerned about splitting with a man who knew so much.

"When I first sent down to pick up these files, I simply had not the faintest idea—truthfully—that it would displease you even the least bit.

"So, all I need to know, just one word of assurance that these unhappy and unfortunate days are behind us," concluded a relieved Hughes, wanting to believe the best. "I am just as willing to assume the blame for the misunderstanding. I dont seek or even want to share that. I only want to know the episode is behind us."

And so it was. But the really wrenching episodes were yet to come.

The Hughes-Maheu marriage was definitely on the rocks. Its special intimacy had been maintained by direct correspondence, and now that was over.

Maheu's only direct link to Hughes now was the telephone. But while Hughes could call Maheu, Maheu could not call Hughes. He could only call the Mormons, who more and more often told him that Hughes was busy, asleep, eating, not well, or simply unavailable.

And the calls from Hughes, in times past all too frequent, first dwindled sharply, then stopped.

Unable to reach Hughes, his calls not returned, his memos not answered, unwilling to sit by his silent telephone like a jilted lover, tired of dialing the penthouse at all hours of the day and night in a futile effort to break through, an angry and frustrated Maheu finally theatened to leave Las Vegas on an extended vacation.

It was the beginning of a final bitter exchange, letters of lost love they dictated to each other through the Mormons.

"I plan to leave immediately for Europe and join my wife, who is already there, for an indefinite period," Maheu told Hughes, after weeks without word from his boss.

"Unless I hear from you to the contrary, I will assume I have your full blessing. I literally hate myself for not having left yesterday with my wife. For over ten years I have promised her a trip to Europe, but have never been able to fulfill my commitment because of my sincere desire to help you with one problem after another.

"Howard, if I cannot get answers from you in matters as important as TWA, Air West, LAA, I really don't know why I should continue worrying about these things alone.

"After all, in the last analysis, the only person who stands to get hurt is yourself and ultimately, however devastating the results may be, they will have very little to do with me personally or my future life. If I do not get answers from you I am stymied.

"I have no reason to believe that I will hear from you for the next two or three months," concluded the cast-aside pen pal. "It appears, therefore, that this might be the propitious time for me to take a much needed vacation, and perhaps this will enable me to stop having these sleepless nights.

"In sincere friendship, Bob."

Maheu's threat to go AWOL finally broke Hughes's silence. In his first memo to Maheu in weeks, the recluse—trapped in his penthouse, unable to make good his own escape, about to lose his own wife (who had finally filed for divorce), beset by financial crises, and in failing health—lashed out bitterly at his deserting lieutenant.

"I don't think the rebuke and hostility expressed in your last message is one damn bit justified," replied Hughes through his aides.

"I have been very ill lately. I have had a personal problem of the enth magnitude involving my wife. And I simply have not been able to keep abreast of the inflow of all these communications. This is not the fault of my staff, it might be my fault, but really it is nobody's fault but just a fault of the system. I am trying to carry the load of 25 normal men.

"The matters to which you refer are still in the pipeline to me," continued the wretched recluse. "If you think this entitles you to go into a fit of rage and sail off to Europe then it certainly is, in my opinion, a peculiar way of demonstrating this loyal, everlasting friendship we have been talking about.

"You may have a lot of political friends and a lot of people who profess to be your friends, but I don't think you have so damn many left who are really, truly reliable friends of yours that you can afford to throw away the one who may be the most reliable and most important of all, namely me.

"If you think you can dispense with me as a friend, go ahead and sail on off to Europe and enjoy yourself," added Hughes, hurling a bitter bon voyage at the man he planned to dump overboard. "Please regard it as the end of what I have considered to be a true and loyal and personal friendship."

It was not so much losing Maheu as the thought of losing control over him that drove Hughes crazy. For years he had been unable to let Maheu free for a day, for a night, for even a few hours, could hardly bear to let him sleep, and now, even as he withdrew behind his Mormons and plotted to escape his alter ego, Hughes could not contemplate letting Maheu escape his control.

But Maheu was not really ready to ship out.

"I am sure that you know that in the last analysis I could not find it within myself to leave for Europe or to be unavailable to you at a time like this for one damn moment," he assured Hughes. "Let us say, therefore, that if the message to which you refer has done nothing more but to reopen communications it perhaps was not in vain.

"I can assure you that if I were not concerned and if I did not care about your well being, I sure as hell would not have spent as many sleepless nights as I have during the last several weeks. Your staff can testify as to the number of telephone calls they have received from me at 3 and 5 AM when I was wide awake because of my deep concern.

"Howard, I do not particularly appreciate your statement relative to my friends and contacts," Maheu continued, heatedly defending his fidelity to his jealous partner. "You better believe that I have them, but it has been many years now since I have thought of them only as they relate to you. I am deeply hurt that you have not recognized this yourself and that I have to be the one to tell you.

"In sincere friendship, Bob."

Hughes was not mollified. That threatened trip to Europe—he couldn't let go of it.

"In view of the numerous expressions of loyalty and undying friendship, that the remainder of your business career will be with me and that if we did come to a parting of the ways, I would not have to worry about another Dietrich, or another Ramo or Wooldridge," the billionaire replied through his Mormons, "it is very difficult for me to reconcile these expressions with the fact that whenever we have some little misunderstanding—the next thing I receive is a threat to take an extended vacation.

"When displeased, your reaction is to desert the ship and let it go to hell. You tell me that my affairs are in a dangerous condition, which I don't seem to realize—instead of telling me how to correct them. I get nothing but a goodbye note on your way to Europe."

And so it came down to that. The "Dear John" letter. With all of his dark suspicions that Maheu was seizing power, stealing his money, plotting a coup, it was instead the pain of rejection, the terrible fear that Maheu would leave him before he could leave Maheu, that at the end gripped Hughes.

"Howard, I am sure that you have a life-size picture of my trouncing off to Europe at a time like this," Maheu quickly responded, desperately trying to reassure his boss. "I would like for you to give me one example of when I have left you in a moment of need.

"I also think it would be difficult for you to say that I have never been prepared to take, personally, all the calculated risks in order to accomplish what it is that you wanted. Hell Howard, if some of the things which I did in order to extricate us from the ABC matter, or to accomplish what we wanted done in the AEC situation, ever surfaced I could never go to Europe because I would be spending the rest of my life in jail."

But it was too late. There was no reply. Once more, just silence from the penthouse.

Hughes was, in fact, ill. Not quite so ill as he claimed to Maheu and not silent because of his sickness, but he did have a mild case of pneumonia and a slight touch of anemia, enough to add an eerie wheeze and an extra pallor to his already extreme condition, enough to prevent his planned escape.

He was in no shape to travel. He needed a quick cure. He called in his local physician but would not allow the doctor to perform any examination, to run any tests, even to touch him. Several months earlier, experiencing an irregular heartbeat, Hughes had reluctantly submitted to an EKG and the doctor got some electrode paste on his beard. Hughes was so shocked by the contamination that he snapped right back into his regular rhythm.

This time, he was taking no chances. Besides, he had already diagnosed his problem and decided on the remedy. What the billionaire wanted was blood—more of that same pure Mormon blood he had received two years earlier.

The transfusions were completely unnecessary. His blood count was close to normal. But Hughes was insistent. "It made me feel so much better last time," he told his doctor. "I want some more."

And sure enough, that last shot of pure Mormon blood did the trick. Right after the transfusion, Hughes finally made good his escape. For the first time in four years, he left his blacked-out bedroom—and moved into a second, identical bedroom in the same suite.

He might have stayed there forever had events outside the penthouse not forced him to flee.

Maheu, suddenly realizing that his rivals were conspiring against him, launched a bold counterattack that brought the hidden power struggle to a head. Early in November, he fired off a telegram to Chester Davis, discharging the billionaire's chief counsel from the TWA case.

Hughes himself had granted Maheu full authority over that litigation shortly after he was hit with the default judgment.

"You have the ball on the TWA situation," he had written, eager to be rid of the hot potato. "It is my understanding that I turned the entire TWA matter over to you lock, stock, and barrel, a long time ago.

"Also, the decision as to what to do about legal representation is up to you. If I am to hold you responsible for the overall outcome, I must give you complete authority to decide which law firm you want to handle each phase of it."

Now, however, when Maheu tried to exercise that power he instead hastened his own downfall. Chester Davis refused to step aside, and the Hughes Tool Company board of directors, controlled by Davis's ally Holliday, revoked Maheu's authority over TWA.

Outflanked, Maheu appealed the decision to Hughes. He hand-delivered a memo to the penthouse, pleading that the billionaire back his play. He received no reply. In fact, Maheu's message got no further than the Mormons. On Bill Gay's orders, they withheld it from Hughes. The palace coup was now in full force.

Unaware that his appeal had been intercepted, feeling himself cruelly abandoned, Maheu sent a second memo to Hughes. This one the Mormons delivered.

"I sometimes think that perhaps the time has come for you either to walk down the nine flights of stairs, or more conveniently utilize the elevator, so as to face the world yourself once and for all," wrote Maheu, daring the recluse to leave his sanctuary. "Perhaps then you might have at least one more ounce of sympathy for someone else who is constantly facing it in your behalf, and who is about ready to go to bed one more evening finding himself on a damned lonely island."

It was about to get a lot lonelier. Two days later, on November 14, Hughes told his aides he was ready to sign the proxy he had proposed back in August, the one that would give Gay, Davis, and Holliday authority over his Nevada empire. Davis had it all prepared. He sent the proxy by telecopier to the Mormons, who brought it in to their boss. The billionaire reached up from the Barcalounger he had installed in his new bedroom, put the proxy on a stack of legal pads, and signed Maheu's death warrant. But he was not yet ready to order the execution.

First Hughes wanted to get out of town. Not even the nerve gas scared him as much as a final showdown with the hot-tempered Frenchman.

On Thanksgiving Eve, November 25, 1970, almost four years to the day from his arrival in Las Vegas, Howard Hughes made his Great Escape.

He did not walk down the stairs or take the elevator, as Maheu had suggested, but instead snuck down a rear fire escape. Rather, he was carried down, a grand invalid held aloft by his loyal Mormons, as they slowly descended nine narrow flights.

The billionaire lay on a stretcher, dressed for the first time since he arrived, again in blue pajamas, his arms and legs poking out bone-thin, a six-foot-four-inch near-skeleton weighing just over one hundred pounds, his scraggly beard reaching down past his sunken chest, his yellowed gray hair, uncut all four years, nearly two feet long—rakishly topped by a snap-brim brown fedora. It was the kind he had worn in his daredevil youth, when he was breaking all the world flying records. Hughes had insisted on that hat. He might be fleeing his kingdom like a thief in the night, an inglorious end to his grand adventure, but that old hat was a sign that he still had the Right Stuff.

Now, however, he took flight down a fire escape, was slipped into a waiting unmarked van, and finally was carried aboard a private jet while his pilots, as ordered, walked off into the darkness. The plane flew its unidentified passenger directly to the Bahamas.

Early the next morning, Hughes was safely ensconced in another blacked-out bedroom of another ninth-floor penthouse in the Britannia Beach Hotel on Paradise Island.

His big getaway was a great success. Hughes had escaped from one self-made prison and locked himself in another, without anyone being the wiser.

It took Maheu a full week to discover that Hughes had disappeared. It took him twenty-four hours to turn it into the most sensational "missing persons" case the world had ever seen.

"HOWARD HUGHES VANISHES! MYSTERY BAFFLES CLOSE ASSOCIATES" read the screaming banner headline in the *Las Vegas Sun*. Maheu had leaked the story to his pal Hank Greenspun, and Greenspun suggested that the billionaire had been kidnapped, drugged, "spirited away," was perhaps even dead.

When the story reached Hughes in his Bahamas bedroom, he was enraged. He immediately released the proxy that stripped Maheu of all power and fired off one final memo dissolving their partnership. It went not to Maheu but to his rival Chester Davis.

"You can tell Maheu for me that I had not fully determined in my mind to withdraw all support from his position until he started playing this cat and mouse game for his own selfish benefit," wrote Hughes.

"In other words, Maheu does not believe for one second that I am dead, disabled, or any of the other wild accusations he has been making. . . .

"Consequently, when he started claiming that my messages were not genuine and that I had been abducted, and all the other wild charges.

"When he demanded entrance to my apartment (to look for foul play, no less!)

"In other words, when this entire TV writer's dream started unfolding, it soon became obvious that Maheu had no concern about the truth in this matter.

"He knew full well where I was," Hughes continued. "I have been planning this trip for more than a year, and I had discussed it with him many times.

"So it became clear that Maheu had decided to milk his relationship with me and my companies to the last possible dollar.

"It was only at this point, that I decided the case against Maheu had been fully and conclusively proven.

"Up to this time, in spite of the massive array of evidence, I would gladly have listened to his side of the issue.

"It was his shocking conduct since my departure that left me feeling all efforts to explain away these actions would be totally without purpose.

"And, if his conduct since my departure consisted of a mass of lies, then I must assume that, in hundreds of other instances wherein his contentions were in direct conflict with other of my associates who had been with me for years and years of honest, loyal service, I repeat, if he has been lying since my departure, then I must assume that he was lying in these many, many other situations wherein I was forced to choose between accepting Maheu's contentions or the equally impassioned and, so far as I could tell, equally genuine and truthful claims of other of my associates whom I have learned to trust.

"Up to this time," Hughes concluded, "I simply had no way to know who was telling the truth, and who was not.

"But Maheu's actions since my departure have made this entire situation very clear."

Not long after, John Ehrlichman encountered Bebe Rebozo coming down the stairway from the president's private quarters inside the White House. They spoke in hushed tones about the strange doings in Las Vegas and the Bahamas. Rebozo wondered aloud whether his pal Richard Danner would survive the big shake-up. His real fear remained unspoken: Would Richard Nixon?

12-9-70

Any word yet from
Chester as to satisfaction
or dissatisfaction with
message?

Chester —

If Mahieu is still
asserting that any mes-
sages from Nassau are
not bona fide, let me
send you a complete
set of finger prints
attached to a copy of my
last message.

If you would make
this offer in front of
members of the press,
with Mahieu present,
I think he would
back down because
he would know that,
upon arrival of the
finger prints, he would

be shown up as the
lyar he has been from
the start of this entire
affair.

You can tell maheu
for me that I had
not fully determined in
my mind to withdraw
all support from his
position until he started
playing this cat and
mouse game for his
own selfish benefit.

In other words,
maheu does not
believe for one second
that I am dead, dis-
abled, or any of the
other wild accusations
he has been making.
There is not the

slightest fragment of a
doubt in Maheu's mind
about the validity and
genuine character of my
messages.

Consequently, when
he started claiming
that my messages
were not genuine and
that I had been ab-
ducted, and all the
other wild charges.

When he demanded
entrance to my apart-
ment (to look for foul
play, no less!)

In other words, when
this entire TV writer's
dream started unfolding,

it soon became obvious
that Maheu had no
concern about the truth
in this matter.

He knew full well
where I was. I have
been planning this trip
for more than a year,
and I had discussed it
with him many times.

So it became clear
that Maheu had decided
to milk his relation-
ship with me and my
companies to the last
possible dollar.

It was only at this
point, that I decided
the case against Maheu
had been fully and
conclusively proven.

in spite of the massive array of evidence,

Up to this time, I would gladly have listened to his side of the issue.

It was his shocking conduct since my departure that left me feeling all efforts to explain away these actions would be totally without purpose.

And, if his conduct since my departure consisted of a mass of lies, then I must assume that, in hundreds of other instances wherein his contentions were in direct conflict with other of my associates who had been with me for years and years of honest,

loyal service, I repeat
— if he has been lying
since my departure in
this manoeuvering game
he obviously has been
playing, then I must
assume that he was
lying in these many,
many other situations
wherein I was forced
to choose between
accepting maker's
contentions or the
equally impassioned
and, so far as I could
tell, equally genuine
and truthful claims
of other of my associ-
ates whom I have
learned to trust.

Up to this time, I
simply had no way
to know who was telling
the truth, and who was

it.

But Maher's actions since my departure have made this entire situation very clear.

Please let me know what further I can do to clear this matter up,

Howard

Epilogue I

Watergate

"This is for Haldeman," said Richard Nixon, speaking into his dictaphone aboard *Air Force One*. The president had just emerged from a ten-day retreat at San Clemente, plotting his reelection campaign and brooding alone with Bebe Rebozo, and now he was flying to the University of Nebraska to "forge an alliance of the generations." But his mind was elsewhere, fixated on another alliance. One he had to destroy, before it destroyed him.

"It would seem that the time is approaching when Larry O'Brien is held accountable for his retainer with Hughes," declared Nixon, going on the attack, dictating his message to Haldeman. "Bebe has some information on this, although it is, of course, not solid. But there is no question that one of Hughes's people did have O'Brien on a very heavy retainer for 'services rendered' in the past. Perhaps Colson should check on this."

It was January 14, 1971. Just six weeks had passed since Howard Hughes made his great escape, and the ugly aftermath of the Hughes-Maheu split had Nixon in mortal terror.

It was not the money O'Brien got from Hughes that really obsessed him. It was his own Hughes money. The hot hundred grand hidden away in Bebe Rebozo's safe-deposit box. Throughout his presidency Nixon had heard that tell-tale heart beating, had grown increasingly fearful that others could also hear it, that soon they would discover the $100,000 payoff his pal Danner had delivered to his pal Rebozo, that again he would be ruined by an ugly Hughes scandal, that it would cost him the White House as it had once before.

Nixon never got over that 1960 defeat. His narrow loss to JFK still haunted him, and he still blamed that loss on the Hughes "loan" scandal—the never-repaid $205,000 his brother had received from the billionaire. Yet Nixon had taken more Hughes money. A cursed bundle of hundred-dollar bills. And now, with the Hughes empire split by a bitter power struggle, Nixon was certain his terrible guilty secret was about to come spilling out.

That very morning, before leaving the western White House, the president had seen a *Los Angeles Times* report that Maheu planned to subpoena his former boss for a fifty-million-dollar lawsuit. Even if the recluse himself failed to appear, secret Hughes memos impounded by the Nevada court were likely to surface. Indeed, the dreaded Jack Anderson already claimed to have seen some.

The more Nixon brooded, the more terrified he grew, and the more he focused on Larry O'Brien. *He* was getting away with it. The hated leader of the Kennedy gang, the man who had beaten him in 1960 by exploiting the Hughes loan scandal, was himself getting $15,000 a month from the billionaire while he served as unpaid chairman of the Democratic National Committee. Nixon wanted revenge. He wanted to unmask O'Brien as a secret Hughes lobbyist. He wanted to make O'Brien pay as he had paid.

But now, aboard *Air Force One,* the president was gripped by a darker thought. The terrible fear that O'Brien *knew*—that he had somehow learned from his hidden masters all about the secret Hughes cash in Bebe's little tin box.

Nixon could not tell that to Haldeman. He could not say to his chief of staff, "My God, O'Brien must know! We've got to find out what he's found out. We've got to get him before he gets me." Nixon could not say that because Haldeman himself didn't know. None of the president's men knew. Only Rebozo shared that secret. So, instead, Nixon ordered Haldeman to get O'Brien.

"We're going to nail O'Brien on this, one way or the other," the president told him back in Washington the next day. He called Haldeman into the Oval Office and said, "O'Brien's not going to get away with it, Bob. We're going to get proof of his relationship with Hughes— and just what he's doing for the money."

It was the beginning of a desperate covert campaign. One that would end with Richard Nixon's burglars caught looking for Howard Hughes's secrets inside Larry O'Brien's office—at the Watergate.

Down in the Bahamas, Hughes was oblivious to the high-stakes intrigue he had unwittingly inspired back in Washington. Indeed, he was oblivious to everything outside his new blacked-out bedroom.

He was finally safe. As safe as a prisoner in solitary confinement, with two armed guards on the penthouse floor of his Paradise Island retreat, one at the elevator, the other behind a locked partition, himself sealed off from Hughes by a second locked partition, but keeping watch on the rest of the hotel through closed-circuit TV cameras, while a third guard patrolled the roof with a vicious attack dog.

But Hughes was no longer entirely his own prisoner. With Maheu out of the picture, his Mormon attendants were firmly in control, determined to keep their boss bedridden and befuddled.

Hughes was completely cut off from the world, thousands of miles from all citadels of his empire, now run by virtual strangers. No longer was he sending secret handwritten memos in sealed envelopes to a trusted regent; indeed he rarely wrote any memos at all. The Mormons controlled all lines of communication. Hughes dictated his messages to them and received all replies through them. And he knew only what they wished him to know.

He no longer read newspapers. He had even stopped watching television. The reception was so bad on his island retreat that he gave up TV after one futile day. To bring a clear picture into his bedroom, he toyed for a few weeks with the idea of using one of the thirty satellites his empire had circling the globe, but soon abandoned that too.

Instead he watched movies, turning his penthouse into a darkened theater of the absurd, screening one film after another, or the same one several times in a row, not infrequently ten or twenty times, and a few real favorites more than a hundred times. Movie soundtracks blared constantly, as his television once had. But unlike TV, the movies told him nothing of the real world beyond.

Caught up in his celluloid fantasies, Hughes spent his days reclining naked on a paper-towel-insulated lounge chair and rarely left his Barcalounger even to sleep. His bedsores got so bad that they required surgery, which Hughes forced his doctor to perform in the hotel room. But one shoulder blade—the bare bone—kept tearing through the parchmentlike skin of his emaciated body, an open sore five inches long continually rubbed raw by his hard Naugahyde lounge chair.

"We should bring in a softer chair," one of his Mormons solicitously advised, "and you should put forth your very best effort to get out of the chair as much as possible—at least do your sleeping in bed. Dr. Chaffin told me that as long as you persist in spending nearly all your time in the chair, you could expect a recurrence. He said I should take your chair and push it off the balcony."

Hughes, however, refused to budge. And his Mormons catered to his whims, kept their prisoner happy. They showed him his movies, they gave him his enemas, and they brought him his codeine.

Hughes was shooting up more than ever now—an incredible fifty to sixty grains of codeine a day, more than twice what he had used in Las Vegas. From time to time his doctors tried to lower the dose.

"The heavy usage of the item," they warned, had affected him "to the extent that you are not in any condition, either physically or mentally, in any 24 hour period to enjoy the day or make any business decisions."

It hardly mattered. Hughes rarely did any real business anymore. Indeed, he rarely did anything at all. His life had fallen into a pattern, one that would change little over the rest of his life, and one that his Mormons carefully chronicled, at his orders keeping a minute-by-minute account of the activities of a man who did virtually nothing.

One day ran into another, with Hughes moving from "chair" to "B/R"—from Barcalounger to bathroom—and back again, his movements meticulously recorded:

SUNDAY 6:55 AM   Asleep.

11:15 AM   Awake, B/R.

11:35 AM   Chair, screening "SITUATION HOPELESS BUT NOT SERIOUS" (completed all but last 5 min. reel 3)

1:30 PM   10 C [10 grains codeine]

1:50 PM   B/R.

2:10 PM   Chair, resumed screening "THE KILLERS"

3:30 PM   Food: Chicken *only*.

4:20 PM   Finished eating. Finished "SITUATION HOPELESS BUT NOT SERIOUS" Screening "DO NOT DISTURB" (OK to return)

6:45 PM   B/R.

7:00 PM   Chair.

7:45 PM	Screening "DEATH OF A GUN-FIGHTER" (1 reel only)
8:25 PM	B/R.
8:45 PM	Chair.
9:00 PM	Screening "THE KILLERS"
9:35 PM	Chicken and dessert. Completed "THE KILLERS"
11:25 PM	B/R.
11:50 PM	Bed. Changed bandages. Not asleep.

Occasionally Hughes had important instructions inscribed in the logs: "Carry the pillow by the bottom seam" or "HRH says not to get any more Italian westerns" or "John must somehow acquire additional #4's" (the Empirin compound containing codeine) or "Hereafter when he asks for his pills, take him the entire bottle (not some on a kleenex)" or, more sadly, "He doesn't want to be permitted to sleep in the bathroom anymore."

Suddenly, after three months locked inside his Bahamas bedroom, Howard Hughes decided to break loose, set sail, move his command post to a yacht.

"I dont know how many more summers I have left," wrote the rapidly failing sixty-five-year-old recluse, "but I dont intend to spend all of them holed up in a hotel room on a barcalounger.

"The choice of boats available in the Miami area now is at its peak. Also, several of the preferred boats are in Europe, and if I should select one of these, I may decide to spend the summer in the Mediterranean area."

Hughes was definitely feeling expansive—he could almost feel the sea breezes already—but his Mormons soon took the wind out of his sails. Their prisoner could not be allowed to escape.

"In connection with the possible plan to move onto a boat, there is an aspect of security which should be considered," the nursemaids warned, raising the specter of Robert Maheu.

The deposed henchman had not been idle. He was still fighting fiercely to recover his lost power and had even sent a crew commanded by his son to spy on Hughes down in the Bahamas. The mission had not gone well. Maheu's gang was routed by a rival cloak-and-dagger outfit—Intertel—the private intelligence agency working for Hughes but reporting to the Mormons.

"Eleven persons were arrested in the rooms directly below us with wiretapping and other apparatus," the Mormons belatedly informed

Hughes. "They had among other things a Peter Maheu check for $10,000 and vouchers from the Frontier.

"All this is bad enough, but the FBI feels that this was very likely not just a case of wiretapping. Based on the number and type of people involved, they think it was more likely an aborted kidnapping attempt.

"If that is so, we really shouldn't go onto a boat where we would be much more vulnerable than we are here, or elsewhere on land."

The unwelcome reminder that the jilted Maheu was still on the loose—and still dangerous—quickly deflated Hughes's yacht fantasy. He settled back into his Barcalounger, back to his movies and his codeine, and once more forgot about the world beyond his bedroom.

But the struggle for control of his empire—the battle between Maheu and the Mormons still raging back in Las Vegas—was steadily feeding Richard Nixon's paranoia and steadily becoming intertwined with the covert activities the president was plotting from the White House.

Chuck Colson was excited. Nixon's bullyboy had just heard some incredible news.

Larry O'Brien was out. He had been replaced by the Mormons with a fellow Mormon. Howard Hughes had a new man in Washington, Robert Foster Bennett. He was a solid Republican, and best of all Bob Bennett and Chuck Colson were old buddies.

"I'm sure I need not explain the political implications of having Hughes's affairs handled here in Washington by a close friend," crowed Colson, spreading the good word through the White House. "This move could signal quite a shift in terms of the politics and money that Hughes represents."

Like the rest of Nixon's gang, Colson was unaware that the president already had a private pipeline to the billionaire, that he wasn't looking for a new way to get Hughes money but for some way to hide the cash already in hand.

And there was also a great deal Colson didn't know about his pal Bob Bennett. Such as the fact that Bennett had another big client. The Central Intelligence Agency. An obscure bureaucrat in the Department of Transportation until he was brought into the Hughes orbit by the Bahamas nerve-gas affair, Bennett had suddenly become the pivot for three powerful forces—Hughes, Nixon, and the CIA—

and it would never be clear where his true loyalties lay. But the mysterious Mormon would never be far from the events that finally drove Nixon from office.

The president, however, remained fixated on O'Brien. His ouster changed nothing. Nixon still wanted him nailed. Haldeman had not assigned that mission to his rival Colson, as Nixon had suggested. Instead he had given the O'Brien hit to a new recruit, an ambitious young White House counsel, John Dean.

But Dean was getting nowhere. He called Bebe Rebozo, but Rebozo only repeated what he had already told Nixon. Nothing really solid. And the president's pal added a disturbing note: "He [Rebozo] requested that if any action is taken with regard to Hughes that he be notified because of his familiarity with the delicacy of the relationships as a result of his own dealings with the Hughes people."

Puzzled and a bit nervous, Dean turned to the White House gumshoe, Jack Caulfield. A former New York City police detective hired on to handle jobs too dirty to entrust to government agencies—wiretapping newsmen, spying on Teddy Kennedy, keeping watch over the president's brother—Caulfield failed to find proof of the O'Brien-Hughes connection.

But the street-wise cop did smell trouble. Big trouble. Digging for dirt on O'Brien, he was coming up instead with dirt on Nixon. He tried to warn Dean off the case.

"The revelation that an O'Brien-Mahew relationship exists poses significant hazards in any attempt to make O'Brien accountable to the Hughes retainer," cautioned Caulfield. "Mahew's controversial activities and contacts in both Democratic and Republican circles suggests the possibility that forced embarrassment of O'Brien in this matter might well shake loose Republican skeletons from the closet.

"Mayhew apparently forwarded Hughes's political contributions, personally, to both parties over the last ten years. Former FBI agent Dick Danner has been an aide to Mayhew. Danner professes a friendship with Bebe Rebozo.

"As one gets closer to Mayhew's dealings, it becomes evident that his tentacles touch many extremely sensitive areas of government, each one of which is fraught with potential for Jack Anderson–type exposure.

"There is a serious risk here for a counter-scandal if we move precipitously."

Dean was all but ready to bail out entirely when Chuck Colson arrived with the mysterious Bob Bennett in tow. Colson was not about to be frozen out of this intrigue, and his pal Bennett had the inside story on O'Brien.

Dean reported it to Haldeman: "Bennett informs me that there is no doubt about the fact that Larry O'Brien was retained by Howard Hughes. He felt confident that if it was necessary to document the retainer with O'Brien he could get the information through the Hughes people, but it would be with the understanding that the documentation would not be used in a manner that might embarrass Hughes."

Urged on by Nixon, afraid that Colson would grab all the credit, Haldeman ignored the danger signs and demanded action.

"Once Bennett gets back to you with his final report," he ordered Dean, "you and Chuck Colson should get together and come up with a way to leak the appropriate information. Frankly, I can't see any way to handle this without involving Hughes, so the problem of 'embarrassing' him seems to be a matter of degree. However, we should keep Bennett and Bebe out of it at all costs."

But Bennett's final report was not what the White House expected. Instead of delivering the goods on O'Brien, he returned to Washington from a meeting with the new Hughes command in Los Angeles to suggest a criminal investigation of Robert Maheu.

The O'Brien deal was "straightforward," said Bennett, and exposing it would only revive the old Nixon scandals. O'Brien probably knew everything that Maheu knew, and Maheu knew everything. It was Maheu who had handled all of Hughes's political activity, and now he was involved with notorious gangsters. Maheu, not O'Brien, was the real problem.

Bennett's convoluted monologue left Dean confused. Was he trying to use the White House to get Maheu on behalf of the Mormons, as it seemed on the surface, or was he subtly playing on Nixon's paranoia: forget about O'Brien, *he knows too much.*

But Dean had heard enough. He told Haldeman they were "treading in dangerous waters." And Haldeman was also ready to let the whole matter drop.

Nixon, however, was not. All the president's men were now queasy about the Hughes probe—even Rebozo seemed nervous—but the president himself only pushed harder. All his worst fears about O'Brien had been confirmed. If O'Brien indeed knew about the Hughes-Nixon dealings, then he certainly had to be neutralized.

"O'Brien's not going to get away with it," Nixon once more told Haldeman. Everybody always went after *him* over any possible Hughes connection—even taking that "cheap shot" at his poor brother—yet nobody was trying to expose O'Brien. Nixon wanted the proof, the full story, all the dirt, and he wanted it now. It became a constant refrain.

While Nixon waited impatiently for his gang to nail O'Brien, the Hughes gang, unable to get White House assistance, made its own move to nail Maheu—and unwittingly caught the president in a deadly crossfire.

Out in Las Vegas, Intertel instigated an IRS probe against Maheu. It was a fateful move. The IRS investigation that began as a plot against Maheu soon mushroomed into a full-scale audit of the entire Hughes empire, turning first against Hughes himself, and finally against Richard Nixon.

Maheu, however, was aware only of his own IRS problems. He was certain that the investigation had been ordered from the White House. Convinced that Nixon had joined forces with Hughes, that the president was conspiring against him, that the FBI and the CIA were also poised to attack, Maheu fired a warning shot at the Oval Office.

Jack Anderson's column appeared on August 6, 1971.

"Howard Hughes directed his former factotum Robert Maheu to help Richard Nixon win the presidency 'under our sponsorship and supervision,' " Anderson reported. "Maheu allegedly siphoned off $100,000 from the Silver Slipper, a Hughes gambling emporium, for Nixon's campaign. The money was delivered by Richard Danner, a Hughes exec, to Bebe Rebozo, a Nixon confidant."

Nixon's worst nightmare had come true. The Hughes payoff was out in the open.

Rebozo immediately called Danner, angrily demanding to know how Anderson found out. Danner's answer was the final blow. Anderson had called him for comment, and said, "Don't deny it, because I have seen the memo describing this in detail." Maheu had shown it to him.

Anderson had documentary evidence. There was no way out. Still, he had called the payoff a "campaign contribution." Obviously a trick. Nixon waited in horror for the full story to explode.

And nothing happened. Nothing that day, nothing that week, nothing that entire month. The story was simply ignored.

Then, without warning, late in September Maheu's pal Hank

Greenspun, publisher of the *Las Vegas Sun,* brought it back sharply to Nixon's attention. The president had stopped off in Portland, Oregon, to meet with West Coast newspaper editors, on his way to Alaska for a meeting with the emperor of Japan. Greenspun approached White House press aide Herb Klein. He said he had a story that could "sink Nixon." He had heard that a contribution of $100,000 from Hughes had been used to furnish the president's San Clemente estate.

When word of Greenspun's bombshell reached John Ehrlichman back in Washington, he immediately sent the president's personal lawyer, Herb Kalmbach, flying out to Las Vegas. Kalmbach checked into the Sahara and met there with Greenspun for nearly four hours. He was slow to get to the Hughes money, as if he didn't want the publisher to realize that was his real concern. And when Kalmbach finally did bring it up, it was only to vehemently deny that any of Hughes's money had gone into San Clemente. "I know where every nickel came from," said the lawyer, "and I can assure you none of it came from Hughes." That done, Kalmbach started pumping Greenspun for dirt on Larry O'Brien.

Kalmbach himself didn't know it, but Greenspun had come uncomfortably close to the truth. He just had the wrong house. Nixon had spent at least some of the $100,000 for improvements at Key Biscayne.

The noose was tightening, and a few weeks later Bob Bennett mentioned to Chuck Colson that Maheu had stolen Hughes documents stashed in Hank Greenspun's safe.

Then, early in December, the same IRS probe that Intertel had instigated against Maheu began to turn against Nixon. An audit of John Meier's mining-claim scam revealed that the president's brother had been involved in the swindle. And worse yet, an informant had told the revenue agents that "Bebe Rebozo advised John Meier not to be available for IRS interview because of Don Nixon's involvement."

Soon a series of IRS "sensitive case reports" started coming into the White House, slipped to John Ehrlichman by Nixon's man in the commissioner's office. Donald's escapades with Meier were detailed—not merely the bogus mining claims but land deals and stock deals with organized-crime figures, Hawaiian vacations paid for by Meier with Hughes ultimately picking up the tab, trips to the Dominican Republic for shady joint ventures with the island's top government leaders.

Meier, now known to have stolen millions from Hughes, even claimed secret meetings with the president himself. "An analysis of expense vouchers submitted by Meier to Hughes Tool Company," one IRS report noted, "shows that Meier and his wife accompanied by Donald Nixon and his wife traveled to Washington for consultation with president-elect Richard Nixon on November 21, 1968."

Ehrlichman kept Nixon informed as the IRS probe zeroed in on the White House. On one such occasion, the president told his domestic-affairs chief the "true story" of the old Hughes "loan" scandal. Nixon, who had personally arranged that entire transaction, now said he had nothing whatever to do with it. He was never even aware that the money had come from Hughes. All he ever knew was that his mother had borrowed some money for his brother from an accountant.

Ehrlichman understood. The president was giving him the official line, rehearsing it, getting ready for the scandal that had cost him the 1960 election to resurface.

Nixon was clearly upset. He railed on and on about his "stupid brother" getting involved all over again with Hughes. Never once did he mention his own $100,000. But Nixon now knew that Rebozo had already been drawn into the IRS investigation. And he had to wonder how long it would be before the revenue agents followed Jack Anderson's lead and opened up Bebe's little tin box.

But it was not Bebe or his brother, not Anderson or the IRS, not Maheu or Bennett or Greenspun who triggered the final series of events that led to Nixon's downfall.

It was Clifford Irving.

Off in Ibiza, the expatriate novelist had been following the lurid story of the struggle for control of the secret Hughes empire. He decided that the billionaire was either dead or disabled—certainly in no shape to make a public appearance—and that gave him an idea. He would concoct his own epic and present it to the world as the autobiography of Howard Hughes.

The coup was announced December 7, 1971. McGraw-Hill said it would soon publish Hughes's personal memoirs, his true life story as told to Clifford Irving.

It became an immediate worldwide sensation. The Hughes organization branded the book a hoax, but with the billionaire himself unseen and silent, that only added to the hoopla. And nowhere did the book arouse more intense interest than at the White House.

Haldeman told Colson and Dean to find out what was in Irving's manuscript. Bennett soon made contact, once more pushing a criminal investigation of Maheu, who he was sure had put Irving up to it, supplied inside information on Hughes, and orchestrated the entire caper.

"Is the book hard on Nixon?" asked Dean. "Yes," replied Bennett, "*very* hard on Nixon."

Haldeman started getting FBI reports on the Irving affair directly from J. Edgar Hoover, and finally the White House managed to obtain a copy of the still secret manuscript from a source at McGraw-Hill.

It came as quite a shock. Irving claimed that Hughes had passed $400,000 to Nixon when the latter was vice-president, in return for fixing the TWA case. It was an inspired guess, the $400,000 figure probably not far off the mark.* To Nixon it must have looked as if Irving had the real story, and it hardly mattered whether he had it from Maheu or Hughes.

And the imaginative Irving had just begun. Next came his tale of the big double-cross. It was Hughes himself who had sabotaged Nixon in 1960. Angry that Nixon had not come through on TWA, the disgruntled recluse had intentionally leaked the "loan scandal" story to columnist Drew Pearson.

"Nobody was raising a hand to help me," Irving quoted Hughes as saying. "So I leaked the details to Drew Pearson. I got someone to whisper it into Mr. Pearson's ear, where to look. Now whether it actually turned the tide of the election or not, I don't know."

And there sat Richard Nixon, reading that in the Oval Office—having just bombed his benefactor in Las Vegas and gassed him in the Bahamas—and now holding another $100,000 in secret cash from Howard Hughes.

Friday, January 7, 1972. A day like any other day in the Paradise Island penthouse. Except that on this day Howard Hughes would break more than fifteen years of public silence and speak to the world.

---

*Counting the $205,000 "loaned" to Donald, the cost of Maheu's covert action to crush the "Dump Nixon" movement in 1956, and unreported campaign contributions, including the "all-out support" Hughes secretly gave Nixon in 1960, Irving's claim of $400,000 was probably just about right. And nobody knew about most of that money. Except Hughes.

He had been awake since 11:30 the night before, not preparing for his big debut, but sitting in his Barcalounger and watching a spy movie, *Funeral in Berlin*. He watched it twice in a row, meanwhile picking at a piece of chicken, interrupting his meal and his movie for frequent but futile trips to the bathroom.

At 12:45 P.M., the double feature finally over, Hughes reached down to his black metal box, pulled out a drug bottle, and counted his codeine tablets. He had fifty left. He took eight of the precious white pills, dissolved them in pure bottled spring water, and shot the big fix into his long spindly arm.

He then eased back into his lounge chair, feeling again that wonderful warm rush, and called for a third showing of *Funeral in Berlin*.

It was 6:45 P.M. when the hopped-up recluse finally reached for his telephone and prepared to meet the press. A month had passed since Clifford Irving made him the unseen center of global attention, and now the mystery man himself was about to speak. Three thousand miles away, at the other end of the line, seven carefully selected reporters waited expectantly in a Hollywood hotel.

The disembodied voice quickly disposed of Irving: "I don't know him. I never saw him. I never even heard of him until a matter of a few days ago when this thing first came to my attention."

A few days ago? Where had he been? And by now there was another big question. Was Hughes still alive, did the phantom exist, or was this voice on the phone some imposter?

Most of the press conference was devoted to "identification questions." At first hesitant, ill at ease, Hughes soon began to enjoy the big quiz game. Off in his isolation booth, not quite sure what these reporters were after, asking all these arcane questions about his past exploits, Hughes nonetheless didn't wish to be stumped. He did very well on the airplane questions, but missed a lot of easy ones about people.

Sitting there naked, with his hair halfway down his back, and his fingernails protruding, Hughes casually dismissed tales of his bizarre appearance.

"I keep in fair shape," he replied when asked about his physical condition, and then launched into a lengthy discussion of his daily manicures. "I have always kept my fingernails at a reasonable length," he said. "I take care of them the same way I always have, the same way I did when I went around the world and at the time of the flight of the flying boat. I cut them with clippers, not with scissors and a nail file the way some people do."

To the press he promised photos, but when his aides later suggested he actually do it—"you should make every effort to get your hair and nails attended to as soon as possible, and if you can bring yourself to do it, have a photograph taken"—Hughes recoiled in horror.

"This is not a beauty contest," he scribbled. "I am only required to demonstrate that I am alive and competent."

But at the press conference, only once did Hughes display any real anger. It was directed not at Clifford Irving, but Robert Maheu. Asked why he had fired his regent, Hughes flew into a rage. "Because he's a no-good, dishonest son of a bitch, and he stole me blind," he shouted. "The money's gone, and he's got it."

Almost in passing, toward the end of the three-hour interview, there was a question about his reported dealings with Nixon and Rebozo.

"Certainly none with Rebozo," replied Hughes, handling this as calmly as the inquiry about his fingernails. "Now, regarding Mr. Nixon, I have tried not to bother him since he's been in office, and I've made no effort to contact him."

The press conference over, Hughes settled back to watch another movie, *Topaz,* shot up four more grains of codeine, then stayed up all night for a fourth and fifth screening of *Funeral in Berlin.* Finally, at eleven the next morning, he swallowed four blue bombers and fell asleep.

All the while his paranoia over Hughes mounted, the president had been pushing his men to set up a covert intelligence operation for his 1972 reelection campaign.

Nixon already had a secret police force operating out of the White House basement, but that gang, the Plumbers, handled "national security leaks." What the president now wanted was a team targeted on the Democrats. The failure of his staff to nail Larry O'Brien showed the need for some real professionals.

To lead the new gang, Nixon's campaign manager, Attorney General John Mitchell, chose a former FBI agent, G. Gordon Liddy. A gun fanatic who liked to watch old Nazi propaganda films, Liddy had already made his bones as a Plumber, staging a break-in at the offices of Daniel Ellsberg's psychiatrist.

He reported for work at the Committee for the Re-election of the President on December 8, 1971, the day after Clifford Irving's book was first announced. And now, as Liddy prepared his espionage plan, the fallout from the Irving caper brought Nixon's paranoia to full boil.

The billionaire's bizarre press conference had only focused yet more attention on Irving, on Hughes himself, and on Nixon.

It all came together January 16, 1972, in a headline on the front page of the *New York Times:* "HUGHES-NIXON TIES DESCRIBED IN BOOK." The story said that Hughes had told Irving all about his Nixon connection, but gave no details.

A week later the *Times* revealed that Bobby Kennedy, as attorney general, had secretly investigated the Hughes-Nixon dealings and considered prosecuting Nixon himself, as well as members of his family. That story particularly enraged the president, and he called Bobby "a ruthless little bastard."

"He wanted to bring criminal charges against my *mother*!" exclaimed Nixon, adding that it was typical of the Kennedys.

And that same day, January 24, the equally feared and hated Jack Anderson repeated his allegation that Nixon had received $100,000 from Hughes through Rebozo, this time adding that he had "documentary evidence" to back it up.

Still, nothing happened, and the president maintained his tortured silence about the payoff, waiting once more for the full story to explode. The press and the Kennedys were clearly out to get him again, to ruin him with another Hughes scandal.

And the ammunition they needed might right now be locked inside a huge green safe, sitting in a Las Vegas newspaper office, under an autographed picture of Richard Nixon.

On February 3, the *New York Times* reported that Maheu's pal Hank Greenspun—who was also known to be close to Jack Anderson—had two hundred secret Hughes memos, some handwritten by the billionaire himself, giving "precise instructions on approaches to be taken in delicate matters."

At eleven o'clock the next morning, G. Gordon Liddy presented his espionage plans to John Mitchell in the attorney general's office. Also at the big meeting were John Dean and Mitchell's deputy campaign chief, Jeb Stuart Magruder.

They had all been there a week earlier to hear Liddy outline a million-dollar operation code-named "Gemstone," for which he had already recruited safecrackers, wiremen, call girls, thugs, and professional killers ("twenty-two dead so far," noted Liddy), a team assembled to carry out his program of kidnapping, blackmail, mugging, bugging, break-ins, and black-bag jobs, all aimed at the president's political foes.

Mitchell had not approved it. "Gordon, that's not quite what we had in mind," said the attorney general. "The money you're asking for is way out of line. Why don't you tone it down a little, then we'll talk again."

Now Liddy was back. He presented a scaled-down version of the same plan, one that concentrated more on burglaries and wiretaps. It would cost half a million.

Mitchell did not give it his final approval—the price still seemed high—but he did suggest two targets. Larry O'Brien's office at Democratic National Committee headquarters. And Hank Greenspun's safe.

Liddy immediately began to plan the Greenspun job, plotting it with his partner in the Ellsberg break-in, a former CIA agent named E. Howard Hunt, who was already working for both Chuck Colson at the White House and Howard Hughes's man in Washington, Bob Bennett.

Indeed, Bennett played a central role in the Greenspun caper. He apparently suggested the burglary to Hunt a few days before Mitchell approved it—as a kind of joint venture—and now he introduced Hunt and Liddy to Hughes security chief Ralph Winte.

They met again the weekend of February 20, in a plush suite at the Beverly Wilshire in Los Angeles. Winte had prepared a hand-drawn diagram of Greenspun's office, the location of his safe marked by a big X. Liddy had the job all figured. The Nixon gang would handle the break-in, bust open the safe, throw the stolen Hughes memos into a canvas bag, and hop on a waiting Hughes jet that would fly them directly to some secret Central American rendezvous point, where the Nixon men and the Hughes men would meet to divide up the booty.

"Gee!" said Winte. "Suppose you get caught?"

"Don't worry about that," replied Hunt. "We're professionals!"

The Hughes high command, however, had no interest in the plot and refused to supply the getaway jet. Liddy was crestfallen. He continued to case Greenspun's office, but without the airplane the mission did not have the same appeal, and it appears that the break-in was never attempted.

Nixon was getting impatient. Months had passed since he first ordered a covert intelligence operation, and still there were no results. In fact, Mitchell still had not approved Liddy's overall plan.

The president called Haldeman into the Oval Office. "When are they going to *do* something over there?" he demanded, drumming his fingers on the desk.

Haldeman told his expediter, Gordon Strachan, to get action, and Strachan called Mitchell's deputy, Jeb Magruder.

"The president wants it done, and there's to be no more arguing about it," Strachan told Magruder, and the pressure from the White House continued.

More and more the pressure focused on Larry O'Brien.

A new scandal had erupted, and O'Brien was leading the attack. Late in February, Jack Anderson revealed that Nixon had killed an antitrust suit against ITT in return for a donation of $400,000 to the Republican convention. It was O'Brien who first made the accusation months earlier, and Nixon believed that he was somehow behind the Anderson exposé. If the two of them could make this much trouble over ITT, imagine what they could do with the Hughes hundred grand.

Day after day O'Brien kept the ITT scandal in the headlines, and an enraged Nixon turned to Chuck Colson. Colson was his ass-kicker, the man who would do anything, the man with whom Nixon shared his darkest fantasies. "One day we will get *them*," he would tell Colson, speaking of all his enemies. "We'll get them on the ground where we want them. And we'll stick our heels in, step on them hard and twist—right, Chuck, right?" And Colson would reply, "Yes, sir, we'll get them."

Now the president called Colson into his hideaway rooms at the Executive Office Building and railed at him about ITT and Larry O'Brien. It was an outrage, said Nixon. O'Brien of all people making noise about ITT underwriting the Republican convention. Shit, Howard Hughes was underwriting the Democratic National Committee. O'Brien was on his damn payroll!

At about that same time, Howard Hunt, who was on Colson's payroll, brought his partner Liddy in to see Colson. Liddy complained that he couldn't get anyone to approve his espionage plan. Colson immediately picked up his phone and called Jeb Magruder.

"Why don't you guys get off the stick and get Liddy's budget approved?" demanded Colson. "We need information, particularly on O'Brien."

Jeb Magruder was tense as he headed over to the attorney general's office to see his boss, John Mitchell. They had been meeting regularly, two or three times a week, ever since Magruder had been named deputy director of the Committee for the Re-election of the President a year earlier, and the young man's open, easy manner had enabled him to develop a close working relationship with his usually reserved boss.

But now in late February, Magruder was troubled. All this pressure from the White House was getting to him. And he didn't want to go ahead with Liddy's intelligence operation.

Magruder met with Mitchell, as always, in a small, cluttered room just off the huge, ceremonial attorney general's office that Mitchell rarely used, and handled some routine campaign business.

Finally, Magruder brought up "Gemstone."

"Why do we even have to do this?" he asked.

"The president wants it done," said Mitchell. "We need to get information on O'Brien."

Magruder already knew that, and not just from Colson or Strachan. He had been in Mitchell's office a few weeks earlier when Nixon himself called. While he could hear only Mitchell's side of the conversation, it was clear that the president was pushing his attorney general to nail O'Brien.

Still, Magruder asked why. Why O'Brien? Everybody knew that party headquarters was a useless place to go for inside information on a presidential campaign.

Mitchell, who rarely showed any emotion, remained impassive as he revealed to Magruder the true motive for Watergate. His disclosure, the only one by anybody directly involved, has never before been made public.

There was some concern about a contribution, said the attorney general. The $100,000 that Howard Hughes had given Nixon through Rebozo, the transaction Jack Anderson had already reported. The money had not gone into the campaign, added Mitchell. Rebozo still had it. In fact, some of the money had already been spent.

And Larry O'Brien knew.

Mitchell said he had heard from Hank Greenspun—it wasn't clear whether he meant directly from Greenspun or through others—that O'Brien knew all about the $100,000 and also knew that it had been passed to Rebozo long after the 1968 campaign.

It was important to find out what else O'Brien knew, and to get solid information on his own Hughes connection—to keep him quiet about Nixon.

A few weeks later, on March 30, at a meeting with Magruder in Key Biscayne, John Mitchell approved Liddy's espionage plan. And he also approved the first target—Larry O'Brien's office at the Watergate.

The first break-in was a great success. On Memorial Day weekend a team led by Liddy and Hunt entered Democratic National Committee headquarters, bugged O'Brien's telephone, photographed papers from his desk, and made a clean getaway.*

But the O'Brien bug never worked, and Mitchell ordered Liddy back in. None of the burglars was ever told the true purpose of the break-in—no one ever told them about the Hughes connection—but this time Magruder did tell Liddy to photograph O'Brien's "shit file" on Nixon, to find out what dirt he had on the president.

They never found out. At 2:30 Saturday morning, June 17, 1972, the police rushed in and broke up the second attempt at a third-rate burglary.

Richard Nixon was with Bebe Rebozo on Robert Abplanalp's private island in the Bahamas when his burglars were caught at the Watergate, just as he had been three years earlier when he first received word that Howard Hughes had approved the $100,000 payoff that led to the break-in.

He returned to Key Biscayne early the next day, Sunday, June 18, and apparently learned of the big bust from his morning newspaper. He called Haldeman at the nearby Key Biscayne Hotel.

"What's the crazy item about the DNC, Bob?" asked the president, affecting a lighthearted tone. "Why would anyone break into a National Committee headquarters? Track down Magruder and see what he knows about it."

The president maintained his bemused air with Haldeman through

---

*A second phone was also bugged. It belonged to Spencer Oliver, one of O'Brien's deputies, whose father happened to work for Robert Bennett and was assigned to the Hughes account. A remarkable coincidence, especially given the fact that Hunt also worked for Bennett, but it seems that this phone was picked by pure chance. Transcripts of that wiretap were passed to both Mitchell and Haldeman but revealed only that a secretary in Oliver's office had an incredibly active sex life.

the long weekend but meanwhile made a frantic series of phone calls to Colson, at one point so agitated he threw an ashtray across the room. On his first day back in Washington, Nixon finally revealed his terror to Haldeman as well.

The tape of their June 20 Oval Office conversation was later erased, creating the famous eighteen-and-a-half-minute gap. But according to Haldeman, it was in this talk—the one some "sinister force" was later so desperate to obliterate—that Nixon himself revealed the Hughes connection to Watergate.

The following account of their meeting is Haldeman's reconstruction.

"On that DNC break-in, have you heard that anyone in the White House is involved?" Nixon asked his chief of staff.

"No one," replied Haldeman.

"Well, I'm worried about Colson," confessed Nixon. "Colson can talk about the president, if he cracks. You know I was on Colson's tail for months to nail Larry O'Brien on the Hughes deal."

Nixon feared it was Colson who had triggered the break-in. He had been pushing all his men to get to the bottom of O'Brien's Hughes connection, and now he seemed not to know which of them had actually sent the burglars into O'Brien's office at the Watergate. He first thought it was Colson, not Mitchell, apparently because he had conspired most directly with his hatchetman.*

"Colson told me he was going to get the information I wanted one way or the other," said Nixon. "And that was O'Brien's office they were bugging, wasn't it? And who's behind it? Colson's boy Hunt. Christ."

Haldeman wasn't so sure. "Magruder never even mentioned Colson," he noted.

"He will," replied Nixon. "Colson called him and got the whole operation started. Right from the goddamn White House. With Hunt and Liddy sitting in his lap."

The president was scared. "I hate things like this. We're not in control. Well, we'll just have to hang tough. In fact, we better go on the attack."

---

*In fact, a Colson aide, Ken Clawson, would later tell Haldeman that Colson had secretly recorded phone calls with Nixon both before and after the break-in, and was using his tapes to blackmail the president. "He's got Nixon on the floor," said Clawson. "He's got on tape just what Nixon said all through the whole Watergate mess." What makes these still hidden Colson tapes special, of course, is that Nixon did not know he was being recorded.

Epilogue II

The Final Days

Howard Hughes awoke at precisely the same moment that Richard Nixon's nightmare began.

It was still Friday night, July 16, in Vancouver, Canada, when the Watergate bust went down. At 11:30 the naked billionaire got up out of bed in his new penthouse hideaway at the Bayshore Inn. He made his way from the bed to his Barcalounger, reached for his remote-control instrument, turned on his television, and started to watch a late movie, *The Brain That Would Not Die*.

He soon switched to a western, *Billy the Kid Outlawed*, and began picking at a piece of chicken that would take him nearly three hours to get down.

Bored with TV, he called for his Mormons to show him a movie on the screen set up in his bedroom. He watched *The Mad Room*, followed it with *The Silencers*, and stayed up all that night, all through the next day, and all through the next night, alternating showings of *Shanghai Express* and *Captain Newman, M.D.*, before finishing his thirty-four-hour weekend film festival with *The World of Suzie Wong* and falling asleep at 10:30 Sunday morning.

It would be more than a year before Hughes discovered there was a Watergate crisis, and he would remain forever puzzled by reports that he might somehow be involved in it.

But Hughes had not merely been watching movies while his specter drove Nixon to Watergate. He had been through quite a few adventures of his own on his way to this new blacked-out bedroom.

Back in February he had been forced to flee Paradise Island when Bahamian immigration authorities raided his penthouse. It was another fallout of the Clifford Irving affair. The publicity triggered an official inquiry and, rather than face it, Hughes left by the fire escape while the local lawmen pounded on his door.

The escape, however, led to the first revelation of his bizarre appearance. The skipper of a yacht chartered to smuggle Hughes off the island got a good look at his strange cargo and some weeks later told his tale to the press.

It was not that the billionaire had hair down past his shoulders or that he was wearing only a bathrobe that struck the captain as weird. It was his toenails. "They were so long they curled up," he told a Miami newspaper. "Never seen anything like that in my life. I had to look twice. Craziest thing I ever saw."

Hughes next took refuge in Nicaragua, under the personal protection of the country's dictator, General Anastasio Somoza. After his narrow escape from the Bahamas, however, Hughes was taking no chances. He decided to offer the general a friendly bribe.

"I think that while Somoza is being so decent to me in the face of all this bad publicity," wrote Hughes, "something might happen tomorrow to change all this.

"The Central and South American people are very emotional and changeable. So before this happens, I think I should make a present to Somoza.

"I suggest a *really* desirable automobile. We should find out whether he likes to drive himself and would prefer a sports car, or a very elaborate limousine with a bar and telephone and TV set, and the very last word in accessories.

"Also, I want to be *damn sure* he (Somoza) is told *loud* and *clear* that this was *my personal idea* because I appreciate the considerate treatment he has shown me."

Somoza, however, had a bigger reward in mind. He asked Hughes to bail out his country's bankrupt airline, which the general himself happened to own. Hughes bought 25 percent of the stock. The dictator was not satisfied. He offered his guest an interest in his plywood factory, his pharmaceuticals company, and some choice local real estate.

Less than a month after his arrival, Hughes decided to leave Nicaragua, before Somoza tried to sell him anything else. But on the way out he made an extraordinary decision. He would break fifteen years of isolation and meet with his host.

Preparations for the big meeting began two days in advance. Hughes watched a movie, *Mirage,* then called in an aide to create his own illusion. For the first time in years he had one of the Mormons cut his hair, trim his beard, and pare those toenails. After four hours of grooming, he even took a shower.

It was a new man who welcomed Somoza and U.S. Ambassador Turner Shelton aboard his Gulfstream jet at 10:45 P.M. on March 13, greeting both with a firm handshake. They chatted until midnight, and when his guests left, Hughes shook hands again.

Hughes, his public image restored, flew off to Vancouver and arrived in broad daylight. Now quite bold, even reckless, he sauntered through the hotel lobby in his bathrobe, and once up in his penthouse paused at the window to watch a seaplane land in the harbor.

The Mormons were not pleased. They quickly hustled Hughes into his new blacked-out bedroom, warning of spies with telephoto lenses—"we know that we are presently being surveilled"—and their boss passively reverted to a life of hiding, of movies, and of drugs.

While the White House burglars plotted the break-in back in Washington, Hughes lay in a stupor watching *Diamonds Are Forever,* a James Bond movie about a reclusive billionaire held prisoner in his Las Vegas penthouse, his empire run by an evil imposter. And Hughes was still in that darkened room, watching *The Brain That Would Not Die,* when the burglars were busted at Watergate.

But if Hughes himself remained oblivious of Watergate, his henchmen were becoming ever more entangled in it. Back in Washington, the mysterious Bob Bennett immediately assumed a central role in the cover-up, acting as go-between for Liddy and Hunt, all the while doing his best to expose it, reporting not to Hughes or even his fellow Mormons, but to the CIA and the *Washington Post.*

On July 10, over lunch at a Marriott Hot Shoppes, Bennett came in from the cold. To his CIA case officer, Martin Lukasky, he passed on everything he had learned about Watergate from Hunt and Liddy. He said that the White House was behind the break-in and pointed the finger at his pal Chuck Colson: "Colson most likely suggested the break-in to Hunt on an 'I don't want to know, just get me the information' basis."

Lukasky deemed Bennett's report so sensitive that he hand-carried it to CIA Director Richard Helms.

The report revealed that Bennett was busy on several fronts, all aimed at undermining the cover-up. He had established "back-door entry" to Edward Bennett Williams, the lawyer representing Larry O'Brien in a million-dollar civil suit filed against Nixon's campaign committee.

And he was talking to the press—to the *Washington Star,* to the *New York Times,* to *Newsweek,* and the *Los Angeles Times.* According to a CIA report, "Bennett took relish in implicating Colson in Hunt's activities, while protecting the Agency at the same time."

But most of all Bennett was talking to the *Washington Post.* He told the CIA he was feeding stories to Bob Woodward, who was "suitably grateful," making no attribution to Bennett and protecting his valued source.

Later, much later, Nixon would tell Haldeman that he believed Bob Bennett was "Deep Throat," and he would wonder whether Hughes and the CIA had plotted together to bring him down.

For the moment, however, Nixon remained obsessed by Larry O'Brien. And just a month after the break-in he saw his chance to go back on the attack.

The president was sitting with his feet up on his desk, sipping a cup of coffee, when John Ehrlichman came to see him on July 24. Ehrlichman had just received the latest IRS "sensitive case report" from the still growing Hughes investigation. There was more bad news about Donald, but that was not the big news. A new name had popped up in the probe—Larry O'Brien. The IRS had turned up the dirt that all the president's men had failed to find: proof of O'Brien's Hughes connection.

Ehrlichman read it to Nixon: "Hughes Tool Company paid $190,000 to Lawrence F. O'Brien and Associates, Washington, D.C., during 1970. Purpose of these payments are unknown."

The president was excited. He took his feet down off his desk, swung around, and leaned toward Ehrlichman. "The American people have a right to know about this!" he declared. "The American people need to know that the chairman of one of its two great political parties was on Hughes's payroll."

Ehrlichman had rarely seen Nixon so excited. Even now, even after his pursuit had led him to Watergate, the president remained determined to nail O'Brien on Hughes.

"This made a lot of trouble for me, and it's going to make a lot of trouble for O'Brien," said Nixon. He was sure that the IRS had uncovered only the tip of the iceberg, that O'Brien had received a lot more Hughes money, and that he had probably failed to report it all on his tax returns. He told Ehrlichman to order a full audit of O'Brien's financial records and to get him for income-tax evasion.

"I want to put O'Brien in jail," said the president, pounding his fist on the desk. "And I want to do it before the election."

Ehrlichman immediately called Nixon's man in the commissioner's office, who took a surreptitious look at O'Brien's returns and found that he had received a whopping $325,000 from Hughes but had reported it all and paid his taxes.

Nixon was not satisfied. He had Ehrlichman call Secretary of the Treasury George Shultz and tell him to push the O'Brien audit. Shultz reported back that O'Brien's returns had been examined and everything was in order.

Nixon was still not satisfied. He had Ehrlichman call Shultz again and demand that O'Brien be interrogated. The IRS interviewed him in mid-August and informed the White House that the audit was closed. Ehrlichman demanded that it be reopened.

Finally, Shultz reviewed the case with IRS Commissioner Johnnie Walters and together they called Ehrlichman to report that there was nothing against O'Brien. "I'm goddamn tired of your foot-dragging tactics," shouted Ehrlichman, and he continued to abuse Walters until the commissioner hung up.

Nixon had been foiled again on O'Brien, but his cover-up of Watergate had succeeded. On September 15, a federal grand jury indicted only the five burglars and their ringleaders, Liddy and Hunt, ignoring their masters in the White House.

Nixon was not content, however, merely to beat the rap. He wanted revenge. Not merely against O'Brien but all his enemies.

"I want the most comprehensive notes on all of those that have tried to do us in," he told Dean that same day. "They are asking for it and they are going to get it. We have not used the power in the first four years, as you know. We have never used it. We haven't used the Bureau and we haven't used the Justice Department, but things are going to change now."

"What an exciting prospect!" exclaimed Dean.

A few weeks later, on November 7, 1972, Richard Nixon was reelected president in an unprecedented landslide.

Howard Hughes did not send in an absentee ballot, but he did send a check. Several checks, in fact, totaling $150,000. But he was still worried that he had not done enough.

"Why didn't Chester do more in the area of contributions?" asked Hughes, now back in Nicaragua.

"We gave as much as we could safely," his aides assured him, adding that his generosity was appreciated. "Because of the polls, which indicated a Republican landslide, contributions dried up and many committees were completely out of money when we came along like angels out of heaven."

Nixon had not waited for Hughes to descend with the manna. In the spring of 1972, even as his fears about the original hundred grand were leading him to Watergate, even as the break-in was being planned and approved, the president had reached out for more Hughes money. It was a fatal attraction he apparently just could not resist.

Rebozo called his pal Danner in March or April and asked if Hughes was going to make another "contribution." Danner explained that he was no longer the bagman, but Rebozo was not put off so easily. "Try to find out," he insisted. Danner checked with his new bosses, Gay and Davis, but was told not to get involved, that the matter was being handled "back East." And so it was.

Bob Bennett was taking care of everything. While he continued to secretly undermine the cover-up with leaks to the *Washington Post* and reports to the CIA, the mysterious Mormon was also slipping more Hughes money to Nixon.

Even before Rebozo called Danner, Bennett had advised his fellow Mormons to make a "voluntary, unsolicited, sizeable contribution," but nothing "so ostentatious as to appear to be an attempt to 'buy' something." They settled on $50,000.

On the morning of April 6, one day before a new law took effect requiring that donors to political campaigns be identified, Gordon Liddy took time off from plotting the break-in and dropped by Bennett's office to pick up the money. So much secret cash was pouring in before the deadline that even Liddy had been pressed into service as a collector.

By the time of the November election, Nixon had accumulated a staggering $60 million and had a huge surplus. But he wanted more. On the weekend before the election, Bennett got a call from Thomas Evans, a partner in Nixon and Mitchell's old law firm (which now shared Washington office space with the president's campaign committee).

"I'm just checking, is Mr. Hughes going to give any more?" asked Evans, claiming that the money was needed to help cover Nixon's "deficit." Bennett asked how much more was needed. Evans said $100,000.

Hughes had planned to give the president only $50,000 more, and give another $50,000 to his opponent, George McGovern, but now he decided to turn over the entire hundred grand to the needy Nixon. Just like an angel out of heaven.

All Bennett asked in return was that the president call Hughes on Christmas Eve to wish him a happy birthday. Although Nixon was preoccupied with planning the Christmas bombing of North Vietnam, he agreed to call his benefactor. It would be their first direct contact.

As it turned out, however, Hughes had more urgent business to handle on his birthday. On December 23, one day before he turned sixty-seven, Howard Hughes was routed from his Nicaraguan penthouse by a massive earthquake that leveled most of Managua.

He was sitting naked in his lounge chair at 12:30 A.M. when the quake struck. He had just finished a twenty-four-hour film festival and called for another movie when the first violent shock toppled a heavy soundtrack amplifier that nearly crushed him. A Mormon rushed in and caught the speaker just before it hit his frail boss.

The room was still heaving, the lights had gone out, and chunks of plaster were falling from the ceiling, but Hughes remained calm. In fact, he refused to leave. "We'll stay right here," he told his frantic aides, and again asked for his movie.

The Mormons, certain the entire hotel was about to collapse, coaxed Hughes onto a stretcher and started to carry him down nine flights of stairs, but Hughes suddenly demanded they go back. He had forgotten his drug box.

The billionaire spent the night huddled under a blanket in the backseat of a Mercedes while the aftershocks continued, the earth split open across the city, buildings crumbled, fires raged out of control, and the death toll mounted to more than five thousand.

At sunrise, the Mercedes drove through the devastation, down streets clogged with rubble and dead bodies, past thousands of dazed homeless victims, taking Hughes to the safety of Somoza's country palace. Secluded in a plush cabana alongside the dictator's swimming pool, Hughes for the first time showed fear. He insisted that a blanket be draped across the windows, afraid that someone might see him.

That night, in the chaos of Managua's airport, Hughes was loaded onto a private Lear jet and flew back for the first time in two years to America, landing just after midnight on the day before Christmas at Fort Lauderdale, Florida.

Where the IRS was waiting for him with a subpoena. Instead of a birthday call from the president, Hughes was greeted by a surprise party of revenue agents. The tax probe that Intertel had instigated against Maheu, the runaway investigation that had already reached into the White House, had finally turned against Hughes himself.

Trapped in his hangared jet, surrounded by tax men demanding to board the plane, Hughes frantically maneuvered to escape the subpoena. His aides called Chester Davis. The gruff attorney ordered the agents to hold off until he contacted IRS headquarters in Washington. They agreed to wait, but only for half an hour.

Twenty minutes later, a triumphant Davis called back. He said he had spoken to IRS Intelligence Chief John Olsiewski, who reportedly roused Commissioner Walters out of bed, and told the agents in Fort Lauderdale they would soon get orders to scuttle their mission.

At 2:15 A.M. the district chief called from Jacksonville. As Davis had predicted, he told his men to back off, forget the subpoena, stay off the plane, and instead merely let a customs inspector read Hughes an IRS statement requesting a voluntary interview.

The besieged Hughes resisted even that. Through the closed door of the jet the waiting agents heard a shouted conversation, and then one voice rising above the others, screaming "No, no!"

Finally, however, the customs man was allowed on board. He made his way to the back of the darkened plane and turned a flashlight on a bearded old man whose face was half hidden by a black hat pulled down past his ears. The agent handed him the IRS interview request and asked if he understood it. The man in the black hat said he did. That was the last time any U.S. government official would see Howard Hughes alive.

He flew off to London, where arrangements had been made with the Rothschilds for a penthouse suite at their posh Inn on the Park Hotel, overlooking Buckingham Palace. By four in the morning, an hour and a half after checking into his new hideout, Hughes had settled back into his familiar routine, picking up where he left off before the earthquake, sitting on his Barcalounger watching a movie, *The Deserter*.

He had been in London less than two weeks, however, when news from the States sent his spirits soaring. On January 10, 1973, the Supreme Court handed down its long-awaited decision in the TWA case. It was a stunning victory for Hughes. Reversing all lower-court findings, the high court dismissed the case he had lost by default when he refused to appear ten years earlier, and threw out the judgment that with interest now totaled $180 million.

Hughes was ecstatic. He decided to celebrate, to break free of his earthbound prison, to relive his past glory—to fly again!

The Final Days

The Mormons were shocked. Hughes had not piloted a plane for a dozen years, had rarely left his bed in the time since, his eyesight was so bad he couldn't read without a magnifying glass, and of course he didn't have a valid pilot's license. No matter. He was going to fly. He sent his aides in search of the proper outfit, a leather flight jacket and a snap-brim Stetson, like the one he had worn back in the 1930s when he had broken all the records. He also started to watch a steady stream of airplane movies—*Zeppelin, Helicopter Spies, Doomsday Flight, The Crowded Sky,* and *Skyjacked.*

Months passed while Hughes readied himself for the big event. Finally it was set for Sunday, June 10. The night before he watched *Strategic Air Command* twice and that morning called in an aide to groom him. It took four hours to cut his hair, trim his beard, clip his long nails, and get him dressed, but shortly before two P.M. he slipped out of the hotel and headed for Hatfield Airport, just north of London.

There a private jet waited. Hughes inspected the Hawker Siddeley 748, settled into the pilot's seat—and stripped off his clothes. Naked now except for the trademark brown fedora, Hughes gripped the controls and took off.

He spent all that day flying, an experienced English co-pilot who hoped to sell him the plane at his side, and he flew twice more in July, by now quite at home again in the skies.

It was during this time of high adventure that Howard Hughes discovered Watergate. He was looking at a picture of an airplane in the *London Express* when he noticed a story about the crisis he had unwittingly caused.

"What's Watergate?" he asked. It was the first time he had seen the word. His Mormons tried to explain, but Hughes didn't understand and soon lost interest.

A few weeks later, on August 9, Hughes got up in the middle of the night to go to the bathroom, lost his footing, fell to the floor, and fractured his hip.

His flying days were over. He would never get out of bed again.

By the time Hughes discovered Watergate, Nixon's condition had also taken a sudden turn for the worse. On the morning of March 21, John Dean came into the Oval Office to give the president his bleak diagnosis.

"We have a cancer—within—close to the presidency, that's growing," said Dean. The malignancy had spread through the entire White House, and the cover-up was about to blow.

"We're being blackmailed," said the shaken young counsel. Already more than $350,000 in hush money had been passed to the burglars, and they were demanding still more.

"It's going to be a continual blackmail operation by Hunt and Liddy and the Cubans," warned Dean. "It'll cost money. It's dangerous. People around here are not pros at this sort of thing. This is the sort of thing Mafia people can do: washing money, getting clean money, things like that."

Nixon was all business. "How much money do you need?" asked the president.

"I would say these people are going to cost a million dollars over the next two years," replied Dean.

"We could get that," said Nixon. "You could get a million dollars. And you could get it in cash. I, I know where it could be gotten."

Nixon was determined to handle Watergate the same way Hughes had tried to handle Nixon—with a big bribe. In fact, Nixon planned to use his accumulated payoffs, the money he had taken from Hughes and others, if need be the entire secret slush fund gathered by Rebozo, to buy his way out of Watergate.

As the scandal engulfed him in mid-April, Nixon sat with his last two stalwarts, Haldeman and Ehrlichman, told them they would probably have to resign—and offered them money from Bebe's little tin box.

"Legal fees will be substantial," said the president, desperate to buy off his two closest aides. "But there is a way we can get it to you, and uh—two or three hundred thousand dollars."

"Let's wait and see if it's necessary," replied Ehrlichman.

"No strain," Nixon quickly assured him. "Doesn't come outta me. I didn't, I never intended to use the money at all. As a matter of fact, I told B-B-Bebe, uh, basically, be sure that people like, uh, who, who have contributed money over the contributing years are, uh, favored and so forth in general. And he's used it for the purpose of getting things out, paid for in check and all that sort of thing."

Nixon was nervous. He stuttered and stammered, barely able to spit out the name of his personal bagman B-B-Bebe. This was the first time he had revealed to anyone that Rebozo maintained a secret fund for his personal use, cash gathered from "contributors" who were "favored and so forth in general." Clearly the Hughes $100,000 was just part of a much larger kitty.

"Very substantial" is all the president now told Haldeman and Ehrlichman, and he was still nervously pushing the money on his reluctant henchmen as they walked out the door.

"I want you to, I hope you'll let me know about the money," he said in parting. "Understand, there's no better use for it. Okay?"

Nixon made the offer all over again two weeks later when he called Haldeman and Ehrlichman out to Camp David to tell them the time had come, that they had to resign.

"It's like cutting off my arms," wailed Nixon, weeping now, but not at all certain this display of emotion was enough. Ehrlichman, especially, remained bitter and suggested that Nixon himself resign.

"You'll need money," said the president, desperately. "I have some—Bebe has it—and you can have it."

Ehrlichman shook his head. "That would just make things worse," he said, turning to go, leaving Nixon alone with his money.

Years later Nixon would tell TV interviewer David Frost that the cash he offered Haldeman and Ehrlichman was the $100,000 Rebozo got from Hughes, and it is tempting to believe that Nixon tried to buy his way out of Watergate with the same payoff that led him into it.

But, in fact, even as the president was trying to bribe his two closest aides, Bebe Rebozo was frantically trying to return that hot hundred grand to Howard Hughes.

There was only one problem. The money was gone.

At eight A.M. the next day, Monday, April 30—as Nixon prepared to announce the purge of his top White House staff in a nationally televised speech from the Oval Office—Rebozo met furtively in a room down the hall with the president's personal lawyer, Herb Kalmbach.

Rebozo was tense. He swore Kalmbach to secrecy, said he was there at the request of the "big man," and then revealed his big problem. It was the Hughes money.

The IRS, Rebozo said, had finally asked to see him about the unreported $100,000 "campaign contribution," the tax interview was just ten days away, and Rebozo told Kalmbach that he no longer had all the money. It had already been spent. And not for any campaign.

Rebozo said he had given some of the secret Hughes cash to

Nixon's two brothers, Edward and Donald, to the president's personal secretary, Rose Mary Woods, and to unnamed "others."

He asked Kalmbach what to do. Kalmbach was not merely the president's lawyer but also his backstage fund-raiser, the chief source of hush money for the Watergate burglars, and he realized that Rebozo was hoping he would volunteer to find fresh cash to replace the missing Hughes money. He figured it was probably all gone. And he had a pretty good idea which unnamed "others" it had gone to. But Kalmbach had had it. He was through playing bagman for the "big man."

He told Rebozo to hire a good tax lawyer, return what was left of the $100,000 to Hughes, and come clean with the IRS.

Rebozo was shocked. "This touches the president and the president's family," he exclaimed. "I just can't do anything to add to his problems at this time, Herb."

On May 10, Rebozo met with the IRS. He did not come clean. He said he had kept the Hughes money intact and untouched in his safe-deposit box for three years and now planned to return it all. The bitter power struggle in the Hughes empire had made him nervous about putting it into Nixon's campaign. The president was not even aware of the contribution, not until Rebozo mentioned it to him a few weeks earlier. Nixon immediately said, "You ought to give it back." That was the whole story.

The IRS agents did not probe. They were not eager to interrogate the president's best friend. Indeed, although Danner had confirmed the $100,000 transaction a full year earlier, agents handling the Hughes case were refused permission to interview Rebozo until now. And before they had come to see him, Nixon's man in the IRS commissioner's office called the White House to ask if it was okay. "We're scared to death," he told Ehrlichman. "He's so close to the president."

As soon as the agents left, Rebozo started calling Richard Danner. He told his old pal to come to Washington immediately, but he didn't tell him why. Danner flew in on May 18. Only when they met over breakfast in Danner's room at the Madison Hotel did Rebozo reveal that he wanted to give back the Hughes money. He said he had the very same hundred-dollar bills Danner had delivered three years earlier. Rebozo stressed that repeatedly. The money was still in the original Las Vegas bank wrappers. It had never been touched. Not once. Not a penny.

Danner refused to take it. For two and a half hours they argued, but Danner wanted no part of it. The cash that Rebozo first feared was too hot to take, and now feared was too hot to keep, Danner feared was too hot to take back.

"It's *your* money," the Cuban shouted at him angrily.

"It's not my money," said Danner. "It's your money. And if I were in your place, I'd go see a lawyer."

Rebozo instead took Danner to see Nixon's other millionaire crony, Bob Abplanalp. "Do you like fresh trout?" asked the aerosol king. "I know just the place." They drove out to the airport, hopped on Abplanalp's private jet, and flew up to his lodge in the Catskills. Just for lunch. It was an impressive display of the rewards of good fellowship. But Danner remained unwilling to take back the Hughes money.

Rebozo was desperate to unload that cursed cash. He told Danner to stay in Washington over the weekend. The president wanted to see him. The three men met at Camp David on Sunday, May 20. It had been a bad week for Nixon. On May 17 the Senate Watergate Committee began its televised hearings. On May 18 Archibald Cox was named special prosecutor. And now Nixon was holed up alone at his rustic retreat preparing a "definitive statement" on Watergate, to be released Tuesday. But he took time off to see Danner.

The president exchanged a few pleasantries, then launched into a lengthy and passionate defense of himself. "I'm not guilty of anything," declared Nixon. He said he would weather the storm. He would *not* resign. The three old friends spoke for more than two hours, but all would later claim that no one mentioned the $100,000 Nixon had personally asked Danner to get from Hughes. Not in the hour they sat in the cabin. Not in the hour they walked together through Camp David in the light misting rain.

But Danner knew why he had been summoned to the mountaintop, and both before and after he met with the president, Rebozo pressed him again to take back the money. Danner refused.

A few days after the failed summit meeting, Rebozo told Nixon's new chief of staff Alexander Haig about the Hughes problem. Haig called Deputy Treasury Secretary William Simon and asked for a status report on the IRS case. Simon informed him that Rebozo was going to be audited.

Rebozo hired a good tax lawyer. On June 18, following his lawyer's advice, Bebe called the FBI's chief agent in Miami, an old friend, and asked him to come over to his Key Biscayne bank. They entered the vault, and there in the presence of the agent and his lawyer,

Rebozo opened safe-deposit box number 224. He slipped out two large manila envelopes and emptied bundles of hundred-dollar bills onto the table. It was the Hughes money, said Rebozo, and they counted it out.

There were no longer twenty bundles in bank wrappers, but ten bundles in rubber bands. Still, it was the same money he received, Rebozo insisted. He had simply removed the Las Vegas wrappers because of "the stigma applied to anything from Las Vegas."

And it was all there, every penny, in fact it had multiplied. The count came to $100,100. Rebozo could not explain the extra hundred-dollar bill.

The next day he brought it all to his lawyer's office, and prevailed on Danner to meet him there. Danner never showed. Finally, however, Danner put Rebozo in touch with Chester Davis, and the bluff Hughes attorney readily agreed to take back the money. "Be glad to accept it," said Davis without ceremony.

Rebozo immediately unloaded the loot on Abplanalp's corporate secretary, who handed it over to a Davis associate in New York on Wednesday, June 27, 1973.

Richard Nixon was finally rid of the Hughes cash, but he had not escaped the Hughes curse.

Out in Los Angeles one week later, on the Fourth of July, Robert Maheu blew the lid off the payoff.

Alone in a room with four lawyers, he celebrated the holiday by giving his deposition for a seventeen-million-dollar slander suit he had filed against Hughes, a suit triggered by his former boss's outburst at the Clifford Irving press conference, the angry accusation that Maheu "stole me blind."

It was the final act of their bitter divorce, and Maheu now openly revealed their most intimate dirty secrets.

"I have religiously protected Howard Hughes relative to political contributions," said Maheu, posing as the still faithful spouse. "I think I should warn you," he told the Hughes lawyers, "that if you want to push into the political world of Howard Hughes, I will put the consequences squarely on your shoulders."

And then he told the tale of the big Nixon bribe.

"Mr. Hughes wanted to own the presidents of the United States," said Maheu, and in the case of Nixon "certain political obligations had to be met." Half of the hundred-thousand-dollar contribution was in direct payment for Attorney General Mitchell's waiver of antitrust laws, the handshake deal he made with Danner that allowed Hughes to continue buying up Las Vegas. "Upon the return of Mr. Danner from Washington, D.C.," said Maheu, "I made available to Mr. Danner the sum of $50,000 for delivery to Mr. Rebozo."

When news of Maheu's sworn revelation reached the Senate Watergate Committee, a team of investigators began to explore the hidden transaction, to push into the political world of Howard Hughes, and to find there the world behind Watergate.

The Hughes connection burst into public view on October 10. For the first time, the hundred-thousand-dollar deal was front-page news across the country, and the senators announced that they planned to subpoena Rebozo, the entire Hughes gang, even Hughes himself, haul them all before the committee and question them live on national television.

Staff investigators had already grilled Rebozo in Key Biscayne. In that and subsequent testimony, the Cuban tried to explain why he had kept the money hidden for three years and then returned it.

"I didn't want to risk even the remotest embarrassment about any Hughes connection with Nixon," said Rebozo. "I was convinced that it cost the president the 1960 election and didn't help him in 1962 in California."

He admitted that he held on to the cash until the IRS came after him, afraid that any public disclosure might destroy Nixon.

"Here was a possibility that we get another Drew Pearson type series about Hughes money, and it goes on and on. It would break him forever."

Rebozo's fears were not unfounded. In the days that followed, Nixon's desperation to hide the Hughes payoff may have led him to take the final fatal step of his presidency—the Saturday Night Massacre.

It was a showdown that could have been avoided. Nixon was about to strike a deal on his White House tapes. He was moving toward a compromise with his respected attorney general, Elliot Richardson, that would bypass the hated special prosecutor, Archibald Cox, and keep the tapes hidden.

Instead of tapes, Nixon would release transcripts authenticated by Senator John Stennis, who was practically stone deaf. No one expected Cox to accept the deal, but Richardson was ready to go along with it, and Nixon was actually hoping that Cox would resign in protest.

Just as the deal was about to go down, however, the specter of the Hughes money apparently spooked Nixon into scuttling it.

On October 18, the day the final details were to be worked out with Richardson, Rebozo suddenly discovered that Cox had joined the Hughes investigation. A friendly IRS agent told him that the special prosecutor had demanded all files on the Hughes $100,000, and that same morning a banner headline in the *Miami Herald* declared: "COX BEGINS TAX PROBE OF REBOZO."

Back at the White House, Nixon flew into a rage. "That fucking Harvard professor is out to get me," he railed. "This proves it."

The president told Haig that he would not have Cox poking into Bebe's private affairs, that the Hughes money was none of his damn business. This was a perfect illustration of how Cox was out to get him, Nixon repeated angrily.*

For the moment, at least, it seemed that Nixon was more angry about the Hughes-Rebozo probe than about Cox's relentless pursuit of the tapes. And his hysteria about Hughes immediately began to undermine the carefully wrought "Stennis Compromise."

Haig called Richardson later that day. Before they even discussed the tapes, Haig let the attorney general know that Nixon would not stand still for a Hughes probe by Cox. The president, he said, didn't see what the special prosecutor's charter had to do with Rebozo or Hughes.

Late that night, Haig and Nixon's lawyers came to see the president. They told him they could still finesse the special prosecutor—force Cox to resign, yet keep Richardson aboard—if only the president would set aside the question of Cox's future access to tapes. Just leave that open, urged the lawyers; make the deal.

By nightfall, however, Nixon was in no mood for subtle strategies. He had been on the phone with Rebozo, he was furious about Cox's intrusion into the Hughes affair, and he wanted above all to get rid of the special prosecutor.

No more tapes, said the president. None, period. And Cox would have to agree to that in writing or be fired.

The next day, as Nixon headed for his inevitable showdown, Rebozo flew into Washington and installed himself at the White House for the duration of the siege.

---

*In fact, Cox had no personal involvement with the Hughes-Rebozo probe. He told his staff not to discuss *any* Hughes matters with him because Cox himself had a Hughes connection—his brother Maxwell was law partner of Chester Davis.

His presence always made Nixon more combative, especially when they were drinking together, and Nixon now began to spend much of his time alone with Rebozo. Haig did not know what they were saying to each other, but he had often before heard the two complain bitterly about the "unfair and unjust persecution" of Bebe over the Hughes money. Clearly it touched a raw nerve.

In a desperate effort to hide that payoff Nixon had already brought himself to the brink of ruin, and now his obsession with Hughes created an atmosphere in the White House that made compromise impossible.

Two days after he learned of the Hughes probe, on Saturday night, October 20, 1973, Nixon fired the special prosecutor. Attorney General Richardson and his chief deputy both resigned. Everyone called it the Saturday Night Massacre.

Within days twenty-two bills had been introduced in Congress calling for Nixon's impeachment.

Howard Hughes was also about to be called to justice.

It was not only Watergate that was closing in on him but also a side deal he had made with Nixon, his illegal Air West takeover the president had agreed to approve the same day Hughes agreed to give him the hundred-thousand-dollar payoff.

Early on the morning of December 20, Hughes fled London one jump ahead of the law. He boarded a jet borrowed from the Saudi arms merchant Adnan Khashoggi and flew back to the Bahamas, where two floors were reserved and waiting in a Freeport hotel owned by shipping magnate Daniel K. Ludwig.

Hughes had hardly settled in when he was indicted by a Las Vegas grand jury, accused of criminal fraud and stock manipulation in the Air West deal. He faced a possible twelve years in jail.

A fugitive from justice now, he desperately needed sanctuary, and the Bahamas seemed a safe bet. Just a few weeks before he arrived, the islands had refused to extradite another fugitive American financier, the notorious swindler Robert Vesco.

Hughes was taking no chances, however. He had not forgotten how he had been forced to flee the Bahamas in the wake of the Clifford Irving affair, and he was determined to buy off his new protector, Prime Minister Lynden O. Pindling.

"Regarding the Honorable P.M.," Hughes wrote Chester Davis,

"I truly admire his courage and the actions he has been brave enough to take.

"I urge you to tell him this: I would like to be of assistance. The question is: how much assistance does he need and how quickly?"

While Hughes dangled dollars in front of Pindling, Chester Davis was unloading the Nixon hundred grand Rebozo had unloaded on him. After resisting for months, he brought the cash under subpoena to the Senate Watergate Committee, opened his briefcase, and angrily dumped the hundred-dollar bills in front of a startled Senator Sam Ervin.

"Here's the goddamn money," shouted Davis. "Take it, burn it, do whatever you damn please with it!"

But the senators were not satisfied with the money. They also wanted Hughes. In mid-January, the committee sent Davis a letter asking the billionaire to appear. Soon after, Ervin approved a subpoena.

Down in the Bahamas, already on the lam, Hughes remained vague about Watergate, even as others began to wonder whether he was somehow at the center of it all.

In a memo dictated to the Mormons, Davis tried to explain the "Hughes connection" to Howard Hughes.

"We are involved in the Watergate affair to this extent:

"1. E. Howard Hunt, convicted for the Watergate break-in, was employed by Bob Bennett (our current Washington representative). In addition, Bennett was maintaining liaison with the White House through Chuck Colson, who was deeply involved in the Watergate cover-up.

"2. Bennett, Ralph Winte (employed by us re: security matters) and Hunt are involved in plans to burglarize Greenspun's safe, and even though those plans were rejected and never carried out, investigators see political motivation related to Watergate.

"3. The political contribution by Danner to Rebozo and visits by Danner to Mitchell, are claimed to be an effort for influencing Governmental decisions, including an alleged change in rulings of the Department of Justice.

"4. Payments made to Larry O'Brien and his employment has been claimed to have been part of the possible motivation for the Watergate break-in because of White House interest in that arrangement as a possible means of embarrassing O'Brien and the Democrats.

"5. The massive political contributions supposedly made by Maheu, particularly those made in cash, is part of the over-all Watergate investigation dealing with the need for reform."

Hughes was not satisfied with the explanation. Alternately puzzled and put upon, seemingly unable to recall the $100,000 payoff, he demanded that Davis bring the entire Watergate investigation to a halt. He was sure it was all a plot designed to force him out of hiding.

"I have not yet received further information identifying exactly who are the persons behind this determined effort to embarrass you in order to compel you to appear," wrote Davis, humoring his mad boss, but suggesting that perhaps it was instead a plot against Nixon.

"Since the Watergate incident, there has been a bitterly fanatic political movement to destroy Nixon. The staggering sums which Maheu is supposed to have paid, allegedly on your behalf and pursuant to your instructions, and the publication of alleged messages from you to Maheu construed as instructions to influence if not control the Administration, has encouraged the Senate Watergate Committee to pursue the contention that Nixon received monies from you (including the $100,000 to Rebozo) for his personal use rather than as a proper contribution to a political campaign.

"To date we have successfully resisted the efforts of the IRS, SEC, and the Senate Watergate Committee from having access to you.

"This has developed into quite a dog fight," concluded Davis, "but I am confident we will prevail."

In fact, Hughes did prevail. He was the only major Watergate figure who eluded all the probes, who was never brought to justice.

Beyond the law in his Bahamas bedroom, under indictment and under subpoena, Hughes watched B-movies in a codeine haze while his past machinations brought down the government of the United States.

If the billionaire was safe, however, his secrets were not.

In the early morning hours of June 5, 1974, the secret papers that Richard Nixon feared were stashed in Larry O'Brien's office or Hank Greenspun's safe were stolen from Howard Hughes's old headquarters at 7000 Romaine Street in Hollywood.

No one dared tell Hughes that his sacred memos were gone.

Nonetheless he was worried. Not that unknown burglars had discovered his dealings with Nixon but that they had made off with an old steam car Hughes had bought when he was twenty or disturbed the movies he had preserved in his vaults. And most of all he was worried that more outsiders would start poking through this ware-house of his past life.

"He wants to know who is actually going to look in the various areas, vaults, and rooms at Romaine to ascertain just what is missing and presumed stolen in the robbery," his aides informed head-quarters.

"He does not want some insurance investigator to take it upon himself to start opening boxes and crates when he has left such rigid instructions through the years on the handling of such sensitive items as his motion picture equipment, etc.

"He wants a detailed report, step by step, on just how it is intended that these searches be made. He wants this report before anything is touched."

While Hughes worried about his memorabilia, his aides back at Romaine discovered that another "sensitive item" was missing—a memo revealing the true mission of the *Glomar Explorer*. The security breach could not have come at a more dangerous time. The *Glomar* was just about to reach its giant claw three miles underwater and scoop up a sunken Russian submarine.

Now, a month after the break-in, CIA Director William Colby had to tell the president the *Glomar* secret was out, apparently in the hands of unknown burglars who had looted Romaine.

The president received that unsettling news just days after he returned from Moscow, where he signed an arms-control treaty that might have saved him had he signed it a few years earlier. It ended the big blasts in Nevada.

But too late. And now Nixon had reason beyond the *Glomar* to worry about the Hughes heist.

Colby knew that. When the CIA compiled its first list of "possible culprits" on July 4, it noted that the Romaine break-in might have been "politically motivated to aid or deter Watergate investigation." And among "possible customers for documents" the Agency listed "anti-impeachment forces if documents are embarrassing."

And now Colby was coming to see Nixon. It could not have been entirely comfortable, this meeting between a CIA director who believed there might be a Watergate motive behind the Hughes break-in, and a president who knew there was a Hughes motive behind the Watergate break-in.

But whatever the CIA suspected, Nixon knew that the Romaine heist was not a White House job. Now he also knew that the secret

Hughes papers he had so long feared had fallen into unknown and perhaps hostile hands.

The president, however, had little time to worry about the "smoking guns" stolen from Romaine.

It was just past nine on Wednesday morning, July 24, when the telephone rang in Nixon's bedroom at San Clemente, jolting him awake. Alexander Haig was on the line.

"It's pretty rough, Mr. President," said Haig. "The Supreme Court decision came down this morning."

Nixon had to surrender his White House tapes.

Watergate, which began with Hughes's dirty secrets spilling out, would now end with Nixon's own dirty secrets spilling. Incredibly, these two most secretive men had both kept a running record of their crimes.

Nixon was now in the dock. That same night the House Impeachment Committee began its televised hearings. The whole appalling story of Watergate would now come out, the president convicted by his own recorded words, all his men already indicted for the cover-up, his burglars already in jail.

Only one aspect of the crime would remain hidden. The motive.

It was not unknown, but it had been suppressed. Just before the Senate Watergate Committee released its final report earlier that month, the senators cut out forty-six pages. In that deleted section staff investigators concluded that the Hughes connection had triggered Watergate.

It all began, the staff reported, with Nixon's fears that Larry O'Brien had discovered the $100,000 payoff while serving simultaneously as the billionaire's Washington lobbyist and chairman of the Democratic National Committee.

None of the senators wanted to publish that. Not the Republicans, not the Democrats. Obviously there was no way to expose Nixon without at the same time exposing O'Brien. But it was more than that. Hughes money exploded in too many directions. Several senators, including at least one on the Watergate committee, Joseph Montoya, had also received contributions from Hughes, and in his lawsuit Maheu had named other prominent political leaders, including Bobby Kennedy, Lyndon Johnson, and Hubert Humphrey. As the committee's maverick Republican Lowell Weicker put it, "Everybody was feeding at the same trough."

But beyond that, none of the senators could believe that $100,000 explained Watergate. It just didn't seem like enough.

Some thought there must be more, that the real payoff, the big bribe that would explain the big risk of the big break-in had not yet been uncovered. Even some in Nixon's own gang were certain there must be more. "Who knows that that's the only $100,000?" said Chuck Colson, shortly before he went to prison.

Surely $100,000 could not have brought the president to the brink. But it had. It was not the amount of money. It wasn't even that it was dirty money. It was the very fact that it was *Hughes* money, the kind of money Nixon had been caught with before, the kind of money that had once cost him the White House. In a desperate effort to keep it from happening again, he had made it happen again.

Haldeman understood. "To take a risk such as that burglary was absurd," he later wrote. "But on matters pertaining to Hughes, Nixon sometimes seemed to lose touch with reality. His indirect association with this mystery man may have caused him, in his view, to lose two elections."

Hughes and Nixon had brought on the cataclysm trying to protect themselves—from each other. Hughes gave Nixon the $100,000 in a desperate effort to stop the bombing, and Nixon brought himself down in a desperate effort to hide the payoff.

Secret money, so central to Watergate, still obsessed Nixon as the end drew near. In one of a series of final phone calls to Haldeman on August 7, the president told his former chief of staff that there was one more unexploded bombshell in the tapes: the secret Rebozo slush fund. At the end, with all his crimes exposed and his soul laid bare, that was still the revelation he most feared.

At nine P.M. the next day, Thursday, August 8, 1974, Richard Nixon announced his resignation as president of the United States.

Hughes and the government fell together.

As Nixon exited the White House for the last time, Hughes described his own terminal condition in a note scrawled on his bedside legal pad.

"I did not leave the stretcher and prone position from time of surgery until arrival in Freeport," he wrote, recalling the operation on his fractured hip a year earlier. "I was put in a bed, and I have not left that bed up until and including this moment, *not even to attempt to go to the bathroom.*"

Yet now, more than ever, even as he went into his final decline, Hughes was seen as the real Mr. Big, the secret center of Watergate, the secret patron of presidents, and the secret partner of the CIA.

Alone in his darkened room atop the Xanadu Princess Hotel, his sixth foreign hideout in four years of exile, the presumed evil genius remained puzzled by events back in the States.

For a moment he thought he had found the key to Watergate. It seemed to be in one White House tape on which the president was heard to say: "I don't give a shit what happens. I want you all to stonewall it, let them plead the Fifth Amendment, cover-up, or anything else if it'll save it—save the plan."

"What's the plan?" asked Hughes. If there was one, he wanted to know about it.

His public relations man in Los Angeles, whose job had long been to refuse all comment, and whose tasks now included keeping Hughes informed on Watergate, sent the answer:

" 'The Plan' apparently refers to an agreement reached by the White House advisors, and accepted by Nixon, that the best method for dealing with the Watergate Committee would be for White House witnesses to refuse to answer questions. The over-all term for this plan was to 'Stonewall it.' "

How disappointing. Hughes had been stonewalling it all his life, and where had it gotten him?

He turned his attention to more immediate concerns, demanding a secret survey of breakfast cereals. "*Please* have them research the serial field—either in Freeport, Miami or L.A. before I consume any more of that turd-like meat," he scribbled to his Mormons. "But plse exercise all caution toward security."

He was equally security-conscious when he closed a deal to buy his Bahamas hotel: "Please send a personal note from me to Mr. Ludwig (just orral—not written—through Mr. Ludwig's chief representative—but with no other man present—) as follows:

" 'It has been a pleasure to do business with you.' "

While Hughes carefully guarded such sensitive messages in Freeport, his biggest secret of all escaped back in Los Angeles, a belated fallout of the heist at his unguarded Romaine Street headquarters. On February 7, 1975, the *Los Angeles Times* broke the *Glomar* story.

While some now began to wonder whether Hughes was a front for the CIA or the CIA was a front for Hughes, whether it was all in fact one dark empire, the naked emperor himself never even heard that the *Glomar* secret was out.

Still, on March 18, when the story broke wide open, banner headlines across the country proclaimed Hughes the CIA's partner in a fantastic three-hundred-fifty million dollar plot to steal a Russian submarine.

And then, at the height of the CIA scandals a few months later, Senate investigators revealed that Robert Maheu had orchestrated a CIA-Mafia conspiracy to assassinate Fidel Castro.

Many were now certain that Hughes was involved in a cabal of sinister dimensions, a secret axis that lay behind all dark events from Dallas to Watergate. The Senate Intelligence Committee began to explore his links to Nixon, the Mob, and the CIA. The only real question seemed to be whether Hughes was master or pawn. "Indeed, was there even a live man named Hughes at the center of it all," asked Norman Mailer, "or was there a Special Committee?"

The IRS had similar concerns. Even as Hughes himself repeatedly asked his aides if it was safe to return to the United States, if the IRS was still after him, an agent involved in the big Hughes probe suggested that he was long dead.

"It is my belief," he reported to headquarters, "that Howard Hughes died in Las Vegas in 1970 and that key officials running his empire concealed this fact in order to prevent a catastrophic dissolution of his holdings."

IRS Commissioner Walters personally tried to determine if Hughes was alive, with no definitive results.

In fact, Hughes was just barely alive, and not master of anything, not even his own empire. His money was disappearing at an alarming rate. Under the new command, corporate losses soared above $100 million in five years, and over the previous decade half a billion in cash and securities had vanished from his bank accounts, apparently the result of mismanagement and waste rather than any conspiracy.

Hughes was oblivious to the loss. He could not even control the name of his empire. Back in 1972 it had been changed without his knowledge to Summa, after he was forced to sell off the foundation of his fortune, the business his father had bequeathed to him, the Hughes Tool Company. Pressured by his lawyers and executives, he reluctantly sold his birthright for $150 million to satisfy the TWA judgment, then watched the stock triple while the TWA case was dismissed.

And now, two years later, he discovered his empire had a new name. "Do you see any reason why we cannot change the name Summa to HRH Properties at the end of this year?" he asked. "Can we change the name Summa now?" he inquired again, and on another occasion instructed, "Don't spend any more money on the name Summa." But the name was never changed.

There were even problems with his drug supply. Hughes was convinced that the Mormons were withholding his blue bombers.

"Of course no one wants you to take any but we don't try to keep them away," soothed an aide. "When you use words and phrases such as 'putting you to sleep,' 'permitting you to go to sleep,' etc. you imply that we have some kind of control over what you or your mind tells you to do."

Actually, the Mormons were firmly in control. Sullen and resentful after fifteen years of servitude, forced to perform absurd and odious tasks, they pressed their dependent boss for ever greater salaries, and while each was paid more than $100,000 a year, they still often treated him with contempt.

"If you knew how much it disturbs me, and how unhappy it makes me when you are completely cold and unfriendly as you were tonight, I really dont think you would turn on the punishment outlet quite all the way," Hughes pleaded in a note to a nursemaid.

"So, all I ask is that the next time you get ready to give me a really harsh expression of your views, you merely take into account the fact that my life is not quite the total 'bed of roses' that I sometimes get the impression you think it is.

"In fact, if we were to swap places in life, I would be willing to bet you would be asking me to permit you to re-swap back to the present position before the passage of the first week."

Hughes had only one last hold over his nursemaids and executives—his will. He had been dangling it in front of them for years, repeatedly assuring them they were all well rewarded, but never letting anyone see it.

"I have had in existance for some time a holographic will," he claimed. "It was carefully written seated at a desk, complying to all the rules governing such wills. It was all done under the supervision of my personal attorney Neil McCarthy, and I assure you no detail was overlooked. It is as binding as a band of steel."

The aides were suspicious. McCarthy was long dead, and the will Hughes claimed to have written was supposedly drafted in the early 1940s, a decade before he assembled his strange crew of Mormons.

"I am sure you dont need this protection," Hughes told them, "as everybody knows that the five of you have been my eyes, ears, and voice for the past five to ten years, so I am sure any one of you could get any exec. position you might care to seek, and with any number of companies to choose from.

"However, as added protection, I have written a codicil to my will which will be delivered to the B. of A. [Bank of America], my trustee in the administration of my will."

The Mormons remained suspicious. As their bedridden boss declined in the summer of 1975, they pressed him repeatedly to show them the will, to update it, or to write a new one.

"We have a little time," replied Hughes. He promised to compose an entirely new will. Soon. But he never would. A man who could not part with his fingernails clearly could not part with his fortune. And Hughes also must have realized that signing a will would be like signing his own death warrant. The nonexistent last testament was his last hold on power.

"We have to get down to it," he nonetheless said, "because I want to fly before I'm seventy."

Hughes, who had not been out of bed since he broke his hip two years earlier, was determined to fly again by his seventieth birthday. He had brought in a former Lockheed executive, Jack Real, made him a member of his entourage, and now spent hours alone with him talking about airplanes.

The Mormons were not pleased. When Hughes asked to see Jack, they told him Real was away. They withheld his messages. They changed the locks on the doors. And finally, on February 10, 1976, they took Hughes off to Mexico.

They told him that the drug supply was drying up in the Bahamas, that they had to go to Acapulco to assure a steady flow of narcotics. It was a lie. The codeine came from a pharmaceuticals firm in New York. But Hughes did not know that. He only knew that he had to have his daily fix.

Saturday, April 3, 1976. Howard Hughes lay motionless in his latest blacked-out bedroom, a luxurious penthouse suite atop the Acapulco Princess Hotel, delirious, dehydrated, starving.

He reached out one spindly arm to a Kleenex box on his bedside night table, withdrew a hypodermic syringe hidden under the flap, and jabbed the needle into his shrunken right bicep. The effort exhausted him. He could not depress the plunger, could not shoot the codeine into his wasted body.

The syringe dangled from his arm, then fell to the floor. Hughes summoned an aide to complete the injection. The Mormon refused. He called for a doctor, who arrived moments later and gave him his shot.

Hughes had been comatose most of the past week. When awake, he refused to eat. His weight had dropped to ninety-four pounds. His six-foot-four-inch frame had shrunk three inches. His brittle bones showed plainly through his parchmentlike skin. His left shoulder was bruised and swollen. He had a gaping wound on the side of his head where he had sheared off an old tumor a few weeks earlier when he fell out of bed. He had four broken needle points embedded in his right arm, another in his left. And inside, his atrophied kidneys, destroyed by a quarter-century of drug abuse, were killing him.

His speech had become incoherent. That Saturday he mumbled repeatedly about an "insurance policy," but none of his aides knew what he was talking about. By the next day he could no longer talk at all. He just lay in bed, staring blankly ahead, his face and neck twitching uncontrollably. Sunday afternoon he slipped into a coma. Still, his aides and doctors kept him hidden, afraid to take him to a hospital. Instead, that night one of the Mormons gave his unconscious boss his third haircut in ten years, while another soaked his hands and feet, then clipped his long nails.

Finally, at eleven o'clock on Monday morning, they lifted a still comatose Hughes out of bed, placed him on a stretcher, loaded him into a waiting ambulance, and rushed him to a private jet. As they carried Hughes aboard, his lips moved slightly, but he made no audible sound.

There were no last words, no "Rosebud." He lay silent on the plane under a bright yellow sheet pulled up to his chin, and at 1:27 P.M. on April 5, 1976, Howard Hughes died three thousand feet in the air, half an hour away from his old hometown, Houston.

His death was front-page news around the world, but he attracted none of the standard public eulogies routinely accorded the famous, the wealthy, and the powerful. Not even his ex-wife, Jean Peters, said much. Just "I'm saddened," that was all, and there were no other loved ones to mourn him.

He was an American folk hero, a man who had lived first the dream then the nightmare—in that sense, perhaps the single most representative American of the twentieth century. But upon his death he had become so loathsome and scandalous a figure that no national leader noted his passing. None of the politicians he had funded said a word. Not Richard Nixon, not Hubert Humphrey, not Larry O'Brien, not even Paul Laxalt.

Only one powerful man stepped forward to praise him, a man who almost never spoke publicly, a man himself so secretive that his name had never appeared in print until just a year earlier, when he was ousted amid scandal from the lofty position he had held for three decades—chief of counterintelligence at the CIA. James Jesus Angleton.

It was entirely fitting that Angleton, the CIA's purest product, the spook's spook, should alone deliver his epitaph:

"Howard Hughes! Where his country's interests were concerned, no man knew his target better. We were fortunate to have him.

"He was a great patriot."

Authenticity Report

As stated in the Author's Note, this book is based primarily on nearly ten thousand Hughes documents stolen from his Romaine Street headquarters on June 5, 1974.

The authenticity of these documents was conclusively established by proof of their origins—clear evidence that the handwritten and typewritten originals I personally photographed and photocopied were the same documents removed from Hughes's penthouse in Las Vegas, taken to Romaine, and finally stolen in the break-in.

Their authenticity was further confirmed by seven years of research— extensive cross-checking of the content against information never made public as well as known facts—and finally through a series of handwriting, typewriting, and other tests performed by the nation's two leading experts, Ordway Hilton, the man who proved Clifford Irving a fraud on behalf of the Hughes organization, and John J. Harris, the man who proved Melvin Dummar's "Mormon Will" a forgery on behalf of the Hughes estate. Both independently authenticated the Romaine documents.

Provenance: Shortly after Hughes left Las Vegas on Thanksgiving eve 1970, a team of his aides led by Kay Glenn, managing director of Romaine, cleaned out his penthouse suite on the ninth floor of the Desert Inn, taking all the documents from both his bedroom and his aides' office in the living room.

"I put everything into transfer cases," Glenn later testified in a sworn deposition. "All of his communications to people, everybody's communications to him. I removed them to Romaine Street. Everything was taken to Romaine."

At the time of the June 5, 1974, break-in, the documents were assembled in a second-floor conference room upon the orders of Hughes's chief counsel, Chester Davis, who according to both FBI and CIA reports said that they were being indexed there for his review in connection with pending litigation. This was confirmed by a secretary in charge of the indexing.

One of the burglars—my source for the documents, the man identified in the Introduction as the Pro—told me in a series of interviews that he removed the documents from the conference room, took them directly to his home, transferred them into steamer trunks, put the trunks into storage for a few months, and then sealed them into a wall for almost two years. No other person saw, touched, or had custody of the documents from the time they were stolen until my source removed them from the wall and showed them to me.

My source had detailed knowledge of the break-in only one of the burglars could have had, information verified in part by confidential police, FBI and CIA records, as well as facts unknown to the authorities confirmed by my own investigation.

Years after I first saw the stolen papers, which had never been made public in any form, xerox copies of several hundred of the same documents were filed in several court cases by the Hughes organization in connection with estate litigation. Obviously, the Hughes organization could not have had photocopies of any of these documents unless they had once had the originals.

Finally, index slips attached to several of the stolen documents were traced back to an IBM typewriter at Romaine used in the indexing under way at the time of the burglary. Typing on the file slips was compared to a known sample from the same typewriter and found to be identical. The known sample was verified by the Los Angeles Police Department.

Handwriting and Typewriting Tests: The two leading authorities on Hughes's handwriting—Hilton, past president of the American Academy of Forensic Sciences, and Harris, past president of the Society of Questioned Document Examiners—both examined memos chosen at random from the material in my possession, and found them authentic.

Hilton examined both originals and photographs of the longhand Hughes memos, comparing them to exemplars of Hughes's handwriting from three sources—a three-page Hughes memo filed in Clark County District Court in Las Vegas, a collection of Hughes memos filed in Federal District Court in San Francisco by the SEC (which Hughes himself identified as his own in a sworn statement), and another group of Hughes memos filed in Federal District Court in Los Angeles by Robert Maheu. All the exemplars were determined to be authentic in judicial proceedings.

"From an examination of each of the documents," Hilton concluded, "and a comparison of them with the known handwriting of Howard Hughes, I am of the definite opinion that all of the documents in question were written by Hughes."

Harris also examined both originals and photographs of the memos— more than a hundred pages of Hughes's handwriting—comparing them to exemplars from two sources: the Maheu lawsuit, and several hundred Hughes memos filed in the "Mormon Will" case in Clark County District Court in Las Vegas. All the exemplars were determined authentic in judicial proceedings.

"I am of the firm opinion that all of the documents I examined were written by Howard Hughes," declared Harris.

One of the originals examined by both Harris and Hilton was a four-page handwritten memo identical to a photocopy filed in the Maheu case. Both found the xerox to be a copy of the original in my possession.

"I performed a series of tests including a line-by-line comparison of the two documents," reported Hilton. "I am convinced that the four-page original letter was the source of the photocopy at hand, and not the converse."

In addition, Hilton examined originals of typewritten documents sent to Hughes—memos dictated by telephone to his Mormons and typed on a machine in his sealed penthouse suite—comparing them to similar memos surrendered under subpoena by the Hughes organization and filed by the SEC in federal court.

Hilton found that both the court exemplars and the documents in my possession were typed on an IBM Selectric, and that identifying characteristics in the typewriting established "a very strong likelihood that each set originated at the same source." Hilton also found that the manufacture dates of the typing paper—as determined by a code in the watermarks—was in all cases consistent with the dates of the memos.

Finally, Hilton identified the index slips attached to several Hughes memos as coming from a typewriter at Romaine. "A number of these slips were typewritten on the same typewriter as the one used to prepare the known sample," he concluded in his report, after comparing the originals in my possession to an exemplar verified by the LAPD and filed in court.

In addition, the documents I obtained included verifiable letterhead correspondence, invoices, memos on Summa Corp. stationary, handwritten letters from both insiders and outsiders dealing with Hughes, hotel bills, travel records, and a notarized affidavit from one of Hughes's personal physicians.

Fact-Checking: Through more than seven years spent writing and researching this book, I checked the information the documents contain by interviewing hundreds of persons with direct knowledge of the events described, reviewing voluminous court files, and obtaining all other available records.

In all instances where corroborating evidence was available, the information in the documents was confirmed by unpublished data as well as known facts. A case in point: dates and places of meetings between Nixon confidant Bebe Rebozo and Hughes representatives chronicled in the memos were corroborated by Senate Watergate Committee records never made public. Other events known only to those present are also accurately described in the memos. For example, a secret meeting between Maheu and Lyndon Johnson recounted in one memo is confirmed in detail by papers on file at the LBJ Library. Those government files also contain a typewritten copy of the letter Hughes sent Johnson, the handwritten original of which is among the documents in my possession. Even Hughes's accounts of television shows were confirmed by videotapes and/or transcripts I obtained—including the "Dating Game" show that caused him to drop his attempt to buy ABC.

There is one final proof, not scientific, yet entirely persuasive to all who read the Hughes memos—only the mind of Howard Hughes could have created them.

Notes on Illustrations

Some of the Hughes documents reproduced in this book are excerpts from longer memos. Wherever material has been excised, the cuts are indicated by tear lines in the facsimiles, and are also noted here:

- The first memo Hughes wrote the night that Robert Kennedy died (following page 39) was misdated 6/7/68 by one of his aides. It was actually written 6/6/68, and the date has therefore been deleted to avoid confusion.
- All the memos in the Hughes-Maheu exchange (following page 74) are excerpts.
- The two Hughes memos regarding his relationship with Maheu (following page 86) are excerpts from separate messages.
- The Hughes memo promising to make Paul Laxalt president (following page 112) is a one-page excerpt from a three-page message that also concerns nuclear testing in Nevada.
- The Hughes handwritten memo offering Laxalt a top job in his empire, and the three typewritten reports from Maheu (following page 114), are all excerpts from separate messages.
- The Hughes memo regarding television and politics (following page 133) is a one-page excerpt from a two-page message.
- The Maheu typewritten memo reporting Laxalt's help in killing the open-housing bill (following page 179) was superimposed on the Hughes handwritten memo as indicated.
- The Hughes memo comparing Las Vegas to Hiroshima (following page 186) is a three-page excerpt from a four-page message.
- The Hughes memo reacting to Lyndon Johnson's refusal to halt a nuclear test (following page 223) is a five-page excerpt from a seven-page message.
- The Hughes memo plotting to play off Humphrey against Kennedy (following page 239) is a one-page excerpt from a two-page message.
- The Hughes memo calling the Kennedy family "a thorn relentlessly shoved into my guts" (following page 265) is a five-page excerpt from a six-page message.

- The Hughes memo about Teddy Kennedy and the RFK funeral (following page 271) is a one-page excerpt from a two-page message.
- The Hughes memos seeking to place in the White House "a candidate who knows the facts of political life" and citing Richard Nixon as such a candidate (following page 296) are excerpts from two different messages.
- The Hughes memo in which he describes himself as "a supposedly successful business man" (following page 334) is a one-page excerpt from an eleven-page message.
- The Hughes memo threatening to leave the country after Nixon's bomb blast (following page 362) is a three-page excerpt from a four-page message.

In addition, the Hughes memos reproduced on the back cover and the title page are excerpts from memos reproduced more extensively elsewhere in the book. The "bagman at the White House" passage on the cover comes from the LBJ memo following page 223, while the two-page extract on the title page was drawn from the Kennedy memo following page 265.

All the facsimiles not cited here are reproduced in full.

Notes

Since Hughes routinely ranged over a variety of subjects in a single memo, and since he often went on at great length, I have rarely quoted any memo in full. Sometimes sentences or paragraphs have been removed without ellipses, but in no case has anything been quoted out of context. Hughes's spelling and punctuation have been retained throughout. He never dated his memos, but his aides often did, sometimes in error. In most cases it was possible to determine the correct date by matching his memos with the dated replies Hughes received.

While this book concentrates on the secret records stolen from Romaine, I have also examined the public record: documents, depositions, and testimony filed in courts throughout the country. Much of that material was never entered into evidence and is also presented here for the first time.

Most of the other information in this book was also obtained from primary sources, identified in these notes.

Introduction **The Great Hughes Heist**

I spent more than six months investigating the Romaine break-in, interviewing at least one hundred persons, reviewing all available records including confidential police reports and grand jury transcripts, contacting all central figures in the case and questioning many others never contacted by the authorities, checking out all possible suspects, and finally tracking down the man who actually had the stolen Hughes papers. I spent several more months confirming his account of the burglary, checking all details against FBI and CIA reports eventually obtained through the Freedom of Information Act, Los Angeles police and district attorney's office files obtained through a confidential source, and other information from interviews with persons directly involved in the official investigation at both the federal and local levels, as well as sources within the Hughes organization.

My description of 7000 Romaine is based on personal observation, and my later description of its interior on accounts from several Hughes employees, one of the burglars, and police reports.

Its mythic security system was described in a typical account by Albert Gerber in *Bashful Billionaire* (Lyle Stuart, 1967, p. 319): "The Romaine Street headquarters is a treasure house of the finest and most sophisticated forms of electronic gadgetry in the counterespionage field. Various warning devices can be triggered by almost anything trespassing in the area. There is a device which will sound an alarm if anyone tried to get information about documents inside the headquarters by use of x-ray outside the headquarters! There are lead-lined safes and burglar-proof vaults. There is electronic equipment to repel radio waves and to neutralize snooping devices." The myth was so powerful that even Hughes's right-hand man Robert Maheu accepted it. "I always heard it was the most impregnable thing," he said in an interview. "It would have been easier to break into J. Edgar's office, that's the way it was described to me."

Mike Davis's account of the break-in is quoted from LAPD reports, grand jury transcripts, and two interviews. Harry Watson's account is from grand jury testimony and an interview.

All descriptions of the police investigation are based on official reports of the LAPD, on interviews with detectives involved in the case, and on information from other law enforcement authorities.

The SEC's Air West probe was detailed by William Turner, a former SEC official who initiated the case and later pursued the criminal prosecution as an assistant U.S. Attorney in Nevada. Turner also made available the quoted SEC report.

The account of the Maheu case was drawn from court records. Summa's claims of a Maheu-Mob link to the burglary are noted in police, FBI, and CIA reports. The quoted FBI report on a possible organized crime connection was dated August 26, 1974.

The Senate Watergate Committee and Special Prosecutor probes of the Hughes-Nixon connection were detailed in published reports, documents obtained through the Freedom of Information Act, and interviews with staff investigators. The Hughes connection to Watergate was first detailed in an unpublished forty-six-page report by the Senate committee staff. The quoted LAPD report log is dated July 5, 1974. FBI agent James G. Karis claimed in an interview not to recall the basis of his suggestion of a Watergate link to Romaine.

The quoted CIA list of "possible culprits" is dated July 4, 1974, and was obtained through the Freedom of Information Act. The discovery of the Castro plot by the Senate Watergate Committee was disclosed by a staff investigator. The details, including Maheu's call to Hughes, were disclosed by the Senate Intelligence Committee in 1975.

The five earlier Hughes break-ins were described in LAPD, FBI, and CIA reports, and further detailed in interviews with detectives involved in the local police investigations. The quoted LAPD report on the Romaine case is dated July 30, 1974. Davis's refusal to submit to a polygraph and

Kelley's failure of his polygraph are noted in the same police report. The FBI report on Kelley's lie-test is also dated July 30, 1974.

Kelley arranged a second polygraph through a private eye named Robert Duke Hall, who was murdered two years later on July 22, 1976. According to Burbank police Lt. Al Madrid, who handled the murder case, the same two men charged with killing Hall—Jack Ginsburgs and Gene LeBell—also staged the April 1974 break-in at Hughes's Encino office and delivered the stolen voice scrambler to Hall, who eventually returned it to Kelley. Madrid said in an interview that he found no evidence that the Encino theft was linked to the Romaine break-in six weeks later, or that Hall's murder was in any way connected to either of the burglaries.

Howard Hunt first revealed Winte's involvement in the aborted Greenspun break-in in sworn testimony before the Senate Watergate Committee, later confirmed by G. Gordon Liddy in *Will* (St. Martin's Press, 1980, pp. 204–205), and by Bennett in statements to both the Senate committee and the Special Prosecutor's Office.

The LAPD's conclusion that the Romaine heist was an "inside job" is quoted from its July 30, 1974, report.

The inside story of the break-in was revealed to me in a series of interviews with one of the burglars, my confidential source called the Pro, and as noted above his account was verified by LAPD, CIA, and FBI records, by interviews with law-enforcement officials, and by my own investigation.

The Chester Brooks ransom calls were detailed by police reports, grand jury testimony, and a transcript of the call recorded by the LAPD. The Hughes memo left by Brooks was later filed in court. The police dragnet for Brooks was detailed in LAPD and FBI reports. Henley's failure to receive the final call and her attendance at the *Glomar* event was noted in LAPD and CIA reports. Henley apparently left instructions for Kay Glenn to receive the ransom call in her absence, but Glenn also missed the call, according to a CIA report.

Glenn's discovery that the *Glomar* document was missing is noted in CIA reports. Sources at the CIA, FBI, and LAPD detailed the series of contacts that ensued. The Sullivan briefing was described by a detective who was present. The CIA suspicion that the Hughes organization staged the break-in and then falsely claimed the *Glomar* document was missing was noted in a July 5, 1974, report by the Agency's task force. CIA Director Colby confirmed his meeting with President Nixon in a series of interviews, and his quoted remarks are from those interviews.

All accounts of the Gordon-Woolbright meetings are based on Gordon's grand jury testimony, further detailed by Gordon in a series of interviews. Woolbright's background was obtained from Los Angeles and St. Louis police records. Their contacts with J. P. Hayes and Maynard Davis were confirmed by both Hayes and Davis in interviews. Winte's report that Korshak and Shenker may have been involved was noted in an LAPD report dated August 25, 1976. Shenker denied any involvement with the burglary or the stolen papers in an interview. Korshak refused comment.

Gordon's contact with the police, and the FBI–CIA reaction was detailed by Gordon, by an investigator for the Los Angeles district attorney's office he first contacted, by LAPD detectives, and FBI and CIA reports. The quoted CIA "payoff" report is dated October 7, 1974. The quoted FBI buy-back scheme is dated September 23, 1974. Gordon described his talks with the authorities and with Woolbright in grand jury testimony and interviews. His account is confirmed by LAPD and FBI reports.

The quoted FBI report of the CIA–FBI strategy meeting is dated November 1, 1974. The CIA's report to the FBI describing the stolen Hughes papers is dated August 5, 1974. The CIA report closing the case is dated November 25, 1974.

Michael Brenner, the assistant district attorney handling the Romaine case, confirmed in a series of interviews that the Hughes organization had not cooperated with the police investigation, that the CIA had interfered with his grand jury probe—at one point actually halting the investigation completely—and Brenner also commented, "The aspect of the case that worries me is that there probably wasn't a burglary."

At his first trial in April 1977, Woolbright was convicted of receiving stolen property and acquitted of attempted extortion. His conviction was set aside on appeal because the trial judge had wrongfully ordered the deadlocked jurors to reach a verdict. His second trial in June 1978 ended in a hung jury, and the district attorney dismissed all charges against Woolbright.

The famous "missing *Glomar* document" was not among the Hughes papers stolen from Romaine. The Pro said in an interview that he never had or saw any such document. Ten months after the break-in, the security guard Mike Davis came forward and told the district attorney that he, not the burglars, had taken the *Glomar* memo. Davis claimed he found it on the floor after the burglars had escaped, stuffed it into his pocket, forgot that he had it, panicked, kept it hidden in a bedroom drawer, and finally flushed it down the toilet, afraid to get "involved." "It was just an absent-minded thing," Davis explained in an interview. "I don't know why I did these things. I can't figure it out myself."

1 Mr. Big

My reconstruction of the first scene, Hughes watching reports of RFK's assassination, comes from one of his own handwritten memos not quoted here but in chapter 9 (page 263). In it, Hughes himself recounts his TV vigil, noting that he was awake for two nights watching CBS and that he "heard Mankiewicz make the fateful announcement." To determine what he had seen, I viewed videotapes of the same CBS reports.

The description of Hughes lying naked in his bedroom is based on interviews with a personal aide who recalled the RFK death watch. The aide also recalled that Hughes had a Zenith Space Commander, and Hughes's own memo shows that he used it to check out all the networks.

Notes

The process by which Hughes sent his orders to Maheu was confirmed both by Maheu and the Mormon attendants, as well as by one of the security guards who made the deliveries. That Hughes summoned his aides by snapping a fingernail against a paper bag was confirmed by the aides, who said they could hear the familiar signal above his blaring TV, even when he kept his door closed.

The timing of the RFK memos was determined both by their content and Maheu's unpublished Senate Watergate Committee testimony that Hughes first ordered him to hire Kennedy's men within minutes of Bobby's death. (The first memo Hughes wrote that night was misdated 6/7/68, but was clearly written 6/6/68, and the date was therefore deleted in the facsimile to avoid confusion.)

A series of memos revealed the outcome—the hiring of O'Brien—and I interviewed O'Brien and his associates for further detail. The link between Hughes's impulsive command to hire the Kennedy team and the Watergate break-in four years later is established in the epilogues, based on sources detailed later in these notes.

Hughes's physical condition at this time has been well established in voluminous court testimony and prior accounts but was verified in specific and in greater detail through extensive interviews with two of his Mormon attendants and one physician, Dr. Harold Feikes, who examined Hughes at least twenty times from 1968 through 1970.

The account of Hughes's codeine addiction and his use of other drugs is based on a 1978 report of the Drug Enforcement Administration, medical records, court testimony from his aides and physicians, and interviews with two of the Mormons who witnessed Hughes preparing and injecting his fix on numerous occasions.

My newsreel-like account of Hughes's early public exploits is based on my viewing of the actual newsreels, on contemporaneous press reports, on interviews with persons involved, and, in the case of the Senate hearings, on the hearings record. The 1957 crisis triggered by the TWA battle, the loss of Dietrich, and his marriage were recounted by aides in interviews and court testimony and by Dietrich in several interviews.

The notes Hughes made for his message to Jean Peters on his train trip to Boston is the only extant handwritten memo to his wife. Peters has testified that she never received a letter from Hughes, and while he often wrote messages for his aides to read to her, all others but this were destroyed on his standing orders to shred and burn all personal memos. The aide who recited a version of this farewell message to Jean recounted the event in a later deposition.

Hughes's arrival in Nevada was detailed in interviews with two aides who were present, one of whom wheeled Hughes's stretcher into the Desert Inn bedroom. "I was with him when we went up to the ninth floor and actually put him in that room so I could look around and see if there might be a room he'd like better," recalled the aide. "But he didn't want to be bothered with moving around any further, so he just stayed in the first room I picked by chance."

The estimate of Hughes's net worth on his arrival in Las Vegas is based on the 1966 U.S. corporate income-tax return filed by Hughes Tool Company, which reports total assets of $759,956,441, including cash and securities of $609.4 million. That does not include almost $100 million of his TWA windfall, eventually paid as a capital-gains tax, nor does it include Hughes's personal bank accounts and other holdings, most notably all the stock of the Hughes Aircraft Company. It is impossible to state with any precision the true worth of his empire, because most of it was in privately held stock never put on the open market and in real estate and other assets never appraised. *Fortune* magazine put his total worth at $1,373,000,000 in 1968, while Hughes himself in a 1969 memo claimed his empire was worth "more than two billion dollars."

The description of Hughes's penthouse suite is based on interviews with two of his Mormon aides, as is the description of Hughes surrounded by his memos. "They were maybe the neatest stacks of papers in the world," commented one.

All of Hughes's aides confirmed either in interviews or court testimony that the four years Hughes spent in Las Vegas was the only time in his life that he regularly risked writing down his orders. While he sometimes wrote longhand memos before and after Las Vegas, he almost always dictated his messages instead, and destroyed most of what little he did write as soon as the business in question was concluded. In his earlier years, Hughes handled most matters by telephone, and only in his Las Vegas years did Hughes ever send handwritten memos to anyone.

The description of Hughes reading his memos is based on accounts from his Mormons. While thoroughly grounded in fact—Hughes did regularly root through his old papers in exactly the manner described—in this one instance I have re-created a typical scene and used it to present a selection of memos obviously not read by Hughes on any one occasion.

Hughes's relationship with his Mormon aides was recounted by all of them in interviews and depositions. His relationship with Jean Peters was described by her in court testimony. That he kept her under surveillance is revealed in his own memos: "HRH wants to know as soon as possible about the surveillance house across the street from the Mrs."

2 Bob and Howard

Maheu himself recounted his first assignment from Hughes in a sworn deposition and provided further details in an interview. An associate of the lawyer who hired him confirmed several details. Maheu also testified in his deposition that Cramer worked for the CIA.

Maheu confirmed his own CIA retainer in an interview and in testimony before the Senate Select Committee on Intelligence in 1975. The committee report reveals that he produced the Sukarno pornographic movie for the CIA, and a staff investigator disclosed that CIA files show that Maheu obtained prostitutes for foreign leaders, including Hussein, on behalf of the Agency.

Maheu's successful effort to scuttle the Onassis contract is also revealed in the Senate report, which notes that he "worked closely with the CIA." A staff investigator said that CIA files reveal Nixon's involvement and that Maheu in fact met at least once with Nixon, and state that "the possibility that he has had continuing contact with Nixon on this or other matters cannot be ruled out."

Maheu himself recounted his early assignments for Hughes in depositions and court testimony. He testified that he first saw Hughes while in the Bahamas to make contact with Sir Stafford Sands, leader of the ruling white clique known as the "Bay Street Boys," to whom Hughes had ordered him to give $25,000 to ease the way for a real estate deal.

The Miss Universe caper (mistakenly identified as a Miss America contest) was described by Maheu in court and also detailed by Jeff Chouinard, a Hughes operative who ran his harem guard. In his memo claiming credit for killing a 1966 Senate probe of the incident, Maheu failed to mention his real coup: killing a Senate probe of Robert A. Maheu Associates, with the help of the CIA. Maheu's firm had acquired a shady reputation, and, according to FBI reports, several of the "associates" were suspected of offenses ranging from wiretapping to extortion to kidnapping, but the CIA managed to quash a subpoena for Maheu's testimony.

Maheu's role in the Castro plot was detailed in a 1975 report of the Senate Intelligence Committee, *Alleged Assassination Plots Involving Foreign Leaders*, and again in a 1979 report of the House Select Committee on Assassinations. According to staff investigators for both committees, an unpublished 1967 CIA report on the plot refers to Maheu as "a tough guy who can get things done." Exactly what Maheu had done to justify such confidence is unknown. There is no evidence of a prior homicide in known CIA files, although one of Maheu's "associates," John Frank, was suspected of the kidnapping and presumed murder of a Dominican dissident on behalf of dictator Rafael Trujillo, one of Maheu's clients. In any event, no one else was even considered for the Castro job. Maheu was the first and only choice.

The passing of the poison pills was described by another Maheu operative, Joe Shimon, who claimed to have witnessed the transfer. There are several other versions of who passed the pills to whom, but every version except Maheu's has him handling it. Roselli claimed that Maheu met with the Cuban in Maheu's hotel room, "opened his briefcase and dumped a whole lot of money on his lap, and also came up with the capsules." Maheu admits only to seeing the pills, not delivering them.

According to a Senate staff investigator, unpublished CIA reports confirm that Maheu informed Hughes of the Castro plot and did so with the approval of his CIA case officer James O'Connell. Maheu himself described his phone conversations with Hughes in Senate testimony and in later interviews.

Maheu's role in handling Hughes's political contributions began in 1961, according to his court testimony, which he reiterated in an interview, but he claims that "the amounts were very nominal for quite a few years" and that he handled no major contributions until Hughes arrived in Las Vegas.

Both Dalitz and Maheu recounted the Desert Inn eviction crisis in depositions later filed in Maheu's slander suit against Hughes, and Maheu gave further details in an interview and in an account quoted by James Phelan in his book *Howard Hughes: The Hidden Years* (Random House, 1976, pp. 63–64). Maheu reported his enlistment of Hoffa in contemporaneous memos sent to Hughes. Dalitz was identified by the Kefauver Committee as Cleveland manager of the national crime syndicate run by Lucky Luciano and Meyer Lansky in the 1930s, and FBI wiretaps made public in 1963 showed that Dalitz was still a Lansky man, also associated with Mafiosi like Roselli and Giancana. "I was seen with them," Dalitz fretted in one bugged conversation. "I don't think that's good. It ties the whole Mob up."

Maheu reported Roselli's role in Hughes's purchase of the Desert Inn in both court and Senate testimony and recounted his threat to resign and Hughes's offer of a half-million-dollar retainer in depositions and court testimony.

In an interview, Maheu noted that his constant fights with Hughes had driven him to drink and said that he had sent some memos "when I was half crocked that I wished I had never dictated." By late 1967 Maheu's drinking problem had become so serious that the CIA worried it would lead to revelation of the Castro plot, according to congressional sources who saw CIA "risk analysis" reports. Curiously, the only person privy to the plot the CIA didn't keep tabs on was Hughes himself.

3 The Kingdom

Paul Laxalt refused repeated interview requests. He failed to answer four letters sent to his home and Senate office, he ignored all requests for an accounting of money received from Hughes, and his campaign treasurer, Jerry Dondero, also refused to make any financial data public. Laxalt's brother Peter, a partner in the family law firm on retainer to Hughes, also declined to answer any questions even after they were submitted in writing at his request.

"The Senator has ducked this question many times," explained his press aide, David Russell. "He's all Hughesed-out."

Laxalt himself has publicly admitted on several occasions that he waived all normal licensing procedures to help Hughes buy up Las Vegas, and two former members of the Gaming Commission confirmed that the governor personally pushed through Hughes's casino applications. Laxalt has stated that he backed Hughes to get rid of the mobsters who owned the casinos, but when he ran for governor in 1966, and again when he ran for the Senate in 1974 and 1980, Laxalt accepted campaign contributions from these same organized-crime figures, including the principal owner of both the Desert Inn and the Stardust, Moe Dalitz. (See Edward Pound, "Some Backers of Laxalt Show Up in FBI Files," *Wall Street Journal*, June 20, 1983.) When asked why he did not return the Dalitz money, Laxalt said, "Moe Dalitz is a friend of mine."

Laxalt's December 1967 meeting with members of Nevada's Gaming Commission and Gaming Control Board is recounted in a December 14, 1967, FBI report obtained through the Freedom of Information Act. The governor's fears about Hughes were also recalled by one of the officials present as well as by the FBI's chief agent in Las Vegas, Dean Elson, who wrote the report. "They didn't know if they had an imposter there or not, they didn't know if they had anyone," said Elson, who quit the FBI to go to work for Hughes in 1968. "There were a lot of discussions with Bob Maheu to try to get prints from a drinking glass or something, to have him remove something from the penthouse, but he was never able to do it."

J. Edgar Hoover's rejection of Laxalt's plea to determine if Hughes was alive was handwritten by Hoover at the bottom of the FBI report.

Hughes's early sojourns in Las Vegas were described by Walter Kane, a longtime employee whose primary job was to sign showgirls and starlets to "movie contracts." "We used to come up here and he didn't want to miss a place—every place in town, we'd go in," recalled Kane in an interview. "He loved show business, he was fascinated by show people, and of course the showgirls."

Hughes bought the Desert Inn for $13.25 million on March 31, 1967, the Sands for $23 million on July 27, 1967, the Castaways for $3.3 million on October 26, 1967, the Frontier for $23 million on December 28, 1967, and the Silver Slipper for $5.4 million on April 30, 1968. His deal for the Stardust, at $30.5 million, was never closed, but later he bought the Landmark for $17.3 million and Harold's Club in Reno for $10.5 million.

Laxalt's phone conversation with Hughes took place on January 5, 1968. In addition to Hughes's tirade about the water, the governor later confided to associates that he was also taken aback by the echo-chamber effect of Hughes's phone amplifier, which he described as "weird, a strange sound, really quite unsettling."

Laxalt has publicly admitted receiving job offers from Hughes while governor but has always claimed that he turned them down, never noting that he did so only after years of negotiations, just as he was about to leave office. His family law firm received $10,000 a month from Hughes as a retainer in 1970, plus fees of at least $60,000, according to Tom Bell, law partner of the governor's brother Peter. Another attorney associated with the firm said that Laxalt himself received legal fees "in excess of $100,000" from Hughes immediately after stepping down as governor, but Laxalt told Jack Anderson that he got only $72,000.

Roselli's claim that the Desert Inn eviction crisis was a Mafia plot was quoted by Jimmy Fratianno in Ovid Demaris, *The Last Mafioso: The Treacherous World of Jimmy Fratianno* (Times Books, 1981, p. 188). According to IRS and Justice Department sources, effective control of Hughes's casinos remained in the hands of the previous Mob owners, and Maheu retained most of the old staff at the Desert Inn and the Sands, while bringing in Lansky's former pit boss at the Flamingo to run the casino at the Frontier.

Notes

Former IRS intelligence chief in Las Vegas, Andy Baruffi, confirmed in a series of interviews that millions—perhaps more than $50 million—were skimmed from Hughes's casinos. "We investigated three possibilities," said Baruffi, who ran a massive audit of the Hughes empire from 1971 through 1973. "That Maheu was stealing the money, that Hughes himself was stealing the money, or that organized crime was doing it either with one or the other or on its own. We knew the Mob was somehow involved because the same Mob people who ran the casinos before Hughes bought them ran them after, and these people would not have run a skim of that magnitude without orders from the top. And we knew that the money had disappeared. But we could never find out where it had gone."

Of the $858,500 drawn from the Silver Slipper and passed to Nevada politicians, Tom Bell, in a sworn deposition and a series of interviews, admitted to handling $385,000. Bell said that another Hughes operative, Jack Hooper, handled other Slipper political funds but did not know how much he disbursed, and Hooper refused to grant an interview. Maheu testified under oath that he passed $50,000 to Senator Bible in 1968 and $70,000 to Senator Cannon in 1970. When Bell revealed the other contributions in court testimony, several of the named beneficiaries claimed they received less—List said he got only $6,200; Fike said he got $25,000. None of the politicians ever signed a receipt, and the payments were always made in cash.

Bell also testified that Laxalt personally solicited contributions: "From time to time during Paul Laxalt's administration he asked me to convey to Mr. Hughes the desirability of making political contributions to certain candidates. He actually visited me personally with reference to supporting particular Republican candidates." In a series of interviews, Bell added that Laxalt requested the funds in visits to the Frontier, on the telephone, and while they played tennis together, and recalled that the governor "pushed very hard" to get Hughes money for his designated successor Fike, who, according to Bell, personally came by to pick up his cash.

The list of Hughes's demands is quoted from Bell's deposition.

Laxalt's letter to Attorney General Clark is reproduced in a report of the Senate Watergate Committee. To the governor's claim that Hughes's purchase of the Stardust was necessary to drive out the mobsters who owned it, the Justice Department replied: "We feel sure that Nevada's interests can be equally well served by means which do not violate federal antitrust laws." The department also noted that Hughes said he planned to retain all the old personnel at the Stardust.

4 Network

The scene of Hughes watching "The Dating Game" is reconstructed from a transcript of the March 29, 1969, show and from a handwritten Hughes memo of the same date quoted later in this chapter (p. 155).

Hughes's TV viewing habits were described by two of his Mormons and also gleaned from information in his own memos. His creation of the "Swinging Shift" is detailed in a series of memos.

Hughes bought KLAS in 1967 from Hank Greenspun, publisher of the *Las Vegas Sun.* "Right after Hughes appeared in Las Vegas, I began getting calls from his Mormons," recalled Greenspun. "At first they asked that I keep the station open a little longer. Then they wanted to know if we'd put on westerns or airplane pictures. Finally I said, 'Why doesn't he just buy the damned thing and run it any way he pleases?' "

On February 14, 1968, the FCC granted Hughes a license for KLAS without holding any hearings, although it had always required other applicants to appear in person. Commissioner Nicholas Johnson issued a stinging dissent: "Before we grant the management of what may become the largest company town in American history one-third control over its television communication, we owe it to the public to air these issues in open hearing." Maheu meanwhile reported to Hughes: "We ran into a problem with the FCC examiner who indicated the necessity of a hearing with you present as sole stockholder. We handled that situation at the Commission level. Sen. Bible was very helpful."

The ABC tender offer Hughes called a two-hundred-million-dollar deal was actually a deal for $148.5 million. With ABC selling at $58.75 a share, Hughes offered $74.25 a share for two million shares, 43 percent of the outstanding stock. However, his memos make it clear that he ultimately planned to buy a controlling interest in ABC, at least 51 percent of the stock, perhaps far more.

My account of the ABC board meeting is based on interviews with then ABC vice-president Simon Siegel and general counsel Everett Erlick, both of whom were present. "It was a total surprise," said Erlick. "Our key strategy was to force Hughes into public, but we never knew why he dropped the bid."

Lyndon Johnson's personal interest in the Hughes-ABC battle was recalled by a member of the White House staff and an associate of one of the president's private attorneys, both of whom noted that Johnson always avoided contact with the FCC for fear it would raise questions about his own TV holdings in Austin. ABC's Erlick also said that "LBJ had people watching it, but never got directly involved." Johnson's belief that Communists controlled the TV networks is quoted by Doris Kearns in *Lyndon Johnson and the American Dream* (Signet, 1977, p. 331).

Four of the seven FCC commissioners confirmed in interviews that the FCC was prepared to approve Hughes's takeover of ABC if he appeared in person. "I regarded him as a much saner man then than I would now," said Kenneth Cox. "We assumed that he would appear, and the FCC had already approved his purchase of KLAS, so we were on record in finding him qualified." Even the maverick Nicholas Johnson, who opposed the KLAS license, was ready to approve the ABC deal. "Obviously he was mad as a hatter," said Johnson. "But we didn't know it at the time. Someone had to own ABC, and there are some who thought he'd do better at it than some guy brought in from some business school who used to work for Allied Chemical or something. It seemed to us to be merely a business deal."

None of the commissioners was aware of Hughes's renewed plans to buy ABC in March 1969, but one noted that the network's worsening financial condition might have made it even easier for Hughes to get FCC approval. "There was concern that ABC was so weak it would go under," said Robert Lee. "We would have had to weigh the problem of one-man control against the network's need for money."

The "beautiful white girl" who won "The Dating Game" was a black actress named Alice Jubert. The child who chose her was the six-year-old son of "Mission: Impossible" star John Copage.

5 Fear and Loathing

The Tony Awards show was broadcast Sunday, April 20, 1969. *The Great White Hope* was named best play; its star, James Earl Jones, was named best actor; and the woman who played his white mistress, Jane Alexander, was named best supporting actress.

My account of the August 23, 1917, Houston race riot was drawn from contemporaneous press accounts and Robert V. Haynes's *A Night of Violence: The Houston Riot of 1917* (Louisiana State University Press, 1976).

Jean Peters described her postmarriage relationship with Hughes in deposition and court testimony, and one of his personal aides provided further details in an interview. Another aide, Ron Kistler, who served Hughes at Goldwyn Studios and lived with him for three months at Nosseck's in 1958, recounted the *Porgy and Bess* episode in a sworn deposition and also gave testimony on Hughes's strange behavior at the projection studio.

"He arrived wearing a white shirt, tan gabardine slacks, and brown shoes," recalled Kistler. "Those were the clothes he wore all the time he was at Nosseck's until finally the clothes got so filthy and foul-smelling that he took them off. Then he became a nudist. . . . He had a lot of telephone talks with Jean Peters. He told her he was in a hospital undergoing treatment for a disease the doctors couldn't diagnose."

Hughes's no-messages decree is transcribed in a Romaine Street log dated August 13, 1958. His breakdown at the Beverly Hills Hotel was described by Kistler in his deposition, and by another aide in an interview.

All of the "germ warfare" memos quoted are from "Operating Memoranda" compiled in a loose-leaf binder entitled "Manual of Instructions/Office Procedures," and also referred to as the "Romaine Street Procedures Manual."

The incident in which Hughes burned his clothes was recounted by Noah Dietrich in an interview. His relationship with "The Party" was described by Kistler; by the chief of his harem guard, Jeff Chouinard; and by an operative working for Chouinard who tapped her telephone on Hughes's orders. The wireman recalled the teen-age mistress calling Hughes an "impotent old slob," and Chouinard quotes her in his book (written with Richard Mathison) *His Weird and Wanton Ways* (Morrow, 1977, p. 153). Despite his playboy image, Hughes had always been shy with women, and a large number of his most famous affairs seem never to have been consummated, at least according to the accounts of several Hollywood actresses who later wrote about their relationships with him. Jean Peters has never discussed the intimate details of their marriage, but it is clear from her court testimony and from interviews with his aides that Hughes had not shared a bed with his wife for five years before he moved alone to Las Vegas.

Of the four Nevada state senators who voted to kill the fair-housing bill, at least two received Hughes money from the Silver Slipper slush fund—James Slattery got $2,500 and James Gibson got $1,500. In a memo to Hughes, Maheu claimed a connection: "I do not claim one iota of credit for the foresight you had when you instructed me to make political contributions to 'worthy' public servants. . . . When I mentioned that Bell had been successful in killing the fair housing bill, please believe me that I had no intent to delete any of the credit which is due to your foresight. Without 'our friends' we would not have had a prayer."

Bell, who described himself as a close personal friend of Laxalt's, refused in an interview to comment on Maheu's report that Laxalt "delivered to Tom the critical vote which enabled Bell to kill it [the fair-housing bill] in committee." As mentioned earlier, Laxalt himself refused repeated requests for an interview.

My account of the October 1969 Las Vegas race riot was drawn from local and national press reports.

Sammy Davis, Jr., could not be reached for comment on Maheu's claim that he promised Hughes "no damage would ever come to you from 'his people.' "

6 Armageddon

The scene of Hughes discovering the impending bomb blast was recounted by an aide who was on duty in the next room. "I had seen the headline, and was watching to see how he would react," said the Mormon. "We were all waiting for the explosion—not from the bomb, but from the boss."

The AEC announcement of the "Boxcar" blast is quoted from local press reports. Emphasis was added to the final lines to reflect Hughes's reaction to the warning that the impact would be greater on "upper stories of high buildings."

In interviews two of the Mormons who were in the penthouse during a major nuclear test described the impact, and in memos to Hughes several of the aides filed after-action reports.

There is now no doubt that Hughes was right about the dangers of nuclear testing. A presidential panel reported in November 1968 that megaton-level underground blasts might trigger major earthquakes (see chapter 8, page 245), and in December 1970 a huge radioactive leak from an underground test forced the AEC to admit that at least sixteen other blasts had spewed radiation beyond the test site, and that the Nevada Test Site itself was "unfit for public use for the forseeable future" due to extensive ground contamination.

Moreover, the forced release of suppressed government records recently revealed that as early as 1953 the AEC knew that above-ground nuclear tests exposed large parts of Nevada and Utah to lethal fall-out, yet continued the tests for ten years and publicly claimed they were entirely safe. In May 1984, in the first of several hundred lawsuits filed on behalf of 375 victims of the test program, a federal judge ruled that the fall-out caused ten cancer deaths.

Hughes was even right about the sheep. Not only had the Utah flock been killed by a March 1968 biological weapons test, but fifteen years earlier, in 1953, more than four thousand Nevada sheep died downwind of the nuclear test site, having absorbed a thousand times the radiation thought safe for humans. It was the first clear evidence of the danger, but the government lied, claimed the sheep had died of natural causes, and continued the blasts.

Accounts of the "Boxcar" operation, of all the other nuclear tests, and of the Nevada Test Site are based on AEC documents, government films of the explosions, interviews with AEC officials, and contemporaneous press reports.

The account of the AEC's fears about Hughes and his impact on the test program is based on records obtained through the Freedom of Information Act. The government's concern about Hughes was so great that his ban-the-bomb campaign generated almost a thousand AEC reports during his four years in Las Vegas.

Hughes's call to Laxalt and the governor's call to the AEC demanding that the tests be moved to Alaska are recounted in AEC reports dated February 8 and 9, 1968. AEC records reveal that Laxalt intervened on Hughes's behalf on at least two other occasions, June 13, 1967, and January 11, 1969.

Senator Gravel's suggestion that the nuclear tests be moved to Alaska is noted in an April 15, 1969, AEC report, as is his appearance on KLAS-TV. In an interview, Gravel admitted that Hughes flew him to Las Vegas and that he had a complimentary suite at a Hughes hotel; while he denied receiving Hughes money, he said he did expect a campaign contribution.

The subpoena threat came from Congressman Craig Hosmer, a member of the Joint Committee on Atomic Energy who later became a lobbyist for the nuclear power industry. Maheu said he killed the subpoena through committee chairman Senator Chet Hollifield: "You will be happy to know that we have been in touch with Holifield. . . . He guarantees that whatever may happen in the fight with the AEC such a subpoena will definitely not be forthcoming."

In the final days before the "Boxcar" blast, Hughes sent three ambassadors to Washington. Gillis Long, at the time a former congressman from Louisiana, now chairman of the House Democratic Caucus, lobbied the AEC. Grant Sawyer, former governor of Nevada, met with Vice-President

Humphrey. Lloyd Hand, an intimate of Johnson's who had recently resigned as White House chief of protocol, tried to get in to see the president. Ultimately Humphrey arranged for Sawyer to see Johnson instead.

7 Mr. President

The scene of Hughes writing his letter to Johnson was described by an aide who was present and also established by Hughes's own memos. Attorney Finney hand-delivered a copy of the letter to White House special counsel Larry Temple, who forwarded it to National Security Advisor Walt Rostow, who sent it to the president at 7:50 P.M. on April 25, 1968, according to documents on file at the LBJ Library in Austin, Texas.

The president's daily diary shows that White House Chief of Staff Marvin Watson was in the Oval Office when Johnson received the letter. Watson claimed in an interview not to recall the incident. But another member of the White House staff said Watson that same day told him Johnson's reaction: "Who the fuck does Howard Hughes think he is?!" A third aide, Devier Pierson, recalls the president saying something similar to him: "Who the hell does Howard Hughes think he is that he can dictate nuclear policy?"

AEC Chairman Seaborg confirmed in an interview that Johnson withheld approval of the bomb test until the last minute, and his account is verified by documents at the LBJ Library. "I remember that the question of whether we should go ahead with 'Boxcar' was under consideration up to the very end," said Seaborg. "I don't remember President Johnson, in holding the test in abeyance, relating it specifically to Hughes, but I do recall that the president was more than a bit concerned by the Hughes protest, because of the potential political impact of Hughes. He talked to me about it at least two or three times."

Several White House aides recalled Johnson showing them Hughes's letter. Special Counsel Pierson said: "There was almost a sovereign-to-sovereign-like quality to the exchange. I think Johnson viewed it as an irritation, and made some caustic comment, but he was also intrigued, fascinated by the direct approach that Hughes had made. And he certainly got very involved in handling it, and stayed involved." White House speech writer Harry McPherson said the president told him Hughes had also telephoned the Oval Office: "Johnson told me that Hughes himself had called, and had gotten his secretary on the line and asked to speak to Johnson. When told that the president was not available he dictated very rapidly a rather long memorandum. And I recall Johnson saying he was quite impressed by the logical and forceful case that Hughes had made." By the time LBJ told the story to another White House aide a few days later, he claimed to have actually talked directly to Hughes and gave a detailed account of the conversation. However, White House files and Hughes's own memos and interviews with his aides make it clear that the billionaire never called or talked to Johnson.

The account of the president's general mental state at the time was drawn from Doris Kearns's *Lyndon Johnson and the American Dream* (Signet, 1977, pp. 324–40 and 358), and was confirmed by several White House aides. Johnson's activities and mood on the day he received Hughes's letter were recalled by aides and detailed by his daily diary and other White House documents. His remark about King Olav was quoted by Merle Miller, *Lyndon* (G. P. Putnam, 1980, p. 552).

Noah Dietrich recalled Hughes's early financial support of Johnson in a series of interviews and also described LBJ's visits to the Hughes Tool Company. "I dealt directly with him; he was a close personal friend of mine," said Dietrich. "He was in my office many times, way back when he was a young upstart congressman. Johnson asked for the billboards, but I think the money—five thousand dollars a year—was on Hughes's initiative. He wanted to buy political influence." Dietrich also said that Hughes may have met with Johnson in a Los Angeles hotel room but could not recall the details. "He was running for some office and we gave him some financial support, but I'm not absolutely sure Howard saw him."

A Hughes lawyer told an associate he handled a cash contribution to Johnson in 1960, but claimed that he did not recall the amount. The attorney said that LBJ regularly received funds from Hughes. Maheu stated in a deposition that he channeled Hughes money to candidates Johnson designated.

Sawyer's meeting with the president is confirmed by files at the LBJ Library. The call to Watson about Hughes's offer to back Humphrey in return for blocking the bomb test is transcribed in a memo dated April 24, 1968. Johnson's mobilization of his White House staff to deal with Hughes is detailed in numerous documents and was confirmed in interviews with Johnson's aides. The Rostow and Seaborg reports were obtained from the LBJ Library.

Press aide Tom Johnson recalled the president showing him Hughes's letter late on the night before the blast. "So many things were coming in to the president, I can't imagine how many pieces of paper a day, but certainly rarely a day without a hundred or two hundred, but that one really struck the president because of the name on it, Howard Hughes. That set it apart from everything else."

Hughes's sleepless vigil is recounted in his own memos and was also recalled by two of his Mormons.

Clark Clifford confirmed in an interview that Hughes personally retained him in 1950. Hughes was mistaken in writing that Clifford had been under retainer for twenty-five years. Clifford denied that he was personally involved in blocking the helicopter probe and lobbying the tax law but admitted that his law firm did assist Hughes on both matters.

Johnson awoke at nine A.M. E.S.T. on April 26 to find the report from Hornig waiting; it was marked "sent for delivery to the president's bedroom at 8:50 A.M." and was immediately handed to Johnson by his personal aide Jim Jones.

Hughes's reaction to the blast was described by an aide who was present.

Notes

The impact of the explosion in the world beyond was detailed in AEC records and press reports.

Johnson's letter to Hughes was obtained from the LBJ Library. Files there show that the president had Seaborg draft a reply, then ordered at least three rewrites by his staff, and had the final version reviewed by national security advisor Rostow. Before sending it to Hughes, Johnson had an aide show the letter to Hughes's lawyer Finney to get his okay.

Maheu's phone conversations with Hughes just before his meeting with Johnson were recounted by Maheu in a sworn deposition. The president's March 1967 discovery of the Castro plot was described by one of his aides, recounted in 1975 reports of the Senate Select Committee on Intelligence, and detailed by a staff investigator of the House Select Committee on Assassinations. An April 4, 1967, FBI report by the Bureau's White House liaison Cartha DeLoach stated: "Marvin Watson called me late last night and stated that the president had told him that he was now convinced that there was a plot in connection with the [Kennedy] assassination. Watson stated the president felt that CIA had had something to do with this plot. Watson requested any further information we could furnish in this connection. I reminded Watson that the director had sent over to the White House some weeks back all the information in our possession in connection with CIA's attempts to use former agent Robert Maheu in contacts with Sam Giancana and other hoodlums, relative to fostering a plot to assassinate Castro." Among the reports Hoover had sent Johnson was one that described Maheu as a "shady character" whose detective agency "has business dealings with a number of foreign governments and has frequently been engaged in wiretapping," and the director also charged that Maheu's "ethics and trustworthiness have been 'questionable.' "

Hughes's order of a million-dollar bribe was described by Maheu in a sworn deposition.

Maheu's visit to the LBJ Ranch was recounted in a memo to Hughes, described by two White House aides who were present, and detailed in the president's daily diary.

White House Appointments Secretary Jim Jones said in an interview that Johnson told him Maheu had offered him money, and that the president had told Maheu "to stick it up his ass." Press aide Tom Johnson, who was also at the ranch that day, said that the president told him Maheu had asked him to halt the bomb tests, and that he later heard from other members of the White House staff that Maheu had offered a donation to the LBJ Library, which the president angrily refused.

Arthur Krim refused an interview request but in a letter confirmed that Johnson asked him to arrange the Hughes library donation and that Krim met with Maheu in Las Vegas in an attempt to get it.

Maheu reported in an interview Hughes's refusal to make the contribution.

8 Poor Hubert

The account of Humphrey's speech was drawn from press reports and television videotapes. On Election Day 1968, Humphrey vividly described his chronic lack of campaign funds in his diary: "I've climbed that damn ladder of politics, and every step has been rough. I wonder what it would have been like with money enough. That top rung is never going to be mine." The quote is from Humphrey, *The Education of a Public Man* (Doubleday, 1976, p. 4), an autobiography in which he also revealed his haunting memories of his 1960 loss to JFK (p. 207).

Humphrey received $91,691 in illegal corporate funds from the Associated Milk Producers, Inc., in 1968, according to a Senate Watergate Committee report. Dwayne Andreas was indicted in 1973 by the Watergate special prosecutor for giving Humphrey's 1968 campaign an illegal corporate "loan" of $100,000.

In the wake of these Watergate revelations, Humphrey told the *New York Times* (October 13, 1974): "Campaign financing is a curse. It's the most demeaning, disgusting, disenchanting, debilitating experience of a politician's life. I just can't tell you how much I hate it. But when you are desperate, there are things you just have to do."

Humphrey lost to Nixon in 1968 by less than 500,000 votes. He spent about $5 million on the race, Nixon at least $20 million.

Humphrey's arrangement of the Sawyer-Johnson meeting was recounted by Maheu in a report to Hughes and confirmed by files at the LBJ Library. His arrangement of the Sawyer-AEC meeting is reported in an AEC memo dated April 24, 1968. His earlier attempts to plead Hughes's case with Johnson were described by White House Chief of Staff Watson in an interview.

LBJ's tormenting of Humphrey was recounted by Humphrey himself in his autobiography (pp. 307–308), by Merle Miller in *Lyndon* (Putnam, 1980, p. 175), by Theodore H. White, *The Making of the President 1968* (Pocket Books, 1970, p. 347), and in interviews with Humphrey and Johnson aides.

Humphrey's outburst over Maheu's phone call was recounted by his friend and adviser Dr. Edgar Berman in his book *Hubert* (Putnam, 1979, p. 205). Berman, who took the call and relayed the message to Humphrey, also detailed the incident in an interview.

Humphrey's son Robert confirmed his employment by Maheu in an interview. He said that he had met Maheu a few years earlier through California Governor Pat Brown but was actually recruited for the job by John Meier. "It happened by accident. I bumped into him while I was with my dad in California. He was doing a press conference, and I was waiting out in the hall, and Meier introduced himself. I was a college graduate, looking for work, and I already knew Bob Maheu."

Maheu described his offer of $100,000 to Humphrey at their May 10, 1968, Denver meeting in sworn court testimony. He said that the vice-president "seemed very grateful." Two Humphrey aides confirmed that Maheu and the vice-president met at that time. A lawyer representing the

Humphrey estate refused me access to Humphrey's activity, appointment, and telephone logs for this and other relevant dates unless I agreed to prepublication censorship of this book, which I, of course, refused.

Humphrey's efforts to establish a White House panel to investigate the bomb tests are recounted in AEC reports dated June 12, 25, and 26, 1968.

Johnson's science adviser Donald Hornig said in an interview that the president appointed his own panel "to preempt the Hughes-Humphrey panel." Johnson's caustic remark about the Hughes-Humphrey dealings—"Hubert had better keep his pants zipped"—was reported by a top White House aide. "There was talk around the White House that Humphrey was getting money from Hughes and that he was in regular contact with Maheu," the aide noted. "The president was not happy about it."

The presidential panel, chaired by former AEC research director Kenneth S. Pitzer, issued its report on November 27, 1968. "The panel is seriously concerned with the problem of earthquakes resulting from large-yield nuclear tests," the report stated. According to a December 13, 1968, AEC memorandum, the White House assured the AEC that "the vice-president was not given the report," and that Hughes therefore would not get access to it.

Maheu described passing the $50,000 to Humphrey on July 29, 1968, in sworn court testimony. He said that when he greeted the vice-president at the fund-raising dinner, he told him, "I have the item we discussed," and that he again referred to "the matter we discussed" when he placed the cash-filled briefcase at Humphrey's feet in the limousine. Maheu testified that he did not show Humphrey the money because "it's not proper to open the envelopes and count the cash in the presence of other people."

Humphrey denied in a sworn statement that he ever personally received any cash from Maheu or that he was personally aware of any contribution made by Hughes to his campaign. However, the evidence of the backseat payoff is overwhelming.

Lloyd Hand, former U.S. Chief of Protocol and a close Humphrey friend, testified that he was in the limousine with Humphrey and Maheu, that Maheu definitely had a briefcase when he entered the car, and that he had "an impression" that Maheu left the briefcase behind when he got out. Gordon Judd, a Hughes lawyer who brought half the cash from Las Vegas to Los Angeles, testified that he watched from the hotel balcony as Maheu entered Humphrey's limousine with the briefcase and that he saw Maheu leave the car without it.

Moreover, Humphrey himself acknowledged the contribution. Although he later claimed to have no personal knowledge of *any* Hughes donation, the vice-president wrote Maheu a letter dated November 1, 1968, thanking him for a second $50,000 Hughes gave his campaign on October 18, and in that letter clearly noted that he had received Hughes money before. "Dear Bob," wrote Humphrey, "Dwayne has told me about the *additional help* you have given us. Bob, you are the greatest! We needed it badly and have put it to good use." (Emphasis added.)

Humphrey's selection of Muskie as his running mate was described by

O'Brien in his book *No Final Victories* (Doubleday, 1974, p. 253). Muskie confirmed in an interview that he had known Maheu for years and visited him in Las Vegas, but denied knowing of any influence Maheu may have had in his selection.

The meeting between Humphrey and O'Brien on the morning after the Chicago convention was described by O'Brien in *No Final Victories* (pp. 253–56), and in two interviews. All the dialogue was quoted by O'Brien. He said that Humphrey called Maheu about eight A.M. on August 30, 1968, and told him: "I understand that you and Larry have worked out a business arrangement, and I'd like to ask you to postpone that arrangement until after the election. It would be a great personal favor to me."

O'Brien claimed that he had no knowledge of the $100,000 Hughes gave Humphrey, although he was in regular contact with Maheu during the campaign. However, Maheu told the Senate Watergate Committee that he kept O'Brien informed of "all political matters," and specifically told him about the money passed to Humphrey.

9 Camelot

Interviews with at least a dozen persons who knew either Joseph P. Kennedy or Hughes during their early days in Hollywood turned up no indication that they ever dealt with each other, ever came into conflict, or even met. Kennedy's mistress in those years, Gloria Swanson, said that she could not recall him even mentioning Hughes. Noah Dietrich, who joined Hughes shortly after he arrived in Hollywood in 1925 and handled the business end of his moviemaking, said he was certain Hughes never dealt with Kennedy.

Information on Joe Kennedy's background was drawn from Richard Whalen, *The Founding Father* (Signet, 1966), as was the "pants pressers" quote (p. 80).

Pierre Salinger confirmed his solicitation of Hughes money for the RFK campaign in a letter: "Steve Smith, who was raising money for the campaign, asked if I might have some special contacts who would help. I met Mr. Maheu in Las Vegas. He did not immediately pledge a contribution, but during the Oregon primary he called me in Portland to say that Mr. Hughes would give the campaign $25,000. After the death of Robert Kennedy, I received a call from Mr. Maheu telling me the contribution would still be made. I reported that to Steve Smith."

FBI Director Hoover reported Bobby Kennedy's revelation of the Castro plot in a memo dated May 10, 1962: "He stated he had been advised by CIA that CIA had hired Maheu to approach Giancana with a proposition of paying $150,000 to hire some gunmen to go into Cuba to kill Castro. I expressed astonishment at this in view of the bad reputation of Maheu and the horrible judgment in using a man of Giancana's background for such a project. The attorney general shared the same views." Less than three months earlier, Hoover had ended John Kennedy's White House affair with

Notes

Giancana's mistress Campbell by bringing a report on her to the president, according to the Senate Select Committee on Assassinations.

Bobby Kennedy's fears that the Castro plot had led to the assassination of his brother were reported by Arthur Schlesinger, Jr., in *Robert Kennedy and His Times* (Houghton Mifflin, 1978, pp. 615–16). According to Kennedy aide Walter Sheridan, Bobby asked CIA Director John McCone, "Did the CIA kill my brother?"

Kennedy called Nixon's Hughes scandal a "decisive factor" in the 1960 election in a *New York Times* interview reported November 13, 1960. Justice Department files leaked to the *Times* January 24, 1972, revealed that as attorney general Kennedy considered criminal prosecution of Hughes, Nixon, and members of Nixon's family over the "loan."

The scene of Hughes watching RFK assassination reports is based on his own memos, on interviews with his aides, and on television videotapes. Teddy Kennedy's eulogy is quoted from press reports of the funeral rites.

O'Brien's "long, sad, emotional journey" on the RFK funeral train is recounted in his *No Final Victories* (Doubleday, 1974, pp. 245–46) and was further detailed in interviews. "After the funeral services," he wrote, "I went home and remained there for several days. It was a mood I had never known before. Following President Kennedy's assassination I had been swept along by Lyndon Johnson, but now I had nothing to do and nothing I wanted to do."

Maheu told the Senate Watergate Committee that Hughes ordered him to hire O'Brien within minutes of Bobby's death, but that he "had the decency to wait some time" before making contact. Maheu finally reached O'Brien on June 28, 1968.

O'Brien described his job negotiations with Maheu in his book (pp. 255–56) and in interviews. "Suddenly Bobby was dead and I had nowhere to go," he said. "There's a cold reality that sets in, and it's very simple. I had to earn a living." But after being shown a copy of the memo Hughes wrote the night that Bobby died, O'Brien added, "Now you make me wonder whether I'd forsaken everything to go to work for a *bum* like Howard Hughes."

O'Brien discussed his work for Hughes in two four-hour taped interviews, but claimed not to recall many matters detailed in Maheu's reports, often went off the record and demanded that the recorder be shut off, and refused access to his own reports to Maheu and all other records relating to O'Brien Associates.

O'Brien confirmed that he had been contacted by Hagerty to represent the three television networks at about the same time he first met with Maheu, but claimed not to recall any discussion with Maheu of Hughes's bid to take over ABC, as reported in Maheu's memos. O'Brien also claimed he was not aware of the Hughes/ABC deal, although it was widely reported in the national press starting July 1, 1968, three days after Maheu first called, and three days before he came to Las Vegas to discuss the Hughes job.

O'Brien's associate Claude DeSautels told the Senate Watergate Committee that Humphrey called while O'Brien was in Las Vegas. O'Brien said in an interview that shortly after he returned to Washington, he agreed to take over Humphrey's campaign and told Maheu he could not go to work for Hughes until after the convention.

O'Brien confirmed that he met again with Maheu in Washington on July 31, 1968, received $25,000 promised to the Kennedy campaign, which he passed on to Smith the next day, and agreed to represent Hughes through O'Brien Associates for at least two years at $15,000 a month.

O'Brien became Democratic national chairman on August 30, 1968, and that same day became chairman of Humphrey's campaign. He confirmed that he met a third time with Maheu in Las Vegas shortly after the November election and made final arrangements to begin work for Hughes on January 1, 1969.

O'Brien confirmed that he "maintained contact" with Maheu while he managed Humphrey's campaign but said that he did not recall discussing Hughes's attempt to take over Air West. He said that he discussed Hughes's TWA battle with Maheu on several occasions but did not recall the plan for a congressional probe of the bankers, which Maheu said he discussed with O'Brien in a memo to Hughes dated October 9, 1968.

O'Brien also said he did not recall having arranged Maheu's August 1968 meeting with Johnson at the LBJ Ranch, but Maheu told the Senate Watergate Committee that O'Brien set up that meeting, and Johnson's appointments secretary Jim Jones confirmed that O'Brien arranged it. Jones recounted LBJ's reaction in an interview.

Maheu confirmed in an interview that Hughes ordered a second million-dollar bribe to Johnson. O'Brien claimed not to recall any "direct contact" with the president in December 1968 regarding the bomb test. "It gets perilously close to suggesting that Maheu's reports to Hughes might not have been accurate, in terms of my opinions and views and activities, and that wouldn't have been the case," said O'Brien. "Because if Maheu told Hughes that O'Brien says Lyndon Johnson's view on the bomb test is this or that, I'm sure I told Bob that was the president's position, and I wouldn't have told him unless some effort was made to find out what the president's position was."

O'Brien claimed that he never discussed with Maheu any offer of money to Johnson, or indeed any political contributions at all, but Maheu told the Senate Watergate Committee that he kept O'Brien informed of "all political matters." Maheu refused in an interview to confirm that he told O'Brien about the proposed million-dollar bribe to Johnson, as he stated he did in his memo to Hughes. "That's none of your business," said Maheu.

An O'Brien associate, who declined to be identified, said in an interview that O'Brien told him that Hughes had once ordered that a million dollars be given to Johnson, but that he refused to get involved.

Colin McKinlay confirmed in an interview that two Hughes representatives, Tom Bell and Jack Entratter, "tried to buy me off not to run the story about Ted Kennedy," and also confirmed that it was Entratter who brought Kennedy to room 1895 at the Sands where the showgirl was seen by a bellhop, a room service waiter, and two detectives assigned to protect Kennedy. Entratter died in 1971, but another Sands executive corroborated McKinlay's account in an interview. Senator Kennedy refused repeated interview requests.

Both Napolitan and DeSautels confirmed their work for Hughes, and both also confirmed that they consulted regularly with O'Brien, as did O'Brien himself. "During my period on Wall Street," said O'Brien, "there were occasions when Claude and/or Joe would check with me on some aspects of their activities with Maheu, and I'm sure I also talked with Maheu directly." However, O'Brien said that he did not recall any involvement with the Air West CAB hearings or seeking congressional support for the fight against nuclear tests, as reported by Maheu.

O'Brien confirmed that he met again with Maheu in Las Vegas in August 1969, after quitting his Wall Street job, and arranged to go to work for Hughes for two years at $15,000 a month starting October 1, 1969. It was not publicly known at the time that O'Brien was working for Hughes, and the fact that O'Brien was on retainer while he was Democratic Party chairman was not reported until July 1974, when leaked by the Senate Watergate Committee.

O'Brien confirmed Maheu's report that his firm played a central role in altering the 1969 Tax Reform Act. "I'm sure that's true," said O'Brien. "Obviously there was involvement on the tax bill through my contract with Hughes, and I'm sure that DeSautels was very active on that. He knew just about everybody on the Hill." O'Brien defended his role but added, "I know I'm going to look a bit illiberal on the tax bill."

The account of Patman's probe of the Hughes Medical Institute was drawn from reports of the House Banking Committee and the hearing record. The account of HHMI's finances was drawn from IRS files and internal documents of the Hughes organization, as well as congressional reports. O'Brien said that he never contacted Patman for Hughes, but that DeSautels probably did.

The Senate Finance Committee revised the Tax Reform bill to allow the Hughes Medical Institute to escape its "private foundation" status by affiliating with a hospital, and the House-Senate conferees gave HHMI a full year to make the change and become a "public charity." The House version of the bill, however, forbid the change unless the foundation repaid with interest all the back taxes it would have paid had it not been tax-exempt as a "private foundation." The Senate Finance Committee revised the bill to allow the change without any tax penalty, and the House-Senate conference adopted the Senate version. The Senate Finance Committee also softened the rules on "self-dealing" in a clause that seemed tailored for Hughes, and in another clause tailored for Hughes allowed foundations to hold 100 percent of stock in a corporation for fifteen years if the foundation already held more than 95 percent of the stock.

Senator Paul Fannin, who received campaign contributions from the Hughes Aircraft Company's "Active Citizenship Fund," confirmed in an interview that he worked with Hughes representatives to revise the Tax Reform Act in the Senate Finance Committee, and also confirmed that committee chairman Russell Long helped push through the Hughes amendments. Both Gillis and Russell Long declined interview requests.

O'Brien confirmed his meeting with Wilbur Mills, but denied that he discussed HHMI with him. Mills, however, supported the Hughes loophole in the House-Senate conference, and two years later opposed an IRS attempt to force HHMI to spend at least 4 percent of its assets each year on medical research.

Nixon's attempt to get a tax break for donating his papers, the backdating of his deed, and his failure to pay $467,000 owed the IRS while he was president was reported by the House Impeachment Committee. Harlow recounted his talks with Nixon about O'Brien in an interview.

The fact that Hughes paid no personal income taxes for seventeen years, from 1950 through 1966, was established by copies of his federal income tax returns. The Hughes Tool Company became a "subchapter S corporation" in 1967, and as a "small business" with ten or fewer shareholders paid no corporate income taxes starting in 1967.

Larry O'Brien continued working for Hughes until February 1971, three months after Maheu was ousted and just a month after the Nixon White House began investigating his Hughes connection. He confirmed that he received $325,000 from Hughes, including a $75,000 severance payment, and that he received at least $165,000 from Hughes while he also served as chairman of the Democratic National Committee for eleven months starting on March 5, 1970.

The Nixon quote regarding Hughes and O'Brien is from volume 2 of his memoirs (*RN: The Memoirs of Richard Nixon*, Warner, 1978, p. 172).

10 Nixon: The Payoff

Dr. Harold Feikes, a Las Vegas heart specialist who administered the transfusions, described Hughes's medical condition in a sworn deposition and in two interviews. Feikes said he first saw Hughes early in November 1968 and memos sent to Hughes by his aides establish that it was on Election Day. One of the Mormons recalled Hughes watching TV reports of the election after receiving his transfusion.

"His life was certainly in danger," said Feikes. "He was anemic enough to be on the verge of congestive heart failure. But even though he was critically ill, he had a very keen understanding of anemia and transfusions. He chose who he was going to take blood from very carefully. His aides said Hughes knew everything about the donors—what they ate, who they slept with, etc., and he only wanted blood from Mormons."

The description of Nixon's election watch was drawn from interviews with his aides, from his memoirs, and from Theodore H. White, *The Making of the President 1968* (Pocket Books, 1970, pp. 484–89). Garment's quote is also from White (p. 484).

Notes

Noah Dietrich confirmed in a series of interviews that Hughes backed Nixon in every race since his first run for Congress in 1946, as did an associate of Hughes's political lawyer Frank Waters, who handled most of the contributions until 1960. Waters refused comment. Maheu described in court testimony the 1956 covert operation to save Nixon.

Nixon refused two interview requests submitted in writing.

The known Hughes money to Nixon and his family includes the "loan" of $205,000 to brother Donald in 1956 (which was never repaid); $50,000 contributed to the Nixon campaign in 1968; $100,000 in cash secretly passed to Rebozo in 1969 and 1970; and $150,000 to the Nixon campaign in 1972. How much Hughes contributed to Nixon's other campaigns remains unknown, including the "all-out support" Hughes himself said he gave Nixon in 1960.

The "loan" of $205,000 was detailed by Noah Dietrich in several interviews, and in his book *Howard: The Amazing Mr. Hughes* (Fawcett, 1976, pp. 282–87). According to Dietrich, Waters told him that Nixon personally called to request the money—"I've been talking to Nixon. His brother Donald is having financial difficulties. The vice-president would like us to help him."—and that Hughes personally approved the transaction. An associate of Waters confirmed Dietrich's account.

Nixon later told both his chief of staff, Haldeman, and his confidant Rebozo that the Hughes loan scandal caused his defeats in 1960 and 1962, according to Rebozo's Senate Watergate Committee testimony and Haldeman in both interviews and his book *The Ends of Power* (Times Books, 1978, p. 20). Bobby Kennedy also called the Hughes scandal a "decisive factor" in the 1960 election, according to a November 13, 1960, *New York Times* report. Nixon's complaints about media coverage of the scandal are quoted from his memoirs, *RN: The Memoirs of Richard Nixon* (Warner, 1978, vol. 1, pp. 300–301).

Danner recounted the 1968 Nixon-Rebozo request for Hughes money in sworn testimony before the Senate Watergate Committee. Maheu testified that Hughes approved the hundred-thousand-dollar contribution in a telephone conversation and that he withdrew $50,000 from Hughes's personal bank account on September 9, 1968, arranging to pick up the balance at a later date. Nadine Henley, Hughes's personal secretary, confirmed Maheu's account.

The meeting between Danner, Rebozo, and Morgan at Duke Zeibert's took place on September 11, according to Danner's diary. "At that time, Morgan relayed the information from Maheu that a contribution would be forthcoming," Danner told the Senate committee. "Rebozo was willing or agreeable to handle it."

Rebozo did not respond to an interview request but in testimony before the Senate Watergate Committee gave his own account of events leading to his receipt of the Hughes $100,000. "Morgan, I presume, had the money with him," said Rebozo, "but he wanted to hand the money to the president, himself, and I told him that the president would never accept it." Morgan told Senate staff investigators that he merely wanted some formal acknowledgment of the transaction, which Rebozo refused. Danner confirmed Morgan's account.

"The atmosphere just didn't seem appropriate to accept the contribution," Rebozo testified. "I recalled, vividly, the 1956 loan to the president's brother, and the fact that Drew Pearson had made a lot of that in the 1960 campaign . . . the fact that Ed Morgan represented Drew Pearson, and the fact that I just did not want to be responsible for anything that might create embarrassment. I declined."

In Senate testimony Rebozo recounted the attempt by John Meier and Donald Nixon to deliver the Hughes money: "I was concerned about the possibility of some more embarrassment, such as he had showered on the president in 1960 and 1962 . . . I just didn't think that Don Nixon should be consorting with a representative of Hughes."

In a Senate interview and in court testimony, Maheu recalled the attempt to deliver the money directly to Nixon in Palm Springs on December 6, 1968: "Through Governor Paul Laxalt arrangements were made for an appointment with president-elect Nixon, at which time Governor Laxalt and I would deliver the money personally to President Nixon. Unfortunately something happened during the day that scuttled the president-elect's schedule."

Just before his trip to Palm Springs, Maheu withdrew another $50,000 from Hughes's personal bank account in two installments on December 5 and 6 "for Nixon's deficit," and on December 5 also apparently received $50,000 from the cashier at the Sands casino. That same day Danner flew to Las Vegas to meet with Maheu and agreed to go to work for Hughes. A week later both Maheu and Danner were down in the Bahamas, but there is no direct evidence that they passed any money to Nixon, as indicated on the Sands withdrawal slip.

Bank records show that Maheu withdrew another $50,000 from Hughes's personal bank account on June 27, 1969, and Hughes lawyer Tom Bell testified that on Maheu's instructions he gave Danner $50,000 from the Silver Slipper on October 26, 1970. Danner denied receiving the money.

In conflicting statements to the IRS, the Senate Watergate Committee, and in court testimony, Maheu at one time or another claimed that each of the withdrawals was the source of the $100,000 eventually passed to Nixon through Rebozo. In any event, Rebozo, Danner, and Maheu all confirmed in sworn testimony that Nixon did receive $100,000 from Hughes in two deliveries of cash to Rebozo.

Danner joined the Hughes organization in February 1969. He testified that in April and May Rebozo began "needling me" about Hughes contributions to Humphrey, and that in May and June Rebozo asked for $100,000, telling him "the president was interested in beginning to raise funds for the 1970 congressional elections." Rebozo, who kept the money past the 1970 elections, denied Danner's account and testified that "it was money that was intended for the president . . . it was for the president's 1972 campaign." In fact, Rebozo admitted that he put the cash in his safe-deposit box, did not use it for any campaign, and kept it until the IRS came after him in 1973.

Danner testified that "sometime during the summer" Maheu told him, and Danner told Rebozo, that "$50,000 was available now, and another $50,000 would be made available later on." Danner's June 26, 1969, meeting with Rebozo in Miami was confirmed by travel records he submitted to the Senate Watergate Committee. According to bank records, Maheu arranged a withdrawal of $50,000 from Hughes's bank account the next day and picked up the cash on July 11. His son Peter testified that he kept the money in his safe a few weeks, and then, on his father's instructions, turned the $50,000 over to Danner for delivery to Rebozo.

Danner's delivery of the Hughes ABM memo to Rebozo on June 26 and Rebozo's delivery of the memo to Nixon on July 4 are established by Maheu's reports to Hughes. Danner also testified that he gave the memo to Rebozo, and that Rebozo told him that "the president and Dr. Kissinger both examined it and were very much impressed and felt that they would like to brief him further . . . Dr. Kissinger would do it." Rebozo himself confirmed the Kissinger offer in Senate Watergate Committee testimony: "I do know that the offer was made to have Kissinger brief him on it."

Nixon's July 16 meeting with Kissinger was established by Maheu's report to Hughes on the same date and by White House logs obtained from the National Archives, and was confirmed by Alexander Haig in an interview. Haig also recounted Kissinger's reaction to Nixon's order that he brief Hughes, and two members of his National Security Council staff independently confirmed Kissinger's tirade. Kissinger himself refused repeated interview requests.

Larry Lynn, a senior aide who handled the ABM, recalled Haig's own reaction to Hughes's memo, and in an interview speculated that the Hughes connection may have led Nixon to propose abandoning the ABM as part of the SALT negotiations a year later: "I have always felt that some of Nixon's zigs and zags on the ABM issue were unexplainable by anything I knew. He seemed to abandon it too quickly, and for all I know if Howard Hughes was stuffing his pockets full of money, that might have made a difference."

Nixon's and Kissinger's review of plans to test the ABM warhead in July 1969 was confirmed by members of the NSC staff and detailed by AEC and State Department documents obtained through the Freedom of Information Act. One "Memorandum for the President" from the NSC Undersecretaries Committee noted that moving the nuclear tests to Alaska would cost $200 million and warned that "the Soviets can be expected to be sensitive to our plans to conduct tests of this magnitude in the Aleutians." Nixon, however, ordered the biggest blasts moved to Alaska, apparently more worried about Hughes.

11 Howard Throws a Party

When Hughes first announced his intention to buy the Landmark late in 1968, the Johnson Justice Department warned Hughes that his acquisition "would violate the Clayton Act" and threatened antitrust action. A month later, on January 17, 1969, three days before Nixon's inauguration, the department told Hughes that it did not "presently intend to take action with respect to the proposed acquisition." Maheu received advance word and flashed the good news to the penthouse: "We just received a telephone call from the anti-trust division advising that they had formally approved our purchase of the Landmark."

The description of the Landmark is based on contemporaneous local press reports and personal observation.

Dean Martin ultimately did perform at the opening, as did Danny Thomas, and even Bob Hope offered to make an appearance, only to drop out at the last minute due to the death of his two brothers. Hughes apparently never forgave Hope. When the comedian called Maheu six months later seeking a donation of $100,000 for the Eisenhower Hospital, Hughes at first refused to give anything and reluctantly agreed to contribute $10,000 only after being told that Nixon had also asked his help.

Martin had points in the Riviera casino, which FBI wiretaps in the early 1960s revealed as being secretly controlled by the Chicago underworld. Mafia informer Jimmy Fratianno also claimed that Sidney Korshak, a reputed organized crime leader, owned "a pretty good piece of the Riviera" (Ovid Demaris, *The Last Mafioso: The Treacherous World of Jimmy Fratianno*, Times Books, 1981, p. 272).

The depth of Hughes's angst over the Landmark opening is demonstrated by the fact that in all the thousands of memos he wrote during his four years in Las Vegas, it was only during the Landmark brawl that he really got into deep introspection, that he summed up his life, that he searched his soul.

And his fight with Maheu over the opening was so intense that years later Maheu's wife would recall that brawl above all others, remembering the shouted phone conversations she heard through many nights (Ron Laytner, *Up Against Howard Hughes: The Maheu Story*, Manor Books, 1972, pp. 34–35).

12 Nixon: The Betrayal

Several Nixon aides recalled the president's intense involvement in planning the moon-walk dinner. "This was not only the big state dinner of his administration, the highpoint of his first year in office, but also was on his home territory, California," said Ehrlichman. "He was certainly involved in preparing the guest list. I know that Haldeman went over the draft guest lists with Nixon in great detail several times." Haldeman himself claimed not to recall the party preparations, but one of his aides said Nixon personally reviewed all 1,440 invitations and also made a list of "enemies" he did not want invited, including one of his wife's best friends.

Several top White House aides noted Nixon's sensitivity toward Hughes. "He was feared in the Nixon White House, where some believed that the 'Hughes loan' scandal had cost Nixon the 1960 election to Kennedy," wrote John Dean in *Blind Ambition* (Simon & Schuster, 1976, p. 67). "On matters pertaining to Hughes, Nixon sometimes seemed to lose touch with reality," wrote Haldeman in *The Ends of Power* (Times Books, 1978, pp. 19–20). "His indirect association with this mystery man may have caused him, in his view, to lose two elections."

Nixon first tried to get the CIA to put a "full cover" on Donald and when the CIA refused turned instead to the Secret Service, according to the final report of the House Impeachment Committee. Ehrlichman confirmed in an interview that the president had him arrange the Secret Service surveillance in May 1969, and that Nixon also ordered Donald's home and office telephones tapped, primarily to keep track of his brother's dealings with Meier. "Don's involvement with Hughes had already caused so much pain in the past, and Nixon was not anxious for another Hughes connection to emerge," said Ehrlichman. "The president was very upset that his 'stupid brother' was involved again in this kind of thing, he was angry."

When Donald was caught at the airport meeting with Meier and Hatsis in July 1969, Ehrlichman immediately called Rebozo, who immediately called Danner. "Do you know where John Meier is?" demanded an angry Rebozo. "I think you'll find that he is at the Orange County airport with Don Nixon." Ehrlichman pulled Hatsis's FBI file, which he said in an interview showed Hatsis to be an " 'unsavory character' with organized-crime connections."

Kreigsman's inquiry about Hughes to the AEC is confirmed by AEC documents dated July 25 and August 2, 1969, obtained through the Freedom of Information Act. The AEC's report on Hughes to the White House is dated August 18, 1969, and was personally reviewed by Chairman Seaborg. Seaborg recalled in an interview that top White House aides contacted him on several occasions to say that Hughes had expressed concern about the bomb tests.

Hoover's report on Hughes was obtained through the Freedom of Information Act. Its description of Hughes was based on a January 7, 1952, report to the FBI by a disgruntled Hughes executive who had also accused the billionaire of income-tax evasion. Hoover had been keeping tabs on Hughes since the 1947 "Spruce Goose" Senate hearings, receiving regular reports from his agents that focused primarily on Hughes's escapades with various starlets. FBI files also reveal that Hughes contacted Hoover directly through his chief Mormon, Bill Gay, on August 20, 1955, to discuss "a very delicate matter," and according to FBI sources shortly thereafter Hughes tried to hire Hoover as his Washington lobbyist. Dean Elson, FBI bureau chief in Las Vegas who later went to work for Hughes, said in an interview that Hoover told him that Hughes came to see the director while Hoover was on vacation in La Jolla, California, and told Hoover he could "name his own price, write his own ticket." Hoover told Elson he turned the job down because he considered Hughes "erratic." FBI files show that before he met with Hughes, Hoover received from his top aide the same report on Hughes he later sent Nixon.

The nuclear test announced on September 10, 1969, and detonated September 16 was code-named "JORUM" and according to AEC reports was "under a megaton."

Maheu's reports to Hughes, pilot logs of the Hughes jet, and Danner's travel records show that Danner and Maheu saw Rebozo in Key Biscayne on September 11 and 12, 1969. The Senate Watergate Committee in its final report called this "the most probable delivery date for the first contribution."

Danner in his first account of the hundred-thousand-dollar payoff told the IRS that it had taken place in Rebozo's home at Key Biscayne in September 1969 and that Maheu was present: "We took the de Havilland, flew to Miami, went to Key Biscayne, met Rebozo at his house. Maheu handed him the package and says, 'Here's $50,000, first installment.' Rebozo thanked him." Maheu also testified that he was present in Key Biscayne when $50,000 was delivered to Rebozo in 1969, but said that Danner handed over the money. Rebozo himself first told the IRS that the initial $50,000 was received from Danner in Key Biscayne in 1969.

Later, all three men gave contradictory accounts. Rebozo, in an effort to explain why some of the hundred-dollar bills he eventually returned to Hughes were issued by the U.S. Treasury after the date he originally said they were delivered, claimed he received all the money late in 1970. Under pressure from Rebozo, Danner changed his account and said he did not recall if the first delivery was in 1969 or 1970, but also testified that it was Rebozo's insistence that led him to change his mind. The only other reason Danner gave for retracting his original testimony was his recollection that the September 1969 trip related to Hughes's concern over the dumping of nerve gas. This is clearly wrong, as the nerve-gas dumping actually took place in August 1970.

All details of the delivery of the first $50,000 to Rebozo are based on Danner's testimony to the IRS and the Senate Watergate Committee, and Maheu's court testimony and statements in interviews with the Senate staff.

Nixon's activities and state of mind in September 1969 were established by his own account in his memoirs, and further detailed by Kissinger in *The White House Years* (Little, Brown & Co., 1979) and interviews with White House and NSC aides. As noted, Kissinger refused repeated interview requests.

Interviews with top White House officials, including Haldeman, Ehrlichman, and Colson, establish that while Nixon was well aware of Hughes's opposition to the bomb tests, the president never indicated that he had any idea of the true extent of Hughes's terror and outrage. Also, Nixon may well have been falsely reassured by the report on Hughes he received from the AEC just weeks earlier, claiming that "Hughes will not object as long as detonations do not exceed a megaton."

The account of the September 1969 blast is drawn from press reports, AEC records, and after-action reports to Hughes from his aides.

Danner's meetings with Attorney General Mitchell on the Dunes deal are established by his Senate Watergate Committee testimony, Justice records obtained through Senate staff investigators, and Maheu's contemporaneous reports to Hughes. In addition, FBI Director Hoover let Nixon and Mitchell know that he knew about the Dunes deal in a March 23, 1970, report sent to Justice: "Information was received by the Las Vegas office of this Bureau that on March 19, 1970, a representative of Howard Hughes . . . stated that Hughes had received assurance from the Department of Justice that no objection would be interposed to Hughes's purchasing the Dunes Hotel."

Maheu described Hughes's orders to give Nixon a million-dollar bribe to halt the March 1970 bomb test in statements to the Senate Watergate Committee, which he confirmed in an interview and detailed in a sworn deposition in his 1973 slander suit against Hughes.

Danner's travel records submitted to the Senate Watergate Committee show that he and Maheu were in Key Biscayne on March 20–22, 1970, and in Senate testimony both Danner and Maheu confirmed meeting with Rebozo on those dates.

13 Exodus

Hughes's fifteen-month effort to escape Las Vegas was described by several of his aides in depositions, further detailed by two of the aides in interviews, and also established by the memos Hughes sent and received during the period.

"It took about a year and a quarter to get going on our trip to Nassau," testified one of the Mormons, John Holmes. "There was some business to attend to. We had a big dust storm in Las Vegas, or it was raining cats and dogs in Nassau. One thing led to another. Also, we required twenty-four-hour advance notice, and he didn't want to commit himself."

The account of the nerve gas dumping was drawn from press reports, confirmed by Defense Department records obtained through the Freedom of Information Act. These records also show that one of the options presented to the president was exploding the gas at the Nevada Test Site.

In addition to contacting Rebozo through Danner, Maheu also attempted to halt the gas through O'Brien's associate Claude DeSautels. "Maheu called at seven in the morning, which was four or five A.M. in Las Vegas," recalled DeSautels in an interview. "I said, 'My God, what are you doing up at this hour?' and he said, 'The old man saw the eleven o'clock news last night and saw the trains and told me to stop them.' And I said, 'Bob! How can I stop the train?' I knew the president had approved it, the secretary of defense had ordered it, and the surgeon general had testified that it was safe. And Maheu said, 'Well, stop it!' So I called some people at the Pentagon, and I called Maheu back and said, 'There's no way to stop those trains, they're already rolling.' And Maheu said, 'I knew you couldn't stop it, but now at least I have something to tell the old man.' "

The account of Danner's delivery to Rebozo of the second $50,000 from Hughes on July 3, 1970, was based on Danner's sworn testimony before the Senate Watergate Committee and confirmed by Rebozo's own Senate testimony. "When I delivered the money to him," said Danner, "he slid it out of the large manila envelope and counted the bundles, and thanked me. The delivery made at San Clemente was in his room in the presidential compound. He laid the bundles out on the bed and counted them, he put them back in the envelope and put them in his handbag. . . . He took me into the president's office and the three of us sat there and chatted for possibly ten or fifteen minutes."

Rebozo testified that he put the $50,000 in his safe-deposit box along with a letter instructing that it be turned over to the finance chairman of the 1972 campaign, but he also testified that he later destroyed that letter and held on to the money himself until the IRS came after him in 1973.

Danner's daily diary submitted to the Senate Watergate Committee confirms that he contacted Rebozo through the White House on August 8, 1970, the day after Hughes discovered the nerve gas. "I relayed to him Hughes's fears that this dumping might lead to catastrophic results," testified Danner.

Defense Department and AEC records obtained through the Freedom of Information Act confirm that Nixon rejected the option of exploding the nerve gas in Nevada and approved the alternative of dumping it in the Atlantic near the Bahamas.

Bennett recounted Gay's contacting him and his own contact with Colson in an interview with staff investigators of the Senate Watergate Committee. Davis's role in the injunction through his legal associate Lea is revealed in memos both Maheu and the Mormons sent Hughes, which also establish his contact with Governor Kirk. The account of court proceedings was drawn from press reports.

Gate logs maintained by the Marine Corps confirm that Rebozo was at Camp David with Nixon the weekend of August 15–16, 1970, as Maheu told Hughes.

The account of the *Glomar Explorer* operation is based on interviews with former CIA director Colby, then deputy secretary of defense David Packard, two confidential sources at the CIA directly involved, Hughes Tool Company Vice-President Raymond Holliday, and a staff investigator for the Senate Select Committee on Intelligence who reviewed CIA records of the operation. In addition, a copy of the contract between the CIA and the Hughes Tool Company signed by Holliday on November 13, 1970, shows that the first *Glomar* proposal was sent to Holliday in August 1970, followed by a formal proposal for the "cover aspect of the project" on November 6, 1970.

Both Colby and the Senate investigator confirmed that the CIA considered Maheu a "bad risk" and kept him out of the *Glomar* dealings. Colby conceded that the CIA had no information of Hughes's actual condition, and CIA records indicate that the Agency knew only that Hughes was reclusive.

While it has been suggested in recent accounts that Hughes himself neither knew of nor approved the CIA cover arrangement, and that he actually believed the *Glomar* was engaged in deep-sea mining, Holliday said in an interview that he personally briefed Hughes by telephone and later sent him "a long, detailed memorandum."

"I was the only one in the company who discussed it with him," said Holliday. "But Chester Davis and Bill Gay both knew he was aware of it, and some of his aides were also aware of it. I discussed it with him extremely thoroughly, I told him the true mission was the submarine-raising, which is what the CIA told me, and Hughes approved our involvement long before the contract was signed." Holliday's account is confirmed by the fact that Davis later sent Hughes a memo referring to the *Glomar*'s "primary mission" and by the fact that a copy of the *Glomar* contract was among the documents found in his Acapulco penthouse after he died.

Hughes's response to the CIA through Holliday was quoted by Holliday in an interview.

While it is impossible to determine how direct a role the *Glomar* deal played in Maheu's ouster, Maheu himself later suggested that his refusal to make a CIA alliance for Hughes was a factor, and it is noteworthy that Hughes first mentioned the proxy that would strip Maheu of his power shortly after Holliday first contacted him about the *Glomar* in August 1970, and that Hughes actually signed the proxy on November 14, 1970, one day after Holliday signed the *Glomar* contract.

Intertel's Peloquin detailed his meetings with Davis and Gay in sworn depositions.

The Mormon who retrieved Hughes's memos from Maheu later recounted the mission in a report to Hughes: "I purposely did not call Bob to tell him I was coming until I was ready to leave (I was there in less than a minute), so he would not have time to plan any other disposition of the papers. He seemed to be in an unhappy mood, and I sensed that he did not like the implication of this action. He asked me the reason behind this, and I gave him some rather vague answer to the effect that you did not want the possibility of your messages being mislaid."

The final breach between Hughes and Maheu was described by Maheu in a series of interviews and in court testimony, and was also recounted by several of the Mormons. One of the aides later testified in a deposition that "during the latter portion of 1970, Gay directed myself and the other aides to hold messages from Maheu to Mr. Hughes; as a result, messages from Maheu piled up without being delivered to Mr. Hughes. At about the same time, I also observed numerous messages from the other aides criticizing Maheu and suggesting that he was disloyal to Mr. Hughes."

Hughes's medical condition just before his departure was described by his physician, Dr. Harold Feikes, in a deposition, and was further detailed in an interview. "I saw Hughes within a few weeks of his leaving Las Vegas," said Feikes. "His primary problem was pneumonia. He was only mildly ill, and not really anemic. His blood count was close to normal. But he wanted more transfusions." Hughes's demand for the blood was quoted by Feikes.

Maheu sent Davis a telegram on November 6, 1970, firing him from the

TWA case. The Hughes Tool Company directors revoked Maheu's authority over the TWA case on November 12, 1970.

One of the Mormons who was present when Hughes signed the proxy ousting Maheu later described the scene in court testimony.

Several of the aides, in depositions, recounted Hughes's departure from the Desert Inn, and one gave further details in an interview. The *Las Vegas Sun* story appeared on December 2, 1970. Two days later Hughes released the proxy, stripping Maheu of power, and on December 7, 1970, at one A.M., Hughes called Governor Laxalt from the Bahamas to confirm that Maheu had been fired.

The White House encounter between Ehrlichman and Rebozo was recounted by Ehrlichman in an interview.

Epilogue I **Watergate**

The story of the Hughes connection to Watergate told in the epilogue is in many ways more a confirmation than a revelation. An unpublished forty-six-page report by the staff of the Senate Watergate Committee first presented significant evidence that the Hughes-Nixon-O'Brien triangle triggered the break-in, and was a primary source for my account. Several staff investigators also provided testimony, transcripts, and documentary material never made public, and provided further details in interviews. I am also deeply indebted to J. Anthony Lukas, the first journalist to fully explore the Hughes-Watergate link in his book *Nightmare: The Underside of the Nixon Years* (Viking, 1976).

Nixon's message to Haldeman was quoted by John Dean in *Blind Ambition* (Simon & Schuster, 1976, p. 66) from a copy of the memo Haldeman passed on to him, and its content was confirmed by Haldeman in an interview.

Nixon's fears that the $100,000 would become public in the aftermath of the Hughes-Maheu split were reflected by Rebozo in his Senate Watergate Committee testimony: "Matters went from bad to worse in the Hughes organization, and I felt that sooner or later this matter would come up and be misunderstood. . . . The concern was principally any disclosure that the president had received Hughes money . . . I didn't want to risk even the remotest embarrassment about any Hughes connection with Nixon. I was convinced that it cost the president the 1960 election."

An aide who was with Nixon in San Clemente recalled seeing the president reading a *Los Angeles Times* story about Maheu's lawsuit against Hughes shortly after Maheu's ouster, and such a story did run on January 14, 1971. In a column five days earlier Anderson wrote, "Some of the confidential documents impounded by the Nevada court in the Hughes case have been slipped to us."

Nixon's orders to "nail O'Brien" were quoted by Haldeman in *The Ends of Power* (Times Books, 1978, p. 155), and while in the book he placed the conversation aboard *Air Force One*, in an interview he corrected his account, placing it in the White House. Haldeman also noted that "O'Brien touched a raw nerve: Nixon's dealings with Howard Hughes, which had cost him two elections" (*The Ends of Power*, p. 155).

Hughes's setup and condition in the Bahamas were described by one of his Mormons in an interview and by other aides in depositions. One of them, George Francom, later testified that "control of Mr. Hughes's communications began to tighten. . . . I observed many messages to and from Mr. Hughes being held by all the other aides."

Hughes's drug use was detailed in a 1978 report of the Drug Enforcement Administration. His activities were recorded for each day from October 1971 through July 1973 in logs kept by his aides. (Logs were also maintained all through the years Hughes spent in Las Vegas and continued until his death, but all these records were destroyed.)

The arrest of Maheu's men in the Bahamas was confirmed by FBI reports obtained through the Freedom of Information Act and by an Intertel agent in an interview.

Colson's memo about Bennett was obtained from Senate Watergate Committee files. In an interview Colson said that he was unaware of the connection to Hughes through Rebozo and also knew nothing about Bennett's CIA ties. Colson also suggested that both Bennett and the CIA instigated the Watergate break-in: "I think Bob Bennett had a tremendous motive— he had more interest in what O'Brien was doing and saying than we did— and I've always felt that the CIA had some motive because of their interlocking ties with both Bennett and Hughes."

Dean detailed his efforts to nail O'Brien on orders from Haldeman in *Blind Ambition* (pp. 66–68), and the memos he sent and received were obtained from files of the Senate Watergate Committee. Haldeman gave a similar account of the Hughes-O'Brien probe in *Ends of Power* (pp. 19– 20, 153–56) and in a series of interviews. The entire operation by the White House was also detailed in an unpublished report by the staff of the Senate Watergate Committee.

Nixon's renewed orders to get O'Brien were quoted by Haldeman in *The Ends of Power* (pp. 19–20, 154–56). "In the case of O'Brien," noted Haldeman, "Nixon was acting very much like Captain Queeg in his search for the strawberries . . . here was Larry O'Brien a secret Hughes lobbyist—and no one cared. . . . And yet, as Nixon often said to me, how the press took after him on any possible connection to Howard Hughes!"

Intertel's instigation of an IRS probe of Maheu was detailed by Andy Baruffi, the IRS agent in charge of the Hughes case, and confirmed by two other IRS agents directly involved. In an interview, Maheu confirmed his belief that he was the target of a conspiracy between the Hughes organization and the federal government. "I felt the pangs of government muscle within hours after I challenged Howard Hughes," he said.

Danner told the Senate Watergate Committee that Rebozo called him right after Anderson's August 1971 column appeared: "I think the subject was how did Anderson learn of this, and the answer was that he had been shown an alleged memo describing the details of the event." Danner also testified that Anderson told him that Maheu had leaked the Hughes memo.

Greenspun's September 1971 warning to Klein was confirmed by both Greenspun and Klein in interviews. Both Ehrlichman and Kalmbach confirmed in interviews that Ehrlichman sent Kalmbach to see Greenspun about the Hughes money, and Kalmbach and Greenspun gave similar accounts of their meeting. "I recall there being a need for someone to talk to Greenspun," said Ehrlichman, "and I recall it being agreed—not just by me, but by a number of people, at the very least Haldeman, possibly Mitchell —that Kalmbach ought to call on him. I probably also discussed it with Rebozo."

The Senate Watergate Committee noted in its final report that Rebozo paid $45,621 for improvements on Nixon's Key Biscayne compound, and concluded that the only apparent source for at least half of that expense was the cash he received from Hughes.

Bennett informed the Senate committee that he told Colson about the Hughes memos in Greenspun's safe late in 1971.

Ehrlichman confirmed in a series of interviews that he received IRS "sensitive case reports" on the Hughes probe, and provided a copy of one such report he received on July 24, 1972, which summarized political aspects of the IRS investigation. The John Meier–Donald Nixon dealings were recounted in that report and further detailed by Ehrlichman, who confirmed in the interviews that he kept Nixon informed on the probe.

Nixon's story of the "loan" scandal was recounted by Ehrlichman. Haldeman gave a similar account of Nixon's claims about that scandal.

The impact of the Clifford Irving affair on Watergate was first suggested by an unpublished report of the Senate Watergate Committee. In *Blind Ambition* (p. 390), Dean reported Haldeman's orders to get a copy of Irving's manuscript and also stated that "somebody from the White House got a copy from the publisher." Bennett told the Special Prosecutor's Office that both Colson and Dean contacted him about Irving's book and recounted his conversation with Dean. FBI files obtained through the Freedom of Information Act revealed that Hoover sent Haldeman reports on the Irving affair.

The account of the Hughes-Nixon dealings in Irving's book was quoted in an unpublished Senate Watergate Committee report and also in part by a February 4, 1972, story in the *New York Times*. A White House aide confirmed that Nixon himself read at least a summary of Irving's account.

Hughes's activities on the day of his press conference were detailed in the logs maintained by his aides. The Hughes quotes are from a tape recording of that conference.

The creation of the Hunt-Liddy team was described in reports of the Senate Watergate Committee and the House Impeachment Committee, by both Hunt and Liddy in their books, and by Haldeman and Dean in their books.

Nixon's reaction to reports that Bobby Kennedy had investigated the Hughes "loan" was quoted by a White House aide in an interview. Nixon himself made similar comments in his memoirs *RN: The Memoirs of Richard Nixon* (Warner, 1978, vol. 1, p. 305), writing that Kennedy's effort to prosecute his mother and brother was "typical of the partisan vindictiveness that pervaded the Kennedy administration."

The February 4, 1972, and January 27, 1972, meetings between Liddy, Mitchell, Dean, and Magruder were detailed by Liddy in his book *Will* (St. Martin's Press, 1980, pp. 196–203), by Dean and Magruder in Senate Watergate Committee and court testimony, by Dean in *Blind Ambition* (pp. 79–86), and by Magruder in *An American Life* (Pocket Books, 1975, pp. 207–12). Both Dean and Magruder testified that Mitchell discussed O'Brien as a target for surveillance. Magruder also told the Senate Watergate Committee, according to an unpublished staff report, that "the attorney general not only brought up the Greenspun entry operation, but also urged Liddy to consider it as more pressing and important than the other targets discussed."

Hunt detailed the Greenspun plot in Senate Watergate Committee testimony and stated that Bennett first suggested that break-in a few days before the Mitchell-Liddy meeting. Bennett gave a similar account but claimed that it was Hunt who suggested a break-in after Bennett told him Greenspun had Hughes memos. Hunt in his testimony and Liddy in his book (*Will*, p. 205) confirmed Winte's involvement.

Nixon's impatience with the lack of action from Liddy's operation was reported by Haldeman in his book (*The Ends of Power*, pp. 10–11). Strachan's call to Magruder was quoted by Magruder in Senate Watergate Committee testimony. Nixon's anger at O'Brien over the ITT affair was noted by Haldeman in his book (*The Ends of Power*, pp. 153–55), by Colson in an interview, and by Nixon himself in his memoirs (*RN*, vol. 2, p. 54). The Hunt-Liddy-Colson meeting was confirmed by all three, and Magruder testified that Colson called to push him on getting approval of Liddy's plan.

The Magruder-Mitchell meeting and Mitchell's revelation of the Hughes motive behind Watergate were described in detail by a confidential source with direct knowledge of their conversation in two hour-long taped interviews. The source agreed to give the information only upon my assurance that he would not be identified.

In Senate Watergate Committee and court testimony, Magruder said that Mitchell approved the Watergate break-in on March 30, 1972. Magruder also testified that Mitchell ordered the second break-in. Liddy stated in *Will* (p. 237) that Magruder ordered him to photograph O'Brien's "shit file" on Nixon. "The purpose of the second Watergate break-in" wrote Liddy, "was to find out what O'Brien had of a derogatory nature about us, not for us to get something on him or the Democrats."

Nixon's reaction to the Watergate arrests was described by Haldeman in his book (pp. 7–13) and by Nixon himself in his memoirs (vol. 2, pp. 109–13).

Haldeman reconstructed his June 20, 1972, conversation with Nixon in *The Ends of Power* (pp. 18–19) and in two interviews confirmed that Nixon himself revealed the Hughes connection to Watergate, probably in that erased conversation, and definitely in one of his talks with Haldeman in the days following the break-in.

Epilogue II   **The Final Days**

Hughes's activities at the time of the Watergate arrests were detailed in the logs maintained by his aides and confirmed by listings for July 16–17, 1972, in a Vancouver edition of *TV Guide*.

The fact that Hughes was oblivious to Watergate for more than a year was established by the memos his aides and attorney sent in response to his belated inquiries and confirmed in an affidavit by one of his Mormons.

Hughes's escape from the Bahamas was described by an aide in an interview, and by several other aides in depositions. His dealings with Somoza were established by memos Hughes wrote and dictated, and by others received from his staff. Hughes's preparations for his meeting with Somoza and Shelton were detailed in his logs, and the meeting itself was described both by an aide who was present and Shelton in an interview with the IRS. Hughes's arrival in Vancouver was described by an aide who was present.

Bennett's role as a double agent in Watergate was detailed in Senator Howard Baker's report of his investigation into "CIA Activity in Watergate," published as an appendix to the final report of the Senate Watergate Committee.

Nixon's suspicion that Bennett was "Deep Throat" and that the Bennett-Hughes-CIA axis was somehow responsible for his downfall was reported by Haldeman in *The Ends of Power* (Times Books, 1978, pp. 134–39) and hinted at by Nixon in his memoirs *RN: The Memoirs of Richard Nixon* (Warner, 1978, vol. 2, p. 578). "Now that few people seemed to care about the question of who had ordered the break-in," wrote Nixon, "there was new information that the Democrats themselves had prior knowledge and that the Hughes organization might be involved. And there were stories of strange alliances."

Ehrlichman detailed his July 24, 1972, meeting with Nixon in an interview and provided a copy of the IRS "sensitive case report" he gave Nixon that revealed Hughes's payments to O'Brien. "He got very, very excited about it, about as excited as I had ever seen him get," recalled Ehrlichman. Ehrlichman also reported Nixon's orders to have the IRS audit O'Brien and put him in jail, and the efforts to use the IRS against O'Brien were confirmed by the final reports of the House Impeachment Committee and the Senate Watergate Committee.

Nixon's September 15, 1972, conversation with Dean is drawn from a transcript of a White House tape.

Hughes's contribution of $150,000 to Nixon's 1972 campaign was reported by Bennett in statements to the Senate Watergate Committee and the Special Prosecutor's Office. Rebozo's call to Danner seeking Hughes money was confirmed by Danner in Senate Watergate Committee testimony. Liddy's involvement in handling the Hughes contribution was noted by Liddy in *Will* (St. Martin's Press, 1980, p. 215), and by Bennett in his Senate staff interviews. Bennett reported Evans's solicitation of another $100,000 in statements to the special prosecutor in which he also noted his arrangement of a birthday call from Nixon to Hughes.

Hughes's reaction to the Managua earthquake was described by an aide who was present, by other aides in depositions, and detailed in logs the aides kept.

The IRS showdown in Fort Lauderdale was detailed in a series of interviews by Richard Jaffe, an IRS agent who played a key role, and confirmed by Andy Baruffi, who was in charge of the Hughes investigation, and by IRS reports of the incident obtained from a confidential source.

Hughes's plans to fly again were described by one of his Mormons, his preparations for the flight were detailed in his logs, and the flight itself was described by his English co-pilot, Tony Blackman, in a later report to lawyers for the Hughes estate. It was the first time Hughes had flown a plane since he slipped out of his seclusion for a flight in 1960, at which time his pilot's license had already expired.

Hughes's belated discovery of Watergate was described by one of his Mormons, George Francom, in an affidavit. "In mid-1973, I gave him a copy of the *London Express* which had a picture of a plane he was interested in," recalled Francom. "There was also a story about Watergate in the paper, and he had no idea what Watergate was about. We prepared several memos explaining Watergate, but I don't know if he ever read them."

Nixon's March 21, 1973, conversation with Dean is transcribed from a White House tape. His conversations with Haldeman and Ehrlichman about money from Rebozo's slush fund were revealed in tapes of April 17 and April 25, 1973, meetings obtained by the special prosecutor. Both Haldeman and Ehrlichman reported Nixon's renewed offers of money at Camp David in their books and in interviews. "In 1976 I asked Nixon where that money would have come from," Haldeman wrote in *The Ends of Power* (pp. 20–22). "He said, 'Bebe had it.' But I reminded him that Bebe had only $100,000 of the Hughes money. Where would the rest have come from? Nixon told me this interesting news. There was much more money in Bebe's 'tin box' than the Hughes $100,000 . . . Bebe Rebozo, in effect, maintained a private fund for Nixon to use as he wished."

Nixon, however, told David Frost in a television interview broadcast May 25, 1977, that the money he offered Haldeman and Ehrlichman was the Hughes $100,000. "Well, as a matter of fact," said Nixon, "I had in mind the campaign contribution that [Rebozo] received from Hughes." It should be noted, however, that Nixon actually offered his two top men up to $300,000, and it is also clear that by the time he made the offer at least some of the Hughes money had already been spent.

The Rebozo-Kalmbach meeting of April 30, 1973, was described by Kalmbach in testimony before the Senate Watergate Committee and further detailed by a confidential source with direct knowledge of their conversation. Rebozo's statement that he had given some of the Hughes money to Nixon's brothers, Woods, and "others" was quoted by Kalmbach under oath.

Rebozo's May 10, 1973, statement to the IRS was reported by the Senate Watergate Committee. The IRS's fears of probing Rebozo were noted by Ehrlichman in an interview. Rebozo's attempts to return the Hughes money to Danner were described by Danner in Senate Watergate Committee testimony. Danner also gave testimony on his May 20, 1973, meeting with Nixon at Camp David.

Both Haig and Simon confirmed in Senate testimony their conversation about the IRS probe of Rebozo. The FBI chief agent in Miami, Kenneth Whitaker, described Rebozo's unveiling of the Hughes $100,000—and the discovery of an extra hundred-dollar bill—in testimony before the Senate Watergate Committee. The return of the money to Chester Davis was described by Davis, Rebozo, and their intermediaries in Senate testimony.

The Federal Reserve later reported that thirty-five of the hundred-dollar bills returned by Rebozo were issued by the U.S. Treasury after the last date Danner, Maheu, and Rebozo himself originally testified the money had been delivered. While Rebozo changed his account to cover all the Hughes cash and tried to pressure Danner to do likewise, Danner would never agree to confirm a delivery date that would cover the thirty-five late-issue bills.

Rebozo's fears about revelation of the Hughes money are quoted from his testimony before the Senate Watergate Committee.

The apparent connection between Cox's probe of the Hughes-Rebozo affair and the Saturday Night Massacre was detailed by a senior aide in the Nixon White House who agreed to provide information only on a not-for-attribution background basis. His account was confirmed in large part by the public testimony of others directly involved and by available government records.

Rebozo's discovery of the special prosecutor's probe on October 18, 1973, was established by the Senate Watergate Committee from the handwritten notes of the IRS agent who tipped him off, and these notes also show that he called Rebozo's lawyer "about disclosure to Cox" and indicate that he also called White House counsel Fred Buzhardt that same morning to inform him of Cox's demand for the IRS files on the Hughes $100,000. In any event, Rebozo could not have missed the eight-column banner headline in the *Miami Herald*.

Nixon's angry reaction to the news, apparently first received in a phone call from Rebozo, was quoted by a member of the White House staff. Haig confirmed in an interview that he discussed the Cox probe with Nixon and that the president said it was "a perfect illustration" of how Cox was out to get him.

Richardson told the Senate Judiciary Committee that Haig called him on October 18 and said that Nixon "didn't see what Mr. Cox's charter had to do with the activities of Mr. Rebozo." Haig confirmed in Senate Watergate Committee testimony that after talking with Nixon he called Richardson:

"I may have expressed this as being of presidential concern and I'm sure if I did I would have had reason to know . . . because he specifically told me so."

Secret Service records obtained from the National Archives show that Rebozo arrived at the White House October 19 and stayed there through October 20 as a "house guest," meeting with the president at least twice in his office, and, according to a member of the staff, he spent "considerable time" alone with Nixon at night.

Haig testified that when he was with the president in Key Biscayne he had "invariably" heard both Nixon and Rebozo complain about the "unfair and unjust persecution" of Rebozo over the Hughes money.

"There's no doubt that the tapes were the big issue," said a senior White House aide, "but there's also no doubt in my mind that Nixon's anger over the Hughes investigation, and quite possibly his fear that it would lead to a broader investigation that would uncover the entire Rebozo slush fund, was a real flash-point in the whole Cox affair. I think it pushed him over the edge."

Hughes was indicted in the Air West deal on December 27, 1973. Maheu and Davis were named co-defendants.

The scene of Davis dumping the Rebozo $100,000 in front of Senator Ervin was described by a member of the committee staff who was present.

One of the Mormons confirmed that Hughes was never told that his secret papers were stolen in the Romaine break-in, and the memos Hughes dictated in the aftermath of the burglary make it clear that he was not aware they were missing.

CIA documents obtained through the Freedom of Information Act show that Gay told the Agency on July 2, 1974, that the *Glomar* document was missing and presumed stolen. Colby confirmed his meeting with Nixon in an interview.

Haig's call to Nixon informing him of the Supreme Court decision about the tapes was described by Nixon in his memoirs (*RN*, vol. 2, p. 640).

The suppressed Senate Watergate Committee staff report on the Hughes connection to Watergate was obtained from one of the staff investigators who wrote it. The chief minority counsel, Fred Thompson, apparently first proposed deleting it from the committee's final report, and Senator Ervin quickly agreed. One of the senators said in a background interview that none of his colleagues, Republican or Democrat, wanted it published. "Too many guilty bystanders would have been hurt," he remarked, "and after two years of Watergate I don't think anyone was ready to accept such a small price tag."

Haldeman's conclusion that the Hughes connection triggered Watergate was stated in *The Ends of Power* (pp. 19–20) and confirmed in a series of interviews. In fact, every top Nixon aide who has publicly expressed an opinion on the cause of the break-in agrees that the Hughes-Nixon-O'Brien triangle lay behind it. It is also the thesis of Dean's *Blind Ambition* (Simon & Schuster, 1976) and Colson said in an interview: "I've always believed that the real motive behind the Watergate break-in was to get dirt on Larry

O'Brien, who was drawing a retainer from Hughes. Beneath it all we'll find some day that the real motive was Hughes."

Colby's discussion of the Romaine-*Glomar* link was quoted in CIA records obtained through the Freedom of Information Act.

The Senate Intelligence Committee's probe of possible Hughes links to Nixon, the Mob, and the CIA was reported in part by the *New York Times* on March 26, 1975, and further confirmed by a staff investigator. Norman Mailer's speculations were published by *New York* magazine, August 16, 1976. The IRS report suggesting Hughes died in 1970 was obtained from a former IRS agent. Commissioner Walters confirmed in an interview that he tried to find out if Hughes was alive.

One of the Mormons, George Francom, stated in an affidavit that Hughes was falsely told that "the drug supply was drying up in the Bahamas and that there would be a better supply in Acapulco."

The description of Hughes's death and of his last fix was recounted by Francom in his affidavit—he was the Mormon who refused to give Hughes the injection—and also by several other aides and doctors in depositions and court testimony.

Angleton's eulogy was reported in *Time* magazine, April 19, 1976. He refused in an interview to explain his remarks.

Acknowledgments

This adventure began as a project for *New Times* magazine. When I had little more than a wild hunch eight years ago, *New Times* editor Jon Larsen supported me without question and gave me the total freedom I needed. Without his backing the entire quest would not have been possible, and the secret papers would never have been found.

Tom Wallace and Irv Goodman, my original editor and publisher at Holt, Rinehart and Winston, displayed rare courage in taking on a book they knew would be more than controversial.

Dick Seaver, who became publisher early on and soon became my editor as well, kept the faith, stood with me through hard times, and remained dedicated to this project throughout. My thanks also to many others at Holt, especially David Stanford, and to Cliff Walter and the entire production team, specifically Catherine Fallin, Randy Lang, and Susan Hood, who performed a miracle to bring this book out in record time.

Rob Fleder, a senior editor at *Playboy*, was among the first outsiders to read the manuscript, and his enthusiasm and that of his magazine meant much.

Very special thanks to my lead attorney, Jerry Gutman, president of the New York Civil Liberties Union, whose wise counsel often went beyond legal advice—a friend who was there from the beginning and never wavered through the years. I am also grateful to Ira Glasser, Aryeh Neier, and Bruce Ennis of the American Civil Liberties Union who all helped at a critical early stage; to Melville Nimmer; and especially to Leon Friedman who played a central role. Men like these keep the First Amendment alive.

Several friends took time to read, criticize, encourage. One, Ron Rosenbaum, did far more. This book is in many ways as much his as my own. Much of what is best in it was suggested by him, and he kept urging me on day after day for years, always generous with his time and intelligence, always full of creative insights. To have had such a brilliant writer as so devoted a friend was truly a godsend. I would not have made it without him.

Finally, my source for the papers, the Pro. He risked everything and gave me total trust. That made it all possible.

Index

Index

Index

Index

Index

Index

530

Index